Basic Food and Beverage Cost Control

Basic Food and Beverage Cost Control

Jack E. Miller, FMP
Professor Emeritus, St. Louis Community College
David K. Hayes, Ph.D., FMP

John Wiley & Sons, Inc.
New York • Chichester • Brisbane • Toronto • Singapore

This text is printed on acid-free paper.

Library of Congress Cataloging-in-Publication Data:

Miller, Jack E., 1930–
Basic food and beverage cost control / by Jack E. Miller and David K. Hayes.
p. cm.
Includes bibliographical references (p.) and index.
ISBN 0-471-57918-1 (alk. paper)
1. Food service—Cost control. I. Hayes, David K. II. Title.
TX911.3.C65M55 1993
647.95'0681—dc20 93-23781
CIP

Printed in the United States of America

10

Contents

Preface

The authors of this text recognize that all foodservice managers, regardless of the type of operation they are involved in, must understand and manage the costs associated with operating their business. If one is to begin the study of managing income and costs, it must be done with an interest in the topic and a conviction that the subject to be studied is of vital importance.

Today's foodservice manager, whether in a commercial restaurant, hotel, or institutional setting, is faced with a variety of responsiblities, from accounting, marketing, human relations, facilities maintenance, and legal issues to sanitation, production, and service methods, to name but a few.

This text intends to focus in a very basic way on helping managers understand the logic and the systems involved with managing costs. The text is intended to be a primer, the first step, in what may be a lifelong and rewarding study of how to be a better manager in this important area of cost control.

Both authors find the topic of cost management to be one of creativity, excitement, and in many cases outright fun. Contrary to the prevalent idea of cost control as drudgery, cost management in this text becomes a challenge to be met by the foodservice manager.

It may be said that there are three kinds of managers: those who know what has happened in the past, those who know what is happening now, and those who know what is about to happen. Clearly, the manager who possesses all three traits is best prepared to manage effectively and efficiently.

This text will give the reader the tools required to maintain sales and cost histories (the past), develop systems for monitoring current activities (the present), and teach the techniques required to anticipate what is to come (the future).

Overviews

Each chapter begins with an **overview**. This is simply a quick and easy guide to each chapter's contents. Overviews make it easy for the reader to quickly find the section of the text he or she is looking for.

Chapter Highlights

Each **chapter's highlights** tell the reader what to expect in that chapter. They are worded is such a way that the reader knows what he or she will be able to *do* at the conclusion of each chapter. These highlights are designed so that the reader will be prepared for and excited about what he or she will be able to achieve when the chapter's materials are successfully mastered.

Test-Your-Skill Exercises

At the conclusion of each chapter, **test-your-skill** exercises allow the reader to immediately determine if he or she has mastered the chapter's content. They relate back to a chapter highlight. In other words, there is one test-your-skill exercise for each chapter highlight presented at the beginning of the chapter. Again, the intent is to allow the reader to immediately practice the skill acquired in the chapter. Through these exercises, the authors seek to reinforce the concepts presented in the chapters.

It is the authors' hope that readers find the book as helpful to use as we found it exciting to prepare. In an effort to make the book an easy reference guide, a section entitled **"Frequently Used Formulas for Managing Costs"** is included in the back of the text. This section will allow the reader to quickly look up the mathematical formula for any of the computations presented in the text. In addition, **"Management Control Forms,"** a section devoted to providing simplified cost-control-related forms is included.

These forms are meant to be used as guideposts in the development of forms for use by a specific operator. They may be used as is or modified as the operator sees fit.

A **glossary** of industry terms will help the reader with the operational vocabulary necessary to understand the language of hospitality management. This is included at the end of the text.

Finally, a **bibliography** is provided for the reader who wishes to pursue his or her study from a variety of excellent books.

This book is intended to serve both the commercial and noncommercial operator. As such, a great deal of effort was given to presenting the information and examples in such a way as to be helpful to both groups. While there are some excellent books on cost control in the hospitality industry, this book is written for a special person, namely, the operator who wants to **begin** the process of developing solid control procedures. In that sense, the book represents a fresh start for the operator.

We hope that this first study of cost management creates in the reader the same interest and excitement for the topic that the authors experience. If that is the case, we have been successful, and our readers will surely feel rewarded and be successful also.

Acknowledgments

We appreciate all the assistance and comments we have received in bringing this book to fruition. We are extremely grateful to those who made contributions to our original concept and idea for the book.

The National Restaurant Association provided up-to-the-minute materials on many industry subjects and helped us track down elusive details for our references.

For comment, encouragement, and constructive criticism on the manuscript, we thank our reviewers: Tom Atkinson, CHA, Columbus State Community College; Carl Riegel, Washington State University; Warren Sackler, CHA, FMP, Rochester Institute of Technology; Andrew Schwarz, Ph.D., FMP, Sullivan Community College; Edward Sherwin, CFE, FMP, Essex Community College. At times, they reminded us of our original concept and kept us from straying from it. We thank our editor, Claire Thompson, who demonstrated enough faith in us and the book concept to go forward with the project.

We hereby proclaim our thanks to Jack Miller's students at St. Louis Community College, and to David Hayes' students at the University of Houston, Texas University, and at Purdue University, who attended our classes as we applied the cost and management theories now put forth in this book. In addition, we thank the many persons who attended seminars and in-house training sessions where we used the theories, formulas, and forms from this text. Their comments and challenges proved the logic and truth of what we had proposed and made this a stronger and more useful text with a practical application for industry and education.

We also want to thank our wives, Anita Miller and Peggy Hayes, and tell them both how much we appreciate their encouragement, patience, and support during the research, writing, and development of the book.

Jack E. Miller
David K. Hayes

About the Authors

Jack E. Miller, FMP, is Professor Emeritus at St. Louis Community College. He is a member of the College of Diplomates of the Educational Foundation of the National Restaurant Association, a past president of CHRIE, The Council on Hotel, Restaurant & Institutional Education, the winner of many education and hospitality industry awards, and the author of six textbooks.

David K. Hayes, Ph.D., FMP, CFBE, has held positions on the hospitality management faculties of Purdue University, Texas Technological University, and the University of Houston. He currently serves on the staff of the Educational Institute of the American Hotel and Motel Association.

Chapter 1

Managing Income and Expense

OVERVIEW

This chapter presents the basic relationship between foodservice income, expense, and profit. Each foodservice manager must understand the relationship between controlling these three areas and the resulting overall success of the operation. In addition, the chapter presents the mathematical foundation necessary to express expense and profit as a percent of income or of budget.

HIGHLIGHTS

At the conclusion of Chapter 1, the manager will be able to

A. Apply the basic formula used to determine profit
B. Express both expense and profit as a percentage of sales
C. Compare actual operating results with budgeted operating results

Foodservice Management

There is no doubt that a successful foodservice manager is a talented individual. Consider for a moment his or her role in the operation of a profitable facility. The foodservice manager is both manufacturer and retailer. He or she is unique because all the functions of product sales, from item conceptualization to product delivery, are in the hands of the same individual. The manager is in charge of securing raw materials, producing a product, and selling it—all under the same roof. Few other types of managers are required to have the breadth of skills that effective foodservice operators must have. Because foodservice operators are in the service sector of business, many aspects of management are more difficult for them than for their manufacturing or retailing management counterparts.

The foodservice manager is one of the few types of managers who actually has contact with the ultimate consumer. This is not true of the manager of a tire factory or an automobile production line. This face-to-face consumer contact requires that foodservice operators be willing to stand behind their own work and that of their employees, in a one-on-one situation with the ultimate consumer, or end user, of the facility's products and services.

The management task checklist in Figure 1.1 shows just some of the areas in which foodservice, manufacturing, and retailing managers vary in responsibilities.

In addition to their role as food factory supervisor, operators must serve as their own cost control managers, because without performing this vital role, the business might cease to exist. Foodservice management provides the opportunity for creativity in a variety of areas. The control of income and expense is just one area in which the effective foodservice operator can excel. In most units of foodservice, excellence in operation is measured in terms of producing and delivering a quality product in a way that assures an operating profit for the owners of the business.

Profit: The Reward for Service

Management's primary responsibility is to deliver a quality product or service to the customer, at a price mutually agreeable to both parties. In addition, the quality must be such that the consumer, or end user of the product or service, feels that excellent value is received for the money spent on the transaction. When this level of service is achieved, the business will prosper. An inherent problem in cost control or, more accurately, cost management is that management may focus more on controlling costs than on servicing guests. When this occurs, problems will certainly surface.

It is important to remember that guests cause us to incur costs. We do not want to get in the mind-set of reducing costs to the point where we think that "low" costs are good and "high" costs are bad. A restaurant with $5,000,000 in sales per year will undoubtedly have higher costs than the same size restaurant with $200,000 in sales per year. If there are no guests, there will be no costs. In a similar vein, when management attempts to reduce costs, with no regard to

Figure 1.1 **Management Task Checklist**

	Foodservice Manager	Manufacturing Manager	Retailing Manager
1. Secure raw materials	Yes	Yes	No
2. Manufacture product	Yes	Yes	No
3. Distribute to end user	Yes	No	Yes
4. Market to end user	Yes	No	Yes
5. Reconcile problems with end user	Yes	No	Yes

the impact on the balance between cost management and guest satisfaction, the business will surely suffer.

The question is not whether costs are high or low. The question is whether costs are too high or too low, given management's view of what represents the value to be received by the guest. We can eliminate all costs by closing the operation's doors. Obviously, however, when we close the doors to expense, we close the doors to profits.

People often assume that if a product is purchased for five cents and sold for ten cents, the profit generated equals five cents. In fact, this is not true. All business operators must realize that the difference between what they have paid for goods and the price at which they sell those goods is not clear, or realized, profit. Actually, all expenses, including labor, that are required to generate the sale must be subtracted before actual profit can be determined. Every foodservice operator is faced with the following profit-oriented formula:

Income − Expenses = Profit

This formula holds even in so-called nonprofit institutions. To illustrate this point, let us examine a business dining operation. Foodservice operators in a business dining situation clearly do not have "profit" as their primary motive. In most business dining situations, food is provided as a service to employees and middle management either as a no-cost benefit or at a greatly reduced price. In some cases, executive dining rooms may be operated for the convenience of senior management. In all cases, however, some provision for profit must be made. Figure 1.2 shows the flow of business for a typical foodservice operation. Note that profit must be taken out at some point in the process, or management is in a position of simply trading cash for cash.

If the foodservice operator finds that income equals expense, with no reserve for the future, he or she will find that there is no money for new equipment, raises will be few and far between, needed equipment maintenance may not be

Figure 1.2 **Foodservice Business Flow Chart**

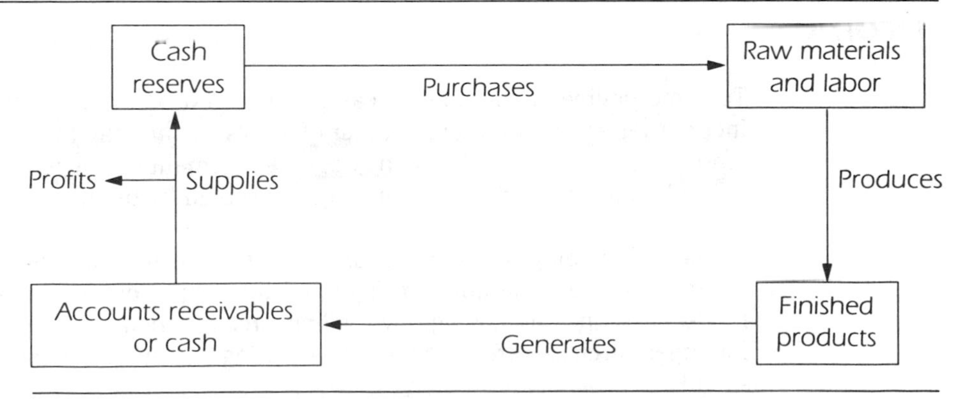

performed and, in general, the foodservice facility will become dated due to a lack of funds needed to remodel and upgrade. One need look no further than to the facilities of many college and hospital feeding operations to see evidence of this type of situation in the not-for-profit sector of the foodservice industry. In fact, all foodservice operations need income in excess of routine expenses to take care of repairs and maintenance, and to plan for future renovations of the facility.

For nonprofit institutions, it is the responsibility of the foodservice manager to communicate this message to those who operate the institution. Profit, whether defined as income minus expense or in terms of reserves for the future, is the result of planning, sound management, and careful decision making.

The purpose of this text is to give the foodservice operator the basic tools necessary to make informed decisions with regard to managing income and expense. If these tools are utilized properly, the potential for achieving desired profits is greatly enhanced.

Profit should not, in reality, be viewed as what is left over after the bills are paid. In fact, careful planning is necessary to earn a profit. Thus a more appropriate formula, which rewards the business owner for the risk associated with business ownership or investment, is as follows:

Income − Desired profit = Ideal expense

Ideal expense, in this case, is defined as management's view of the correct or appropriate amount of expense necessary to generate a given quantity of sales. **Desired profit** is defined as the profit level that management desires to achieve on a given quantity of sales.

This formula clearly places profit as a reward for providing service, not a left-over. Ideal expense is not, however, easily achieved. In these competitive times, it takes an astute foodservice operator to consistently make decisions that will lead to maximizing income while holding expenses to the ideal or required amount.

Income

To some degree, income levels can be managed by the foodservice manager. Income varies with both the number of guests frequenting the business and the amount of money spent by each guest. Management is able to increase income either by increasing the number of guests served or by increasing the amount each guest spends. Adding seating or drive-in windows, extending operating hours, and building additional foodservice units are all examples of management efforts to increase the number of guests choosing to come to the restaurant or foodservice operation. Suggestive selling, creative menu pricing, and discounts for larger purchases are examples of increasing the amount of money each guest spends.

It has been said that management's primary task is to deliver customers to the front door. While one may or may not agree with such a statement, it is clearly true that the profit formula begins with income. Experienced foodservice operators know that increasing income through adding customers, suggestive selling, or possibly raising menu prices is an extremely effective way of increasing overall profitability *if* effective cost management systems are in place.

The focus of this text is on managing expense, not generating income. While the two are clearly related, they are different. Marketing efforts, restaurant design and site selection, employee training, and food preparation methods are all critical links in the income-producing chain. No amount of effective control can take the place of poor sales volume or income.

Effective cost control, when coupled with management's aggressive attitude toward meeting and exceeding guests' expectations, can result in outstanding profit performance.

Expenses

There are four major expense categories that must be controlled by management. They are

1. **Food costs**
2. **Beverage costs**
3. **Labor costs**
4. **Other expenses**

Food Costs

These are the costs associated with producing the menu items a customer selects. They include meats, dairy, fruits, vegetables, and other categories of food items produced by the foodservice operation. When computing food costs, many operators include the cost of minor paper and plastic items, such as the paper wrappers used to wrap sandwiches, when they compute food costs. In general, these items make up the largest or second largest expense an operator faces.

Beverage Costs

Beverage costs are those related to the sale of alcoholic beverages. It is interesting to note that costs for nonalcoholic beverages usually are accounted for in the food costs category. Alcoholic beverages accounted for in the beverage costs category include beer, wine, and liquor. This category may also include the costs of ingredients necessary to produce these drinks, such as cherries, lemons, limes, olives, and other items commonly used in the production and service of alcoholic beverages. Food costs are sometimes combined with beverage costs to yield **food and beverage costs.**

Labor Costs

Labor costs include the cost of all employees necessary to run the business. This amount includes taxes required to be paid by the employer for having the employees on the payroll. Some operators include the cost of management in this category. Others prefer to place the cost of managers in the other expenses category. In most operations, labor costs are second only to food costs in total dollars spent.

Other Expenses

This category includes all expenses that are not food, beverage, or labor. Examples include utilities, rent, linen, and equipment. While these expenses are sometimes called "minor expenses," the successful operator knows that their control is critical to the overall profitability of the foodservice unit.

Consider the case of Greg Larson, the food and beverage director in a 200-room hotel, located near an interstate highway. Greg has just received his year-end operating reports for the current year. He is comparing the results to those of last year. The numbers he received are shown in Figure 1.3.

Greg is concerned, but he is not sure why. Income is higher than last year, so he feels his customers must like the products and services they receive from his operations. In fact, repeat business is actually really beginning to develop. Profits are up also, but Greg has the uneasy feeling that things are not going so well. The kitchen appears to be running smoothly. The staff, however, often run out of needed items, and there seems to be a large amount of food thrown away. Theft may be occurring, but who has time to watch every storeroom? Greg also senses that his boss, Ruth Richards, is less than pleased with his department's performance. He would really like to get a handle on the problem (if there is one), but how and where should he start?

The answer for Greg, and for anyone who wants to develop a serious control package, is very simple. Start with basic mathematics and build from there. The mathematics used in this text consist only of addition, subtraction, multiplication, and division. These tools will be sufficient to build a cost control system

Figure 1.3 **Highway Hotel Operating Results**

	This Year	Last Year
Income	$1,106,040	$850,100
Expense	1,017,557	773,591
Profits	88,483	76,509

that will help food service operators effectively manage the expenses they incur on a daily basis.

Getting Started

What would it mean if a foodservice manager said that he or she spent $500 on food yesterday? Obviously, it means little unless we know more about the operation. Should the manager have spent $500 yesterday? Was that too much? Too little? Was it a "good" day? These questions raise a difficult problem. How can we compare today with yesterday, or one foodservice unit with another, so that we can see how well we are doing? A restaurant with sales of $1,000 per day in 1954 is very different from the same restaurant with daily sales of $1,000 today. The value of the dollar today is quite different from what it was in 1954.

We know that the value of dollars has changed over a period of time. Generally, inflation causes the purchasing power of a dollar today to be less than that of a dollar during a previous time period. While this concept of changing value is useful in the area of finance, it is vexing when one wants to answer the simple question "Am I doing as well today as I was five years ago?"

Or consider the problem of a multiunit foodservice manager. Two units sell tacos on either side of a large city. One uses $500 worth of food products each day; the other unit uses $600 worth of food products each day. Does the second unit use an additional $100 worth of food each day because it has more customers or because it is less efficient in utilizing the food?

The answer to all of the above questions, and others, can be determined by using percents to relate expenses incurred to sales generated.

Expressing Percent

Percent (%) means "out of each hundred." Thus 10 percent would mean 10 out of each 100. If we asked how many customers will buy blueberry pie on a given day, and the answer is 10 percent, then 10 people out of each 100 we serve will select blueberry pie. If 52 percent of our employees are female, then 52 out of each 100 employees are female.

There are three ways to write a percent, as shown in Figure 1.4.

Common Form

In its common form, the percent sign (%) is used to express the percent. If we say 10%, then we mean 10 out of each 100, and no further explanation is necessary. In common form, the percent is equivalent to the same amount expressed in either the fraction or decimal form.

Figure 1.4 **Forms for Expressing Percent**

	Percent		
Forms	**1%**	**10%**	**100%**
Common	1%	10%	100%
Fraction	1/100	10/100	100/100
Decimal	.01	0.10	1.00

Fraction Form

In fraction form, the percent is expressed as the part, or a portion, of 100. Thus 10 percent is written as 10 over 100 (10/100). This is simply another way of expressing the relationship between the part (10) and the whole (100).

Decimal Form

A decimal is a number developed from the counting system we use. It is based on the fact that we count to ten, then start over again. In other words, each of our major units—tens, hundreds, thousands, and so on—is based on the use of tens, and each number can easily be divided by ten. Instead of using the percent sign (%), the decimal form uses the decimal point (.) to express the percent relationship. Thus 10% is expressed as 0.10 in decimal form. The numbers to the right of the decimal point express the percent.

Each of these three methods of expressing percentages is used in the foodservice industry, and the foodservice manager must develop a clear understanding of how a percent is computed. Once that is known, the foodservice manager can express the percent in any form that is useful or comfortable to him or her.

Computing Percent

To determine what percent one number is of another number, divide the number that is the **part** by the number that is the **whole**. Usually, this means dividing the smaller number by the larger number. For example, 840 customers were served at a hotel banquet; 420 of them had coffee. To find what percent ordered coffee, divide the part (420) by the whole (840). The process looks as follows:

$$\frac{\textbf{Part}}{\textbf{Whole}} = \textbf{Percent} \quad \textit{or} \quad \frac{\textbf{420}}{\textbf{840}} = \textbf{0.50}$$

Thus 50% (common form), 50/100 (fraction form), or 0.50 (decimal form) represents the proportion of people who ordered coffee at the banquet. A great number of new foodservice managers have difficulty computing percent figures. It is easy to forget which number goes "on the top" and which number goes "on the bottom." In general, if one attempts to compute a percent and gets a whole number (a number larger than one), either a mistake has been made, or costs are extremely high! Percent calculations are important, however, for at least two major reasons. First and foremost, percents are the most common standard used for evaluating costs in the foodservice industry. Therefore, a knowledge of what a percent is and how it is calculated is vital. Secondly, individuals in the foodservice industry are evaluated primarily on their ability to compute and control these percent figures. They are used extensively in this text and are a cornerstone of any effective cost control system. Many people also get confused converting from one form of percent to another. If that is a problem, remember the following conversion rules:

1. **To convert from common form to decimal form, move the decimal two places to the left, that is, 50.00% = 0.50**
2. **To convert from decimal form to common form, move the decimal two places to the right, that is, 0.40 = 40.00%**

In a commercial foodservice operation the "whole" is usually a sales or income figure. Expenses and profit are the "parts," which are usually expressed in terms of a percent. It is interesting to note that in the United States the same system used for numbers is used for money. Each dime contains 10 pennies, each dollar contains 10 dimes, and so on. Thus, it is true that a percent, when discussing money, refers to "cents out of each dollar" as well as "dollars out of each one hundred dollars." When we say 10% of a dollar, we mean 10 cents or 10 cents out of each dollar. Likewise, 25% of a dollar represents 25 cents, 50% of a dollar represents 50 cents, and 100% of a dollar represents $1.00.

Sometimes, when using percent to express the relationship between portions of a dollar and the whole, we find that the part is indeed larger than the whole. Figure 1.5 demonstrates the three possibilities that exist when computing a percent.

Great care must always be taken when computing percents so that the percent arrived at is of help to the manager and does not represent an error in mathematics.

Figure 1.5 **Percent Computation**

Possibilities	Examples	Results
Part is smaller than the whole	$\frac{61}{100} = 61\%$	Always less than 100%
Part is equal to the whole	$\frac{35}{35} = 100\%$	Always equals 100%
Part is larger than the whole	$\frac{125}{50} = 250\%$	Always greater than 100%

Using Percent

Imagine that our sales (income) for a week are $561. Expenses for the same week are $490. Given these suggested facts, our profit formula for the week would look as follows:

Income − Expense = Profit

or

$561 − $490 = $71

If we had hoped for $100 profit for the week, we would have been "short." Using the alternative profit formula, we would find the following:

Income − Desired profit = Ideal expense

or

$561 − $100 = $461

Note that expense in this example ($490) exceeds ideal expense ($461) and thus, too little profit was achieved.

These numbers can also be expressed in terms of percent. If we want to know what percent of our income went to expenses, we would compute it as follows:

$$\frac{\textbf{Expense}}{\textbf{Income}} = \textbf{Expense \%}$$

or

$$\frac{\$490}{\$561} = 87.30\%$$

Another way to state this relationship is to say that each dollar of sales costs 87.3 cents to produce. Also, each sales dollar yields 12.7 cents profit.

$1.00 Income − $0.873 Expense = $0.127 Profit

As long as expense is smaller than income, some profit will be generated, even if it is not as much as we had hoped for. We can compute profit percent using the following formula:

$$\frac{\textbf{Profit}}{\textbf{Income}} = \textbf{Profit \%}$$

In our example

$$\frac{\$71 \text{ profit}}{\$561 \text{ income}} = 12.7\% \text{ profit}$$

We can compute what we had hoped would be our profit percent by dividing desired profit ($100) by income ($561).

$$\frac{\$100 \text{ desired profit}}{\$561 \text{ income}} = 17.8\% \text{ desired profit}$$

In simple terms, we had hoped to make 17.8% profit, but made only 12.7% profit. Excess costs could account for the difference. If these costs could be identified and corrected, we could perhaps achieve the **desired profit** percent. Most foodservice operators compute many cost percents, not just one. The major cost divisions used in foodservice are as follows:

1. **Food and beverage expense**
2. **Labor expense**
3. **Other expense**

A modified profit formula therefore looks like this:

$$\textbf{Income} - \left(\begin{array}{l}\textbf{Food \& beverage}\\ \textbf{expense}\end{array} + \begin{array}{l}\textbf{Labor}\\ \textbf{expense}\end{array} + \begin{array}{l}\textbf{Other}\\ \textbf{expense}\end{array}\right) = \textbf{Profit}$$

Put in another format, the equation looks as follows:

	Income
less	Food and beverage expense
less	Labor expense
less	Other expense
equals	Profit

Developing the Profit and Loss Statement

Consider the example of Cynthia's Steak House shown in Figure 1.6.

All of Cynthia's expenses and profits can be computed as percents by using the income figure ($400,000) as the whole, with expenses and profit representing the parts as follows:

Figure 1.6 **Cynthia's Steak House Expenses and Profits**

Income	$400,000
Expenses	
Food and beverage	150,000
Labor	175,000
Other	25,000
Total expense	350,000
Profit	50,000

1. $$\frac{\textbf{Food and beverage expense}}{\textbf{Income}} = \textbf{Food and beverage expense \%}$$

or

$$\frac{\$150{,}000}{\$400{,}000} = 37.50\%$$

2. $$\frac{\textbf{Labor expense}}{\textbf{Income}} = \textbf{Labor expense \%}$$

or

$$\frac{\$175{,}000}{\$400{,}000} = 43.75\%$$

3. $$\frac{\textbf{Other expense}}{\textbf{Income}} = \textbf{Other expense \%}$$

or

$$\frac{\$25{,}000}{\$400{,}000} = 6.25\%$$

4. $$\frac{\textbf{Total expense}}{\textbf{Income}} = \textbf{Total expense \%}$$

or

$$\frac{\$350{,}000}{\$400{,}000} = 87.50\%$$

5. $$\frac{\textbf{Profit}}{\textbf{Income}} = \textbf{Profit \%}$$

or

$$\frac{\$50{,}000}{\$400{,}000} = 12.50\%$$

A simplified statement that details income, expenses, and profit for a given period of time is called the **profit and loss (P&L) statement.** It lists income, food and beverage related expense, labor expense, and other expense. The P&L also identifies profits, since profits are generated by the following formula:

Income − Expense = Profit

Figure 1.7 is a simplified P&L statement for Cynthia's. Note the similarity to Figure 1.6. This time, however, expenses and profit are expressed in terms of both dollar amount and percent of income.

Cynthia knows, from the following P&L, that her food and beverage expense percent equals 37.50%. The labor expense percent in her steak house equals 43.75%; other expense percent equals 6.25%; and in total, her expense percent is 87.50% (37.50 + 43.75 + 6.25 = 87.50%). Her profit percent equals

Figure 1.7 **Cynthia's Steak House P&L**

Income	$400,000	100%
Expenses		
Food and beverage	150,000	37.50%
Labor	175,000	43.75%
Other	25,000	6.25%
Total expense	350,000	87.50%
Profit	50,000	12.50%

12.50%. Thus, for each dollar in sales, Cynthia earns a profit of $0.125. This profit percent is very important. Many items affect the profit percent, and the foodservice manager must be aware of, and in control of, all of them. All of the items that impact profit percent are discussed in later chapters of this text.

Performance to Budget

Some foodservice managers do not generate income or sales on a daily basis. Consider for a moment the foodservice manager at Camp Eureka, a summer camp for children. In this case, parents pay a fixed fee to cover housing, activities, and meals for a set period of time. The foodservice director in this situation is just one of several managers who must share this income. If too many dollars are spent on providing housing or activities, too few dollars may be available to provide an adequate quantity or quality of food products. On the other hand, if too many dollars are spent on providing foodservice, there may not be enough left to cover other needed expense areas such as housing and activities. In a case like this, foodservice operators usually prepare a budget. A budget is simply a forecast or estimate of projected income, expense, and profit.

Budgets may be used by both commercial and noncommercial foodservice operators. They are most frequently used, however, by effective managers, whether in the commercial or noncommercial sector. Budgeting is simply planning for income, expense, and profit. If these items are planned for, managers can determine how close they are to the plan or budget.

In the summer camp example, the following information is known:

1. **Number of campers = 180**
2. **Number of meals daily = 3**
3. **Length of campers' stay = 7 days**

With 180 campers eating 3 meals each day for 7 days, 3,780 meals will be served (180 campers × 3 meals × 7 days = 3,780 meals).

Generally, in a case such as the summer camp, the foodservice director is given a dollar amount for each meal to be served. For example, if $0.85 per meal is the amount budgeted for this director, the total income budget would equal $3,213.00 ($0.85 per meal × 3,780 meals = $3,213.00). From this figure, we can begin to develop an expense budget. In this case, we are interested in the amount budgeted, the amount actually spent, and the percent of budget used each day.

A childhood example may help to firmly establish the idea of budget and performance to budget. Assume a child has $0.25 per day to spend on candy. On Monday morning, the child's parents give the child $0.25 for each day of the week, or $1.75 total ($0.25 × 7 days = $1.75). If the child spends $0.25 per day, he or she will be able to buy candy all week. If, however, too much is spent in any one day, there may not be any money left at the end of the week. A good spending pattern is shown in Figure 1.8.

The % of total column is computed by dividing $0.25 (the part) by $1.75 (the whole). Notice that we can determine the percent of total that should have been spent by any given day when we know that each day equals 14.28% or 1/7 of the total.

Figure 1.8 **Child's Spending for Candy**

Weekday	Budgeted Amount	% of Total
Monday	$0.25	14.28%
Tuesday	0.25	14.28
Wednesday	0.25	14.28
Thursday	0.25	14.28
Friday	0.25	14.28
Saturday	0.25	14.28
Sunday	0.25	14.28
Total	1.75	100.00

Figure 1.9 **Common Foodservice Budget Periods**

Budget period	Portion	% of Total
One week	One day	1/7 or .143
One month (28 days)	One day	1/28 or .036
One month (30 days)	One day	1/30 or .033
One month (31 days)	One day	1/31 or .032
One month	One week	1/4 or .250
Six months	One month	1/6 or .167
One year	One day	1/365 or .003
	One week	1/52 or .019
	One month	1/12 or .083

This same logic applies to the foodservice operation. Figure 1.9 represents commonly used budget periods and their accompanying proportions.

In the summer camp, after one week's camping was completed, we found the information shown in Figure 1.10. Assume we used the expense records from last year to develop the expense budget figures for this summer.

In this case, we are interested in both the plan (budget) and our actual performance. Figure 1.11 shows a performance to budget summary, with income and expenses presented in terms of both budget amount and actual amount. In all categories, percents are used to compare actual expense with the budgeted amount, using the following formula:

$$\frac{\textbf{Actual}}{\textbf{Budget}} = \textbf{\% of budget}$$

In this example, income remained the same although some campers skipped (or slept through!) some of their meals. This is often the case when one fee or price buys a number of meals, whether they are eaten or not. In some

Figure 1.10 **Camp Eureka Budget for One Week**

Item	**Budget**	**Actual**
Meals served	3,780	3,615
Income	$3,213	$3,213
Expenses		
Food	1,600	1,416
Labor	1,200	1,290
Other	300	465
Profit	113	42

Figure 1.11 **Camp Eureka Performance to Budget Summary**

Item	**Budget**	**Actual**	**% of Budget**
Meals served	3,780	3,615	95.60%
Income	$3,213	$3,213	100.00%
Expenses			
Food	1,600	1,416	88.50
Labor	1,200	1,290	107.50
Other	300	465	155.00
Total Expense	3,100	3,171	102.30
Profit	113	42	37.20

other cases, only meals actually eaten are allowed to be charged for. In either case, budgeted amount, actual expense, and percent of budget or **performance to budget** are important management tools. In looking at the Camp Eureka performance to budget summary, we can see that we served fewer meals than planned and thus spent less on food than we estimated, but spent more on labor than we thought necessary. We also spent much more than we estimated for other expenses (155% of the budget in this category). As a result, our profit dollars were too low. We have some problems, but they are not everywhere in our operation.

How do we know that? If our budget was accurate and we are within reasonable limits of our budget, we are said to be "in line" or in compliance with our budget. If, as management, we decided that plus or minus 15% of budget in each category would be considered in line or acceptable, we are in line with regard to meals served, food expense, labor expense, and total expense. We are not in line with other expense (+155%) or profit (+37.20%). Note that figures over 100% mean too much (other expense), while figures below 100% mean too little (profit).

Many operators use the concept of **significant variation** to determine whether a cost control problem exists. In this case, a significant variation is any variation in expected costs that management feels is a case for concern. This variation can be in costs that were either higher or lower than the normal or standard amount that was expected. When significant variation exists, management must

1. **Define the problem**
2. **Determine the cause**
3. **Take corrective action**

It is crucial to know the kind of problem we have if we are to be effective problem solvers. Management's attention must be focused on the proper place. In this case, the proper areas for concern are other expense and profit. If, in the future, food expense became too low, it too would be an area of concern. Why? Remember, expenses create sales, and thus it is not the goal of management to eliminate expense. In fact, those managers who focus too much on eliminating expense, instead of building sales, often find that their expenses are completely eliminated when they are forced to close the restaurant's door permanently! Control and management of income and expense are important. Elimination of either is not desired.

As we have demonstrated, income and expense directly impact profit. The manager's role is to control this balance. It can be done and it can be fun.

The remainder of this text discusses how the foodservice operator can best manage and account for income and expense. With a good understanding of the relationship between income, expense, and profit, we are ready to begin the cost control or cost management process.

TEST YOUR SKILL

A. At the conclusion of her first month of operating Val's Donut Shop, Val has computed the following income and expense figures:

Week	Income	Expense
1	$ 894.50	$ 761.80
2	1,147.60	522.46
3	1,261.80	879.14
4	1,345.11	1,486.20

Prepare both weekly and monthly profit formulas so that Val has a good idea about her current profit situation. Also, tell her how much her expenses should have been for the month to realize the $1,000 profit she had hoped for.

B. The dining room at the Roadrock Inn is extremely popular. Jeremy Graves, the food and beverage director, is pleased to see that his sales are higher than last year. Of course, expenses are higher also. Express Jeremy's expenses and profit as a percentage of total sales, both this year and last year.

	This year	%	Last year	%
Income	$965,971		$875,421	
Expenses				
Food and beverage	367,069		350,168	
Labor	338,090		315,151	
Other	144,896		140,068	
Total Expense	?		?	
Profit	?		?	

Comparing this year to last year, how is Jeremy doing in managing his expense? How do changes in income affect his performance?

C. Pamela Burgoyn operates a school foodservice department in a small rural community. She feeds approximately 1,000 students per day in three different locations. Her budget, set at the beginning of the school year by the superintendent, is developed in such a way that a small amount is to be reserved for future equipment purchases and dining room renovation. These funds are available, however, only if Pamela meets her budget. She hopes to use this year's reserve to buy a $5,000 refrigerated salad bar for the high school. Since it is the midpoint of her school year, help her determine her performance to budget.

Item	Budget	Actual	% of Budget
Meals served	290,000	146,105	?
Expenses			
Food	$170,000	$84,961	?
Labor	125,000	63,752	?
Other	60,000	31,460	?
Total Expense	355,000	?	?
Reserve	5,000	?	—

Is Pamela likely to meet the reserve requirement and thus be able to purchase the salad bar?

CHAPTER 2

Determining Sales Volume

OVERVIEW

In this chapter, we present methods and procedures for developing accurate projections and records of food and beverage sales volume. This includes both number of guests served and amount spent per guest. The use of these techniques is required if the manager is to develop a sales history for his or her unit.

HIGHLIGHTS

At the conclusion of this chapter, the manager will be able to

A. Develop a plan to record actual sales
B. Develop a procedure to estimate future sales
C. Compute percentage increases or decreases in sales over time

Determining Sales Volume

The first questions operating managers must ask themselves are very simple: "How many guests will I serve today?" "How many this week? This year?" The answers to questions such as these are critical, since these customers will provide the income from which the operator will pay basic operating expenses. Simply put, if too few customers are served, total income may be insufficient to cover costs, even if these costs are well managed. In addition, purchasing decisions regarding the kind and quantity of food or beverage to buy depend on knowing the number of guests who will be coming to consume those products. Labor required to serve the guests is also determined based on the manager's "best guess" of projected sales volume or number of guests to be served. Forecasts are normally based on history, since what has happened in the past is generally our best predictor of what will happen in the future.

In the hospitality industry, we have many ways of counting or defining sales. In its simplest case, **sales** is the dollar amount of income collected during some predetermined shift or meal period. When sales is defined in this way, the cash register or guest check helps us determine how many sales, in general, were completed. In other areas of the industry, for example, in college dormitory foodservice, it is customary that no cash actually changes hands during a particular meal period. There is still, however, a need for the college foodservice director to know "How many individuals will I serve?"

In some cases, the food and beverage operation may be a blend of cash and noncash sales. Consider for a moment the hospital foodservice director, who is very likely involved in serving both cash customers (public cafeteria) and noncash patients (tray line), as well as employees who pay cash for meals at a reduced or subsidized rate.

A knowledge of sales, in terms of cash or customers, helps the effective foodservice manager plan to have the right number of workers, at the right time, and with the right amounts of product available. In this way, the hospitality manager can begin to manage his or her costs effectively. In addition to the importance of accurate sales records for purchasing and staffing, sales records are valuable to the operator when developing labor standards. Consider, for example, a large restaurant with 400 seats. If an individual waitperson can serve 25 guests at lunch, we could need as many as 400 / 25 or 16 waitpersons per lunch shift. If no accurate sales records or forecasts are kept by management, too few or too many waitpersons could possibly be scheduled on any given lunch period. With accurate sales records, a sales history can be developed for each sales outlet operated by management, and better management decisions can be made with regard to planning for its operation.

Developing the Sales History

A sales history is no more than the systematic record of all sales achieved during a given time period. Before operators can develop a sales history, it is necessary that they determine which measure of sales will be most important. In the restaurant business, sales are generally recorded in terms of dollar sales *and* customers served. Figure 2.1 shows a typical format for recording sales of a cash nature only.

In this most basic of cases, we determine daily sales from either actual sales rung up on the cash register or the sum of the individual sales recorded on the guest checks. We transfer that number to the daily sales history in the column titled **cash sales**. **Sales to date** is the cumulative total of sales reported in the unit. Sales to date is the number we get when we add today's sales to the sales of all prior days in the reporting period.

Sales to date on Tuesday, January 2, is computed by adding Tuesday's sales to those of the prior day ($851.90 + $974.37 = $1,826.27). The sales to date column is a running total of the sales achieved by the unit for a given accounting period, in this case, one week. Should an operator prefer, the sales period could be defined in blocks other than one week. Common alternatives are meal periods, days, weeks, two-week periods, months, quarters, or any other period that makes sense to the operator.

Figure 2.2 shows the type of format used when no cash sales typically are reported. For purposes of demonstration, a sales period is defined in terms of time of day rather than a 24-hour period. This type of form can be used in an institutional setting such as a nursing home, college dormitory, prison, or summer camp, or in any other situation where a knowledge of the number of guests served during a given time period is important for planning purposes.

Figure 2.1 **Sales History**

		Able's Restaurant	**1/1/93 to 1/7/93**
Sales Period	**Date**	**Cash Sales**	**Sales to Date**
Monday	1/1	$ 851.90	$ 851.90
Tuesday	1/2	974.37	1,826.27
Wednesday	1/3	1,004.22	2,830.49
Thursday	1/4	976.01	3,806.50
Friday	1/5	856.54	4,663.04
Saturday	1/6	1,428.22	6,091.26
Sunday	1/7	1,241.70	7,332.96
Week's total			7,332.96

Figure 2.2 **Sales History**

Camp Eureka

	Guests Served							
Serving Period	**Mon**	**Tues**	**Wed**	**Thurs**	**Fri**	**Sat**	**Sun**	**Total**
7:00–9:00 A.M.	121							
9:00–11:00 A.M.	40							
11:00–1:00 P.M.	131							
1:00–3:00 P.M.	11							
3:00–5:00 P.M.	42							
5:00–7:00 P.M.	161							
Total served	506							

Given the data in Figure 2.2, the implications for staffing service personnel at Camp Eureka are obvious. Fewer service personnel are needed from 9:00 to 11:00 A.M. than from 7:00 to 9:00 A.M. The reason is obvious. Fewer campers eat between 9:00 and 11:00 A.M. (40) than between 7:00 and 9:00 A.M. (121). With this information, the effective manager can now either reduce staff during the slower service period or shift those workers to some other necessary task. Notice also that we know *not* to continue to produce as many items for consumption during this time period. We make more efficient use of both labor and food products when we know the answer to the question "How many guests will I serve?"

Computing Averages

Foodservice operators use two major types of averages when computing average sales or average customer count. Since future customers can be expected to mirror the activities of customers in the past, using historical averages can be quite useful in projecting future volume.

An **average** is defined as the value arrived at by adding the quantities in a series and then dividing the sum of the quantities by the number of items in the series. Thus, the average of 6 + 9 + 18 is 11. The sum of the quantities in this case equals 33 (6 + 9 + 18 = 33). The number of items in the series is three (6, 9, and 18). Thus 33 / 3 = 11, the average of the numbers. The two major types of averages used in foodservice are as follows:

1. **Fixed average**
2. **Rolling average**

Fixed Average

A **fixed average** is an average in which an operator determines a specific time period, say the first 14 days of the month, and computes the mean or average amount of sales or customer activity for that period. Note that this average is fixed; in other words, the first 14 days of the month will always contain the same numbers, as shown in Figure 2.3. This average (total sales ÷ number of days) is fixed or constant because management has identified 14 specific days that are used to make up the average.

Rolling Average

The **rolling average** is the average amount of sales or volume over a changing time period rather than a specific time period. Whereas the fixed average is computed using a specific or constant set of data, the rolling average is computed using data that change regularly. To illustrate the rolling average, consider the case of Ubalda, who operates a sportsbar in a university town in the Midwest. Ubalda is interested in knowing what the average sales dollars were in her operation for *each prior seven-day period.* Obviously, in this case the prior seven-day period changes or rolls forward each day. Note that Ubalda could have been interested in average sales last week (fixed average), but she prefers to know her average sales for the last seven days. This means that she will, at times, be using data from both last week *and* this week to compute the last seven days' average. Using the sales data in Figure 2.4, the seven-day rolling average for Ubalda's bar would be computed as shown in Figure 2.5.

Figure 2.3 **14-Day Fixed Average**

Day	Sales
1	$ 350.00
2	320.00
3	390.00
4	440.00
5	420.00
6	458.00
7	450.00
8	460.00
9	410.00
10	440.00
11	470.00
12	460.00
13	418.00
14	494.00
14-day total	5,980.00

$$\frac{\$5,980.00}{14} = \$427.14 \text{ per day}$$

Figure 2.4 **Ubalda's 14-day Sales**

Date	Sales	Date	Sales
1	$350	8	$460
2	320	9	410
3	390	10	440
4	440	11	470
5	420	12	460
6	458	13	418
7	450	14	494

Figure 2.5 **Seven-Day Rolling Average**

	Seven-Day Period							
Date	**1–7**	**2–8**	**3–9**	**4–10**	**5–11**	**6–12**	**7–13**	**8–14**
1	$350	—						
2	320	$320	—					
3	390	390	$390	—				
4	440	440	440	$440	—			
5	420	420	420	420	$420	—		
6	458	458	458	458	458	$458	—	
7	450	450	450	450	450	450	$450	—
8		460	460	460	460	460	460	$460
9			410	410	410	410	410	410
10				440	440	440	440	440
11					470	470	470	470
12						460	460	460
13							418	418
14								494
Total	2,828	2,938	3,028	3,078	3,108	3,148	3,108	3,152
7-day rolling average	404.00	419.71	432.57	439.71	444.00	449.71	444.00	450.29

Note that each seven-day period is made up of a group of daily sales figures that changes over time. Each day we add today's sales to the seven-day total and drop the day that is now eight days past. This gives us the effect of continually rolling the most current seven days forward. The rolling average, while more complex than the fixed average, is extremely useful in recording data to help management make effective forecast decisions. This is true because in many cases rolling data are more current and thus more relevant than some fixed historical averages. Some operators choose to compute fixed averages for some items and rolling averages for others. In either case, managers should record sales volume and track it in a way that is meaningful to them.

Cash Sales, Customer Counts, or Both?

As previously mentioned, some operations do not handle cash. For them, developing sales histories with customer counts, as in the case of Camp Eureka, makes sense. For others, such as Able's Restaurant, cash sales are generated and thus should be tracked.

For many operators, both sales *and* customer counts are important. In fact, when an operator tracks both cash sales and customer counts, he or she may record a third variable, namely, **average sales per guest**.

Average sales per guest is determined by the following formula:

$$\frac{\textbf{Total sales}}{\textbf{\# of guests served}} = \textbf{Average sales per guest}$$

Consider the table in Figure 2.6 in which the operator is concerned with monitoring the following:

1. **Sales**
2. **Guests served**
3. **Average sales per guest**

Guests served may be determined by an actual customer head count, a count of utensils or trays issued, or the total number of individuals listed on the guest checks. In the case of Brothers' Family Restaurant, average sales per guest for Monday, January 1, is determined to be $4.90 ($1,391.60 / 284 = $4.90). On Tuesday, average sales per guest was $5.15 ($1,602.22 / 311 = $5.15).

It might be considered logical to think that the two-day average sales per guest would be ($4.90 + $5.15) / 2. This is *not* the case. It is an error many operators seem to make. The correct computation would be as follows:

Figure 2.6 **Sales History**

Brothers' Family Restaurant

Sales Period	Date	Sales	Guests Served	Average Sales per Guest
Monday	1/1	$1,391.60	284	$4.90
Tuesday	1/2	1,602.22	311	5.15
Wednesday	1/3			
Thursday	1/4			
Friday	1/5			
Saturday	1/6			
Sunday	1/7			
Total				

$$\frac{\textbf{Monday sales + Tuesday sales}}{\textbf{Monday guests + Tuesday guests}}$$

or

$$\frac{(\$1{,}391.60 + \$1{,}602.22)}{284 + 311} = \$5.03$$

The correct computation is a weighted average, that is, an average that uses the proper denominator. To demonstrate further, consider the following example:

Sales Period	Sales	Guests Served	Average Sales per Guest
Monday	$ 10.00	4	$2.50
Tuesday	120.00	40	3.00
Wednesday	1,600.00	400	4.00

Overall average sales per guest, using an unweighted average, would be $3.17 [($2.50 + $3.00 + $4.00) / 3 = $3.17]. The weighted and correct average would be as follows:

$$\frac{\$10.00 + \$120.00 + \$1{,}600.00}{(4 + 40 + 400)} = \$3.90$$

The correct answer to the question "What is the average sale per guest" is, in this case, clearly $3.90 and *not* $3.17.

Maintaining Sales Histories

It is very important that a hospitality operator keep copies of his or her completed sales history documents. These documents will become the basis for the development of **profit and loss statements**, which detail income and expenses for a given accounting period. Just as important, a knowledge of past and present sales levels provides a clue to estimating future sales volume levels. Projecting sales is a key factor in separating good managers from excellent ones. Simply put, good managers know what happened to sales last Monday; excellent managers have a good idea what will happen *next* Monday. This is only possible by keeping records of past sales activities.

In most cases, sales records should be kept for a period of at least two years. This allows the operator to have a good sense of what has happened in his or her business in the past. Of course, the manager of a new operation or one that has recently undergone major concept changes does not have the luxury of accurate sales histories. In such cases, the astute manager begins immediately to build his or her sales data base.

Figure 2.7 details a convenient method for compiling sales on a regular basis. In addition, a column has been added to identify the change in sales when comparing this year with last year. In this case, the operator is interested in looking at performance in the first three months of this year and then comparing that with performance in the first three months of last year.

The **variance** column in Figure 2.7 is determined by subtracting the **sales last year** column from the **sales this year**. In January, the variance figure is obtained as follows:

$$\textbf{Sales this year} - \textbf{Sales last year} = \textbf{Variance}$$

or

$$\$37{,}702.73 - \$34{,}861.51 = \$2{,}841.22$$

Percentage variance is obtained as follows:

$$\frac{\textbf{Variance}}{\textbf{Sales last year} \times 100} = \textbf{Percentage variance}$$

In the example in Figure 2.7, January percentage variance is determined by the following computation:

Step 1. $$\frac{\textbf{January variance}}{\textbf{January sales last year}} \quad \text{or} \quad \frac{\$2{,}841.22}{\$34{,}861.51} = .0815$$

To convert to common percentage variance from decimal form, move the decimal point two places to the right.

Step 2. .0815 (decimal form) = 8.15% (common form)

As you can see, first-quarter sales for Richard's Restaurant #16 are approximately 7.6% higher than they were last year. If the manager of Unit #16 were to use the 7.6% average for projection purposes, a planning sheet for the next quarter, as presented in Figure 2.8, could be developed.

Projected sales increase is determined by the following formula:

$$\textbf{Sales last year} \times \textbf{(Predicted change / 100)} = \textbf{Projected sales increase}$$

Figure 2.7 **Sales History**

Richard's Restaurant #16

Month	**Sales This Year**	**Sales Last Year**	**Variance**	**Percentage Variance**
January	$ 37,702.73	$ 34,861.51	$2,841.22	+ 8.15%
February	33,472.03	31,485.60	1,986.43	+ 6.31
March	36,492.98	33,707.79	2,785.19	+ 8.26
First quarter total	107,667.74	100,054.90	7,612.84	+ 7.61

Figure 2.8 **Sales Projection**

Richard's Restaurant #16

Month	**Sales Last Year**	**Predicated Change**	**Projected Sales Increase**
April	$ 39,845.62	+ 7.6%	$3,028.27
May	41,011.98	+ 7.6	3,116.91
June	40,852.65	+ 7.6	3,104.80
Second quarter total	121,710.25	+ 7.6	9,249.98

Projected sales increase for April would be determined as follows:

$$\mathbf{\$39{,}845.62 \times (7.6 / 100) = \$3{,}028.27}$$

Monthly sales figures from last year plus projected sales increase for the month give this operator a good idea of what might be expected during the second quarter of the year. Clearly, this operator will have a better idea of what volume to expect than the one who does not have the advantage of sales histories to help guide his or her planning.

Estimating Change in Customer Counts

Using the same techniques employed in estimating increases in sales, the non-cash operator can estimate increases in the number of guests served, and the cash operator can estimate increases in **average sales per guest** or **per person check average**. Figure 2.9 demonstrates how operators can project changes in either guests served or check average. For purposes of this example, let us assume that sales histories indicate 10% average increases in customer count and 5% increases in check average.

The manager of Bennie's is now prepared to complete the sales forecast necessary for 1993. To compute **total expected**, the following formula is used:

Customer count last year + Estimated increase = Total expected

In the case of Bennie's, the January **customer count last year** (8,486) is added to the estimated January increase. We determine the estimated increase by multiplying our **projected % increase** times **last year customer counts** (8,486 × .10 = 849). This number (**estimated increase**) is then added to the original 8,486 to yield 9,335, the total number of customers expected (8,486 + 849 = 9,335).

This process can be simplified, if desired, by using a math shortcut as follows:

Figure 2.9 **Sales Forecast 1993**

Bennie's

	Customer Counts			Check Average			
Time Period	**Last Year**	**Projected % Increase**	**Total Expected**	**Last Year**	**Projected % Increase**	**Check Average Forecast**	**Projected Sales 1993**
January 92	8,486	10%	9,335	$5.94	5%	$6.24	$58,250.40
February 92							
March 92							
First quarter total 92							

Customer count last year × **(1.00 + Projected % increase)** = **Total expected**

In our example,

8,486 × (1.00 + .10) = 9,335

This process works in exactly the same way as the one previously described. Each manager is free to use the method he or she is most comfortable with.

Forecasting Changes in Average Sale per Guest

We use the same basic technique to forecast next year's per person check average as follows:

Last year's check average + **Estimated increase** = **Average sale per guest forecast**

Last year's January **check average** ($5.94) is added to the estimated increase to achieve the **check average forecast**. We determine this number by multiplying our **projected % increase** times **last year's check average** ($5.94 × 0.50 = $0.30). This number (**estimated increase**) is then added to the original $5.95 to yield $6.24 ($5.94 + $0.30 = $6.24).

Projected sales is determined by multiplying **total expected customers** times **check average forecast**. In the case of Bennie's in January, the computation is as follows.

Total expected customer count × **Check average forecast** = **Projected sales**

Or

9,335 × $6.24 = $58,250.40

Estimating Future Volume

It is important to note that sales histories alone are not sufficient to accurately predict future sales. A manager's knowledge of potential price changes, new competitors, facility renovations, and improved selling programs are just a few of the many factors that he or she should consider when predicting future sales. There is no question, however, that every foodservice operator must develop and monitor daily a sales history report appropriate for his or her unit. A sales history report is easily developed and will serve as the cornerstone of other management systems. Without accurate sales data, control systems, regardless of their sophistication, are destined to fail.

When added to a manager's knowledge of the factors that impact his or her own unit, properly maintained histories help answer two important control questions, namely, "How many people are coming tomorrow?" and "How much is each person likely to spend?" The judgment of management is critical in forecasting answers to these questions. Since we can answer those questions, we are now ready to develop systems that will allow us to prepare an efficient and cost-effective way to serve those guests, be they customers in a hotel lounge or tourists visiting our restaurant as part of their overall travel experience. We want to be ready to provide them with quality products and enough people to properly serve them. We have done our homework with regard to the number of individuals that may be coming. Now we need to prepare for their arrival!

TEST YOUR SKILL

A. Peggy Richey operates a small interstate highway restaurant. She keeps a record of daily sales for each of three meal periods. She also records customers served during those same periods.

Complete her forms so that she can close out her sales records for the week.

Cash Sales

	Mon	Tues	Wed	Thurs	Fri	Total
Breakfast 7–11 A.M.	$189.50	$ 205.53	$197.22	$ 241.60	?	$1,048.91
Lunch 11 A.M.–3 P.M.	$487.90	?	$596.20	?	$799.82	?
Dinner 3 P.M.–close	$715.22	$ 487.51	$622.80	$ 685.90	$792.40	?
Total	?	$1,299.04	?	$1,527.50	?	?

Customer Counts

	Mon	Tues	Wed	Thurs	Fri	Total
Breakfast 7–11 A.M.	48	52	50	60	54	?
Lunch 11 A.M.–3 P.M.	81	97	?	83	120	501
Dinner 3 P.M.–close	65	?	68	62	?	325
Total	?	199	238	?	254	?

B. Don Lopez is developing his sales forecast for next year. His company has asked him to assume a 5% increase in his monthly customer counts. Don is not aware of any anticipated menu price increases and assumes, therefore, that his check average will remain stable.

Using last year's sales and customer counts, estimate Don's sales for next year.

Current Year	Cash Sales	Customer Count	Projected Cash Sales Next Year
January	$ 45,216	4,800	
February	48,538	5,120	
March	50,009	5,006	
April	45,979	4,960	
May	49,703	5,140	
June	48,813	5,300	
July	55,142	5,621	
August	59,119	6,002	
September	55,257	5,780	
October	50,900	5,341	
November	54,054	5,460	
December	50,982	5,482	
Total	613,712	64,012	

Did you decide to use each month's check average for your projection, or the yearly total average? Why?

C. Simon Seegrist is a district manager responsible for five quick-service units. His sales records for the region show an 8% increase in sales during this period over last period.

Help Simon know more about his sales increase by analyzing sales performance for each of his five units.

	Sales			
Unit #	**This Period**	**Last Period**	**Variance**	**% Increase or Decrease**
1	$ 5,276	$ 4,885		
2	6,006	5,997		
3	5,640	6,180		
4	7,700	7,850		
5	7,567	4,891		
Total	32,189	29,803	2,386	8%

CHAPTER 3

Managing the Cost of Food

OVERVIEW

This chapter presents the techniques and methods used to effectively plan for buying, receiving, and storing food products. It also presents a method for computing actual cost of food consumed and a method for estimating food cost percentage on a daily or weekly basis.

HIGHLIGHTS

At the conclusion of this chapter, the manager will be able to

A. Use sales histories and standardized recipes to determine the amount of food products to buy in anticipation of sales
B. Compute the actual cost of food consumed
C. Estimate food cost percentage on a daily basis

Menu Forecasting

The success of a foodservice operation is determined mainly by the menu. When selecting a restaurant, many people start the process with the question "What do you feel like eating?"

The importance of the answer to this question can be demonstrated by the following example. A restaurateur has used sales histories (see Chapter 2) to project 300 customers for lunch today. This restaurateur serves only three items: roast chicken, roast pork, and roast beef. How many of each item should the restaurateur produce so that he or she does not run out of any one item? If this were to happen, the customers would be upset. Producing too much of any one item, on the other hand, would create excess products and cause costs to rise to unacceptable levels. Clearly, it would be unwise to produce 300 portions of each item. While we would never run out of any one item, that is, each of our 300 estimated customers could order the same item and we would have enough, we would always have 600 left-overs at the end of our lunch period. The answer to the question of how many servings of roast chicken, pork, and beef to prepare lies in accurate menu forecasting.

Referring to the example cited above, if we are wise, we will have recorded last week's sales on a form similar to the one presented in Figure 3.1.

As you can see, we made an estimate for 300 customers because our weekly total (1,500) averages to 300 per day (1,500 / 5 days = 300 / per day). We also know that on an average day we sold 73 roast chicken (365 sold / 5 days = 73 per day), 115 roast pork (573 sold / 5 days = 115 per day), and 112 roast beef (562 sold / 5 days = 112 per day).

Once we know the average number of people selecting a given menu item and the total number of customers making the selections, we can compute the **percent selecting** figure for any menu item. In the case of this restaurant, we can improve our "guess" about the quantity of each item to prepare if we use the sales history to help guide our decision. If we assume that it is likely that future customers will select menu items much as past customers have done, given that the list of menu items and their order on the menu remains the same, the sales history can be used to improve our predictions with the following formula:

$$\textbf{Percent selecting} = \frac{\textbf{Total \# of specific menu items sold}}{\textbf{Total \# of all menu items sold}}$$

In fact, customers do tend to behave in fairly predictable ways. The best predictor of what customers will do today is to know what they did yesterday.

Put in another way, we know that 24.3% of our customers typically order roast chicken (365 roast chicken / 1,500 total all items sold = 24.3%). Similarly, 38.2% (573 roast pork / 1,500 total all items sold = 38.2%) prefer roast pork, while 37.5% (562 roast beef / 1,500 total all items sold = 37.5%) select roast beef.

If we know, in a general way, what we can expect our customers to select, we are better prepared to make good decisions about the quantity we should produce of each item. In our example, Figure 3.2 demonstrates our best guess of what our 300 customers are likely to order when they arrive.

Figure 3.1 **Sales History**

1/1/92–1/5/92

Menu Item	**Mon**	**Tues**	**Wed**	**Thurs**	**Fri**	**Total**	**Week's Average**
Roast chicken	70	72	61	85	77	365	73
Roast pork	110	108	144	109	102	573	115
Roast beef	100	140	95	121	106	562	112
Total	280	320	300	315	285	1,500	

Figure 3.2 **Predicting Number to Be Sold**

Menu Item	Forecast	% Selecting	Predicted # to Be Sold
Roast chicken	300	.243	73
Roast pork	300	.382	115
Roast beef	300	.375	112
Total			300

The basic formula for forecasting, based on past menu item sales history, is as follows:

$$\text{\# guests expected} \times \text{\% selecting a given menu item} = \text{Predicted \# of that item to be sold}$$

The **predicted number to be sold** is simply the number of a specific menu item likely to be sold if the total number of guests expected is known.

Once we know what our guests are likely to select, we move to the next step: determining the number of each item that should be prepared. It is important to note that foodservice managers face a great deal of uncertainty when attempting to determine the number of customers who will arrive on a given day. Many factors come together to influence the number of customers an operator will serve on any given day. Among these are the following:

1. **Competition**
2. **Weather**
3. **Special events**
4. **Hotel occupancy**
5. **Promotions**
6. **Conventions**

The interplay of these and other factors that may impact sales volume makes accurate customer count prediction very difficult.

In addition, sales histories track the general trends of an operation. They are not able to predict precisely the number of guests who may arrive on any given day. Sales histories, then, are a guide to what might be expected. In our example, last week's customer counts range from a low of 280 (Monday) to a high of 320 (Tuesday). In addition, the percentage of people selecting each menu item changes somewhat on a daily basis.

The foodservice manager must take into account possible increases or decreases in customer count and possible fluctuations in **predicted number to be sold** computations. The projection of customer counts and predicted number to be sold are tools to help the manager make better decisions about the kind and quantity of items to be produced. It would not be wise to produce only 300 servings for our expected guests. We certainly would not want to tell guest number 301 that we had run out of food! Depending on a variety of factors, including cooking time, preparation method, and reusability, the food production manager must determine exactly how many portions of each item to prepare.

A more thorough discussion of forecasting as it relates to production planning is presented in Chapter 5, "Managing the Food and Beverage Production Process."

In Chapter 2, we began to discuss the concept of sales forecasting. Forecasting can involve estimating the number of guests we expect, the dollar amount of sales we expect, or what those guests may want to purchase. This forecasting, as we have seen, is critical to effectively plan food production, and it is just as important as we make decisions about what and how much to buy.

Standardized Recipes

While it is the menu that determines what is to be sold and at what price, the **standardized recipe** controls the end product. The standardized recipe ensures that each time customers order an item from the menu, they get the same item! All critical factors of a standardized recipe have been tested and retested, and thus remain constant. The standardized recipe, therefore, is the key to menu item consistency and, ultimately, operational success. It is always true that customers expect to get what they pay for. The standardized recipe helps the foodservice operator make sure that this is always the case. Inconsistency is the enemy of any quality foodservice operation. It makes little difference to unhappy customers if we tell them, for instance, that they should remember how good we were the last time they dined with us!

Standardized recipes must be appropriate for the operation using them. If they are not, they will simply not be used or followed. In general, standardized recipes contain the following information:

1. **Item name**
2. **Total yield**
3. **Portion size**
4. **Ingredient list**
5. **Preparation/method section**
6. **Cooking time and temperature**
7. **Special instructions, if necessary**

*8. **Recipe cost (optional)**

***Note:** This information is optional. If the recipe cost is *not* included in the standardized recipe, a standardized cost sheet must be developed for each recipe item. The authors prefer the standardized cost sheet method (see Chapter 5).

Figure 3.3 demonstrates the use of a standardized recipe form. If this recipe is followed, we can expect to produce a consistent product of management-approved quantity and quality.

Figure 3.3 **Standardized Recipe**

Roast Chicken

Special Instructions:	Serve with Crabapple Garnish (see Crabapple Garnish standardized recipe). Serve on 10″ plate.
Recipe Yield:	48
Portion Size:	¼ chicken
Portion Cost:	See cost sheet.

Ingredients	Amount	Method
Chicken quarters (twelve 3–3½-lb chickens)	48 ea	Step 1. Wash chicken; check for pinfeathers; tray on 24″ x 20″ baking pans.
Butter (melted)	1 lb 4 oz	
Salt	¼ C	Step 2. Clarify butter; brush liberally on chicken quarters; combine all seasonings; mix well; sprinkle all over chicken quarters.
Pepper	2 T	
Paprika	3 T	
Poultry seasoning	2 t	
Ginger	1½ t	
Garlic powder	1 T	Step 3. Roast at 325°F in oven for 2½ hours, to an internal temperature of at least 165°F.

Many operators refuse to take the time to develop standardized recipes. The excuses used are many. The following list contains some of the arguments often used against developing standardized recipes:

1. **They take too long to use.**
2. **My people don't need recipes; they know how we do things here.**
3. **My chef refuses to reveal his or her secrets.**
4. **They take too long to write up.**
5. **We tried them but lost some, so we stopped using them.**
6. **They are too hard to read, or many of my people cannot read English.**

Of the above arguments, only the last one, an inability to read English, has any validity. Perhaps it is as one seasoned veteran in hospitality has stated, "When I don't want to do something, one excuse not to do it is as good as the next one!" Standardized recipes have far more advantages than disadvantages. Reasons **for** incorporating a system of standardized recipes include the following:

1. **Accurate purchasing is impossible without the existence and use of standardized recipes.**
2. **Dietary concerns require some foodservice operators to know exactly the kind of ingredients and the correct amounts of each that must be included in each serving of food consumed.**
3. **Accurate recipe costing and menu pricing is impossible without standardized recipes.**
4. **Matching food consumed to cash sales is impossible without standardized recipes.**
5. **New employees cannot be trained without standardized recipes. If the chef quits, for instance, you are stuck!**
6. **The computerization of a foodservice operation is impossible unless the elements of standardized recipes are in place.**

In fact, standardized recipes are so important that they are the cornerstone of any serious effort to produce consistent, high-quality food products at an established cost. Without them, cost control efforts become nothing more than raising selling prices, reducing portion sizes, or lessening quality. This is not effective cost management. It is hardly management at all. Without established standards, however, this happens frequently.

The importance of standardized recipes should not be underestimated. The effective operator should have them printed in the language of his or her production people, or accept the responsibility of providing the training needed to read them in their current form.

Any recipe can be standardized. The process can be quite complicated, however, especially in the areas of baking and sauce production. It is always best to begin with a recipe of proven quality. Frequently, we have a recipe designed to serve 10, but we want it to serve 100 people. In cases like this, it may not be possible to simply multiply each ingredient used by 10. A great deal has been written regarding various techniques used to expand recipes. Computer software designed for that purpose is now on the market. As a general rule, however, any item that can be produced in quantity can be standardized in recipe form and can be adjusted, up or down, in quantity.

Recipe adjustment can be done in many ways. Some work better than others, but in all methods some principles must be remembered. The first principle is that the measurement standard must be consistent. Weighing with a pound or an ounce scale is the most accurate method of measuring any ingredient. The food item to be measured must be **recipe ready**. It must be cleaned, trimmed, cooked, and generally completed, save for its addition to the recipe. For liquid items, the measurement of volume—a cup, quart, or gallon—may be the preferred process. Of course, some operators prefer to weigh all ingredients, even liquids, for improved accuracy.

When adjusting for recipe quantities, the following two general methods may be employed:

1. **Factor method**
2. **Percentage technique**

Factor Method

When using the factor method, the operator would use the following formula to arrive at a recipe conversion factor:

$$\frac{\textbf{Yield desired}}{\textbf{Current yield}} = \textbf{Conversion factor}$$

If, for example, our current recipe makes 50 portions, and the number of portions we wish to make is 125, the formula would be as follows:

$$\frac{125}{50} = 2.5$$

Thus, 2.5 would be the conversion factor. To produce 125 portions, we would multiply each ingredient in the recipe by 2.5 to arrive at the proper amount of that ingredient. Figure 3.4 illustrates the use of this method in a three ingredient recipe.

Figure 3.4 **Factor Method**

Ingredients	Original Amount	Factor	New Amount
A	4 lbs	2.5	10 lbs
B	1 qt	2.5	2½ qts
C	1½ T	2.5	3¾ T

Percentage Method

The percentage method deals with recipe weight, rather than with a conversion factor. In this regard, it is more accurate than using a conversion factor alone. Essentially, the percentage method involves computing the percentage of each ingredient in relation to the total weight needed. In this method, the original recipe is used to determine the total weight of all ingredients used to prepare the item. A percentage is then established for each ingredient.

To facilitate the computation, many operators convert pounds to ounces prior to making their percentage calculations. These can, of course, be converted back to standard pounds and ounces when the conversion is completed. To illustrate the use of the percentage method, let us assume that an operator has a recipe with a total weight of 10 pounds 8 ounces or 168 ounces. If the portion size is 4 ounces, the total recipe yield would be 168 / 4 or 42 servings. If the operator wishes to prepare 75 servings, he or she would need the following total recipe weight:

$$\textbf{75 servings} \times \textbf{4 oz per serving} = \textbf{300 oz}$$

The operator now has all the information necessary to use the percentage method of recipe conversion. Figure 3.5 details how the process would be accomplished. Note that % of total is computed as recipe ingredient amount divided by total amount required.

To compute the new recipe amount, we multiply the % of total figure times the total amount required, as follows for ingredient A:

$$\mathbf{61.9\% \times 300\ oz = 185.7\ oz}$$

The proper conversion of weights and measures is important in recipe expansion or reduction. The judgment of the recipe writer is critical, however, since such factors as cooking time, temperature, and utensil selection may vary as recipes are increased or decreased in size. In addition, some recipe ingredients like spices or flavorings may not respond well to mathematical conversions. In the final analysis, it is the manager's assessment of product taste that should determine ingredient ratios in standardized recipes. Recipes should be standardized and used as written. It is management's responsibility to see that this is done.

Figure 3.5 **Percentage Method**

Ingredient	Original Amount	Ounces	% of Total	Total Amount Required	% of Total	New Recipe Amount
A	6 lb 8 oz	104 oz	61.9%	300 oz	61.9%	185.7 oz
B	12 oz	12	7.1	300 oz	7.1	21.3 oz
C	1 lb	16	9.5	300 oz	9.5	28.5 oz
D	2 lb 4 oz	36	21.5	300 oz	21.5	64.5 oz
Total	10 lb 8 oz	168	100.0	300 oz	100.0	300.0 oz

Inventory Control

With a knowledge of what is likely to be purchased by our customers (sales forecast) and a firm idea of the ingredients necessary to produce these items (standardized recipes), the foodservice operator must make decisions about desired inventory levels. The desired inventory level is simply the answer to the question "How much of each needed ingredient should I have on hand at any one time?"

It is clear that this question can only be answered if our sales forecast is of good quality and our standardized recipes are in place so we don't "forget" to stock the necessary ingredient. Inventory management seeks to provide appropriate **working stock,** which is the amount we feel will be used between deliveries, and a minimal **safety stock,** which is the extra amount of a food product we will keep on hand. Safety stock seeks to reduce outages when item demand is higher than anticipated.

Foodservice managers face a much more difficult task in attempting to control inventory than their counterparts in general manufacturing. Demand for a given menu item can fluctuate greatly between delivery periods, even when the delivery occurs daily. The ability to effectively manage the inventory process is one of the best skills a foodservice manager can acquire.

Determining Inventory Levels

Inventory levels are determined by a variety of factors. Some of the most important ones are as follows:

1. **Storage capacity**
2. **Item perishability**
3. **Vendor delivery schedules**
4. **Potential savings from increased purchase size**
5. **Operating calendar**
6. **Relative importance of stock outages**
7. **Value of inventory dollars to the operator**

Storage Capacity

It is apparent that the foodservice operator will be unable to purchase for inventory in quantities that cannot be adequately stored and secured. Many kitchens lack adequate storage facilities. Those kitchens constructed before the mid-1970s, especially, are often short on space for frozen and refrigerated foods, and have excess capacity in dry storage areas. Operators must be careful not to determine inventory levels in a way that will overload storage capacity. This may mean scheduling more frequent deliveries and holding less of each product on hand than would otherwise be desired. When storage space is too great, the tendency by some managers is to fill the space. It is important that this not be done, as increased inventory of items generally leads to greater spoilage and loss due to theft. Moreover, large quantities of goods on the shelf tend to send a message to employees that there is "plenty" of everything. This may result in the careless use of valuable and expensive products. Never overload refrigerators or freezers. This not only can result in difficulty in finding items, but may cause carryovers (those items produced for a meal period but not sold) to be "lost" in the storage process, if not stored and labeled properly.

Item Perishability

If all food products had the same shelf life, that is, if all items would retain their freshness, flavor, and quality for the same number of days, the foodservice operator would have less difficulty in determining the quantity of each item he or she should keep on hand at any given time. Unfortunately, the shelf life of food products varies greatly.

Figure 3.6 demonstrates the difference in shelf life among some common foodservice items when properly stored.

The foodservice operator must balance the need for a particular product with the optimal shelf life for that product. Serving items that are "too old" is a sure way to develop customer complaints. In fact, one of the quickest ways to determine the overall effectiveness of a foodservice manager is to "walk the boxes." This means to take a tour of a facility's storage area. If many products, particularly in the refrigerated area, are moldy, soft, overripe, or rotten, it is a good indication of a foodservice operation that does not have a feel for inventory levels based on item perishability. It is also a sign that sales forecasting methods either are not in place or have broken down. Stock rotation problems may also exist in an operation like this.

Vendor Delivery Schedules

It is the fortunate foodservice operator who lives in a large city with many vendors, some of whom may offer the same service and all of whom would like to have the operator's business. In some cases, however, the foodservice operator does not have the luxury of daily delivery. The operation may be too small to warrant such frequent stops by a vendor, or the operation may be in such a remote location that daily delivery is simply not possible. Consider for a moment the difficulty faced by a foodservice operator on an offshore oil rig. Clearly, daily donut delivery is not going to work in this case! In all situations, it is important to remember that the cost to the vendor for frequent deliveries will be reflected in the cost of the goods to the operator.

Figure 3.6 **Shelf Life**

Item	Storage	Shelf Life
Milk	Refrigerator	5–7 days
Butter	Refrigerator	14 days
Ice cream	0°F or lower freezer	30 days
Ground beef	Refrigerator	2–3 days
Steaks (fresh)	Refrigerator	14 days
Bacon	Refrigerator-freezer	30 days
Canned vegetables	Dry storeroom	12 months
Flour	Dry storeroom	3 months
Sugar	Dry storeroom	3 months
Lettuce	Refrigerator	3–5 days
Tomatoes	Refrigerator	5–7 days
Potatoes	Dry storeroom	14–21 days

Vendors will readily let an operator know what their delivery schedule to a certain area or operator can be. It is up to the manager to use this information to make educated decisions regarding the quantity of that vendor's product he or she will require to have both in working stock and safety stock.

Potential Savings from Increased Purchase Size

Some foodservice operators find that they can realize substantial savings by purchasing large quantities and thus receiving a lower price from the vendor. This certainly makes sense if the total savings actually outweigh the costs of receiving and storing the larger quantity. For the large foodservice operator who once a year buys canned green beans by the railroad car, the savings are real. For the smaller operator, who hopes to save by ordering two cases instead of one, savings may be negligible. There are costs associated with extraordinarily large purchases. They may include storage costs and those related to spoilage, deterioration, insect or rodent infestation, and theft.

As a general rule, operators should determine their actual product inventory levels and then maintain their stock within that need range. Only when the advantages of placing an extraordinarily large order are very clear should such a purchase be attempted.

Operating Calendar

When an operation is involved in serving meals seven days a week to a relatively stable number of customers, the operating calendar makes little difference to inventory level decision making. If, however, the operation opens on Monday and closes for two days on Friday, as is the case in many school foodservice accounts, the operating calendar plays a large part in determining desired inventory levels. In general, an operator who is closing out, either for a weekend (as in school foodservice), or for a season (as in the operation of a summer camp), should attempt to reduce overall inventory levels as the closing period approaches. This is especially true when it comes to perishable items. If this is not done, opening-day spoilage rates can be extensive. Many operators actually plan menus to steer clear of highly perishable items at week's end. They prefer to work highly perishable items such as fresh seafood and some meats into the early or mid- part of their operating calendar. This allows them to minimize the amount of perishable product that must be carried through the shutdown period.

Relative Importance of Stock Outages

In many foodservice operations, not having enough of a single food ingredient or menu item is simply not that important. In other operations, the shortage of even one menu item might spell disaster. While it may be all right for the local

French restaurant to run out of one of the specials on Saturday night, it is not difficult to imagine the problem of the McDonald's restaurant manager who runs out of french fried potatoes on that same Saturday night!

For the small operator, a mistake in the inventory level of a minor ingredient that results in an outage can often be corrected by a quick run to the grocery store. For the larger facility, such an outage may well represent a substantial loss of sales or customer goodwill. Whether the operator is large or small, being out of a key ingredient or menu item is to be avoided, and planning inventory levels properly helps prevent it. A strong awareness and knowledge of how critical an outage can be helps determine the appropriate inventory level. A word of caution, however, is necessary. The foodservice operator who is determined never to run out of anything must be careful not to set inventory levels so high as to actually end up costing the operation more than if realistic levels were maintained.

Value of Inventory Dollars to the Operator

In some cases, operators elect to remove dollars from their bank accounts and convert them to product inventory. When this is done, the operator is making the decision to value product more than dollars. When it is expected that the value of the inventory will rise faster than the value of the banked money, this is a good strategy. All too often, however, operators overbuy, causing too many dollars to be tied up in non-interest-bearing food products! If the dollars to purchase inventory must be borrowed from the bank rather than obtained from one's own funds, an even greater cost to carry the inventory is incurred, since interest must be paid on the borrowed funds. In addition, a foodservice company of many units that invests too much of its capital in inventory may find that funds for acquisition, renovation, or marketing are not readily available.

In contrast, a state institution that is given a one-year budget at the beginning of a fiscal (financial) year may find it advantageous to use this purchasing power to acquire inventory at very low prices. Inventory represents real dollars waiting to be converted from products to sales. Alternative uses of those dollars must be considered when establishing the correct inventory level of each product.

Setting the Purchase Point

A **purchase point,** as it relates to inventory levels, is simply that point in time when an item should be reordered. This point is typically designated by one of two methods:

1. **As needed**
2. **Par level**

As Needed

When operators use the **as-needed** method of determining inventory level, they basically are purchasing food based on their prediction of unit sales and on the sum of the ingredients (from standardized recipes) necessary to produce those sales. When this system is used, the purchasing agent, chef, or manager compiles a list of needed ingredients and submits them to management for approval to purchase. In a hotel foodservice operation, the demand for 500 servings of a raspberries and cream torte dessert, to be served to a group in the hotel next week, would cause the responsible person to check the standardized recipe for this item, and thus determine the amount of raspberries that should be ordered. This is an example of ordering for inventory by using the as-needed system.

Par Level

Foodservice operators may set predetermined purchase points, called **par levels,** for some items. In the case of our raspberries and cream torte dessert, it is likely that the cream torte will require vanilla extract. It does not make sense, however, to expect our food production manager to order vanilla extract by the tablespoon! In fact, we may find that we are restricted in the quantity we can buy due to the vendor's delivery minimum, namely bottle or case, or the manufacturer's packaging methods. In situations such as this, or when demand for a product is relatively constant, we may set inventory level by determining purchase points based on par levels that we feel are appropriate. In determining par levels, management must establish both minimum and maximum amounts required. In addition, it must establish a purchase point. If, for example, management has decided that the inventory level for coffee shall be based on a par system, the decision may be made that the minimum that should be on hand at all times (given our usage) is four cases. This would be the minimum par level. The maximum par level has been set at ten cases. While the inventory level in this situation would vary from a low of four cases to a high of ten cases, management could be assured that it would never have too little or too much of this particular menu item.

If coffee were to be ordered under this system, the manager would always attempt to keep the number of cases between the minimum par level (four cases) and the maximum (ten cases). The purchase point in this example might be six cases; that is, when the operation had six cases of coffee on hand, an order would be placed with the coffee vendor. Management's intention would be to get the total stock up to ten cases before the supply got below four cases. Since delivery might take one or two days, six cases might be an appropriate purchase point.

Whichever method is used—the as needed, par level, or as in the case of most operators, a combination of both—each ingredient or menu item should have a management-designated inventory level. As a rule, highly perishable items should be ordered on an as-needed basis, while items with a longer shelf life can often have their inventory levels set using a par level system. The answer to the question "How much of each ingredient should I have on hand at any point in time?" must come from management. Many factors impact this decision. The decision, however, must be made and monitored by management on a regular basis.

Purchasing

Regardless of the method used to determine inventory levels, each foodservice operator must now turn his or her attention to the extremely important area of purchasing. If we know the number of guests who will be coming (sales forecast) and what they are likely to select from our menus, we must purchase the ingredients needed so that our workers can prepare those items. This means having inventory levels in line with customer demand. Purchasing is essentially a matter of determining the following:

1. **What should be purchased?**
2. **What is the best price to pay?**
3. **How can a steady supply be assured?**

What Should Be Purchased?

Just as it is not possible to determine inventory levels or items to be purchased without standardized recipes, it is not possible to manage costs where purchasing is concerned without the use of product specifications, or **specs.** A product spec is simply a detailed description of an ingredient or menu item. A spec is a way for the foodservice director to communicate specifically with a vendor so that the operator receives the *exact* item requested, delivery after delivery. A foodservice specification generally lists the following types of information:

1. **Product name or spec number**
2. **Packaging or unit on which a price is quoted**
3. **Standard or grade, if established**
4. **Weight range**
5. **Type of processing or packaging**
6. **Size of the basic container**
7. **Other information such as product yield**

Other information may be included if it helps the vendor understand exactly what the operator has in mind when the order is placed. For extremely detailed specifications, it is important that the person receiving the product apply good judgment about whether the product does or does not meet the specification.

Figure 3.7 **Product Specification**

Product Name:	Bacon, sliced	Spec #.	117
Pricing Unit:	lb		
Standard/Grade:	Select No. 1,		
	moderately thick slice.		
	Oscar Mayer item 2040 or equal		
Weight Range:	14–16 slices per pound		
Packaging:	2/10 lbs cryovac packed		
Container Size:	Not to exceed 20 lbs		
Other Information:	Flat packed on oven-proofed paper		
	Never frozen		

It is also important to note that the product specification determines neither the "best" product nor the product that costs the least. The specification determines the product that management has decided is **most appropriate** for the intended use in terms of both quality and cost.

Let us listen in on Louie, who is about to place an order for bread with a new vendor, Sam's Uptown Bakery.

Louie: "Sam, I need bread for sandwiches."
Sam: "Louie, you know I have the best in town!"
Louie: "Well, send me five loaves as soon as possible."
Sam: "No problem Louie, we will deliver this afternoon!"

Little does Louie know that Sam's definition of bread for sandwiches is *quite* different from Louie's. Louie is expecting 1¼-pound white, split, thin-sliced, 45-slices-to-the-bag bread. From Sam's exotic shop, however, he may well receive 2-pound, thick-sliced, sesame seed Italian. Even for a product as common as bread, a spec must be developed. Fortunately, the process is relatively simple for it depends mainly on management's view of appropriate product quality.

Figure 3.7 demonstrates a form used to develop product specifications. Each menu item or ingredient should have its own spec. In fact, management should make it a habit to ensure that only telephone conversations such as the following take place:

Louie: "Sam, I need five loaves of my spec #617 as soon as possible."
Sam: "Spec #617? Let's see, I've got it right here. That's *your* bread for sandwiches spec, right?"
Louie: "That's right, Sam."
Sam: "No problem Louie, we will deliver this afternoon!"

Product Name

This may seem self-explanatory, but in reality it is not. Mangoes are a fruit to those in the southwestern United States but may mean a green pepper to those in the Midwest. Canned hams are usually pear-shaped, but a Pullman canned ham is square. With meats and seafood, especially, different regions in the country may have different names for the same product. In addition to using the correct name in assigning the product specification, a number may help when multiple items of the same type, such as cheese, ham, and milk, are used by an operator.

Pricing Unit

A pricing unit may be established in terms of pounds, quarts, gallons, cases, or any other commonly used unit. Parsley, for example, is typically sold in the United States by the bunch. Thus, it is also priced by the bunch. How much is a bunch? The operator should know. Grapes are sold by the **lug.** Again, knowledge of the pricing unit, whether it be a gallon, pound, case, or bunch, is critical when developing a product specification. Figure 3.8 lists some of the more common pricing units in the United States.

Standard or Grade

Standards have been developed by the U.S. Department of Agriculture, the Bureau of Fisheries, and the Food and Drug Administration for many products. In addition, grading programs are in place for many commonly used foodservice items. Trade groups such as the National Association of Meat Purveyors publish item descriptions for many of these products. Often a trade name or location can be included in the standard/grade section, for example, A-1 Steak Sauce, Cure-81 Ham, or Texas grapefruit.

Weight Range

This term is generally used when referring to meats, fish, poultry, and some vegetables. In our standardized recipe example of roast chicken, the quarters were to have come from chickens in the 3–3½-pound range. In the case of products requiring specific trim or maximum fat covering, such as 10-ounce strip steak, maximum tail 1 inch, or fat covering ½ inch, that should be designated also.

Figure 3.8 **Selected Container Net Weights**

Items Purchased	**Container**	**Approximate Net Weight In Lbs**
Apples	Cartons, tray pack	40–45
Asparagus	Pyramid crates, loose pack	32
Beets, bunched	½ crates, 2-doz bunches	36–40
Cabbage, green	Flat crates (1¾ bushel)	50–60
Cantaloupe	½ wirebound crates	38–41
Corn, sweet	Cartons, packed 5 doz ears	50
Cucumbers, field grown	Bushel cartons	47–55
Grapefruit, FL	4/5-bushel cartons & wirebound crates	42½
Grapes, table	Lugs and cartons, plain pack	23–24
Lettuce, loose leaf	4/5-bushel crates	8–10
Limes	Pony cartons	10
Onions, green	4/5-bushel crates (36 bunches)	11
Oranges, FL	4/5-bushel cartons	45
Parsley	Cartons, wax treated, 5-doz bunches	21
Peaches	2-layer cartons & lugs, tray pack	22
Shallots	Bags	5
Squash	1-layer flats, place pack	16
Strawberries, CA	12 one-pint trays	11–14
Tangerines	4/5-bushel cartons	47½
Tomatoes, pink and ripe	3-layer lugs and cartons, place pack	24–33

Four-ounce hamburger patties, 16-ounce T-bones, and ¼-pound hot dogs are additional examples of items of the type that require, not a weight range, but a high degree of accuracy. It is important to note that while operators may specify such a specific weight, it is likely that they will pay a premium for such accuracy, especially in items such as steaks, where the supplier's ability to perfectly control product weight is somewhat limited.

Packaging

Packaging refers to the product's state, namely fresh, canned, frozen, and so on, when delivered. It is important to note that the term **fresh** is one with varying degrees of meaning. Fish that has been frozen and then thawed should be identified as such. Clearly, that product is not fresh in the sense of fish that has never been frozen. Packaging is extremely important when determining product yield. Three pounds of canned corn, for example, will not yield the same number of 3-ounce servings as three pounds of frozen corn, since the canned corn is packed in liquid whereas the frozen corn is not. Fresh fruits and vegetables may be of excellent quality and low in cost per pound, but the effective foodservice operator must consider actual usable product when computing price per pound. Also, the labor cost of washing, trimming, and otherwise preparing fresh products must be considered when comparing their price to that of a canned or frozen product.

Container Size

This term refers to the can size, number of cans per case, or weight of the container in which the product is delivered. Most operators know that a 50-pound bag of flour should contain 50 pounds. Many are not sure, however, what the appropriate weight for a lug of tomatoes would be.

Product Yield

Most foodservice products are delivered in the **AP** or as-purchased state. This refers to the weight or count of a product, as delivered to the foodservice operator. **EP** or edible portion refers to the weight of a product after it has been cleaned, trimmed, cooked, and/or portioned. Thus, AP refers to food products as they are received by the operator; EP refers to food products as they are received by the customer. If the purchasing agent attempts to fill required inventory levels and considers only AP weight, shortages are sure to occur. To demonstrate the reason for this, let's examine a typical foodservice occurrence. Jerry hopes to serve 40 guests each a 4-ounce portion of roast beef, for a total of 160 ounces.

$$\textbf{40 desired servings} \times \textbf{4 oz per portion} = \textbf{160 oz required}$$

Since he begins with a 10-pound roast, he knows he has the following in AP weight:

$$\textbf{10-lb roast} \times \textbf{16 oz per lb} = \textbf{160 oz}$$

What Jerry has failed to calculate is the loss that will result from normal cooking, trimming, and portioning. This loss can be computed, and thus forecasted. If past experience tells Jerry that he will lose 50 ounces of product in the preparation process, he can compute his **waste %** using the following formula:

$$\textbf{Waste \%} = \frac{\textbf{Product loss}}{\textbf{AP weight}}$$

In this example, our waste % is computed as follows:

$$\textbf{Waste \%} = \frac{\textbf{50 oz}}{\textbf{160 oz}} = \textbf{.3125}$$

Once waste % has been determined, whether due to cooking, trimming, portioning, or cleaning, it is possible to compute the **yield %,** since waste % plus yield % equals 1.00, as shown in the box below:

$$\textbf{Yield \%} = 1.00 - \textbf{Waste \%}$$

In this example, our yield % is computed as follows:

$$\textbf{Yield \%} = 1.00 - .3125 = .6875$$

From the yield % we can compute the AP weight required that will yield the appropriate EP weight required, by using the following formula:

$$\frac{\textbf{EP required}}{\textbf{Yield \%}} = \textbf{AP required}$$

In this example, with an EP required of 160 ounces and a yield % of .6875, the computation to determine the appropriate AP required is as follows:

$$\begin{aligned} \frac{\textbf{160 oz}}{\textbf{.6875}} &= \textbf{232.73 oz} \\ &= \textbf{232.73 oz / 16 oz} \\ &= \textbf{14.55 lbs AP required} \end{aligned}$$

To check the above figures to see if we should use the yield % of .6875 when purchasing this item, we proceed as follows:

$$\textbf{EP required} = \textbf{AP required} \times \textbf{yield \%}$$

In this example, **EP required = 14.55 lbs × .6875 = 10.00 lbs.**

As we can see, with this product a yield % of .6875 will indeed help us determine exactly the right amount of product to purchase. Obviously, yield % is important also in the area of recipe costing. This is true because a recipe cost must take into account the difference in price of products in their AP or EP state.

Waste % and yield % can be determined if records are kept on the cooking of meat, the cleaning and processing of vegetables and fruits, and the losses that occur during portioning. Since most recipes assume some consistency in these areas, the good foodservice manager takes the losses into account when making purchasing decisions. Good vendors are an excellent source for providing tabled information related to trim and loss rates for standard products they carry. Many operators list yield % as part of their product specification. This could be done in the **other information** section (see Figure 3.7).

What Is the Best Price to Pay?

Once purchase specifications have been developed and quantities to be purchased have been established, the operator's next step is to determine the best price. Many would say that determining price should be a simple matter of finding who has the lowest-cost product and placing an order with that person. In fact, that is almost always a sure sign of an operator who lacks understanding of the food wholesale business. The **best price,** in fact, is more accurately stated as a fair price, for both operator and vendor.

When the operator has a choice of vendors, each supplying the *same* product according to specs, it is possible to engage in comparison shopping. A vehicle used to do this comparison is the **bid sheet** (Figure 3.9).

A bid sheet typically has a place to list the category being bid, namely, produce, dairy products, meats, and so on; the name of the vendors available to bid; bid date; items and quantities to be bid; and the prices quoted by the vendor. This information may then be used to select a vendor, based on the best price.

A bid sheet may be used to determine the specific vendor who can supply the lowest price, but it does not give enough information to determine a fair or best price. We would not expect our foodservice customers to go only to the restaurant with the lowest price steak if that were the item they wanted to eat. If that were true, there would be little hope for the operator who tried to provide a better cut of meat, in a better environment, with better service. In fact, most foodservice operators would resent customers who came into his or her operation and claimed they could get the same item for a lower price down the street.

Any product can be sold a little cheaper if quality is allowed to vary. Even when product specifications are used, vendor dependability, quality of vendor service, and accuracy in delivery can be determining factors when attempting to ascertain the best price.

In Figure 3.9, Ready Boy has the lowest overall price and may be the preferred vendor if price alone is the issue. If, however, Ready Boy is frequently late in delivery, has questionable sanitary habits, and frequently is short or unable to deliver the promised product, the lower price may be no bargain. Davis Foods, on the other hand, may have a reputation for quality products and service that make it the vendor of choice. Any foodservice operator who uses price as the **only** criteria when shopping will find it very difficult to develop any meaningful relationship with a supplier.

In some cases, the vendor to be used by the foodservice operator has been determined in advance. This is often true in a large corporate organization or in a franchise situation. Contracts to provide goods may be established by a central purchasing department of these organizations. When that happens, the designated vendor may have a national or a long-term contract to supply products at a predetermined or fixed price. In all cases, however, products to be ordered must conform to predetermined specifications.

How Can a Steady Supply Be Assured?

Unfortunately, very little has been written in the field of foodservice about managing costs through cooperation with vendors. An operator's food salesperson can be his or her most important ally in controlling costs. Operators who determine their supplier only on the basis of cost will find that they receive only the product they have purchased, whereas their competitors are buying more than

Figure 3.9 **Bid Sheet**

Vendors:

A. Joe's Produce

B. Davis Foods

C. Pauline, Inc.

D. Ready Boy

Category: Produce

Date Bid: 1/1/92

Item	Quantity	Vendor A		Vendor B		Vendor C		Vendor D	
		Unit	**Total**	**Unit**	**Total**	**Unit**	**Total**	**Unit**	**Total**
Bananas	25#	$.18/#	$ 4.50	$.21/#	$ 5.25	$.19/#	$ 4.75	$.25/#	$ 6.25
Cabbage	50#	.10/#	5.00	.12/#	6.00	.08/#	4.00	.12/#	6.00
Grapes	2 lugs	17.00/lg	34.00	18.25/lg	36.50	18.50/lg	37.00	19.00/lg	38.00
Lemons	3 cs	12.00/cs	36.00	11.50/cs	34.50	11.75/cs	35.25	8.00/cs	24.00
Oranges	1 cs	16.00/cs	16.00	15.50/cs	15.50	16.25/cs	16.25	17.00/cs	17.00
Parsley	2 bchs	.40/ea	.80	.30/ea	.60	.38/ea	.76	.39/ea	.78
Total			$96.30		$98.35		$98.01		$92.03

Bid Method: Telephone X Written

Bid Reviewed: M. Hayes

just food! Or as one food salesperson said when asked why he should be selected as the primary food vendor, "With my products, you also get me!" And thus it is; just as good foodservice operators know that customers respond to both products and service levels, so too do effective food suppliers. Assuring a steady supply of quality products at a fair price is extremely important to the long-term success of a foodservice operator, yet many operators treat their suppliers as if they were the enemy. In fact, suppliers can be of immense value in assuring a steady supply of quality products at a fair price if the foodservice operator remembers the following points.

1. Suppliers Have Many Prices, Not Just One

Unlike restaurants, which tend to hold prices steady between menu reprints and generally charge the same price to all who come in the door, suppliers have a variety of prices based on the customer to whom they are quoting them. Therefore, when an operator gets a quote on a case of lettuce, the telephone conversation may sound like this:

Foodservice operator:	"Hello, is this Ready Boy Produce?"
Ready Boy:	"Yes, how can I help you?"
Foodservice operator:	"What is *your* price on lettuce?"
Ready Boy:	"$18.50 per case."

This conversation should really be interpreted as follows:

Foodservice operator:	"Hello, is this Ready Boy Produce?"
Ready Boy:	"Yes, how can I help you?"
Foodservice operator:	"What is *my* price on lettuce?"
Ready Boy:	"Based on *our* relationship, it is $18.50 per case."

2. Suppliers Reward Volume Customers

It is simply in the best interest of a supplier to give a better price to a high-volume customer. The cost of delivering a $1,000 order is not that much different than the cost of delivering a $100 order. It still takes one truck and one driver. Those operators who decide to concentrate their business in the hands of fewer suppliers will, as a general rule, pay a lower price.

3. Cherry Pickers are Serviced Last

Cherry pickers is the term used by the suppliers to describe customers who get bids from multiple vendors, then buy only those items each vendor has on sale or at the lowest price. If an operator buys only a vendor's low-end item, the vendor will usually respond by providing limited service. It is a natural reaction to the foodservice operator's failure to give credit for varying service levels, long-term relationships, dependability, or any other characteristic except cheapest price.

4. Slow Pay Means High Pay

Those operators who do not pay their bills in a timely manner would be surprised to know what their competitors are paying for similar products. In most cases, operators who are slow to pay will find that the vendor has decided to add the extra cost of carrying this account to the price the operator pays for his or her products.

5. Vendors Can Help Reduce Costs

Vendors have a knowledge of the products they sell that exceeds that of the average foodservice operator. This skill can be used to help the competition, or it can be harnessed for an operator's own good use. Vendors can be a great source of information related to new products, cooking techniques, trends, and alternative product usage.

One Vendor versus Many Vendors

Every operator is faced with the decision of whether to buy from one vendor or many vendors. In general, the more vendors there are, the more time must be spent in ordering, receiving, and paying invoices. Many operators, however, fear that if they give all their business to one supplier, their costs may rise because of a lack of competition. In reality, the likelihood of this occurring is extremely small. Just as foodservice operators are unlikely to take advantage of their best customers (and in fact would tend to offer services not available to the occasional customer), so too does the vendor tend to behave in a manner that is preferential to the operator who does most of his or her buying from that vendor. In fact, it makes good business sense for the vendor to do so. It is never advisable, however, to be at the mercy of a particular vendor. A good business relationship can occur only among equals; thus many operators strive to maintain both a primary and secondary supplier of most products.

Using one or two vendors tends to bring the average delivery size up and should result in a lower per item price. On the other hand, giving one vendor all of the operation's business can be dangerous and costly if the items to be purchased vary widely in quality and price. Staples and nonperishables are best purchased in bulk from one vendor. Orders for meats, produce, and some bakery products are best split among several vendors, perhaps with a primary and secondary vendor in each category. This helps to reduce product variability and allows an operator to have a second alternative should the need arise.

Preparing the Purchase Order

Some items will be purchased daily, others weekly, and some, perhaps monthly. In all cases, however, it is critical that a written purchase order be prepared. The purchase order (PO) should be made out in triplicate (3 copies). One copy goes to the receiving area for use by the receiving clerk. One copy is retained by management for the bookkeeping area. The original, of course, is sent to the vendor. If the purchase order is developed by telephone, the original copy is retained by management, with a notation in the comment section stating that the vendor has not seen the PO. In all cases, however, it is important to place *all* orders using a purchase order form. If this is not done, the receiving clerk will have no record of how much is expected to be delivered. This will result in "blind" receiving, the process of signing an invoice without checking the product delivered because the amount ordered was not known, and thus could not be verified.

Purchase order preparation can be simple or complex, but in all cases the written purchase order form should contain space for the following information:

1. **Item name**
2. **Spec number, if appropriate**
3. **Quantity ordered**
4. **Quoted price**
5. **Extension price**
6. **Vendor name**
7. **Date ordered**
8. **Delivery date**
9. **Ordered by ___________**
10. **Received by ___________**
11. **Delivery instructions**

Figure 3.10 is an example of a simplified yet effective purchase order form.

Each vendor should have a purchase order prepared for each delivery. This is true even if the vendor is delivering on a daily basis. A written purchase order has many advantages, including the following:

1. **Written verification of quoted price**
2. **Written verification of quantity ordered**
3. **Written verification of the receipt of all goods ordered**
4. **Written and special instructions to the receiving clerk, as needed**
5. **Written verification of conformance to product specification**
6. **Written authorization to prepare vendor invoice for payment**

Figure 3.11 shows the completed purchase order following a thorough inspection of a produce walk-in at the Ardmoor Hotel. The chef has used a sales forecast to determine the quantity of products needed for next Thursday's deliv-

Figure 3.10 **Purchase Order**

Vendor: ____________ Delivery Date: ____________

Vendor's Telephone #: ____________

Item Purchased	Spec #	Qty Ordered	Quoted Price	Ext Price
1.				
2.				
3.				
4.				
5.				
6.				
7.				
8.				
9.				
10.				
11.				
12.				
13.				
14.				
15.				
16.				

Order Date: ____________ Comments: ____________

Ordered by: ____________

Received by: ____________

Delivery Instructions: ____________

Figure 3.11 **Purchase Order**

Vendor: Scooter's Produce Delivery Date: 1/3

Vendor's Telephone #: 999-0000

Item Purchased	Spec #	Qty Ordered	Quoted Price	Ext Price
1. Bananas	81	30 lbs	$ .12/lb	$ 3.60
2. Parsley	107	4 bchs	.80/bch	3.20
3. Oranges	101	3 cs	15.50/cs	46.50
4. Lemons	35	6 cs	14.80/cs	88.80
5. Cabbages	85	2 bags	6.50/bag	13.00
6.				
7.				
8.				
9.				
10.				
11.				
12.				
13.				
14.				
15.				
16.				

Order Date: 1/1

Ordered by: Joshua David

Received by:

Delivery Instructions:

After 1:00 P.M.

Comments:

Faxed on 1/1

Transmitted by Joshua David

ery. A check of the produce walk-in lets the chef know what is on hand and what quantity of each product is required, either on an as-needed or par basis. This information allows for the accurate preparation of the purchase order. The order is then faxed to Scooter's Produce. The receiving clerk at the Ardmoor is now prepared with the information necessary to effectively receive the product from Scooter's Produce.

We will discuss the process of developing the purchase order in more detail in Chapter 5, "Managing the Food and Beverage Production Process."

The Receiving Area

Once the purchase order has been prepared by the purchasing agent, it is time to prepare for the acceptance or receiving of the goods. In a large operation, this function is performed by the receiving clerk; in a smaller operation, it may be performed by the manager or his or her designee. In all cases, however, it is wise to establish the purchasing and receiving functions so that one individual is responsible for placing the order, while another individual is responsible for verifying delivery and acceptance of the product. When this is not done, the potential for fraud or theft is substantial. Owners have frequently found that the purchasing agent ordered a product and signed for its acceptance, thus authorizing invoice payment, when in fact, no product was ever delivered! In this case, the purchasing agent could be getting cash payment from the purveyor or supplier without the owner's knowledge. Proper control procedures will eliminate the possibility of this happening. Again, it is imperative to remember that the purchasing agent and the receiving clerk should be two different individuals, or if that is not possible, the work of the purchasing agent/receiving clerk must be carefully monitored by management to prevent fraud.

There is probably no area of the foodservice establishment more ignored than the area in which receiving takes place. This is truly unfortunate since this is the area where we are ensuring the quality of products we ordered. Proper receiving includes all of the following features:

1. **Proper location**
2. **Proper tools and equipment**
3. **Proper delivery schedules**
4. **Proper training**

Proper Location

The "back door," which is usually reserved for receiving, is often no more than that—just an entrance to the kitchen. In fact, the receiving area must be adequate to handle the job of receiving, or product loss and inconsistency will result.

First, the receiving area must be large enough to allow for checking products delivered against both the invoice, which is the supplier's record of products delivered and price charged, and the PO, which is the operation's record of the same thing. If physical space is insufficient to allow for this cross-check, receiving duties will not be performed adequately.

In addition to the space required to allow for counting and weighing, accessibility to equipment required to move products to their proper storage area and to dispose of excess packaging is important. A location near refrigerated areas is helpful in maintaining refrigerated and frozen products at their desired temperatures. The area should be free of trash and clutter, as these make it too easy to hide delivered food items that may be taken home at the end of the dishonest employee's shift. It is important to remember that the delivery person is also a potential thief. While most suppliers are extremely careful to screen their delivery personnel for honesty, a delivery person does have access to products and a truck available to *remove* as well as deliver goods. For this reason, it is important that the receiving clerk work in an area that has a clear view of both delivery personnel and their vehicles.

The receiving area should be kept extremely clean, since we do not want to contaminate incoming food, nor provide a carrying vehicle for pests. Often, suppliers themselves are responsible for delivering goods that can harbor roach eggs or other insects. A clean receiving area makes it easier to both prevent and detect this type of problem. The area should be well lit and properly ventilated. Excessive heat in the receiving area can quickly damage delivered goods, especially if they are either refrigerated or frozen products. Too little light may cause product defects to go unnoticed; therefore, the receiving area should be well lit. Flooring should be light in color and of a type that is easily cleaned. In colder climates, it is important that the receiving area be warm enough to allow the receiving clerk to carefully inspect products. If it is February and the temperature is 10 degrees below zero, the outside dock area is no place to conduct an inspection of products!

Proper Tools and Equipment

While the tools and equipment needed for effective receiving vary by type and size of operation, some items are standard in any receiving operation. These include the following:

Scales

Scales should be of two types: those accurate to the fraction of a pound and those accurate to the fraction of an ounce. The larger scale is used, of course, for large items. Fifty-pound sacks of onions, for example, would be weighed on the large scale. The smaller scale, accurate to the fraction of an ounce, would be used to verify the proper weight of smaller items, for example, to ensure that the 10-ounce strip steaks weigh in fact 10 ounces. In both cases, scales should be checked regularly for accuracy.

Wheeled Equipment

These items, whether hand trucks or carts, should be available so that goods can be moved quickly and efficiently to their proper storage areas.

Box Cutter

This item, properly maintained and used, allows the receiving clerk to quickly remove excess packaging and thus accurately verify the quality of delivered products. Of course, care must be taken when using this tool, so proper training is essential.

Calculator

Vendor calculations should always be checked, especially when the invoice has been prepared by hand. The calculator should also be available in case the original invoice is either increased or decreased in amount.

Records Area

This area, in the best of cases, should include a desk, telephone, file cabinet, and ample office supplies like pens, pencils, and staples. Obviously, larger operations are more likely to have such an area. In a smaller operation, however, the need for basic equipment still exists. Some managers solve this problem by supplying a clipboard with a pen or pencil attached to the wall! In any case, the records area should be appropriate to the size of the operation. In *all* cases, the records area should include a copy of all product specifications.

Proper Delivery Schedules

In an ideal world, the foodservice manager would accept delivery of products only during designated hours. These times would be scheduled during slow periods, when there would be plenty of time for a thorough checking of the products delivered. In fact, some operators are able to demand that deliveries be made only at certain times, say between 9:00 A.M. and 10:30 A.M. These are called **acceptance hours.** In a case such as this, the operation may refuse to accept delivery at any other time. Some large operations prefer to establish times in which they will *not* accept deliveries, say between 11:00 A.M. and 1:00 P.M. These are called **refusal hours.** Since a busy lunchtime may make it inconvenient to accept deliveries at this time, some operators will simply not take delivery then. In both cases, however, the assumption is that the operator is either a large enough or a good enough customer to make demands such as these.

For many operators, however, the supplier will determine when goods are delivered. While this may seem inconvenient (and often is), remember that all foodservice units would like to have their deliveries made during the slow periods between peak meal times. It is simply not possible for the supplier to stop his or her trucks for several hours to wait for a good delivery time. In fact, in a remote location, some foodservice operators will be told only the day a delivery will be made, not a specific time!

The key to establishing a successful delivery schedule with suppliers is, quite simply, to work with them. If an operator is seen as especially difficult or costly to do business with, the supplier will pass those costs on in the form of higher prices. On the other hand, the foodservice operator must make the supplier understand that there are certain times of the day when it is just not possible to accept delivery. While every relationship between operator and supplier is somewhat different, both sides, working together, can generally come to an acceptable solution.

If the operator decides to post either acceptance hours or refusal hours, these should be equally enforced with all vendors.

Proper Training

Receiving clerks should be properly trained to verify the following product characteristics:

1. **Weight**
2. **Quantity**
3. **Quality**
4. **Price**

Weight

One of the most important items to verify when receiving food products is, of course, their weight. Fourteen pounds of bulk-packaged ground beef looks exactly like 15 pounds. There is no way to tell the difference without putting the product on the scale. Receiving clerks should be required to weigh all meat, fish, and poultry delivered. The only exception to this rule would be unopened cryovac packages, such as hot dogs, bacon, and the like. In this situation, the entire case should be weighed to detect shortages in content. Often, meat deliveries consist of several items, all of which are packaged together. When the receiving clerk or supplier is very busy, the temptation exists to weigh all of the products together. The following example shows why it is important to weigh each item rather than the entire group of items as a whole.

Joseph ordered 40 pounds of product from Beaners Meats. The PO showed the information in Figure 3.12. When Beaners came to deliver, all three items were in one box and the delivery person was in a hurry. He therefore suggested that Joseph simply weigh the box. Joseph did just that and found that the contents

Figure 3.12 **Ordered**

Item Ordered	Unit Price	Total Ordered	Total Price
Hamburger	$1.25/lb	10 lbs	$ 12.50
N.Y. strips	4.00/lb	20 lbs	80.00
Corned beef	3.60/lb	10 lbs	36.00
Total		40 lbs	128.50

weighed 40½ pounds. Since the box weighed about ½ lb, Joseph signed for delivery. When he began to put the meat away, however, he weighed each item and found the information shown in Figure 3.13.

When Joseph called the supplier to complain about the overcharge ($128.50 total price − $112.75 actual value = $15.75 overcharge), he was told that the driver must have made a mistake. Joseph wondered about this, but decided that he would always weigh the items individually in the future, even if he was in a hurry.

When an item is ordered by weight, its delivery should be verified by weight. It is up to the operator to train the receiving clerk to *always* verify that the operation is charged only for the product weight delivered. Excess packaging, ice, or water (in the case of produce) can all serve to increase the delivered weight. The effective receiving clerk must be aware of, and on guard against, deceptive delivery practices as far as the delivery of the agreed-upon product is concerned. Verifying the weight of product alone, however, will not ensure that all the goods ordered have been received.

Quantity

The counting and weighing of product are equally important. Suppliers make more mistakes in *not* delivering products than they do in excessive delivery. Products delivered but not charged for cost the supplier money. Products not delivered but charged for cost the foodservice operation money. If five cases of green beans have been ordered, then five cases must be delivered. This is important for two reasons. First, we want to pay only for product that has been delivered. Second, if we have prepared our purchase order correctly, we truly need five cases of green beans. If only four are delivered, we may not be able to prepare the menu items that are necessary to service our guests. If this means we run out of an item, we will have to deal with unhappy customers. If a supplier consistently shorts an operation on products, that supplier is suspect in terms of both honesty and concern for the foodservice operation's long-term success.

The counting of boxes, cases, sacks, barrels, and the like must be routine behavior for the receiving clerk. Counting items, such as the number of lemons or oranges in a box, should be done on a periodic basis, but the value of counting items such as these on a regular basis is questionable. While an unscrupulous supplier might be able to remove one or two lemons from each box delivered, the time it would take for an employee to detect such behavior is hardly worth

Figure 3.13 **Delivered**

Item Ordered	Unit Price	Total Delivered	Actual Value
Hamburger	$1.25/lb	15 lbs	$ 18.75
N.Y. strips	4.00/lb	10 lbs	40.00
Corned beef	3.60/lb	15 lbs	54.00
Total		40 lbs	112.75

the effort expended. It is preferable to do a periodic check and to work with reputable vendors.

The direct delivery of products to a foodservice operator's storeroom or holding area is another cause for concern. Some items, such as bread, milk, and soda are brought by the delivery person directly to the storage area, thus bypassing the receiving clerk. This should not be allowed if at all possible. After such an activity, it is simply impossible to accurately verify the quantity of items delivered. If this process must be used, product dates on each item can help assure that all products listed on the invoice were indeed delivered.

Quality

No area is of greater concern to the foodservice operator than that of the appropriate quality of product delivered. An operation that goes to the trouble of developing product specifications, but then accepts delivery of products that do not match these specifications, is simply wasting time and effort. Without product specifications, verification of quality is difficult because management itself is unsure of the quality level that is desired. Many foodservice operators think that all food items are basically alike. Nothing could be further from the truth. Suppliers know their products. They also know their customers. Some customers will accept only those items they have specified. Others will accept anything that comes in the back door. If you were a supplier and had a sack of onions that was getting a bit old, which customer would you deliver it to?

Unscrupulous suppliers can cost an operation its customers because of both overcharging and shortchanging. Imagine, for example, a restaurant manager who requests a ¼-inch fat cover on all New York strip steaks ordered. Instead, the meat company delivers steaks with a ½-inch fat cover. The operation will, of course, pay too much for the product, since steaks with a ¼-inch fat covering sell at a higher price per pound than those with a ½-inch covering. Customers, however, will hold the operator responsible for steaks that suddenly seem to be a little "fatter" than they used to be. Coincidentally, the guests who eat the fatter steaks may tend to be a bit fatter themselves in the future!

Checking for quality means checking the entire shipment for conformance to specifications. If only the top row of tomatoes in the box conforms to specs, it is up to the receiving clerk or manager to point that out to the vendor.

Vendors sometimes run out of a product, just as foodservice operators sometimes run out of a menu item. In cases such as these, the receiving clerk must know whether it is management's preference to accept as a substitute a product of higher quality, a product of lower quality, or no product at all. If this information is not known, one can expect that suppliers will be able to downgrade quality simply by saying that they were out of the requested product and did not want the operator to be shorted on the delivery.

Training to assess and evaluate quality products is a continual process. The effective receiving clerk should develop a keen eye for quality. This is done not merely to protect the operation and ensure that it gets what it pays for, but also to ensure that the consumer gets what he or she pays for. The receiving clerk might accept a lower quality. Our guests, however, may not. In fact, accepting a lower-quality substitute merely because it costs less is almost always a sure sign that management is unclear about the concept of establishing quality standards and sticking to them.

Price

In the area of training for price, the following two major concerns are to be addressed:

1. **Matching PO unit price to invoice unit price**
2. **Verifying price extensions**

Matching Purchase Order Unit Price to Invoice Unit Price. When the person responsible for purchasing food for the operation places an order, the confirmed quoted price should be written on the purchase order. There can then be no mistake about the cost of an item when it is delivered. It is never safe to assume, however, that the delivered price will match the price on the purchase order. While most suppliers are honest, it is amazing how often the price quoted on the telephone or in person ends up being lower than the price the operation is charged at delivery time. Often, this variation is said to be "computer error" or a "clerical mistake." It is interesting to note, however, that the errors most often result in an overcharge for the foodservice operator and rarely result in an undercharge.

The effective foodservice manager is happy with neither an overcharge nor an undercharge situation. We would hope that a customer would inform us if a waiter forgot to add the price of a bottle of wine to the dinner check. Similarly, a good receiving clerk works with the supplier to ensure that the operation is fairly charged for all items delivered. The acceptance of products puts the integrity of both supplier and operator on the line. Honesty and fair play must govern the actions of both parties in this area.

If the receiving clerk has a copy of the purchase order, it is a simple matter to verify the quoted price and the delivered price. If these two do not match, management should be notified immediately. If management notification is not possible, both the driver and the receiving clerk should initial the comment section of the purchase order, showing the difference in the two prices. Obviously, if the receiving clerk has no record of quoted price, either from a purchase order or an equivalent document, price verification of this type is not possible. An inability to verify quoted price and delivered price *at the time of delivery* is a sure indication that all is not well in the food cost control system.

Some operators deal with suppliers in such a way that a **contract price** is established. A contract price is simply a price agreed to by both operator and supplier. The contract price covers a certain product for a prescribed amount of time. For example, Harold uses Dairy O milk. Dairy O agrees to supply Harold with milk at the price of 98 cents per gallon for three months, from January 1 through March 31. Harold is free to buy as much or as little as he needs. The milk will always be billed at 98 cents per gallon; 98 cents then is the contract price. The advantage to Harold is that he knows exactly what his milk cost will be for the three-month period. The advantage to Dairy O is that it can offer a lower price in the hope of securing all of Harold's milk business. Even in the case of a contract price, however, management must insist that the receiving clerk verify invoice delivery price against the established contract price.

Verifying Price Extensions. Price extension is just as important as the ordered or unit price. Price extension or extended price is simply the unit price multiplied by the number of units delivered. If the price for a case of lettuce is $8, and the number of cases delivered is six, the price extension is as follows:

Unit price × # of units = Extended price

or

$8 × 6 = $48

Price extension verification is extremely important. Consider, for a moment, the case of Bruce, the foodservice director for the Downtown Society Club, a private dining club in the heart of a major city. Bruce is receiving the produce order for the day. He has been well trained to check for product weight, quantity, and quality. He also has a copy of the purchase order used to place the day's order with Larson's Produce. The Larson's invoice contains the following information:

Item	Unit Price	# Delivered	Extended Price
Tomatoes	$18.50	3	$55.50
Potatoes	12.90	6	83.40
Carrots	18.29	4	82.30

Bruce has verified both that the unit price matches the purchase order and that the number of items delivered is correct. That is, there are three boxes of tomatoes, six sacks of potatoes, and four bags of carrots. Should Bruce sign the invoice verifying acceptance of the product? *No!* The extended price of both potatoes and carrots is wrong. The potatoes should be $77.40 ($12.90 × 6 = $77.40, *not* $83.40), and the carrot extended price should be $73.16 ($18.29 × 4 = $73.16, *not* $82.30). If Bruce does not check the extended price, the operation will pay more (in this case $15.14) than it should for the products delivered. There seem to be two major reasons why operators do not always insist that the receiving clerk verify the extended price. The most common reason is the belief that there is not enough time to do so. The driver may be in a hurry and the operation may be very busy. If that is the case, the process of verifying the extended price can be moved to a slower or more convenient time. Why? Because there is a written record provided by the vendor of both the unit price and number delivered. Extension errors are vendor errors, in the vendor's own handwriting! Or more accurately, today they are in the vendor's own computer. Verification of price extensions is the only part of the receiving verification process that need not be done at the time of delivery.

The second reason operators sometimes ignore price extension is related to these same computers. Some operators believe that if an invoice is computer generated, the mathematics of price extension must be correct. Nothing could be further from the truth. Anyone familiar with computers knows that there are many possible methods that can result in extension errors.

For the effective manager, the conclusion is to verify extension prices. If it cannot be done at the time of delivery, it must be done as soon thereafter as possible. Errors are made, and they can cost the operation greatly if they go undetected.

Receiving Record or Daily Receiving Sheet

Some large operations use a receiving record rather than a copy of the actual purchase order when receiving food. This method, while taking more administrative time to both prepare and monitor, does have some advantages.

A receiving record generally contains the following information:

1. **Name of supplier**
2. **Invoice number**
3. **Item description**
4. **Unit price**
5. **Number of units delivered**
6. **Total cost**
7. **Storage area**
8. **Date of activity**

Figure 3.14 is an example of a receiving record, specifically designed for the receiving area of a large hotel.

Note that some items are placed directly into production areas (direct use), while others may be used in specific units or sent to the storeroom. Sundry items, such as paper products, ashtrays, matches, and cleaning supplies, may be stored in specific nonfood areas. Note also that subtotals for storage areas can be determined in terms of either units or dollars, whichever the operator prefers. In all cases, the sum of the totals for the distribution areas should equal the total for all items received during the day.

Receiving reports can be useful to management if it is important to record where items are to be delivered or where they have been delivered. Some foodservice operators will find the receiving report useful; many will not, since most of the information it contains is also included in the receiving clerk's copy of the purchase order.

Figure 3.14 **Hotel Pennycuff**

Receiving Report **Date 1/1**

Supplier	Invoice #	Item	Unit Price	# of Units	Total Cost	Unit Distribution A	B	C	D	E
Dairy O	T-16841	½ pt milk	$ .24	800	$192.00	75	200	125	—	400
Tom's Rice	12785	Rice (bags)	12.00	3	36.00	—	1	—	2	—
Barry's Bread	J-165	Rye	.62	25	15.50	—	25	—	—	—
		Wheat	.51	40	20.40	20	—	20	—	—
		White	.48	90	43.20	40	10	—	30	10
Total units				958		135	236	145	32	410
Total cost					$307.10					

Distribution Key:

A = Coffee shop
B = Banquet kitchen
C = Direct use
D = Storeroom
E = Sundry (nonfood items)

Comments:

Storage

The ideal situation for any foodservice operator would be to store only the food needed between deliveries. Storage costs money, both in terms of providing the storage space for inventory items and in terms of money that is tied up in inventory items, and thus unavailable for use elsewhere. It is always best, whenever possible, to order only the products that are absolutely needed by the operation. In that way, the vendor's storeroom actually becomes the operator's storeroom! In all cases, however, foodservice operations must have an adequate supply of products on hand to service the guests, who are the main concern. If we are doing our job well, we will have many guests and will need many items in storage!

Once the food products have been properly accepted by the receiving clerk, the next step in the control of food costs is the storage process. In most foodservice establishments, the storage process consists of essentially four main parts:

1. **Placing products in storage**
2. **Maintaining product quality and safety**
3. **Maintaining product security**
4. **Determining and using inventory value**

Placing Products in Storage

Food products are highly perishable items. As such, they must be moved quickly from the operation's receiving area to the area selected for storage. This is especially true for refrigerated and frozen items. An item like ice cream, for example, can deteriorate substantially if it is at room temperature for only a few minutes. In foodservice, most often, this high perishability dictates that the individual responsible for receiving the items be the same individual responsible for their storage.

Kathryn, the receiving clerk at the Speedway Motel, has just taken delivery of seven small boxes of coffee creamers. They were delivered in accordance with the purchase order and now must be put away. While Kathryn has many decisions to make as she stores her items, the first decision is whether management requires her to use the **LIFO** (last-in, first-out) or **FIFO** (first-in, first-out) method of storage.

Methods of Storage

LIFO System. When using the LIFO storage system, the storeroom operator intends to use the most recently delivered product (last in) before he or she uses any part of *that same product* previously on hand. If Kathryn decides, for example, to use the seven *new* boxes of creamers before she uses the product already on hand, she would be electing the LIFO system. Using the new boxes (last in) before using the product already on hand would assure her customers of the freshest possible product. Unfortunately, it might also assure the operation, at some point, of spoiled creamers, since the old product will now be used only if the operation runs out of fresh product.

While most authorities on food cost control do *not* recommend the use of the LIFO system, there are areas where its use does make sense. Imagine for a moment a truckstop restaurant that sells donuts and pastries. These are delivered daily. It makes no sense, in this case, to sell yesterday's few remaining donuts before starting to sell today's fresh product. It would be better to sell all of today's delivery first and thus ensure a quality product, since leftover donuts will not have the same desirability as today's delivery. The older donuts should be rotated out of stock, back to an area where they can be used as a carryover, or discarded. Some operators would say that the few remaining donuts from yesterday should be sold *before* selling the new product. Wrong! If we expect to gain repeat business, we must set our quality standards and stay with them. If our quality standard is "fresh today" donuts, each customer deserves that standard. If our standard is "fresh yesterday," we should buy Tuesday's donuts on Monday so they can age properly! In all cases, the foodservice operator must strive to maintain a consistent product standard. In the case of *some* bread, pastry, dairy, fruit, and vegetable items, the storeroom clerk could practice the LIFO system if these items have been designated as LIFO items by management.

To be successful, the operator must take great care to order only the quantity of product needed between deliveries. If too much product is ordered, loss rates will be very high. Cost can rise dramatically when LIFO items must eventually be discarded or used in a way that reduces their revenue-producing ability. In most cases, however, the operation will employ the FIFO system.

FIFO System. First-in, first-out (FIFO) means that the operator intends to rotate stock in such a way that products already on hand are sold before more recently delivered products are sold. If the FIFO system is to be used, the storeroom clerk must take great care to place new stock behind or at the bottom of old stock. It is the tendency of employees not to do this. Consider, for example, the storeroom clerk who must put away six cases of tomato sauce. The cases weigh about 40 pounds. The FIFO method dictates that these six cases be placed *under* the five cases already in the storeroom. Will the clerk place the six newly delivered cases underneath the five older cases? In many instances, the answer is no. Unless management strictly enforces the FIFO rule, employees may be tempted to take the easy way out. Figure 3.15 demonstrates the difference between LIFO and FIFO when dealing with cases of food products.

FIFO is the preferred storage technique for most perishable and nonperishable items because it is generally a good idea to sell oldest stock first. Failure to implement a FIFO system of storage management will result in excessive product loss due to spoilage, shrinkage, and deterioration of quality. All of these must be avoided if the foodservice operator is to effectively manage food expenses.

Decisions about storing food items according to the LIFO or FIFO method are management decisions. Once these decisions have been made, they should be communicated to the storeroom clerk and monitored on a regular basis to ensure compliance. Some foodservice operators require the storeroom clerk to mark or tag each delivered item with the date of delivery. These markings provide a visual aid in determining which product should be used first. If the supplier has computerized his or her delivery, the box or case may already bear a strip identifying both the product name and the delivery date. When this is not the case, the storeroom clerk should assume this function.

Figure 3.16 demonstrates the visual aspect of products in a dry storage area when management requires that the storeroom clerk mark each item with its date of delivery.

Storage Areas

Products are generally placed in one of the following three major storage areas:

1. **Dry storage**
2. **Refrigerated storage**
3. **Frozen storage**

Dry Storage. Dry storage areas should generally be maintained at a temperature ranging between 65 °F and 75 °F; therefore, a thermometer in the storeroom

Figure 3.15 **FIFO and LIFO Storage Systems**

FIFO	LIFO
Oldest	Newest
Oldest	Newest
Oldest	Newest
Newest	Oldest
Newest	Oldest
Newest	Oldest

Figure 3.16 **FIFO Stacking System**

Napkins	2/10	Straws	2/10	12-oz cups	3/8
Napkins	3/8	Straws	2/10	12-oz cups	3/8
Napkins	3/8	Straws	3/8	12-oz cups	4/6
Napkins	4/6	Straws	4/6	12-oz cups	4/6

is a good idea. Temperatures lower or higher than this can be harmful. Dry storage temperatures more often get too high than too low, exceeding by far the upper limit of temperature acceptability. This is because storage areas are frequently in poorly ventilated, closed-in areas of the building. Excessive temperatures damage dry storage products.

Shelving in dry storage areas must be easily cleaned and sturdy enough to hold the weight of dry products. Shelves must be kept at least 10 inches above the ground to enable the room to be easily cleaned and to ensure proper ventilation. Dry good products should never be stored directly on the floor. Can labels should face out for easy identification. Wheeled bins and cans should be used whenever possible so that heavy lifting can be avoided. Most importantly, dry storage space must be sufficient in size to handle the operation's needs. Cramped and cluttered dry storage areas tend to increase costs because inventory cannot be easily rotated, maintained, and counted. Theft can go undetected, and operators may find themselves accidentally using the FIST method of inventory storage (first-in, still-there!) because products get "lost" in the storeroom.

Refrigerated Storage. Refrigerator temperatures should be maintained between 32 °F and 40 °F. Temperatures will vary as much as four degrees between the refrigerator's coldest and warmest spots. The bottom tends to be coldest in a refrigerator because warm air rises and cold air falls. Refrigerators actually work by removing heat from the contents rather than "making" food cold. This is an important point to remember when refrigerating food. Foods that are boiling hot should be precooled to 160 °F before being placed in the refrigerator. This results in lower operating costs for the refrigerator but is still well above the food danger zone of 45 °–140 °F.

Refrigerators should have easily cleaned shelving units. They should be properly cleaned on a regular basis, and doors should be opened and closed quickly, both to lower operational cost and to ensure that the items in the refrigerator stay at their peak of freshness. Carryover items should be properly labeled, wrapped, and rotated.

Frozen Storage. Freezer temperatures should be maintained between 0 °F and −10 °F. What is usually called a freezer is more properly a **frozen food storage unit.** The distinction is an important one. To be frozen at its peak of freshness, a food item must be quickly frozen. This involves temperatures of −20 °F or lower. Freezer units in a foodservice operation do not generally operate at these temperatures; thus they really are best at "holding," not freezing, frozen food.

It is anticipated that in the future more and more foodservice storage space will be devoted to frozen food. Therefore, the conversion of dry or refrigerated space to frozen food storage is highly recommended. Most foodservice operators also find that their carryover items will, in many cases, have a longer shelflife when held frozen rather than refrigerated. Frozen foods should be wrapped securely to reduce moisture loss, and they should be carefully checked when received to ensure that they have not been thawed and refrozen. It is a good idea to periodically check that gaskets on freezers tightly seal the food cabinet. This will not only reduce operating costs but will also maintain food quality for a longer period of time.

Storage Basics

Regardless of the storage type, food and related products should be stored neatly in some logical order. Some operators store items alphabetically; others have their own system. Canned vegetables, for example, might be stored alphabetically (asparagus, beets, corn, and so on); canned fruit (apples, cherries, cranberries, and so on) would be stored separately. Many operators store products according to how often they use them. In this case, time may be saved by storing frequently used items near the door of a storeroom or the front of a refrigerator or freezer. When a few items constitute a majority of the sales volume in a unit, this can be an effective storage technique. It is important to note that the objective of a neat storage area is to both maximize storage space and minimize the time it takes to locate an item in storage.

In this regard, proper storage techniques, while assisting in lowering the cost of food products, also help in reducing costs associated with labor. It is sometimes amazing how long it can take an employee to go to the storeroom for a can of beans! In an improperly maintained storage area, employees can claim that it took a long time to find the desired product. When a storage area is properly labeled, kept clean, and regularly monitored, problems such as this will not occur.

Maintaining Product Quality and Safety

It is important that the storeroom clerk understand his or her role in maintaining product quality. Food product quality rarely improves with increased storage time. For most foodservice operators, quality of ingredients is at its peak when the product ordered is delivered to the operator. From then on, the product can only decline in freshness, quality, and nutrition. The only exception to this might be the gourmet restaurant that elects to age some of its own products. The general case, however, is that the storeroom clerk must make every effort to maintain food quality in all of the operation's storage areas, since food quality tends to diminish during the storage process.

The primary method for ensuring product quality while in storage is through proper product rotation and high standards of storeroom sanitation. Storage areas are excellent breeding grounds for insects, rodents, and bacteria. To protect against these potential hazards, the operator should insist on the regular cleaning of all storage areas. Compressor units on refrigerators and frozen food holding units should be checked regularly for the buildup of dust and dirt. Interior racks should be kept free of spills and soil. Since refrigerators and frozen food holding units actually remove heat rather than "add" cold, they also remove product moisture, thus causing shrinkage in meats and produce, and freezer burn in poorly wrapped items kept at freezing temperatures. Both refrigerators and frozen food holding units should be mounted at least ten inches off the ground or sealed to the floor to prevent cockroaches and other insects from living beneath them. Both types of units should be kept six to ten inches from the walls to allow for the free circulation of air around the units. Drainage systems in refrigerators should be checked at least weekly. Frozen food holding units should have *externally visible* internal thermometers, whether they use a digital display or the more traditional temperature scale.

In larger storage areas, hallways should be kept clear of storage materials or boxes. This helps both in finding items in the storage area and in reducing the number of hiding places for insects and rodents.

Maintaining Product Security

Food products are like money to the foodservice operator. In fact, one should think of food inventory items in exactly that way. The apple in a produce walk-in is not just an apple. It represents $1 in income to the airport foodservice director who hopes to sell a crisp, fresh apple to a weary traveller. If the apple disappears, sales income of $1 will disappear also. When we think of inventory items in terms of their sales value, it becomes clear why product security is of the utmost importance to the foodservice operator. As such, systems must be in place to reduce employee, vendor, and guest theft to the lowest possible level. All foodservice establishments will experience some amount of theft, in its strictest sense. The reason is very simple. Some employee theft is impossible to detect. Even the most sophisticated computerized control system is not able to determine if an employee or vendor's employee walks into the produce walk-in and eats one green grape. Similarly, an employee who takes home two sugar packets per night will likely go undetected for a great length of time. In neither of these cases, however, is the amount of loss significant, certainly not enough to install security cameras in the walk-in or to frisk all employees as they leave for home at the end of their shift. What we want to do, however, is to make it difficult to remove food from storage without authorization so that we can know when food has been removed. Again, good control systems must be in place if we are to achieve this goal.

It is amazing how large the impact of theft can be on profitability. Consider the following example. Jesse is the receiving clerk at the Hole in the Wall hotel. On a daily basis, Jesse takes home $2 worth of food products. How much, then, does Jesse, or an employee like him, cost the hotel in one year? The answer is a surprising $14,600 in sales revenue! If an employee steals $2 per day for 365 days, the total theft amount is $730 (365 days × $2 per day = $730). If the hotel makes a profit of 5% on each dollar of food products sold, the operation must sell $\frac{\$1.00}{.05} \times \$730.00 = \$14,600.00$ to recover the lost $730.

In order to recover the dollar amount of this theft, the hotel must sell $14,600 of food per year and make 5 cents per dollar on these sales. Clearly, small thefts add up to large dollar losses!

Most foodservice operators attempt to control access to the location of stored products. This may be done, in some areas, by a process as simple as keeping the dry storage area locked and requiring employees to get the keys from the manager or supervisor. In other situations, cameras may be mounted in both storage areas and employee exit areas. It is generally a good idea to limit access to storage areas. While the physical layout of the foodservice operation may prevent management from being able to effectively lock and secure all storage areas, too much traffic is sure to cause theft problems. This is not because employees are basically dishonest. Most are not. Theft problems develop because of the few employees who feel that either management won't miss a few of whatever is being stolen or they "deserve" to take a few things because they work so hard and are paid so little!

It is management's responsibility to see that the storeroom clerk maintains good habits in securing product inventory. As a general rule, if storerooms are to be locked, only one individual should have the key during any shift. The temptation sometimes exists for management to hang the key by the door, that is, to lock the storeroom but give the key to any employee who says he or she needs it. This obviously defeats the purpose of the locked system. In reality, it is simply not possible to keep all inventory items under lock and key. Some items must be received and immediately sent to the kitchen for processing or use. Also, what would happen if the manager or other key holder were gone from the operation for a few minutes? Most operators find that it is impossible to operate under a system where *all* food products are locked away from the employees. Storage areas should not, however, be accessible to customers or vendor employees. Unlocked storage areas near exits are extremely tempting to the dishonest individual. If proper control procedures are in place, employees will know that management can determine if theft has occurred. Without such control, employees are aware that theft can go undetected. This must be avoided and can be.

Determining and Using Inventory Value

It is the responsibility of the storeroom clerk, or other person selected by management, to maintain the inventory in a way that makes it easy to count items and determine the monetary value of the inventory. The concepts of both inventory management and product issuing are discussed more fully in Chapter 5, "Managing the Food and Beverage Production Process." Placing products into the production system, or **issuing,** impacts inventory levels and must be carefully accounted for. Issuing, in fact, begins the food production process.

Regardless of the inventory system or issuing system in place, however, all foodservice managers must be able to answer this fundamental question: "What is the dollar value of the products I currently have on hand?" The answer to this question is important for many reasons. Foremost, it is not possible to know actual food expense without an accurate inventory. Indeed, the formula used to determine the cost of food consumed (food expense) is driven primarily by knowing the dollar value of all food products in inventory. The process of determining inventory value is quite simple, even if the actual task is time-consuming.

Valuing inventory is done by using the following inventory valuation formula:

Item amount × Item value = Inventory value

Item Amount

Item amount may be determined by counting, as in the case of cans, or weighing, as in the case of meats. If an item is purchased by the pound, it is generally weighed to determine item amount. If it is purchased by the piece or case, then the appropriate unit to determine item amount can be either piece or case. If, for example, canned pears are purchased by the case, with six cans per case, management might decide to consider the item as either case or can. That is, 3 cases might be considered as 3 items (by the case) or 18 items (by the can). Either method is acceptable.

Item Value

Item value, generally speaking, is determined by using either the LIFO or FIFO method. When the LIFO method is in use, the item value is the price paid for the most recent addition to item amount. When the FIFO method is in use, the item value is the price paid for the oldest product on hand. In the hospitality industry, most operators value inventory at its most recently known value; thus, LIFO is the more common method. A simple illustration may help. Peggy Sue purchased grapes on Monday and paid $30 per lug. On Friday, she again purchased grapes, but paid $40 per lug. On Saturday morning, she took inventory and found that she had 1½ lugs of grapes. What is their inventory value? According to the LIFO system, it would cost Peggy Sue $60 ($40 current price × 1.5 lugs = $60) to replace the grapes; therefore, their value is $60. Peggy Sue did not pay that much for them, but that is their replacement value. Valuing inventory at the most recently paid price is the best method for establishing item value for the majority of hospitality operators.

Inventory value is done on a form similar to the inventory valuation sheet shown in Figure 3.17. This valuation sheet has a place for all inventory items, the quantity on hand, and the unit value of each item. There is also a place for the date the inventory was taken, the name of the person who counted the product, and the name of the person who extended or established the value of the inventory. It is recommended that these persons be two different individuals to reduce the risk of inventory valuation fraud.

Figure 3.17 **Inventory Valuation Sheet**

Unit Name: ____________ Inventory Date: ____________

Counted by: ____________ Extended by: ____________

Item	Item Amount	Item Value	Inventory Value
		Page Total	

Page ____ of ____

Thus, if we have five cases of beets in our inventory, and each case has a value of $20, the inventory value of our beets is as follows:

5 × $20 = $100
or
Item amount × Item value = Inventory value

The process of determining inventory value requires the foodservice operator to count all food products on hand and multiply the value of the item by the number of items on hand. The process is more difficult than it would first appear when one realizes that the average foodservice operation has hundreds of items in inventory. Thus, taking the inventory can be a very time-consuming task. A **physical inventory,** one in which the food products are actually counted, must, however, be taken to determine actual food usage. Some operators take this inventory monthly, others weekly or daily! Some, unfortunately, feel that there is no need to ever take inventory. These operators cannot effectively control their costs, because they do not know what their costs are. Without taking inventory, operators have no way to determine their actual costs.

Computing Actual Food Expense

Consider for a moment the case of Lester, the manager of a hand-dipped ice cream store. Lester has received his records for January and found the following:

Ice cream sales = $68,000
Ice cream purchases = $39,000

Lester determined his sales figure by adding all of his daily sales receipts (see Chapter 2). He has determined his food expense by adding the dollar value of all the delivery invoices that he has accumulated for the month. Would it be correct to say that Lester's food expense for the month of January is $39,000? *No.* Why not? Because Lester may have more, or less, ice cream in inventory on the last day of January than he had on the first day. If Lester has more ice cream in inventory on January 31 than he had on January 1, Lester's food expense is less than $39,000. If Lester has less product in inventory on the 31st than he had on the 1st, then his food expense is higher than $39,000. To understand why this is so, we must understand the accounting formula for computing food expense. The formula follows.

Food Cost Formula

Beginning inventory

plus

Purchases

Goods available

less

Ending inventory

less

Employee meals

Cost of food consumed

Cost of food consumed is the dollar amount of all food sold, thrown away, wasted, or stolen. It represents for the foodservice operator all food that is gone, for whatever reason.

Beginning Inventory

Beginning inventory is the dollar value of all food on hand at the beginning of the accounting period. It is determined by completing a physical inventory.

Purchases

Purchases are the sum cost of all food purchased during the accounting period. This sum is determined by adding all relevant invoices for the accounting period.

Goods Available for Sale

Goods available for sale are the sum of beginning inventory and purchases. They represent the value of all food that was available for sale during the accounting period.

Ending Inventory

Ending inventory refers to the dollar value of all food on hand at the end of the accounting period. It also is determined by completing a physical inventory.

Employee Meals

Employee meal costs are a labor-related, *not* food-related, cost. Therefore, the value of this benefit, if provided, is more accurately charged to labor expenses. This expense is removed from the food expense group and added to the labor expense group.

Cost of Food Consumed

As stated earlier, the cost of food consumed is the actual dollar value of all food used by the operation. Again, it is important to note that this not merely the value of all food sold, but rather the value of all food no longer in the establishment.

In our example, Lester has no idea what his actual cost of food consumed is, since he has no inventory figures. Nor is he able to determine cost of food consumed at this point because it is impossible to turn back the clock to January 1 and thus establish a beginning inventory.

Figure 3.18 illustrates a recap sheet used to determine cost of food consumed. Had Lester completed such a form, he would have known what his cost of goods consumed actually was. Every manager should compute on a regular basis actual cost of goods consumed. It is not possible to improve the cost picture unless the manager knows what his or her costs are.

Figure 3.18 **Recap Sheet**

Cost of Food Consumed

Accounting Period: __________ to __________

Unit Name: ______________________

Beginning inventory	$ ________	
plus		
Purchases	$ ________	
Goods available		$ ________
less		
Ending inventory		$ ________
less		$ ________
Employee meals		$ ________
Cost of food consumed		$ ________

Variations on the Basic Cost of Food Consumed Formula

While Figure 3.18 demonstrates the format most commonly used to determine cost of food consumed, some operators prefer slightly different formulas, depending on the unique aspects of their units. The important point to remember, however, is that all of these formulas should seek to accurately reflect actual cost of food used by the operation for a given time period. Two variations of the formula follow.

1. No employee meals are provided. When an operation has no employee meals at all, the computation of cost of food consumed is as follows:

Beginning inventory	$ ________	
plus		
Purchases	$ ________	
Goods available		$ ________
less		
Ending inventory		$ ________
Cost of food consumed		$ ________

2. Food or beverage products are transferred from one food service unit to another. This is the case when, for example, an operator seeks to compute one cost of goods consumed figure for a bar and another for the bar's companion restaurant. In this situation, it is likely that fruit juice, vegetables, and similar items are taken from the kitchen for use in the bar, while wine, sherry, and similar items may be taken from the bar for use in the kitchen. This concept of transferability is covered in detail in Chapter 4. The formula for cost of goods consumed in this situation would be as follows:

Beginning inventory	$ ________	
plus		
Purchases	$ ________	
Goods available		$ ________
less		
Ending inventory		$ ________
less		

(continued)

Transfers out	$ ________
plus	
Transfers in	$ ________
Cost of goods consumed	$ ________

It is important for the effective foodservice operator to know exactly which formula or variation is in use when analyzing cost of food consumed. The variations, while slight, can make big differences in the interpretation of this cost data. In all cases, it is critical that accurate beginning and ending inventory figures be maintained if accurate cost data are to be computed.

In Chel's operation, a restaurant in Miami, Florida, called Flanders' Poppies, both beginning inventory and ending inventory figures are known, thus enabling her to determine with the following information her cost of food consumed.

Beginning inventory	$ 8,420.60
Purchases	31,642.20
Ending inventory	9,006.14
Employee meals	706.00

Figure 3.19 **Recap Sheet**

Cost of Food Consumed

Accounting Period: 1/1 to 1/31

Unit Name: Flanders' Poppies Restaurant

Beginning inventory	$ 8,420.60	
plus		
Purchases	$ 31,642.20	
Goods available		$ 40,062.80
less		
Ending inventory		$ 9,006.14
less		$ 31,056.66
Employee meals		$ 706.00
Cost of food consumed		$ 30,350.66

She is now able to complete her recap sheet as illustrated in Figure 3.19.

In this example, employee meals were determined by assigning a food value of $2 per employee meal consumed. If records are kept on the number of employees eating per day, monthly employee meal figures are easily determined. Some operators prefer to estimate the dollar value of employee meals each month rather than record employee meals. This is not a good practice, both from a control point of view and in terms of developing accurate cost data.

It is important to note that the ending inventory figure for one accounting period becomes the beginning inventory figure for the next period. For example, in the case of Flanders' Poppies, the January 31 ending inventory figure will become the February 1 beginning inventory figure. It is clear that in this manner physical inventory need only be taken once per accounting period, not twice. Again, while the physical inventory process can be time-consuming, it must be performed in order to determine actual food expense.

While there is no reliable method for replacing the actual counting of inventory items on hand, there are many computer programs on the market to compute inventory value, thus making a time-consuming task less tedious and more efficient.

Food Cost Percentage

We know from Chapter 1, "Managing Income and Expense," that food expense is often expressed as a percentage of total income or sales. Since we can now determine actual cost of food consumed, we can also compute an actual food cost percentage. Again, this is both the traditional way of looking at food expense and generally the method used by operators when preparing the profit and loss statement.

The formula used to compute actual food cost percentage is as follows:

$$\frac{\textbf{Cost of food consumed}}{\textbf{Sales}} = \textbf{Food cost \%}$$

Food cost percentage represents the portion of our income that was spent on food expenses. In the case of Flanders' Poppies Restaurant, we know that cost of food consumed equals $30,350.66 (Figure 3.19). If, for example, the restaurant experienced $95,000.00 in sales for the period of January 1 to January 31, the food cost percentage for the period would be as follows:

$$\frac{\textbf{\$30,350.66 (cost of food consumed)}}{\textbf{\$95,000.00 (sales)}} = \textbf{31.95\% (food cost)}$$

Thus, Chel knows that her cost of food consumed is exactly $30,350.66 for the accounting period and her food cost percentage for the same period is exactly 31.95%. Since she knows her costs exactly, she is better able to control her costs over time.

Estimating Daily Cost of Food Consumed

Many operators would like to know their food usage on a much more regular basis than once per month. When this is the case, the physical inventory may be taken as often as desired. Again, however, physical inventories are time-consuming.

It would be convenient if the foodservice operator could have a close estimate of his or her food usage on a weekly or daily basis without the effort of a monthly inventory count. Fortunately, such an approximation exists. Figure 3.20 illustrates a six-column form that can be used for a variety of purposes. One of them is to estimate food cost percentage on a daily or weekly basis.

As an example, consider Margo's, an Italian restaurant that serves no liquor and caters to a family-oriented clientele. Trisha, the manager of Margo's, would like to monitor food cost percentage on a more regular basis than once a month,

Figure 3.20 **Six-Column Form**

Date: ____________

Weekday	Today	Todate	Today	Todate	Today	Todate

which is her regular accounting period. She has decided to use a six-column form to estimate food cost percentage. Since she keeps track of both daily sales and purchases, she can easily do so. In the space above the first two columns, she writes **sales.** Above the middle two columns, she writes **purchases,** and above the last two columns, she writes **cost %** (see figure 3.21).

Trisha then proceeds each day to enter daily sales figures in the column labeled **sales today.** Her invoices for food deliveries are totaled daily and entered in the column titled **purchases today.** Dividing the purchases today column by the sales today column yields the figure that is placed in the **cost % today** column. **Purchases todate** (the cumulative purchases amount) is divided by **sales todate** (the cumulative sales amount) to yield the **cost % todate** figure. A quick summary of the six-column food cost percentage estimate is as follows:

$$1.\quad \frac{\textbf{Purchases today}}{\textbf{Sales today}} = \textbf{Cost \% today}$$

$$2.\quad \frac{\textbf{Purchases todate}}{\textbf{Sales todate}} = \textbf{Cost \% todate}$$

Figure 3.21 shows this information for Margo's operation for the time period January 1 to January 7.

As can be seen, Trisha buys most of her food for Margo's at the beginning of the week, while sales are strongest in the later part of the week. This is a common occurrence at many foodservice establishments. As can also be seen, Margo's daily cost formula ranges from a high of 130% (Monday) to a low of 0% (Sunday), when no deliveries are made. In the cost % todate column, however, the range is only from a high of 130% (Monday) to a low of 39.20% (Sunday).

What is Trisha's best guess about what her food cost percentage actually is as of Sunday? The answer is that it will be slightly less than 39.20%. Why? Let us go back to the formula for cost of food consumed. First, we must make the important assumption that for any time period we are evaluating, beginning inventory and ending inventory are the same. In other words, over any given time period, we will have approximately the same amount of food on hand at all times. If this assumption is correct, the six-column food cost estimate is, in fact, a good indicator of our food usage. The reason is very simple. The formula for cost of food consumed asks us to *add* beginning inventory and then later *subtract* ending inventory (see page 79). If these two numbers are assumed to be the same, they can be ignored, since adding and subtracting the same number will result in no effect at all. For example, if we start with $50, add $10, and subtract $10, we are left with $50. In terms of the cost of food consumed formula, when beginning inventory and ending inventory are assumed to be the same figure, it is the mathematical equivalent of adding a zero and subtracting a zero. To continue our example, if we start with $50, add 0, and subtract 0, we are left again

Figure 3.21 **Six-Column Form**

Food Cost Estimate
Margo's

Date: 1/1–1/7

	Sales		Purchases		Cost %	
Weekday	**Today**	**Todate**	**Today**	**Todate**	**Today**	**Todate**
Mon	$ 850.40	$ 850.40	$1,106.20	$1,106.20	130.00%	130.00%
Tues	920.63	1,771.03	841.40	1,947.60	91.40	110.00
Wed	1,185.00	2,956.03	519.60	2,467.20	43.80	83.50
Thurs	971.20	3,927.23	488.50	2,955.70	50.30	75.30
Fri	1,947.58	5,874.81	792.31	3,748.01	40.70	63.80
Sat	2,006.41	7,881.22	286.20	4,034.21	14.30	51.20
Sun	2,404.20	10,285.42	0	4,034.21	0	39.20

with $50. Thus, when beginning inventory and ending inventory are equal, or assumed to be equal, the cost of food consumed formula would look as follows:

	Beginning inventory	$0
plus	Purchases	
equals	Purchases	
less	Ending inventory	$0
equals	Purchases	
less	Employee meals	
equals	Cost of food consumed	

Therefore, as stated earlier, if Trisha assumes that her inventory is constant, her cost of food consumed for the one-week period is a little less than $4,042.21, or 39.20% of sales. Why a little less? Because we must still subtract the value of employee meals if any are provided, since they are a labor expense and not a food expense. How accurate is the six-column form? For most operators, it is quite accurate and has the following advantages:

1. **It is very simple to compute, requiring ten minutes or less per day for most operations.**
2. **It records both sales history and purchasing patterns.**
3. **It identifies problems before the end of the monthly accounting period.**
4. **By the ninth or tenth day, the degree of accuracy in the todate column is very high.**
5. **It is a daily reminder to both management and employees that there is a very definite relationship between sales and expenses.**

The use of a six-column food cost estimate is highly recommended for the operator who elects to conduct a physical inventory less than every two weeks.

The control of food expense is critical to all foodservice operations. From the purchase of the raw ingredient to its receiving and storage, the effective foodservice operator strives to have the proper quality and quantity of product on hand at all times.

Food represents a large part of a manager's overall expense budget. Protecting this product and accounting for its usage are extremely important in helping to manage overall costs.

TEST YOUR SKILLS

A. Anita operates a lunchroom in a large but exclusive health club. The members demand high-quality service and are especially concerned about reducing fat in their diets. They like high-protein items for their lunches, which are light and generally consumed prior to or immediately after a workout. The menu in Anita's restaurant consists of five main lunch specials. Each meat, poultry, or fish item is purchased by the pound (using product specifications), then prepared and served in a four-ounce portion (EP), according to the standardized recipe. Anita keeps excellent sales records and thus knows her % selecting figures, which are tabled below. She also carefully monitors waste % data, which are also tabled below for each item. How much of each item should Anita order for next week, given that Anita expects 500 customers for lunch next week, each of whom will order one of her five menu items?

Item	% Selecting	Waste %	Purchase Price
Beef	21%	30%	$3.20/lb
Pork	18	25	1.70/lb
Chicken	15	10	.89/lb
Sole	30	10	3.20/lb
Tuna	16	5	4.10/lb

What should the total of Anita's purchases for these items be next week if she buys at the purchase price listed above? Do you think Anita should buy these items on a par or as-needed basis? Why?

B. Saint John's Hospital foodservice director, Herman, has a problem. He has the following information about his operation for the month of April but has forgotten how to compute cost of food consumed for the month. Use Herman's figures to compute actual cost of food consumed for his operation.

Inventory on March 31		$22,184.50
April purchases		
Meats	$11,501.00	
Dairy	$ 6,300.00	
Fruits and vegetables	$ 9,641.00	
All other foods	$32,384.00	
# of employees eating daily	85	
Cost per employee for employee meals	$1.25	
Inventory on April 30		$23,942.06

Could Herman have computed this figure if he had not taken a physical inventory on April 30? Why or why not?

C. "Fast Eddie" operates a restaurant in the casino town of Taloona. He is checking over the work of his assistant manager, who has been newly hired. One of the jobs of the assistant manager is to complete daily the six-column food cost estimate. "Fast Eddie" finds that while data are listed for the first ten days of the accounting period, the form has not been completed. Complete the form for "Fast Eddie" so that he can go home.

Six-Column Form

Date: 1/1–1/10

Weekday	Sales Today	Sales Todate	Purchases Today	Purchases Todate	Cost % Today	Cost % Todate
1/1	$3,482.50	3,482.50	$1,645.80	1645.80	47	47
1/2	2,970.05	6,812.55	2,006.40	3652.20	68	53
1/3	2,855.20	9,667.75	1,107.20	4759.40	39	49
1/4	3,001.45	12,669.20	986.24	5745.64	33	45
1/5	3,645.20	16,314.40	1,245.60	6991.24	34	43
1/6	4,850.22	21,164.60	2,006.40	8997.64	41	43
1/7	6,701.55	27,866.15	–0–	8997.64	0	32
1/8	3,609.20	31,475.35	1,799.90	10797.54	50	34
1/9	2,966.60	34,441.95	851.95	11649.49	29	34
1/10	3,105.25	37,547.20	924.50	12573.99	30	33

Chapter 4

Managing the Cost of Beverages

OVERVIEW

This chapter begins with a review of the special responsibilities associated with the purchase and sale of alcoholic beverages. Discussions focus on the use of sales forecasts and standardized recipes to develop product inventory levels. The method of accounting for kitchen transfers and the method for computing cost of beverages consumed are presented.

HIGHLIGHTS

At the conclusion of this chapter, the manager will be able to

A. Use sales histories in conjunction with standardized drink recipes to develop a beverage purchase order
B. Compute the dollar value of bar transfers both to and from the kitchen
C. Compute actual cost of goods consumed for beer, wine, and spirits

Managing the Cost of Beverages

It might seem unusual that a book about cost management would have to separate the study of cost control into a segment dealing with food and another one dealing with alcoholic beverage products. In fact, it might seem unusual that the very term **beverages,** in this chapter, will always refer to those beverages with an alcoholic content.

Alcoholic beverages refer to those products that are meant for consumption as a beverage, and that contain a significant amount of ethyl alcohol. These products are generally classified as follows:

1. **Beer: a fermented beverage made from grain and flavored with hops**

2. **Wine: a fermented beverage made from grapes, fruits, or berries**
3. **Spirits: fermented beverages that are distilled to increase the alcohol content of the product**

The foodservice operator who combines the sale of food products with that of beverages, or who sells beverages exclusively, faces a unique set of challenges that deserve special discussion. In many ways, the foodservice operator will treat beverage products in a manner similar to that of food products. The products will be specified, ordered, received, and stored in much the same fashion as are food products. In other ways, however, the operator must make special accommodations because these beverage products create control issues beyond those of normal food products. Thus, control systems must be modified to meet the increased responsibility inherent in the sale of alcoholic beverages.

In general, there are two primary classifications of establishments that serve alcoholic beverages. The first includes restaurants where alcoholic beverages are served primarily as an accompaniment to food products and are consumed in conjunction with a meal. The second includes establishments where the beverages are sold as the primary offering. Generally, bars, taverns, and nightclubs fall into this category.

People have long been fond of alcoholic beverages, whatever the location of their consumption, because they add greatly to the enjoyment of food or other people. In moderate doses, ethyl alcohol, the type found in beverage products, is a mild tranquilizer. In excessive doses, it can become toxic, causing impaired judgment and, in some cases, death. Clearly, a foodservice manager whose establishment serves alcoholic beverages must take great care in the serving and monitoring of customer alcohol intake.

Many states have now developed third-party liability legislation that holds the foodservice operator responsible, under certain conditions, for the actions of his or her patrons who consume excessive amounts of alcoholic beverages. This series of legislative acts, commonly called **dramshop laws,** shifts the liability for acts committed by an individual under the influence of alcohol from that individual to the server or operation that supplied the intoxicating beverage.

Dramshop is derived from the word **dram,** which refers to a small drink, and **shop,** where such a drink was sold. Dramshop laws, then, cover situations involving the sale and consumption of alcoholic beverages. Because of these laws, operators are becoming increasingly concerned with alcohol awareness. This means training employees to serve alcoholic beverages properly and to notice telltale signs of customer intoxication.

The service of alcoholic beverages in the United States is highly restricted. A drinking age of 21 in most states, warning labels on bottles, religious beliefs, drinking and driving laws, and other factors all will continue to tightly control consumption of beer, wine, and spirits. While the special requirements involved in serving alcoholic beverages are many, the control of beverage costs is similar, in most respects, to that of the control of food-related costs.

This chapter details the unique aspects of sales forecasting, purchasing, receiving, and storage of beverage products. In some areas, beverage control is no different from that of nonalcoholic food products. In others, the differences are pronounced.

Forecasting Beverage Sales

The number of possible "menu items" in the average bar or lounge is staggering. Human imagination has few limits, and thus the number of different mixtures a skilled bartender can concoct makes forecasting customer item selection a difficult process indeed. Of course, number of guests served and average customer sale are easy to track. This is done exactly as previously discussed (Chapter 2). However, percentage selecting—the proportion of people who will buy a particular drink, given a choice of many different drink types—must be modified somewhat if it is to be applied to forecasting beverage sales. In fact, beverage sales forecasting varies also by the type of beverage sold.

Forecasting Beer Sales

Forecasting beer sales is essentially the same as forecasting a regular menu item. That is, given a choice of beverage products, some percentage of customers will choose beer. The questions for the operator are, of course, "What percent of my customers will choose beer *and* which kind of beer will they choose?"

Consider the case of Ray. He operates a small bar in a trendy section of a large West Coast city. His clientele generally consists of upscale office and managerial professionals. For the time period January 1–8, Ray served a total of 1,600 customers, 400 of whom selected a beer product, 160 a wine product, and the balance some other beverage type. Ray has monitored his percentage selecting data and has determined that one out of four customers coming to Ray's bar will order beer. He needs to determine, however, which beers they will buy. By charting current beer sales, he knows what his customers' beer preferences are. Figure 4.1 demonstrates that for the period January 1–8, a total of 400 of Ray's customers selected beer. It also details which specific beer his customers ordered.

If he is to build the information data base necessary to accurately develop purchase orders based on projected sales, Ray must know both what percentage of his customers select beer, and which kind of beer they select. Fortunately, Ray has invested in a POS (point of sales) system that lets him know exactly which beers, by brand, have been sold in his bar on a daily basis. A tally of his guest checks would have furnished him with the same information.

Figure 4.1 **Ray's Bar**

	Beverage Sales	**Date: 1/1–1/8**
Product	**# Sold**	**% Sold**
Beer		
Brand A	45	11.25%
Brand B	18	4.50
Brand C	61	15.25
Brand D	68	17.00
Draft A	115	28.75
Draft B	93	23.25
Total	400	100.00

Forecasting Wine Sales

The forecasting of wine sales must be divided into two main parts:

1. **Forecasting bottled wine sales**
2. **Forecasting by-the-glass sales**

Forecasting Bottled Wine Sales

When forecasting wine sales by the bottle, the foodservice operator treats an individual type of bottled wine exactly as he or she would treat a menu item. A wine list, or wine menu, detailing the selections of wines available, can be presented to the customer who then makes a choice. Percentage selecting figures are computed exactly as they would be when analyzing food item sales. For the operator, however, it is possible to offer wines with very small percentage selecting figures because wines in a bottle are not highly perishable. Thus, many operators develop wine lists consisting of a large number of wines, many of which rarely sell. While this selling strategy has its place, it must be remembered that excessive product inventory, whether food or beverage, must be avoided. Dollars invested in excessive inventory are not available for use in other areas of the foodservice organization. While bottled wine is not highly perishable, all wine products are perishable to some degree, and thus excessive inventory can result in increased product loss through oxidation and theft.

Forecasting By-the-Glass Sales

Generally, forecasting the sale of house wines or other wines sold by the glass is done in a manner similar to that used in forecasting beer sales. Once the operator has determined the number of guests who will select wine, the type of wine selected must be monitored.

In Figure 4.2 Ray has tracked his by-the-glass sales of wine for the period January 1–8. He knows that one out of ten customers buy wine by the glass. Thus, 160 (from a total of 1,600 customers) select this beverage.

If Ray's customers remain consistent in their buying habits, he will have a good idea of the total demand for his by-the-glass products and will be better able to ascertain the amount that must be on hand on any given day.

Forecasting Spirit Sales

The number of customers who order a mixed drink can be determined in the same way as the number of customers who order beer and wine. Unlike beer and wine, however, the exact item the customer will request is very difficult to determine. For example, two customers order bourbon and soda; one customer specifies Old Crow brand of bourbon, whereas the other one prefers Heaven Hill. From the customers' point of view, they both ordered bourbon and soda. From the operator's point of view, two distinct items were selected. To make matters a bit more complicated, a third customer comes in and orders bourbon and soda without preference as to the type of bourbon used. In this case, it is the operator who will decide which product is to be sold. Obviously, a different method of sales forecasting is necessary in a situation such as this, and in fact, several are available. One method requires that the operator view customer selection not in terms of the drink requested such as bourbon and water, bourbon and soda, bourbon and cola, and so on, but rather in terms of the particular spirit that forms the base of the drink. For example, four customers order the following:

1. **Kahlua on the rocks**
2. **Kahlua and coffee**
3. **Kahlua and cream**
4. **Kahlua and Coke**

Each customer could be considered as having ordered the same item: a drink in which Kahlua, a coffee-flavored liqueur, forms the base of the drink. The

Figure 4.2 **Ray's Bar**

	Beverage Sales	**Date: 1/1–1/8**
Product	**# Sold**	**% Sold**
Wine by-the-glass		
White	30	18.75%
Red	16	10.00
Blush	62	38.75
House Blush	52	32.50
Total	160	100.00

purpose of this method, of course, is to simplify the process of recording customer preferences.

Depending on the degree of accuracy desired by the operator, tracking spirit sales can be done by any of the following methods:

1. **Generic product name**
   a. **Bourbon**
   b. **Gin**
   c. **Scotch**
   d. **Etc.**
2. **Specific product name**
   a. **Kahlua**
   b. **Old Crow**
   c. **Heaven Hill**
   d. **Etc.**
3. **Specific drink requested**
   a. **Kahlua on the rocks**
   b. **Kahlua and coffee**
   c. **Kahlua and cream**
   d. **Kahlua and Coke**

As the amount of time and effort required to track specific drink sales increases, so does accuracy. Each operator must determine the level of control appropriate for his or her own operation. This is because there must be a relationship between the time, money, and effort required to maintain a control system, and the cost effectiveness of such an endeavor.

Standardized Drink Recipes/Portions

If a beverage operation is even moderately busy, it is simply unrealistic to assume that the bartender can stop each time an order comes in, consult a standardized recipe as discussed in Chapter 3, and then prepare the drink requested. Imagine the resulting chaos and time delay if such a system were in place! Yet standardization of products served in the bar is critical. The demand for consistency and control in the bar is even greater than that required in the kitchen. The reason is simple. The potential for employee theft and waste is greater in the bar than in the kitchen. Consider for a moment just a few of the unique aspects of beverage operations that require strict adherence to control procedures.

1. **Beverage operations are subject to tax audits. In some states, these audits can be unannounced.**
2. **Beverage operations can be closed down "on the spot" for violation of law.**

3. **Employees in a bar may attempt to become operational "partners" by bringing in their own products to sell and keeping sales revenue.**
4. **Detecting the disappearance of small amounts of beverage products is extremely difficult, as for example the loss of 8 ounces of beer from a 1,984-ounce half barrel.**

For these reasons and others, using standardized recipes is an absolute must for the beverage operation. Consider the case of Paul, who knows that each bourbon and water he produces should require 60 cents in product cost. His selling price is $2.75. Thus, his beverage cost percentage should be as follows:

$$\frac{\$0.60}{\$2.75} = 21.8\%$$

Yet Paul's beverage cost percentage on this item is much higher. How can this be, on an item as uncomplicated as bourbon and water? The answer is simple. The bartender did not follow the standardized recipe. Even on an item as ordinary as bourbon and water, the bartender must know exactly the amount of product to use. It is not simply a matter of bourbon and water, but rather a matter of how much bourbon with how much water. Figure 4.3 shows the beverage cost that would be achieved with different drink sizes and a standard one-liter bottle.

As shown, the difference in the drink recipe can make a big difference in total beverage cost percentage. For purposes of accuracy, we assume a 0.8-ounce-per-liter evaporation loss, thus leaving us with 33 ounces of usable product from a 33.8 oz liter of bourbon. We assume a product cost of $19.80 per liter, with a selling price of $2.75 per portion and a normal portion size of one ounce of bourbon. Obviously, the quantity of alcohol used makes the liquor cost percentage vary greatly.

For example, assume that a large convention hotel has a beverage sales volume in spirit drinks of $2,000,000 per year. If the bartenders pour 1½-ounce drinks rather than 1-ounce drinks, and we assume costs and selling prices as

Figure 4.3 **Beverage Cost Comparison**

Beverage: Bourbon Container Size: One liter (33.8 oz)

Product Cost: $19.80/liter

Portion Size	# of Portions	Portion Cost	Liter Cost	Selling Price	Total Income	Beverage Cost %
1.00 oz	33.0	$ .60	$19.80	$2.75	$90.75	21.8%
1.25 oz	26.4	.75	19.80	2.75	72.60	27.3
1.50 oz	22.0	.90	19.80	2.75	60.50	32.8
1.75 oz	18.8	1.05	19.80	2.75	51.70	38.3

related in Figure 4.3, then beverage costs will be 32.8 − 21.8 = 11.0 percentage points out of line. The loss represents $2,000,000 × 11% = $220,000 for this one operation in just one year! A loss as sizeable as this is certainly career-threatening for any manager!

While standardized recipes, including step-by-step methods of preparation may be necessary for only a few types of drinks, standardized recipes detailing the quantity of product that management has pre-determined as appropriate should be strictly adhered to. That is, if management has determined that bourbon and water should be a one-ounce portion of bourbon and a two-ounce portion of water, then *both* items should be measured by a proper jigger or other automated device. Some mechanized/computerized bar systems on the market today will premeasure both items simultaneously. The capabilities of such a system are many and are outlined in Chapter 5 of this text. Regardless of method of measurement, however, both bourbon and water, in this case, must be delivered to the customer in the proper ratio if product quality is to be maintained. Thus, standardized portion size is critical.

Consider for a moment the case of a manager who determines that a particular brand of bourbon, while expensive, can be sold at a premium price. The manager sets the drink price and instructs the bartender that the portion size is to be one ounce of spirit with two ounces of water. Consider the following customer reactions when the bartender varies the quantity of water added to the bourbon.

Drink Ratio	Possible Customer Response
A. 1-oz bourbon 1-oz water	1. Gee, the drinks sure are small here! 2. Gee, this sure is strong! Can you add a splash of water?
B. 1-oz bourbon 2-oz water	1. Gee, this sure tastes good! Just right!
C. 1-oz bourbon 3-oz water	1. Gee, this tastes watered down. Can you add a splash of Bourbon? 2. Gee, these drinks cost a lot for such a small amount of alcohol!

Remember that the quantity of **spirit** used, and thus the product cost percentage, did not change under scenarios A, B, or C. In this case, the bartender was very careful not to use more product than he or she had been instructed to use. In effect, the bartender put the profitability of the operation before guest satisfaction. It is important to remember that happy guests provide profits; profits do not provide happy guests. The manager of this operation might be pleased with the bartender's precise product control, since the cost of one ounce versus three ounces of water is miniscule. Customers, however, will react to sloppy drink preparation in the same way they do to sloppy food preparation.

In summary, each drink in the bar must have a standardized recipe, or if the preparation of the drink is simple, a standardized portion size. These recipes will affect the guaranteed profitability of the operation and customer satisfaction.

Since it is necessary to cost beverage recipes just as it necessary to cost food item recipes, a standardized recipe sheet (see Chapter 3) should be prepared for each drink item to be sold. A notebook of these recipes should be available at each beverage outlet. If questions about portion size or preparation arise, the standardized recipe sheet should be referred to.

Purchasing Beverage Products

Most foodservice operators select only one quality level for food products. Once a determination on necessary quality level has been made and a product specification written, then only *that* quality of egg, lettuce, milk, bread, and so on is selected. In the area of alcoholic beverage products, however, several levels of quality are chosen. This ensures that a beverage product is available for those consumers who wish to purchase the very best, while a product is also offered for those consumers who prefer to spend less. Thus, the beverage manager is faced with deciding not only whether to carry wine on the menu, but also how many different kinds of wine to carry and of what quality. The same process is necessary for spirits and to a lesser degree for beers.

Determining Beer Products to Carry

Beer is the most highly perishable of beverage products. The pull date, or expiration date on these products, can be as short as a few weeks or months. Because of this, it is important that the beverage operator only stock those items that will sell relatively well. This generally means selecting both brand and packaging methods.

Brand Selection

Beverage operators typically carry between three and ten types of beer. Some operations, however, stock as many as 50 or more! Generally speaking, geographic location, clientele, ambiance, and menu help determine the beer product that will be selected. Obviously, we would not expect to see the same beer products at Hunan Gardens Chinese Restaurant that we would at Three Pesos Mexican Restaurant. Most foodservice operators find that one or two brands of light beer, two or three national domestic brands, and one or two quality import beers meet the great majority of their customers' demand. One must be very careful in this area not to stock excessive amounts of products that sell poorly.

Again, beer is perishable, and great care must be taken to ensure proper product movement. It is important, however, to train bartenders to make a notation on a product request log (see Figure 4.4) so that customer requests that **cannot** be filled are noted and monitored by management. This log should be easily accessible to service personnel. Its purpose is to maintain a record of customer product requests that are not currently available. In the case of beverages, those items that customers wish to purchase that are *not* available are nearly as important to track as the sales of the items that are available.

Referring to the requests in Figure 4.4, management may wish to investigate the possibility of stocking brand Y beer.

Packaging

Beer typically is sold to foodservice operators in either cans, bottles, or kegs. While each of these containers has its advantages and disadvantages, most foodservice operators with active beverage operations will select some of each of these packaging methods. Many beer drinkers prefer draft beer (beer from kegs) over bottled or canned beer, and the cost per glass to the foodservice operator is generally lower with beer from a keg. Special equipment and serving techniques are required, however, if quality draft beer is to be sold to guests. Also, the shelf life of keg beer, ranging from 30 to 45 days for an untapped keg, is shorter than for other packaging types. Kegs can be difficult to handle because of their weight, and it is difficult to keep an exact count of the product served without special metering equipment. Despite these drawbacks, many operators serve draft beer. Draft beer is sold in a variety of keg and barrel sizes as listed in Figure 4.5.

Figure 4.4 **Product Request Log**

Date	Item Requested	Entry by
1/1/92	Brand Y beer	P. J.
1/1/92	Cherry schnapps	T. R.
1/2/92	Brand Z beer on draft	T. A.
1/4/92	Brand Y beer	P. J.
1/5/92	Soave wine	J. D.
1/6/92	Texas wine	S. H.
1/6/92	Brand Y beer	T. R.

Figure 4.5 **Draft Beer**

Container	Liters	Ounces
Barrel	111.33	3,968
½ barrel (keg)	58.67	1,984
¼ barrel (½ keg)	29.33	992
⅛ barrel (¼ keg)	14.67	496

Determining Wine Products to Carry

Determining which wines to carry, as in determining which beers to carry, is a matter of selecting both product and packaging, or bottle size. Typically, an operator must determine to sell wine by the:

1. **Glass**
2. **Bottle**
3. **Split or Half Bottle**

In addition, some operations will find that wine for cooking must also be purchased. In general, these products will be secured from the beverage wholesaler rather than the grocery wholesaler. It makes little sense to use extraordinarily fine wine in cooking. Again, the guiding principle for the foodservice operator should be to select the appropriate quality food or beverage product for its intended use. Some operators add salt to their cooking wines in an effort to discourage the kitchen staff from drinking them. This method, if used, should be clearly communicated to kitchen personnel if the operator is to avoid possible liability.

Wine Lists

Each foodservice operator will build a wine list that fits his or her own particular operation. In wine list development, several points must be kept in mind. First, the operator must seek to provide alternatives for customers who want the best, as well as for those who prefer to spend less. Second, wines that either complement the food or, in the case of a bar, are popular with the guests must be available. The operator must avoid the temptation to offer too many wines on a wine list. Excess inventory and use of valuable storage space make this a poor idea. In addition, when selling wine by the glass, those items that sell poorly can lose quality and flavor rapidly. Third, wine sales can be diminished due to the complexity of the product itself. The effective foodservice manager makes the purchase of wine by the bottle a pleasant, nonthreatening experience. Waitstaff, who help in selling wine, should be knowledgeable but not pretentious.

In general, when foodservice operators have trouble selling wine (the world's most popular alcoholic beverage), the difficulty lies in the delivery of the product rather than with the product selected. It would almost appear as if some operators go out of their way to make the ordering, presentation, and service of wine so pretentious as to intimidate many would-be customers into not purchasing wine at all. This is unfortunate, since wine is perceived as the beverage of moderation and is enjoyed by so many! The foodservice operator can seek help from his or her wine supplier in the effective marketing of wine, either by the bottle or the glass. This is a valuable resource that far too few operators use to their advantage.

Determining Spirit Products to Carry

Distilled spirits have an extremely long shelf life. Thus, an operator can make a "mistake" and purchase the wrong spirit product without disastrous results if that product can be sold over a reasonable time frame. Customer preference will dictate the types of liquor that are appropriate for a given operation, but it is management's responsibility to determine product quality levels in the beverage area. Nowhere is this more important than in the area of distilled spirits.

Consumer preferences with regard to alcoholic beverages can change rapidly. The wise beverage manager stays abreast of changing consumption trends by reading professional journals and staying active in his or her professional associations. These associations can be major providers of information related to changes in consumer buying behavior as far as wine, beer, and spirits are concerned. What is hot one year may be out of the fashion the next! It is important to spot these trends and respond to them quickly.

Packaging is not a particular issue, as it is for beer and wine, in the selection of spirits for an establishment's use. In the United States, as in most parts of the world, bottle sizes for spirits are fairly standard. Since the early 1980s, the bottle sizes shown in Figure 4.6 have represented those most commonly offered for sale to the hospitality market.

The minibottle (50 milliliters) is typically offered for sale on airlines and in some situations, such as room minibars and room service, in the hotel segment of the hospitality industry. In the state of South Carolina, for instance, liquor by the drink may be purchased in the 1.7-ounce bottle, and prior to 1991, Utah required producers of spirits to offer a 1.7-ounce bottle size.

Figure 4.6 **Bottle Sizes**

Bottle Type	Capacity
50 ml (mini)	1.7 oz
750 ml	25.4 oz
1 liter	33.8 oz
1.5 liter	50.7 oz
1.75 liter	59.2 oz

While packaging is not a major concern of the operator selecting a spirit product, brand quality is crucial. As a comparison, consider brand Y beer, a standard product that tastes the same from coast to coast. An operator who chooses to carry *that* beer need only decide whether it will be sold in bottles, in cans, or on draft. Should that same operator elect to carry scotch, however, an extremely wide selection of products at widely varying prices is available for purchase. In general, restaurant operators will select spirits in two major categories: **well liquors** and **call liquors.**

Well Liquors

Well liquors are those spirits that are poured when the customer does **not** specify a particular brand name. The name stems from the concept of **well,** or the bottle holding area in the bar. The wise operator will choose well liquors very carefully. By electing to buy spirits that are very low in cost as well items, the operator may find that the quality is accordingly low. Make no mistake, customers who order well liquors may be price conscious, but that does not mean they are not quality conscious also. It is fairly easy to tell the difference between a well liquor of average quality and one of very poor quality. Managers who shop for well liquors considering only price as a criterion for selection will find that customer reaction is extremely negative. Conversely, if exceptionally high quality products are chosen as well items, liquor costs may be excessive unless an adequate price structure is maintained.

Call Liquors

Call liquors are those spirits that are requested by name, such as Jack Daniels, Kahlua, and Chivas Regal. Extremely expensive call liquors are sometimes referred to as **premium** liquors.

Operators generally charge a higher price for those drinks prepared with call or premium liquors. Customers understand this and in fact, by specifying call liquors, indicate their preference to pay the price required for these special products.

Figure 4.7 **Spirit Cost Percentage**

Original Portion Cost

Spirit	# Sold	Portion Cost	Total Cost	Selling Price	Total Sales	Beverage Cost %
Well	50	.45	$22.50	$2.50	$125.00	18.0%
Call	50	.60	30.00	3.00	150.00	20.0
Total	100		52.50		275.00	19.1

Figures 4.7 and 4.8 illustrate the effect of changes in the selection of well liquors. As Figure 4.7 shows, 50 well drinks and 50 call drinks are sold. Total beverage costs, in this example, equal 19.1%.

In Figure 4.8, the portion cost of our well brand is reduced from 45 cents to 30 cents, due to a reduction in the quality of product selected for this purpose. This results in a decrease in beverage cost percentage to 16.4%.

While the decision to lower the quality of well liquor used did in this case reduce overall liquor cost percentage, the question of the long-term effect on customer satisfaction and loyalty is not being answered. In fact, changes in customer behavior may seem negligible in the short run. Successful foodservice operators, however, remember that one cannot fool all of the people all of the time. *Quality products at fair prices build customer loyalty.* It is wise to select well products that are in keeping with an operator's clientele, price situation, and desired image. Anything less cheats both the operator and the guest.

Beverage Purchase Orders

The form in Figure 3.10 (page 57) can be used to document the beverage purchase order in the same way it is used for food purchases. Special laws, depending on the state and county, may influence how beverage purchases are to be made or paid for. One of the first responsibilities of an effective beverage manager is to become familiar with all applicable state and local laws regarding beverage purchase. As with food, the goal in purchasing is to have an adequate but not excessive amount of product on hand at all times. Unlike distributors of most food products, however, beverage distributors will sometimes sell products in less than one-case lots. This is called a **broken case** and occurs when several different brands or products are used to completely fill the case. Take for example the operator who orders a case of scotch, consisting of 12 bottles. The case, however, might contain four bottles of brand A scotch, four bottles of brand B, and four bottles of brand C.

As a general rule, wine, beer, and spirits are purchased by the case. Beer, of course, may also be bought by the ¼, ½, or full keg. As with food products,

Figure 4.8 **Spirit Cost Percentage**

Reduced Portion Cost

Spirit	# Sold	Portion Cost	Total Cost	Selling Price	Total Sales	Beverage Cost %
Well	50	.30	$15.00	$2.50	$125.00	12.0%
Call	50	.60	30.00	3.00	150.00	20.0
Total	100		45.00		275.00	16.4

smaller container size usually results in higher cost per ounce. It is important to remember that both product quality and container size are critical when determining what to buy.

Receiving Beverage Products

The skill required to receive beverage products is somewhat less than what is needed to receive food. The reason is that beverage products do not vary in quality in the same manner food products do. As with food, the receiving clerk needs the proper location, tools, and equipment. In addition, proper delivery schedules must be maintained. The training required, however, is reduced due to the consistent nature of the product received. A case of fresh Coors beer will be consistent in quality regardless of the vendor. And assuming that the product is freshness dated, very little inspection is required to ensure that the product is exactly what was ordered. In fact, when matching the purchase order to the vendor delivery slip, only quantity ordered and price must be verified, unlike the process for food deliveries, which requires the verification of weight, quantity, quality, and price. It is possible, however, that the goods delivered will not match those ordered. Or, in fact, the goods delivered are defective in some manner. Thus, appropriate receiving procedures must be in place.

When receiving beverage products, the following key checkpoints should be verified:

1. **Correct brand**
2. **Correct bottle size**
3. **No broken bottles or bottle seals**
4. **Freshness dates (beer)**
5. **Correct vintage (wine)**
6. **Correct unit price**
7. **Correct price extension**

If errors are detected, a credit memo must be filled out and signed by both the delivery person and the receiving clerk.

Credit memo

A credit memo is an addendum to the delivery invoice. Its purpose is to correct any differences between the purchase order prepared by the foodservice establishment and the delivery slip or invoice that is signed at the time the ordered goods are delivered. If, for example, ten cases of brand A gin have been ordered on a given day, but only five cases of brand A and, erroneously, five cases of brand B are delivered, the vendor's delivery invoice will not match the purchase order. In this situation, the foodservice operator may want to refuse delivery of the five cases of brand B gin, while accepting the five cases of brand A. A credit memo, deleting the charge for the five cases of brand B gin, would be filled out and signed by both the beverage receiving clerk and the liquor delivery person. A copy would then be attached to the invoice prior to payment. This would ensure that the respective parties received and were paid for the proper merchandise. Figure 4.9 shows the method for completing a credit memo. Credit memos are as useful for receiving food and paper products as they are for receiving beverages. The documents may be numbered, if so desired. For good control, they should be made in duplicate so that one copy can be returned to the purchasing agent, while the second one, attached to the invoice, is being forwarded for payment.

Beverage Storage

While the shelf life of most beverage products is relatively long, alcoholic beverages, especially wine, must be treated in a very careful manner. Beverage storage rooms should be easily secured, since beverages are a favorite target for both employee and customer theft. These storage areas should, of course, be kept clean and free of insect or rodent infestations, and they should be large enough to allow for easy rotation of stock. Many beverage managers use a two-key system to control access to beverage storage areas. In this system, one key is in the possession of the individual responsible for the beverage area. The other key is kept in a sealed envelope in the safe or other secured area of the operation. Should this key be needed, management will be aware of its use, since the envelope will be opened. Of course, it is up to management to ascertain the validity of the use of this key should the envelope be opened.

Liquor storage

Spirits should be kept in a relatively dry storage area at 70 °F–80 °F. Since these products do not generally require refrigeration, they may be stored along with food products, if necessary. An organized, well-maintained area for spirits also ensures that purchasing decisions can be simplified, since no product is likely to get overlooked or lost. In addition, care should be taken so that access to liquor storage areas is severely limited.

Beer Storage

Beer in kegs, or other unpasteurized containers, should be stored at refrigeration temperatures of 36 °F–38 °F. The temperatures are ideal for both keg and bottled or canned beer that is not pasteurized. When receiving and storing beer, it is important to examine freshness dates. If these dates are not easily discernable,

Figure 4.9 **Credit Memo**

Credit Memo #: 001 Operation: Millie's Date: 1/1/92

Vendor: Bugy's Liquor Vendor Invoice Number: 307J571

Item	Quantity	Correction: Short	Correction: Refused	Price Error	Credit Amount
Brand B gin	5 cases		X		$360.45
Total					$360.45

Explanation: Ordered 10 cases brand A gin. Received 5 cases brand B by mistake.

Vendor Representative: T. J. Laroor

Operation Representative: I. M. Thinkin

the effective foodmanager should demand that the vendor explain the coding system being used. Canned beer, especially, should be covered to eliminate the chance of dust or dirt settling on the cans' rims. Nothing is quite as disturbing to a beer drinker as to find the top of a cold beer can covered with dirt that cannot be removed. It is a good idea for the storage clerk to rinse beer can tops prior to issuing these products for use in the bar. Pasteurized beer, in either cans or bottles, should be stored in a cool, dark room at 50 °F–70 °F but does not, of course, require refrigeration.

Product rotation is critical if beer is to be served at its maximum freshness, and it is important that management devise a system to ensure that this happens. The best method is to date each case or six-pack as it comes in. In this manner, management can determine at a glance whether proper product rotation has occurred.

Wine Storage

Wine storage is the most complex and time-consuming activity required of beverage storeroom personnel. Depending on the type and volume of the restaurant, extremely large quantities of wine may be stored. In general, the finer wines in the United States are sold in bottles of 750 milliliters. Foreign wines are generally sold in bottles of approximately this size, but the contents may vary by a few ounces more or less. Sometimes, larger bottle sizes may be sold, especially of sparkling wine such as champagne. A tremendously underutilized bottle size that may also be stored is the half bottle or split, which is about half the size of the 750-milliliter bottle. If a restaurant finds that its average table size is a table for two, it is simply unrealistic to assume that a couple will have before-dinner drinks, a full 750-milliliter bottle of wine with dinner, and then coffee and after-dinner drinks to finish the meal. In today's age of caution about drinking and driving, the trend is away from this kind of consumption, and if wine sales are to maintain their current levels, operators would do well to provide the option of the half bottle to their customers.

Regardless of bottle size, the techniques for proper wine storage must be followed in all cases if the quality of the product is to be maintained and product losses are to be kept at a minimum. Despite the mystery associated with wine storage, the effective manager will find that proper storage can be achieved if the following factors are monitored:

1. **Temperature**
2. **Light**
3. **Cork condition**

Temperature

A great deal of debate has centered around the proper temperature at which to store wine. All can agree that red wine should be served at cellar temperature. There is, however, less agreement about what exactly is meant by "cellar" temperature. When serving white wine by the glass, we may find that the proper storage temperature, at least for the container currently being used, is refrigerator temperature. Obviously, this would not do for a case of fine red wine. But generally speaking, most experts would agree that wines should be stored at a temperature of 50 °F–65 °F. If the food service operation finds, however, that wines must be stored at higher temperatures than this, the wine storage area should be as cool as can reasonably be achieved. It is important to remember that while wine may improve with age, it improves only if it is properly stored. Heat is an enemy of effective wine storage.

Light

Just as wine must be protected from excess heat, it must also be protected from direct sunlight. In old times, this was achieved by storing wines in cellars or caves.

In today's foodservice establishment, this means using a storage area where sunlight cannot penetrate and where the wine will not be subject to excessive fluorescent or incandescent lighting. With regard to light, the rule of thumb for storing wine is that it should be exposed only to the minimum amount necessary.

Cork Condition

It is the wine's cork that protects it from its greatest enemy, that is, oxygen. Cork has proven over the years to be the bottle sealer of choice for most wine producers. Quality wines demand quality corks, and the best wines are fitted with cork sealers that should last many years *if* they are not allowed to dry out. This is the reason why wine should be stored in such a manner that the cork remains in contact with the wine and thus stays moist. In an effort to accomplish this, most foodservice managers store wines on their sides, usually on specially built wine racks. Corks should be inspected at the time the wine is received and periodically thereafter to ensure that there are no leaks and thus no damaged products. If a leak is discovered when the wine is received, it should be refused, or if the leak occurs during storage, the wine should be examined for quality and then either consumed or discarded, as appropriate.

In general, the foodservice manager can be an effective storer of wine if he or she remembers that storage should be designed to keep the **cork** and thus the wine

1. **Cool**
2. **Dark**
3. **Moist**

Beverage storage techniques are important if we hope to have the desired amount of product available for service during the beverage production process. In most instances, wine and beers will be consumed directly from their original containers. With spirits, on the other hand, the bartender will probably find that the customer prefers the spirit mixed with some other product to make the beverage fit his or her personal preference. While this presents no particular production problem, it does raise a unique costing/control issue for the beverage manager.

Bar Transfers

While the great majority of product loss related to bar operations is in the area of beverages, the effective foodservice manager must also consider the cost of those items associated with the preparation and service of beverage products. In the case of wine and beer, there are, in general, no additions to the beverage prior to serving and thus no additional product costs. As far as spirits are concerned, however, a great number of nonalcoholic food products may be served as a part of the drink order. To illustrate this, assume that a customer in the bar orders Irish coffee. This popular drink has as its two primary ingredients Irish whiskey and brewed coffee. The spirit cost should clearly be charged to the bar. A question arises, however, on how to account for the coffee. In this case, coffee is as central to the preparation of the drink as the whiskey itself. If the operation is a stand-alone bar, accounting for the cost of purchasing the coffee is not complex. If the bar is operated, however, as part of a larger foodservice, the ground coffee used to make the brewed coffee in the bar may have to come from the general foods storeroom. When that is the case, the **transfer** of product from the kitchen to the bar must be controlled and accounted for. If this is not done, the food cost percentage in the restaurant will be artificially inflated, while the total beverage cost percentage in the bar will be understated. This same issue exists with cherries, limes, lemons, coffee, cream, sugar and a host of other items that may be ordered as regular food products for the kitchen but are needed by and transferred to the bar area. Similarly, many foodservice operators use items from the bar when preparing menu items for service in the dining room. Using a bottle of beer from the bar to prepare bratwurst in the kitchen would be an example of a transfer of products from the bar *to* the kitchen. Wines may frequently be used by the kitchen to produce some items. In fact, a close working relationship between kitchen and bar management is helpful as both areas attempt to assist each other to the best of their ability in providing needed ingredients and in helping to utilize any carryover products.

The control procedure for kitchen and bar transfers is quite simple. To be effective, it requires nothing but consistency. Figure 4.10 shows the type of form that can be used to monitor products flow either to or from the bar. Should management prefer, a separate form can be used for each transfer area, but for most operators the form in Figure 4.10 would be sufficient. Note that the form requires the initials of both the person receiving and the person issuing the product. In addition, space is available to total product values at the end of the accounting period. These figures would then be used to adjust, as needed, either cost of food consumed data or cost of beverage consumed data. In either case, the principle is that product cost should be assigned to the area that is reporting the sales of that product.

Computing Cost of Beverages

The proper computation of beverage cost percentage is identical to that of food cost percentage with two important differences. First, there is typically no equivalent for **employee meals,** since the consumption of alcoholic beverage products by employees who are working should be strictly prohibited. Thus, **employee drinks** would never be considered as a reduction from overall beverage cost. Second, transfers to or from the kitchen and bar, if applicable, must be included.

Figure 4.10 **Transfer Record**

Location: Surfside Bar Date: January 1–7

Date	**Item**	**Quantity**	**Product Value** To Bar	**Product Value** From Bar	**Issued by**	**Received by**
1/1/92	Lemons	6	$ .36		T. S.	B. H.
	Limes	2	.14		T. S.	B. H.
	Cream	2 qt	2.31		T. S.	B. H.
1/2/92	Chablis	1 gal		$5.55	B. H.	T. S.
1/3/92	Coffee	2 lbs	5.35		T. S.	B. H.
1/4/92	Cherries	1/2 gal	6.47		T. S.	B. H.
1/4/92	Lemons	4	.24		T. S.	B. H.
	Limes	2	.14		T. S.	B. H.
	Ice cream (vanilla)	1 gal	6.66		T. S.	B. H.
1/5/92	Pineapple juice	1/2 gal	1.50		T. S.	B. H.
1/6/92	Tomato	1 cs	10.00		T. S.	B. H.
1/6/92	Sherry	750 ml		3.35	B. H.	T. S.
1/7/92	Celery	1 bch	.27		T. S.	B. H.
Total product value			$33.44	$8.90		

Consider the case of Luigi, whose Mexican restaurant is very popular and does a high volume of alcoholic beverage sales. To prepare his drinks, Luigi uses limes, lemons, and fruit juices from the kitchen. He would like his beverage cost percentage to reflect all the costs associated with the actual ingredients used in drink preparation. He keeps excellent daily records of all food products he transfers from the kitchen to the bar, including their value. In Luigi's operation, there are no transfers from the bar to the kitchen as there might be, for instance, in a French restaurant that uses wine extensively in its recipes. Figure 4.11 details

Figure 4.11 **Recap Sheet**

Cost of Beverage Consumed

Accounting Period: 1/1/92 to 2/1/92

Unit Name: Luigi's

Beginning inventory	$ 24,405.00	
plus		
Purchases	$ 21,986.40	
Goods available		$ 46,391.40
less		
Ending inventory		$ 18,741.25
less		$ 27,650.15
Transfers from bar		$ 0
plus		$ 27,650.15
Transfers to bar		$ 2,140.00
Cost of beverage consumed		$ 29,790.15

how Luigi would compute his actual cost of beverage consumed for a month where the following data represent his operating results.

1. **Beverage sales = $100,000.00**
2. **Beginning inventory = 24,405.00**
3. **Ending inventory = 18,741.25**
4. **Purchases = 21,986.40**
5. **Transfers to bar = 2,140.00**
6. **Transfers from bar = 0**

Note again that beginning inventory for this accounting period is the ending inventory figure from the prior accounting period.

Special Features of Liquor Inventory

Determining beginning and ending inventory levels for beverage products is generally more difficult than determining these same levels for food. Food items can generally be weighed, counted, or measured for inventory purposes. Any of these methods may be used for liquor inventory, should the operator choose. Unopened bottles can, of course, be counted. Opened bottles, however, must be valued also. It is the process of valuing these opened bottles that presents a challenge to the beverage manager. Three methods are commonly in use to accomplish this goal. They are:

1. **Weight**
2. **Count**
3. **Measure**

Liquor Inventory by Weight

The weight method uses a scale to weigh open bottles of liquor. This system is effective if operators remember to subtract the weight of the empty bottle itself from the total product weight and if operators remember that each liquor, due to its unique specific gravity, must be weighed separately.

Liquor Inventory by Count

Counting full bottles is easy; when operators use the counting method to determine amounts in **open** bottles, the **tenths** system is often used. This involves the operator assigning a value of 10/10 to a full bottle, 5/10 to a half bottle, and so on. While this system results in an approximation of the actual amount in a bottle, many managers feel the tenths system is accurate enough for their purposes. It does have the advantage of being a rather quick method of determining inventory levels of open bottles.

Liquor Inventory by Measure

Some foodservice operators determine product levels of open bottles by using a ruler to determine the amount the bottle contains. Dollar values are then assigned to each inch or portion of an inch for inventory evaluation purposes. This method has a high degree of accuracy and is favored by many.

In general, it is important to take liquor inventories at a time when the operation is closed so that nothing changes when the inventory is being taken. It is also important that product contained in the lines of mechanical drink-dispensing systems be counted if the quantity of product in these lines is deemed to be significant.

With sales of $100,000.00 and a cost of beverage consumed of $29,790.15, Luigi applies the beverage cost percentage formula as follows:

$$\frac{\textbf{Cost of beverage consumed}}{\textbf{Beverage sales}} = \textbf{Beverage cost \%}$$

Thus,

$$\frac{\$29{,}790.15}{\$100{,}000.00} = 29.79\%$$

Again, it is important to note that transfers both to and from the bar must be accounted for, if and when they occur. These adjustments will affect the overall product cost percentages in the kitchen and the bar. In addition, computing transfers to the bar helps the bar staff remember that the use of fruit juices, milk, cherries, lemons, limes, and the like do impact the total cost effectiveness of the bar.

Often, foodservice managers who operate beverage facilities wonder whether their beverage cost percentages are too high or what they in fact should be. Incidentally, there is a popular tongue in cheek story about why a 20 percent beverage cost was chosen by many as the preferred operating figure.

> In the year 500 B.C., a man built a tavern on the road to Rome. His first customer was an accountant who happened to stop to have a drink. When he finished, he said: "Say, I think you have a pretty good thing going. It looks as if this tavern business may develop into something that will spread all over the world. How would you like it if I kept books for you?" The owner had no one working on the books, so he hired the accountant/customer to keep the books for his first month of operation. At the end of the month, the accountant came back to the tavern operator and reported, "You have a 20 percent beverage cost." The owner asked, "Is that good?" The reply was, "That is very good." So from that time forward, it has been accepted that all beverage operations should maintain a 20 percent beverage cost.

Unfortunately, a great number of factors can produce negative results and cause beverage cost percentages to escalate. Many of these factors are discussed in Chapter 5, "Managing the Food and Beverage Production Process." Note, however, that **customers themselves can contribute to relatively major changes in food or beverage cost percentages,** both on the plus and the minus side of the ledger. This is due to the concept that food and beverage operators call the **sales mix** or **product mix.** Our preferred term is the former.

Sales Mix

Sales mix is defined as the series of consumer purchasing decisions that result in a specific food or beverage cost percentage. Sales mix affects overall product cost percentage anytime consumers have a choice among several menu selections, each one having its own unique product cost percentage.

To illustrate the effect of sales mix on beverage cost percentage, consider the case of Cynthia. She is the food and beverage director at the Nothil Resort, a 400-room beachfront property on the coast of Texas. In addition to her normal restaurant, Cynthia serves beverages in three basic locations. They are as follows:

1. **Banquet beverages for receptions prior to meal events are typically served in the grand ballroom foyer or outdoors; beverages are also served during banquets.**
2. **The Surfside Bar is an upscale bar with soft piano music that appeals to the 50-plus customer.**
3. **Harry O's is a bar with indoor and poolside seating. Contemporary top-40 music in the evenings draws a younger crowd interested in dancing.**

Cynthia computes a separate beverage cost percentage for each of these beverage outlets. Figure 4.12 details the separate operating results for each outlet and an overall percentage for the three units, using the standard beverage cost percentage formula as follows:

$$\frac{\textbf{Cost of beverages consumed}}{\textbf{Beverage sales}} = \textbf{Beverage cost \%}$$

Cynthia knows that each beverage location uses the same portion size for all standard drinks. Brands for well and call liquors, as well as for wine by the glass, are constant in all three locations. Since she dislikes the difficulty sometimes associated with draft beer, she serves beer in cans or bottles only. In addition, bartenders are typically rotated on a regular basis through every serving location. Should Cynthia be concerned that her beverage cost percentage varies so greatly by service location? The answer in this case is that she has no cause for concern. In this situation, it is sales mix, not poor control, that governs her overall beverage cost percentage in each individual location. A close examination of #1, #2, and #3 in Figure 4.13 will reveal how this can happen.

Although product cost percentages for beer, wine, and spirits are constant in each location, the *overall* beverage cost percentage is not. The reason that each unit varies in total beverage cost percentage is due to sales mix or customer selection. In other words, customers, not management, have made the beverage cost percentage determination. While the effective foodservice manager can certainly help shape customer selection by such techniques as controls, effective pricing, menu design, and marketing, it is often the customer who will determine overall cost percentage, through sales mix. This is true in both the beverage and

Figure 4.12 **Nothil Resort**

Monthly Beverage Percentage Report

Location	**Sales**	**Cost of Beverage**	**Beverage Cost %**
Banquets	$ 80,000	$20,500	25.6%
Surfside Bar	45,500	10,350	22.7
Harry O's	67,000	16,350	24.4
Total	192,500	47,200	24.5

Figure 4.13 **Nothil Beverage Outlets**

Monthly Beverage Percentage Recap

1 Outlet Name: Banquets Month/Year: January 92

Product	Sales	Cost of Beverage	Beverage Cost %
Beer	$10,000	$ 2,500	25%
Wine	40,000	12,000	30
Spirits	30,000	6,000	20
Total	80,000	20,500	25.6

2 Outlet Name: Surfside Bar

Product	Sales	Cost of Beverage	Beverage Cost %
Beer	$15,000	$ 3,750	25%
Wine	5,000	1,500	30
Spirits	25,500	5,100	20
Total	45,500	10,350	22.7

3 Outlet Name: Harry O's

Product	Sales	Cost of Beverage	Beverage Cost %
Beer	$45,000	$11,250	25%
Wine	7,000	2,100	30
Spirits	15,000	3,000	20
Total	67,000	16,350	24.4

food areas. In the case of Nothil Resort, it is easy to see the sales mix by looking at Figure 4.14.

Each sales percentage in Figure 4.14 was computed using the following formula:

$$\frac{\textbf{Item dollar sales}}{\textbf{Total sales}} = \textbf{Item \% of total sales}$$

Therefore, in the case of beer sales in the banquet area, the following formula applies:

$$\frac{\textbf{Beer sales}}{\textbf{Total sales}} = \textbf{\% of beer sales}$$

Figure 4.14 **Nothil Resort**

Sales Percentage Recap

Unit	Beer	Wine	Spirits	Total Sales
Banquets	12.5%	50%	37.5%	100%
Surfside Bar	33%	11%	56%	100%
Harry O's	67%	10.5%	22.5%	100%

Or, using the amounts from Figure 4.13, the formula is as follows:

$$\frac{\textbf{Banquet beer sales}\quad \$10{,}000.00}{\textbf{Banquet total sales}\quad \$80{,}000.00} = 12.5\%$$

As indicated, each beverage outlet operates with a unique sales mix. Figure 4.14 shows that in the banquet area, the mix is heavy in wines and spirits, the choice of many guests when they are at a reception or dining out. The Surfside Bar clientele is older, and their preferred drink tends to be spirits. Harry O's, on the other hand, caters to a younger crowd that prefers beer and wine. Thus, Cynthia may rest assured that her controls are in place, costs are in line, and variations can still occur due to sales mix rather than to other confounding factors.

Beverages are, and will remain, an important part of the hospitality industry. Marketed and consumed properly, they enhance many an occasion, and in the hands of the thoughtful foodservice operator, they are a powerful profit center.

Now that we know who is coming (Chapter 2), and have enough food (Chapter 3) and beverages (Chapter 4) available to be served, we enter into the most challenging aspect of foodservice cost management, which is "Managing the Food and Beverage Production Process," Chapter 5.

TEST YOUR SKILL

A. Thomas is planning for the wedding of the mayor's daughter in his hotel. The reception, to be held in the grand ballroom, will be attended by 1,000 people. From his sales histories of similar events, Thomas knows that the average drinking habits of those attending receptions of this type are as follows:

25% select champagne
50 % select white wine
25% select spirits

Assuming three drinks per person and a portion size of 3 ounces for champagne, 4 ounces for wine, and 1 ounce for spirits, how much of each product should Thomas make available? If you were Thomas, would you order more than you think you would need? Why? How much?

B. Elvin operates a magical restaurant called Shazam!, in which he features both excellent food and magic shows. The lounge is popular, since that is where the magic is viewed. Elvin wants to compute his cost of beverage consumed percentage and finds that he has the following data for the month of January. What is his actual dollar value of transfers to the bar? What is the dollar value of transfers from the bar?

Transfer Record

Location: Shazam! Date: 1/1/92–1/7/92

Date	Item	Quantity	Product Value To Bar	Product Value From Bar	Issued by	Received by
1/2	Lemons	40	$ 2.40		T.A.	B.P
1/3	Coffee	12 lbs	25.20		T.A.	B.P
	Cream	2 qts	1.60		T.A.	B.P.
1/4	Chablis	1 gal		$5.20	B.P.	T.A.
	Ice cream	1/2 gal	3.33		T.A.	B.P.
1/5	Pineapple juice	1 gal	3.00		T.A.	B.P.
	Sherry	1/2 gal		7.10	B.P.	T.A.
1/6	Celery	1 cs	9.72		T.A.	B.P.
1/7	Olives	1 gal	8.50		T.A.	B.P.
Total product value			53.75	12.30		

C. Missy operates a popular French restaurant in a large midwestern city of the United States. Her establishment is a favorite both for its cozy cocktail area and its superb cuisine, patterned after that of the Nantes area in France. Missy keeps excellent records on all her product usage. She wishes to compute for the month of January cost of goods consumed in the food, beer, wine, and spirits areas. In effect, she desires a separate product cost percentage for each of these four areas. In addition, she has determined that the value of all transfers from the kitchen to the bar will be assigned to the spirits area for cost purposes. Given the following data, compute these four cost percentages.

Sales	
Food	$175,000
Beer	12,000
Wine	45,000
Spirits	51,000
Employee meals	3,500
Transfers from Bar	
Beer	$ 125
Wine	1,800
Spirits	425
Transfers to Bar	$ 960.00

	Beginning Inventory	Purchases	Ending Inventory
Food	$45,800	$65,400	$41,200
Beer	4,500	2,900	4,400
Wine	65,000	15,400	66,900
Spirits	6,400	11,850	8,050

CHAPTER 5

Managing the Food and Beverage Production Process

OVERVIEW

In this chapter we will discuss the methods used to issue and produce food and beverage products as well as arrive at their cost of production. Methods for pricing both food and beverage products, reducing theft and waste, and computing attainable costs in the production process are presented. The chapter concludes with a discussion of the techniques used to reduce overall food and beverage costs.

HIGHLIGHTS

At the conclusion of this chapter, the manager will be able to

A. Determine a portion cost using a standardized recipe

B. Compare actual cost of goods sold with attainable cost of goods sold

C. List the six methods available to reduce cost of goods sold percentage

Managing the Food and Beverage Production Process

Once the foodservice manager has ordered and received the product he or she believes will be purchased by the customer, the manager's concern turns toward the most important function of all, that is, that of controlling the food and beverage production process. If any activity is at the heart of foodservice management and control, it is this. To view this process, let us observe Sparky, the manager of Scotto's Supper Club. Scotto's is a high-volume, upscale-clientele steak house. Business is good both during the lunch period and in the evenings. Volume is especially heavy on Friday and Saturday nights, as well as for Sunday brunch. As Sparky prepares for another week, he reviews his sales history, purchase orders, and menu specials. He does so in order to take the first step in the production process—developing his kitchen production schedules.

Production Schedules

Fundamentally, each foodservice manager is in charge of kitchen production. How much of each item to prepare may be a joint decision between chef and foodservice manger, but it is the manager who must *ultimately take the responsibility* for proper production decisions.

Ideally, the process of determining how much of each menu item to prepare would look as follows:

Prior day carryover	+	**Today's production**	=	**Today's sales forecast**	+	**Margin of error**

The margin of error amount should be small; however, since projecting sales and customer counts is an imprecise science at best, most foodservice managers will find that they must produce a small amount more than they anticipate selling each day. In some cases, management may elect to produce slightly less product than it anticipates selling in a given meal period. Using this approach, management may attempt to sell out of a given product toward the end of the meal period. This action, which is especially appropriate if the food item is not easily carried over to a future meal period, ensures that no product will be left over for the following day. Care must be taken, however, not to plan to run out of so many menu items that customer choice is severely restricted. Strip steak, for example, will not be cooked until it is ordered. An order for coconut cream pie, however, cannot be filled in the same manner. It is because of items like coconut cream pie, that production sheets are necessary. Figure 5.1 demonstrates the production sheet in use at Scotto's.

Sparky had 15 servings of prime rib left over from the prior day's operation. He would know this by looking at the carryover section of the *prior* day's production sheet. Since Sparky anticipates sales of 85 servings of prime rib, one might assume that 70 servings should be prepared. In fact, Sparky will prepare 75 servings to allow for slightly higher than anticipated demand. In the case of broccoli, Sparky makes the decision not to carry over any broccoli that was not sold on the prior day. If any such product exists, it may be used for soup or, if there is no use for it, discarded. Some items simply do not retain their quality well when they are carried over. Sparky prefers not to serve broccoli to his guests if it is not freshly cooked. Again, in the case of broccoli, production exceeds anticipated demand by a small margin (10 servings). In the case of the peanut butter pie, Sparky makes the decision to produce none on this particular day because this item, which is made in large quantities, is not made each day. With 70 servings available and an anticipated demand of 41, Sparky has enough to

Figure 5.1 **Production Schedules**

Unit Name: Scotto's Date: 1/1/92

	Menu Item	Sales Forecast	Prior Day Carryover	New Production	Total Available	# Sold	Carryover
1.	Prime rib	85	15	75	90		
2.	Broccoli	160	0	170	170		
3.	Peanut butter pie	41	70	0	70		
4.							
5.							
6.							
7.							
8.							
9.							
10.							
11.							
12.							
13.							
14.							
15.							
16.							
17.							
18.							

Special Instructions: Thaw turkeys for Sunday preparation

Prepared by: S.A.

carry him at least through the day. At the end of the night, Sparky will enter the number sold in the appropriate column and also make a determination on how much, if any, of each product he will carry over to the next day. Some foodservice managers preprint their production sheets listing all menu items and thus ensure that production levels for each major menu item is considered on a daily basis. Others prefer to use the production sheet on an as-needed basis. When this is the case, it is used daily, but only for the items to be prepared that day. Either method is acceptable, but production schedules in and of themselves are important to operational efficiency.

Now that Sparky's kitchen production people have been notified by management about what they are to prepare for the day, they move to the next logical step, which is to requisition food from the storage area. In both the food and beverage production process, the issuing of products from the storage area is a critical part of the control process.

Product Issuing versus Inventory Control

Getting necessary beverage, food, and supply products from the storage area in smaller establishments may be as simple as entering the locked storeroom, selecting the product, and locking the door behind you. In a more complex operation, and especially one that serves alcoholic beverages, this method is simply inadequate to achieve appropriate control.

The act of requisitioning products from the storage area need not be unduly complex. Often, however, foodservice managers create difficulties for their workers by developing a requisition system that is far too time-consuming and complicated. The difficulty in such an approach usually arises because management hopes to equate products *issued* with products *consumed* without taking a physical inventory. In reality, this process is difficult, if not impossible, to carry out. Consider, for example, Scotto's bar. If, on a given night, Sparky hopes to relate liquor issued to liquor sold, he must assume that all liquor issued today is sold today, *and* that no liquor issued on a prior day is sold today. This generally will not be the case. In the kitchen, some items issued today, for example, peanut butter pie, will be sold over several days; thus, in the same way as for liquor, food products issued will not relate exactly to products sold. When this occurs, management may elect to allocate the cost of producing a product over several days. It is simply good management to regard an issuing system as one of providing basic product security, and an inventory control/cost system as a separate entity entirely. Given that approach, let us observe how Scotto's issuing system is designed to protect the security of food and beverage products, and then move to the process of inventory control, with a view toward achieving effective cost control and purchasing.

Product Issuing—Food and Supplies

The process of issuing food and supply products to employees, often called **requisitioning**, need not be overly complicated. While special care must be taken to ensure that employees use the products for their intended purpose, maintaining product security can be achieved with relative ease if the following issuing principles are observed:

1. **Food and supplies should be issued only with management approval.**
2. **If a written record of issues is to be kept, each person removing food or supplies from the storage area must sign, acknowledging receipt of the products.**
3. **Unused products should be returned to the storage area, and their return recorded.**
4. **Food and supplies should be issued only as required by timed production schedules.**

Some foodservice operators who employ a full-time storeroom person prefer to operate with advance requisition schedules. This process can sometimes be helpful because requisition schedules for tomorrow's food, for instance, can be submitted today, thus allowing storeroom personnel the time to gather these items prior to delivery to the kitchen. Occasionally, products are even weighed and measured for kitchen personnel, according to the standardized recipe to be prepared. When this system is in place, the storeroom is often called an **ingredient room**. Figure 5.2 illustrates the kind of requisition form typically in use by a foodservice operation for food and supply products. If so desired, the unit cost and total cost columns may be omitted. If they are to be included, it is important to remember that their primary role is to remind employees that *all food items have a cost*. It is not recommended that these dollar amounts be considered equal to the cost of goods consumed or sold. That system might work in a manufacturing or shipping company but is not sufficiently accurate for use in foodservice.

It is vital that the storeroom requisition forms be sent to the purchasing agent after they have been used so that this individual will have a sense of the movement of product in and out of the storage areas. The form in Figure 5.2 or one similar to it could be used by the bar managers if a record were to be kept of product transfers from the kitchen or food storage area to the bar.

Product Issuing—Beverages

The basic principles of product issuing that apply to food and supplies also apply to beverages. There are, however, special concerns that must be addressed when

Figure 5.2 **Storeroom Requisition**

Unit Name: Scotto's

Requisition #: 001 Date: 1/1/92

Item	Storage Unit	Requested Amount	Unit Cost	Total Cost
Rice	1 lb	5 lb	$0.25/lb	$ 1.25
Broccoli	1 lb	30 lb	0.60/lb	18.00
Rib roast	1 lb	100 lb	3.40/lb	340.00
Total				$359.25

To: Kitchen X Requisition Approved by: S.A.R

Bar Requisition Filled by: T.A.P

issuing beverage products. At Scotto's, beverage issues routinely are one of two types:

1. **Liquor storeroom issues**
2. **Wine cellar issues**

Liquor Storeroom Issues

While several methods of liquor issues could be in place, Sparky practices the **empty-for-full** system of liquor replacement. Each bartender is required to hold empty liquor bottles in the bar or a closely adjacent area. At the conclusion of the shift, or at the start of the next shift, each empty liquor bottle is replaced with a full one of the same brand or type turned in. The empty bottles are then either broken or disposed of, under management supervision, as local beverage law requires.

Figure 5.3 illustrates the requisition form used to issue liquor products at Scotto's. Note that this requisition form does not include unit or total price on product issued, since monitoring those costs should be a function of the liquor storeroom personnel or management, and not the bartender.

It is important to note that all liquor issued from the liquor storage area should be stamped or marked in a manner that is not easily duplicated. This allows management to ensure at a glance that all liquor sold is the property of the foodservice operation, and not that of a bartender who has produced his or her own bottle for the purpose of going into partnership with the operation. In a partnership of this type, the operation supplies the customer, while the bartender provides the liquor and keeps the product sales and profits! While bottle stamping will not prevent dishonest bartenders from bringing in their own liquor, it will force them to pour their product into the operation's bottles and dispose of their empties, which does make the process more difficult.

Occasionally, it may be necessary for a bartender or supervisor to enter the liquor storeroom during a shift. In preparation for this possibility, management should have a key, sealed in an envelope with a signature over the seal so that

Figure 5.3 **Liquor Requisition**

Unit Name: Scotto's

Shift: P.M. Date: 1/1/92

Service Area: Cocktail lounge

Product	# Empties	Bottle Size	Verified by Management Bar	Management
Old Crow	6	750 ml	P.O.F.	S.A.R.
Scotch A	4	750 ml	P.O.F.	S.A.R.
Scotch B	2	Quart	P.O.F.	S.A.R.
Scotch C	3	750 ml	P.O.F.	S.A.R.
Bourbon A	8	750 ml	P.O.F.	S.A.R.
Bourbon B	2	Quart	P.O.F.	S.A.R.
Total empties	25			

it cannot be opened without detection. It should be made clear that an adequate explanation of use of the key will be expected. It is wrong not to give employees controlled access to the products desired by the customer, but it is equally wrong to allow employees this access without management's knowledge and close control.

Wine Cellar Issues

The issuing of wine from a wine cellar is a special case of product issuing because these sales cannot be predicted as accurately as sales of other liquor products. This is especially true in an operation where a large number of valuable wines are routinely stored. If the wine storage area contains products valuable enough to remain locked, it is reasonable to assume that each bottle of wine issued should be noted. The form in Figure 5.4 can be used in such a situation.

This form may be used to secure wine for either the bar or the kitchen, as well as for the dining room. In the case of transfers to the kitchen or the bar, it should be noted that the product has been directed to one of these two locations rather than assigned to a guest check number. Forcing the waitstaff to identify a guest check number when requesting wine will ensure that at the conclusion of the shift wine issues will match wine sales. If the wine is to be sent to a guest as complimentary, or "comp," that can be noted as well, along with the initials of the management personnel authorizing the comp. In the case of the wine cellar issue, the form itself should remain in the wine cellar for use by the wine purchasing agent.

Estimating Daily Costs Using the Issues System

For operations who prefer to use a strict issue and requisition system, it is still possible to estimate product usage on a daily basis. This is done using the six-column estimate. In an issues system, rather than using purchases, as discussed in Chapter 3, the dollar amount of issues is used to form the basis of the estimate.

In Chapter 3, the rationale for estimating cost of food consumed on a regular basis was presented using a six-column format. This same technique can be used to estimate other product costs also. Consider the case of Marvin, who operates a busy Irish pub in a large hotel and would like to have a daily estimate of his beverage costs. He completes his physical inventory on the last day of each month, yet it is often the seventh or eighth day of the next month before he is informed of the prior month's beverage cost percentage. At that point, of course, the previous month has come and gone. Marvin has been "surprised" by high costs in this process more than he can bear! In an effort to generate more current data about his operation, Marvin analyzes his daily beverage issues, shown in Figure 5.5.

Marvin determines his daily issues amount by simply adding the total of all beverage requisitions he has filled during the day. That is, Marvin keeps a copy

Figure 5.4 **Wine Cellar Issues**

Unit Name: Scotto's

Date: 1/1/92

	Product	Vintage	# of Bottles	Guest Check #	Removed by
1.	Soave	1988	2	60485 L	T.A.
2.	Brand A chablis	1990	1	60486 L	S.J.
3.	Brand C bordeaux	1954	1	Comp	S.A.R.
4.	Brand B chablis	1992	1	Kitchen	S.A.R.
5.	Soave	1989	1	60500 M	S.J.
6.					
7.					
8.					
9.					
10.					
11.					
12.					

Remarks: #4 requested by chef 1/1/92

of each requisition and notes the total dollar value of these before submitting them to the purchasing agent. At the end of each day, Marvin records total operational sales and, using his beverage issues totals, fills in the six-column beverage estimate form shown in Figure 5.6. Data for the period January 1–10 have been entered.

As can be seen, the six-column form requires only that the manager divide today's issues by today's sales to arrive at today's estimate. The formula for January 1 is as follows:

$$\frac{\textbf{Issues today}}{\textbf{Sales today}} = \textbf{Beverage cost estimate today}$$

Or

Figure 5.5 **Marvin's Beverage Issues Recap**

Date: 1/1–1/10

Date	Total Issues
1/1	$ 945.00
1/2	785.00
1/3	816.50
1/4	975.40
1/5	1,595.50
1/6	1,100.20
1/7	18.40
1/8	906.50
1/9	1,145.25
1/10	546.25
Total	8,834.00

$$\frac{\$945.00}{\$1{,}450.22} = 65.2\%$$

The todate columns represent cumulative totals of both issues and sales. Therefore, Marvin adds today's issues to the issues total of the prior day. He does the same with the sales figure. Thus, on January 2, the todate estimate would be as follows:

$$\frac{\textbf{Issues todate}}{\textbf{Sales todate}} = \textbf{Beverage cost estimate todate}$$

Or

$$\frac{\$1{,}730.00}{\$3{,}138.62} = 55.1\% \text{ todate}$$

Marvin's ten-day beverage cost estimate is 38.0%. Marvin's daily cost estimate varies greatly. Notice, however, that the todate column settles in the mid to high 30s range despite rather major changes in the daily cost estimates. This is because each passing day adds to both the issues and sales cumulative total. By the 10th or 11th day, it is unlikely that normal changes in daily issues activity will move the todate figure in a substantial way.

It is important to note that Marvin does not know at this point what his actual cost of beverage consumed really is for this ten-day period. That, of course, can only be determined by a physical inventory and the application of the cost of beverage consumed formula. Marvin's estimate, however, will be *extremely* close to his actual cost of goods consumed percentage if one assumption he makes is either true or nearly true. That assumption is, if you remember, that

Figure 5.6 **Six-Column Beverage Cost Estimate**

Unit Name: Marvin's Date: 1/1/92–1/31/92

Date	Issues Today	Issues Todate	Sales Today	Sales Todate	Beverage Cost Estimate Today	Beverage Cost Estimate Todate
1/1	$ 945.00		$1,450.22		65.2%	
1/2	785.00	$1,730.00	1,688.40	$ 3,138.62	46.5%	55.1%
1/3	816.50	2,546.50	2,003.45	5,142.07	40.8%	49.5%
1/4	975.40	3,521.90	1,920.41	7,062.48	50.8%	49.9%
1/5	1,595.50	5,117.40	5,546.50	12,608.98	28.8%	40.6%
1/6	1,100.20	6,217.60	5,921.27	18,530.25	18.6%	33.6%
1/7	18.40	6,236.00	495.20	19,025.45	3.8%	32.8%
1/8	906.50	7,142.50	1,292.20	20,317.65	70.2%	35.2%
1/9	1,145.25	8,287.75	1,381.51	21,699.16	82.9%	38.2%
1/10	546.25	8,834.00	1,548.21	23,247.37	35.3%	38.0%
Subtotal		8,834.00		23,247.37		38.0%
+/–						
Total						

Marvin's inventory remains constant or nearly constant in total dollar value from month to month.

Of course, it is unlikely that inventory levels are exactly the same from month to month or from accounting period to accounting period. It is true, however, that these values should not change a great deal. In fact, if changes are slight, the monthly estimate will be extremely close to the actual cost of food consumed figures. Note that Figure 5.6 has at the bottom an entry point to adjust issues back to actual inventory levels at the end of the accounting period. If, for example, ending inventory is higher than beginning inventory, the difference between these two numbers will be subtracted from the issues total. If ending inventory is lower than beginning inventory, the difference between the two numbers is added to the issues total. In this way, management can determine actual cost of goods consumed if all issues have been accounted for and an ending physical inventory has been taken. It is recommended that the issues cost estimate be posted where all employees can see it. It communicates both sales and costs to employees and lets them see the importance of controlling product usage.

Inventory Control

Regardless of the methods used by employees to requisition food and beverage products, or management to issue these, inventory levels will be affected. It is the responsibility of the foodservice manager and the purchasing agent to monitor this movement and purchase additional products as needed. Restocking the inventory is critical if product shortages are to be avoided and product necessary for menu item preparation is to be available. Nothing is quite as traumatic for the foodservice manager as to be in the middle of a busy meal period and to find that the operation is out of a necessary ingredient or frequently requested menu item. Therefore, the effective foodservice manager carefully monitors inventory levels. It would obviously be very expensive and time-consuming to monitor all ingredients, food products, and supplies on an individual daily basis. The average foodservice operation stocks hundreds of items, each of which may or may not be used every day. The task could be overwhelming.

Imagine, for example, the difficulty associated with monitoring on a daily basis the use of each sugar packet or cube in a high-volume restaurant like Scotto's. Taking a daily inventory of the use of such a product would be akin to spending $10 to watch a penny! The effective foodservice manager knows that proper control involves spending time and effort where it is most needed and can do the most good. It is for this reason that many operators, including Sparky at Scotto's, practice the ABC method of inventory control.

ABC Inventory Control

In order to fully understand the principles of ABC inventory control, one must first be very familiar with the concepts of physical inventory and perpetual inventory.

A **physical inventory** is one in which an actual physical count and valuation of all inventory on hand is taken at the beginning and close of each accounting period. A **perpetual inventory** system is one in which additions to and deletions from total inventory are recorded as they occur. Both the physical and the perpetual inventories have advantages and disadvantages for the foodservice operator. The physical inventory, properly taken, is more accurate, since each item is actually counted and then valued. It is the physical inventory taken at the beginning of the accounting period (beginning inventory) and the physical inventory taken at the end of the accounting period (ending inventory) that are used to compute the cost of food consumed. In turn, the cost of food consumed determines actual product usage and is used to compute food cost percentage (see Chapter 3). Despite its accuracy, the physical inventory suffers from being extremely time-consuming. Even with the use of software programs that can extend inventory (multiply number of units by unit cost), counting each food and beverage item in storage can be a cumbersome task. It is important that the individuals who actually count the inventory be well trained. Guessing at the weights of products like prime ribs and roasts must not be tolerated. If management is to control overall costs, accuracy in taking the physical inventory is critical.

The perpetual inventory seeks to eliminate the need for frequent counting by adding to the inventory when appropriate (receiving slips) and subtracting from the inventory when appropriate (requisitions or issues). The perpetual inventory is especially popular in the area of liquor and wine, where each product may have its own inventory sheet or, in some cases, a **bin card**. A bin card is simply an index card that details additions to and deletions from a given product's inventory level. Figure 5.7 illustrates the use of such a card.

Of course, the accurate use of a perpetual inventory system requires that each change in product quantity be noted. In the ideal situation, the perpetual inventory, whether using bin cards or perpetual inventory sheets, needs to be verified by the physical inventory, when taken for costing purposes. Again, in the ideal situation, perpetual inventory quantities would match actual product counts. The reasons for discrepancies in quantity are many, not the least of which is that employees, when in a hurry, simply forget to update the perpetual system. For example, products like canned green beans may be removed from inventory in the morning, but not used and thus returned in the afternoon. Knowing this,

Figure 5.7 **Bin Card**

Bin Card

Product Name: Brand A bourbon Bottle Size: 750 ml

Balance Brought Forward: 24 Date: 12/31/93

Date	In	Out	Total on Hand
1/1/92	4		28
1/2/92		6	22
1/3/92		5	17
1/4/92	12		24

the employee may elect to wait and adjust the perpetual inventory just once, at the end of the day. Obviously, shortcuts like these begin to wear at the accuracy of the perpetual inventory.

In the foodservice industry it is not wise to depend **solely** on a perpetual inventory system. While exclusive use of a perpetual inventory system may make sense for some businesses, the foodservice industry, because of its complexity, does not appear to be one of them. There are, however, advantages to the perpetual inventory system that must be acknowledged, among them the ability of the purchasing agent to quickly note quantity of product on hand without resorting to a daily physical inventory count.

Physical or Perpetual Inventory

When making the decision about which inventory system to use, the question is "Which of the two systems is best?" The answer is "Neither is best, so use the best of both." This is exactly what the ABC inventory system attempts to do. It separates inventory items into three main categories.

Category A items are those that require tight control and the most accurate record keeping. They are typically high-value items, which can make up 70% to 80% of the total inventory value.

Category B items are those that make up 10% to 15% of the inventory value and require only routine control and record keeping.

Category C items make up only 5% to 10% of the inventory value. These items require only the simplest of inventory control systems.

Follow the steps outlined below to develop the A, B, and C categories.

1. **Calculate monthly usage in units (pounds, gallons, cases, and the like) for each inventory item.**
2. **Multiply total unit usage by purchase price to arrive at the total monthly dollar value of product usage.**
3. **Rank items from highest dollar usage to lowest.**

In a typical ABC analysis, 20% of the items will represent about 70% to 80% of the monthly product usage. This represents the A product category. It is not critical that the line between A, B, and C products be drawn at any given point. Many operators use the following guide, but it can be adapted as the individual operator sees fit.

Category A—Top 20% of items
Category B—Next 30% of items
Category C—Next 50% of items

It is important to note that while the percentage of items in category A is small, the percentage of monthly dollar value the items account for is large. Conversely, while the number of items in category C is large, the monthly dollar value these items account for is small. It is important to note that the ABC inventory system deals with monetary value of products, not product count. An example from Scotto's may help make this distinction clear. One item on Scotto's menu is a New York strip steak. The preparation of this item is simple. The cook sprinkles the steak with garlic salt and cooks it to the customer's specification. The steak is then garnished with one large onion ring, which Sparky buys frozen. In this example, the inventory items would likely be grouped as follows:

Ingredient	Inventory Category
New York strip	A
Onion ring	B
Garlic salt	C

The ABC inventory system attempts to direct management's attention to the critical area of cost. Reducing product costs, especially for category A items, is extremely important and is discussed more fully later in this chapter. The chart in Figure 5.8 details the differences in handling items in the A, B, and C categories.

Some foodservice managers misunderstand the concept behind the ABC system. Of course, all essential menu ingredients are important. The ABC system, however, attempts to focus more of management's attention on the few critical items in inventory and focus less of management's attention on the many trivial items. Again, it is important to note that time is best spent on the items of most

Figure 5.8 **ABC Inventory System**

Category	Inventory Management Techniques
A	1. Order only on an as-needed basis. 2. Take physical inventory on a daily or at least weekly basis. 3. Have clear idea of purchase point and estimated delivery time.
B	1. Maintain normal control systems, and order predetermined inventory (par) levels. 2. Monitor more closely if sale of this item is tied to sale of an item in category A. 3. Review status quarterly for movement to category A or C.
C	1. Order in large quantity to take advantage of discounts if item is not perishable. 2. Stock constant levels of product. 3. Conduct monthly physical inventory.

importance. In the case of inventory management, these are category A, and to a lesser degree category B, items.

The ABC system can be used to arrange storerooms or to determine which items should be stored in the most secure area. Regardless of the inventory management system used, however, whether it is the physical, perpetual, or ABC inventory, management must be strict in monitoring both withdrawals from inventory and the process by which inventory is replenished. The reasoning behind this is quite simple. In addition to enabling the operator to compute the cost of goods consumed and thus the food cost percentage, accurate inventory records allow the effective operator to know much more about his or her operation. To illustrate, note Figure 5.9, which details Sparky's food usage in five major inventory categories. Many operators prefer to categorize their product usage in terms of broad categories of food. In other words, they are interested in their meat cost percentage, produce cost percentage, and so on. When the storeroom inventory is set up as a series of mini-inventories, this approach is possible. It simply requires management to determine desired subcategories and then use inventory valuation sheets that match these groups.

These groups may be determined in any manner management feels is appropriate. Sparky selects meat, seafood, dairy, produce, and other as his five basic inventory categories. Figure 5.9 details food usage at Scotto's when monthly food sales are \$190,000 and total cost of food consumed equals \$66,500, thus yielding a food cost percentage for the month of \$66,500 / \$190,000 = 35%.

Given sales of \$190,000 for the month of January, Sparky can now determine both food cost percentage by category and product usage ratios. He computes his **category** food cost percent by using the standard formula of cost of food consumed divided by sales. This is illustrated in Figure 5.10.

In each category, including the total, Sparky uses \$190,000 as the denominator in his food cost percentage equation. Proportion of total cost percentages are developed by the following formula:

$$\frac{\textbf{Cost in product category}}{\textbf{Total cost in all categories}} = \textbf{Proportion of total product cost}$$

Figure 5.9 **Inventory Recap**

Scotto's January 31, 1992

Category	Beginning Inventory	Purchases	Goods Available	Ending Inventory	Cost of Food Consumed
Meat	\$26,500	\$33,800	\$ 60,300	\$28,000	\$32,300
Seafood	4,600	17,700	22,300	10,900	11,400
Dairy	7,300	4,400	11,700	6,000	5,700
Produce	2,250	15,550	17,800	4,500	13,300
Other	23,000	1,800	24,800	21,000	3,800
Total	63,650	73,250	136,900	70,400	66,500

Figure 5.10 **Food Cost Category Percentage/Proportion**

Scotto's Sales: $190,000.00

Category	Cost of Food Consumed	Food Cost %	Proportion of Total Cost
Meat	$ 32,300.00	17%	48.6%
Seafood	11,400.00	6	17.1
Dairy	5,700.00	3	8.6
Produce	13,300.00	7	20.0
Other	3,800.00	2	5.7
Total	66,500.00	35	100.0

For the meat category, the formula would be as follows:

$$\frac{\textbf{Cost in meat category}}{\textbf{Total cost in all categories}} = \textbf{Meat cost proportion of total cost}$$

In this example,

$$\frac{\$32{,}300.00}{\$66{,}500.00} = 48.6\%$$

By using the categories listed in Figure 5.10, Sparky is better able to determine when his costs are getting out of line. Sparky knows, for example, that meats accounted for 48.6% of his total food usage in the month of January. He can compare this figure to the meat expense of prior months to determine whether his meat costs are rising, declining, or staying constant. When category percentages are higher than anticipated, management must turn its attention to areas of potential concern. The largest area, and one that requires a great deal of attention, is the food production process itself.

Managing Food Production

Managing the food production process entails control in the following five areas:

1. **Waste**
2. **Overcooking**
3. **Overserving**
4. **Improper carryover utilization**
5. **Inappropriate make-or-buy decisions**

Waste

Food losses through simple product waste can play a large role in overall excessive cost situations. This waste may be simple to observe, as when an employee does not use a rubber spatula to get all of the salad dressing out of a one-gallon jar, or it may be difficult to detect, as when a salad preparation person trims the lettuce just a bit more than management would prefer. This would, of course, change the EP yield on the lettuce and result in higher costs. Management must show its concern for the value of products on a daily basis. Each employee should be made to realize that wasting food affects the profitability of the operation, and thus their own economic well-being. In general, food waste is the result of poor training or management inattentiveness. Unfortunately, some managers and employees feel that small amounts of food waste are unimportant. The goal of the effective foodservice manager should be to maximize product utilization and minimize the it's-only-a-few-pennies'-worth syndrome.

Overcooking

Prolonged cooking reduces product volume, whether the item is roast beef or vegetable soup! Cooking times on standardized recipes must be carefully calculated and meticulously followed. It is important to remember that in many ways heat is the enemy of well-prepared foods. Too much time on the steam table line or holding oven removes moisture from products, and thus fewer portions are available for service. Figure 5.11 details the change in portion cost when yield is reduced in a roast of beef due to overcooking.

If we assume that a properly cooked pan of roast beef yields 50 pounds EP and costs \$3.00 per EP pound, the total product cost equals \$150.00 (50 lbs × \$3.00/lb = \$150.00). In its properly cooked state, the beef would yield 100 eight-

Figure 5.11 **Prime Ribs**

Effect of Overcooking on Portion Cost of 50 Pounds (800 Ounces) of Roast Beef

50 # EP cost = \$150.00

Preparation State	Ending Weight (oz)	# of 8-ounce Portions	Portion Cost
Properly prepared	800	100.0	\$1.50
Overcooked 15 min	775	96.9	1.55
Overcooked 30 min	750	93.8	1.60
Overcooked 45 min	735	91.9	1.63
Overcooked 60 min	720	90.0	1.67
Overcooked 90 min	700	87.5	1.71
Overcooked 120 min	680	85.0	1.76

ounce portions, for a cost of $1.50 per portion. As you see, increased cooking time or temperature can cause product shrinkage that increases average portion cost.

While the difference between a portion cost of $1.50 and $1.76 may seem small, it is the control of this type of production issue that separates the good foodservice manager from the outstanding one.

In attempting to control loss due to overcooking, management must strictly enforce standardized recipe cooking times. This is especially true for meats, soups, stews, baked goods, and the like. Moreover, extended cooking times can result in loss of both quantity and quality if items are placed in an oven, fryer, or broiler and then "forgotten." It is therefore advisable to supply kitchen production personnel with small, easily cleanable timers for which they are responsible. This can help substantially in reducing product loss due to overcooking.

Overserving

No other area of food and beverage cost control has been analyzed and described as fully through articles, speeches, and even books, as the control of portion size. There are two reasons for this. First, overportioning on the part of service personnel has the effect of increasing operational costs and may cause the operation to mismatch its production schedule with anticipated demand. If, for example, 100 guests are expected and 100 products are produced, yet overportioning causes us to be out of the product after only 80 guests have been served, the 20 others will be left clamoring for *their* portions, which of course, have already been served to others. Second, overportioning must be avoided because customers want to feel that they have received fair value for their money. If portions are large one day and small the next, customers may feel that they have been cheated on the second day. Consistency is a key to operational success in foodservice. Customers want to know exactly what they will get for their money.

It is not possible, of course, to set one standard portion size for all foodservice operations. The proper portion size of an entrée in a college dormitory feeding male athletes will clearly be different than that of an extended-care facility whose residents might be, on average, 85 years old. It is important for management to consider clientele, ambience, pricing structure, and quality prior to establishing appropriate portion size.

Once portion size **has** been established, it is up to management to strictly enforce it. Often, management's efforts are resisted by employees. When this is the case, it is a clear indication that management has failed in its mission to provide employees with a basic understanding that underlies the foodservice industry. Employees must be made to see that strict adherence to predetermined portion size is a benefit both to the customer and to the operation. Management must also be sensitive to the fact that it is the line server or waitperson who must deal with the customer who complains about the inadequacy of portion size.

Therefore, waitstaff must be made to feel comfortable about predetermined portion sizes so that they, along with management, will want to maintain them.

In most cases, tools are available that will help employees determine proper portion size. Whether these are scales, scoops, ladles, dishes, or spoons, employees must have an adequate number of easily accessible portion control devices, if they are to use them. Scoops, for example, are sized based on the number of servings per quart. Thus, a #12 scoop will yield 12 servings per quart, or 48 servings per gallon, a #20 scoop, 20 servings per quart, and so on.

Many portion sizes are closely tied to the purchasing function. In order to serve a ¼-pound hot dog, for instance, one must begin with ¼-pound hot dogs. In a similar vein, if one banana is sliced for addition to breakfast cereals, the purchasing agent must have been diligent in ordering and accepting only the banana size for which management has developed a specification.

Constant checking of portion size is a key task of management. When incorrect portion sizes are noticed, they must be promptly corrected. If not, considerable cost increases can be incurred. Consider the case of Sparky, the manager of Scotto's. Sparky purchases, on occasion, three-pound boxes of frozen yellow corn, to be served as his vegetable of the day. Each box costs $1.40. With a total of 48 ounces (3 lbs × 16 oz = 48 ounces) and an established portion size of 3 ounces, Sparky knows that he should average 48 ounces / 3 ounces = 16 servings per box. Figure 5.12 demonstrates the effect on total portion cost if either 1, 2, or 3 servings are lost to overportioning.

As Figure 5.12 demonstrates, a small amount of overportioning on an item as inexpensive as corn costs the operation only a few cents per serving. Those few cents per serving, however, multiplied time after time can mean the difference between a profitable operation and one that is only marginally successful. If Sparky's portion cost should have been 8.7 cents ($1.40 / 16 = 8.7 cents) but, due to overportioning, rises to 10.8 cents ($1.40 / 13 = 10.8 cents), his costs are 2.1 cents higher than they should be on this item. If Sparky is open seven days a week and serves an average of 200 portions of corn per day, his total loss for a year would be 365 × 200 × .021 = $1,533.00, enough to buy Sparky's operation proper portioning tools. It is also an amount worthy of Sparky's attention!

Figure 5.12 **Scotto's**

Corn Portion Cost Chart
@ $1.40 per 3-pound Box

# of Portions per 3-lb Box	Portion Size	Portion Cost
16	3.0 oz	8.7¢
15	3.2 oz	9.3¢
14	3.5 oz	10.0¢
13	3.7 oz	10.8¢

Improper Carryover Utilization

As was discussed earlier in this text, predicting customer counts is an inexact science at best. Because this is true, and because most foodservice operators want to offer the same broad menu to the evening's last diner as to its first, it is inevitable that some food that has been prepared will remain unsold at the end of the operational day. In some areas of the hospitality industry, this is a particular problem; in others, it is less of a concern. Consider for a moment the operation of a shaved ice or snow cone facility. At the end of the day, any unsold ice is simply held until the next day, with no measurable loss of either product quantity or quality. Contrast that situation, however, with a full-service cafeteria. If closing time is 8:00 P.M., management wishes to have a full product line, or at least some of each item, available to the customer who walks in the door at 7:55 P.M. Obviously, in five more minutes a large number of items will become carryover items. Indeed, management's ability to effectively integrate carryover items on subsequent days can make the difference between profits and losses. Food products are at their peak of quality when they are delivered to the back door. From then on, storage, temperature, and handling work against product quality. These forces are especially at work in the area of carryovers. It is for this reason that production schedules must note carryover items on a daily basis. If this is not done, these items tend to get stored and lost in walk-in refrigerators or freezer units.

Management should have a clear use in mind for each menu item that may have to be carried over. Broiled or sauteed fish may become seafood chowder or bisque. Today's prime rib roast may be the key ingredient in tomorrow's beef stroganoff, and so on. This process can be creative and, if management involves the employee, quite effective.

It is important to understand that carryover foods seldom can be sold for their original value. Today's beef stew made from yesterday's prime rib cannot be sold at a prime rib price. Thus, it is critical for the effective foodservice manager to strive for a minimal carryover situation. Carryovers generally mean reduced income relative to product value, and thus reduced profit levels.

There are very few items that do not have some value in their carryover state. Akin to the idea of using carryover items is the idea of using products that were intended for sale, but for which sales did not materialize. Consider the case of a hotel that has been made inaccessible due to a severe snowstorm. A banquet function, planned for the evening, had to be cancelled. The items intended to be sold must be used, and quickly! Menu specials, substitutions, and employee meals can be sources of utilization for products like these.

Inappropriate Make-or-Buy Decisions

Many foodservice operators elect to buy some food products that are prepre-pared in some fashion. The items, called convenience or ready foods, can be of great value to the foodservice operation. Often they can save dollars spent on labor, equipment, and hard-to-secure food products. They can also add menu variety beyond the skill level of the average kitchen crew. A disadvantage, however, is that these items tend to cost more on a per-portion basis. This is to be expected, since these items include a charge for labor and packaging, as well as for the food itself.

Convenience items are not, of course, an all-or-nothing operational decision. Nearly all foodservice operations today use canned products, sliced bread, and the like—items that would have been considered convenience items years ago. Therefore, the question is not whether to use convenience items or not, but rather, how many of a certain kind of convenience item to use. In general, the following guidelines may be of value when determining whether to adopt the use of a convenience product.

1. **Is the quality acceptable? This question must be answered from the point of view of the customer, not management alone.**
2. **Will the product save labor? Identifiable labor savings must be discovered if management is to agree that the convenience item will indeed save labor costs.**
3. **Would it matter if the customer knew? If an operation has built its image on made-on-premise items, customers may react negatively to boil-in-a-bag or microwave type products.**
4. **Does the product come in an acceptable package size? If convenience items are not sold in a size that complements the operation, excessive waste can result.**
5. **Is storage space adequate? With the new *sous-vide* type convenience items, this may in the future become less of an issue. Frozen convenience items, however, can take up valuable storage space.**

Controlling the Beverage Production Area

Controlling beverage production is as important as controlling food production. The beverage manager, however, has a greater choice in automated equipment than does the food production manager. Each beverage manager must make the determination of how much, if any, automation is desirable in the bar area or areas. In its simplest form, beverage production consists of a bartender pouring a measured amount of liquor into a glass. This method is not complicated and requires only a bartender and a jigger to work. The jigger is the device used to measure alcoholic beverages, typically in ounces and portions of an ounce. This system is obviously inexpensive. It is also quite portable; in other words, it is a good system to use in remote serving locations like a pool area, beach, or reception hall. The disadvantage, of course, is the room for employee error and the potential for fraud and waste.

At the other extreme are some of the total bar systems available to beverage managers today. Depending on the level of sophistication and cost, these liquor/computer systems can perform one or all of the following tasks:

1. **Record beverage sale by brand**
2. **Record who made the sale**
3. **Post sale to room folio (in hotel)**
4. **Measure liquor**
5. **Add predetermined mixes to drink**
6. **Reduce liquor from inventory**
7. **Prepare liquor requisition**
8. **Compute liquor cost by brand sold**
9. **Calculate gratuity on check**
10. **Identify payment method, that is, cash, check, credit card**
11. **Record guest check number**
12. **Record date and time of sale**

Managers must determine exactly where on the automation scale they prefer to operate. At Scotto's, Sparky uses a relatively simple beverage production control system. The special preportion devices Sparky uses on his liquor bottles pour only a predetermined amount of liquor, yet give each customer the sense of a drink made to order by the bartender. In addition, mixers can be varied, if requested by the customer, to create a drink that has the strength the customer prefers. Sparky is also very careful to designate a proper glass size and ice quantity for each drink. This ensures that the portion size of the drink is consistent with the customer's visual perception of a full glass. Furthermore, he looked long and hard to find an ice machine whose ice shape best fit his view of proper spacing in the glass and melting characteristics. Sparky uses the full-for-empty system of replenishing his bar. Thus, he knows exactly how many bottles of every type of liquor should be on hand at any given time. He also conducts on a periodic basis an attainable versus actual cost comparison for his bar, as discussed later in this chapter.

The question of automated versus manual bars will continue for some time. There are other issues of beverage production, however, that should be of concern to the effective beverage manager. They fall in the following areas:

1. **In-room mini bars**
2. **Bottle sales**
3. **Open bars**
4. **Banquet operations**

Minibars

Minibars, serving 50-milliliter bottles, have become popular in hotels that cater to the upscale business traveler. The control issue here is one of matching requests by housekeeping for replenishment bottles with guest usage of product. Some large operations deal with this issue by having a single individual or department charged with the responsibility of filling the minibars. If this is not practical, it is critical that bottles be issued only after consumption has been determined. While this will necessitate two trips to the guests' rooms per day, the control features inherent in such a system make it preferable to issuing bottles prior to determining guest usage.

Bottle Sales

When liquor sales are made by the bottle, either through room service, in the case of a hotel, or at a reception area, the control issue is one of verifying bottle count. The customer and the operation must be treated fairly in such a transaction. In the case of full-bottle sales to a guest room, the customer must be required to sign a receipt accepting the product. It is the only way to avoid potential misunderstandings about cost. In the case of receptions or banquets, customers should be charged only for empty bottles or, in the case of a purchase of a specified number of bottles, should be shown both full and empty bottles equal to the number used and charged for the event. In an effort to protect both the establishment and the customer from employee theft, the thoughtful beverage manager will mark the bottles for that reception or banquet in a way that is not easily duplicated, thus preventing employees from bringing in their own empty bottles and then removing full ones at the customer's expense.

Open Bars

The production control issues associated with open bars fall into one of two main categories: portion size and accountability. Open bars are, by definition, ones in which no charge is made for individual drinks, thus establishing an all-you-can-drink environment. In this environment, customers can cajole bartenders into pouring larger than normal drinks. This must, of course, be resisted through management's strict enforcement of the use of jiggers, premeasured pour spouts or mechanical systems. Bartenders, and customers too, must understand that while it may be an open bar, someone will be paying the bill at the end of the event, and they, whoever they are, have the right to expect reasonable portion control if they are paying on a per-drink or per-bottle-used basis. If the foodservice operation has established a per-person charge for the open bar, overportioning costs will have to be absorbed by the operation. This obviously necessitates strict control of portion size and total liquor consumption per guest.

As great an issue as overportioning is, accountability looms larger and larger on the horizon as an area of legitimate cost control concern for the effective beverage manager. With more states holding liquor sellers responsible for the actions of their patrons, the entire concept of reasonable and prudent care in beverage operations is called into question. Bartenders who work open bars should be specially trained to spot signs of customer intoxication. As difficult as it may sometimes be, customers should be made aware that it is illegal to serve an intoxicated guest. To do so puts the entire food and beverage operation at risk. Fewer and fewer operations allow the open bar concept, preferring to go to a coupon system, where each coupon issued is good for one drink, and the number of coupons issued, rather than the number of drinks, can be controlled. While the possibility exists that coupons can be shared and thus given to an intoxicated guest, the coupon system does show an attempt by management to exercise reasonable and prudent care.

Banquet Operations

The sale of alcoholic beverages during a banquet usually takes the form of bottle wine sales. Guests usually are provided with a set number of bottles on the table, to be shared by those seated at the table. Alternatively, as they consume their wine, they can be served by the waitstaff. It is the latter method that presents cost control problems, as the host of the event will be charged either by the number of bottles served or the number of guests served. If the payment is based on the number of bottles served, the bottles should be marked and the empties made available for inspection by either the customer or the waiter captain. If the sale is based on the number of glasses poured, then both the customer and the foodservice operation must be in agreement as to the desired portion size and total number of portions to be served.

Employee Theft

Loss of product can happen when systems of control are too slack to prevent employee theft. While all kitchens and beverage operations can expect to experience small amounts of product slippage, such as an apple eaten in secret or a carrot nibbled where the supervisor cannot see it, extensive loss of product is, of course, to be avoided. Product theft can occur in either the bar or kitchen production areas yet is probably more prevalent in the bar areas.

Reducing Bar-Related Theft

Experienced food and beverage managers seem to have an endless supply of stories related to theft in bar operations. Indeed, bar theft is one of the most frequent types of thefts in the foodservice industry. While it may well be impossible to halt all kinds of bar theft, the following are areas that management should check periodically to ensure proper safeguards.

1. Order filled but not rung up

In this case, the bartender delivers the drink as requested by the customer or waitstaff, but never rings up the drink on the cash register, and the bartender simply pockets the sale. All drinks should be rung up on the cash register to prevent this type of theft. Management's vigilance is critical to ensure that no drink is prepared until **after** the ticket is rung up.

2. Bringing in extra product

In this scenario, mentioned earlier in this text, the bartender sells products that he or she has brought in and, of course, pockets the sales. Bottle stamps or markings help prevent this type of theft, since nonmarked bottles can be easily detected.

3. Over- and underpouring

When bartenders overpour, they are stealing from the operation; when they underpour, they are stealing from the customer. Bartenders will pour the appropriate amount if management demands it. When bartenders underpour, they may be making up for drinks they have given away or sold, but have not rung up. When they overpour, they may be doing so for their friends or for the extra tips this activity may yield. In either case, management must prevent such behavior.

Proper portion size in the spirits area is preserved through the enforced use of jiggers, spouts or mechanical equipment. In the case of draft beer, head size, that is, the amount of foam on top of the glass, directly affects portion size and portion cost, and thus must be controlled.

4. Incorrect change making

If a bar is extremely busy and customers are paying little attention, bartenders may be greatly tempted to give incorrect change for drinks that are sold. This can be as simple as "forgetting" that a customer paid with a $20 bill and returning change from a $10 bill, or as clever as maintaining that the change was returned to an overindulgent guest when, in fact, no change was returned at all!

5. Dilution of product

Often called "watering the drinks," this method of bar or storeroom theft involves adding water to the product in order to make up for spirits that have been either stolen or given away. It is especially easy to water products such as gin, vodka, rum, or tequila, since these clear spirits will not change color with the addition of water. Detection of this type of theft is rather difficult. Periodic sampling of a known proof alcohol against bar stock by a knowledgeable food and beverage director may be the only defense against such bartender fraud. Since each alcohol product has a particular specific gravity or weight associated with it, management may also check for product dilution through the use of a **hydrometer**, which identifies specific gravity. If water has been added to the bottle, the specific gravity will change from the value originally associated with that liquor.

6. Product theft

Alcohol is a highly desirable product; therefore, its theft is always a possibility. This is especially true in a beverage service area that is secluded, or in which the bartender has access both to product inventory and ease of exit. Proper controls, as well as strict rules restricting the access of employees to liquor, beer, and wine storage areas, should help detect this sort of theft.

7. Product substitution

If a call brand liquor has been ordered and paid for, it should, of course, be served. If the bartender, however, substitutes a less expensive well liquor for the call brand, he or she may pocket the difference in price between the two items. This has the effect of shortchanging the customer, who has paid a premium for something he or she did not receive. Conversely, if the customer has ordered a well drink, but the bartender serves from the premium or super premium stock, the customer has received more value than he or she has paid for, and the operation is shortchanged.

While it is impossible to list all types of bar thefts, it is important to note that they can and do occur. Conscientious managers should hire honest bartenders, train them well, and demand that they follow all house policies. Perhaps the best advice of all is simply to be vigilant. Watch the bar area carefully or enlist the aid of a **spotter**, a professional who, for a fee, will observe the bar operation with an eye toward reporting any unusual or inappropriate behavior by the bartender.

While theft may occur during the normal operation of the bar, it may also occur during receptions and special events. Consider for a moment the case of a father of the bride who wishes to serve champagne to his guests at the wedding reception, to be held in a local hotel. It is estimated that ten cases of champagne will be used. The food and beverage director orders 12 cases, since it would not be appropriate to run out of champagne. The father of the bride will pay for each bottle used. Potential difficulties loom in two areas, neither of which bode well for the father of the bride. In the first scenario, more champagne is used than should have been because the bartenders use larger than normal glasses or pour larger than normal portions. Obviously, this could also happen when serving spirits. In the second scenario, ten cases are served, as predicted, yet one case ends up in the bartender's automobile trunk. The result is that 11 cases are gone. The bartender maintains that all 11 were used. The customer must pay for one extra case. Imagine, however, the embarrassment if management is asked by the customer to produce the empty bottles from 11 cases!

While bartenders suffer from a poor reputation in many parts of the foodservice industry, it is important to remember that anytime the same individual is responsible for both the preparation of a product and the collection of money for its sale, the opportunity for theft is greatly increased. In a small beverage operation, this situation is common. Again, management vigilance is critical.

Reducing Kitchen-Related Theft

Most kitchen-related theft deals with the removal of products from the premises, since few kitchen workers also handle cash, as is the case with bartenders. Kitchen workers can, however, work with waitstaff personnel to defraud the operation (see Chapter 9). In addition, kitchen workers have access to valuable food and beverage products. The following product security tips are helpful when designing control systems to ensure the safety and security of food and beverage products.

1. **Keep all storage areas locked and secure.**
2. **Issue food only with proper authorization and management approval.**
3. **Monitor the use of all carryovers.**
4. **Do not allow food to be prepared unless a guest check is prerung with the appropriate order.**
5. **Maintain an active inventory management system.**
6. **Ensure that all food received is signed for by the appropriate receiving clerk.**
7. **Do not pay suppliers for food products without an appropriate and signed invoice.**
8. **Do not use petty cash to pay for food items unless a receipt and the product can be produced.**
9. **Conduct periodic physical inventories of all level A, B, and C products**
10. **Do not allow employees to remove food from the premises without management's specific approval.**

If management has determined that purchasing, receiving, storage, issuing, and production controls are well in line, yet food and beverage costs are out of line, the problem may well lie in the fundamental areas of menu design, product pricing, or both. It makes good sense to analyze menu first, as menu design decisions drive most pricing decisions.

Menu Design

Menus in foodservice establishments generally fall into one of the following three major categories:

1. **Standard menu**
2. **Daily menu**
3. **Cycle menu**

Each of these can be an asset in the manager's effort to control food costs. The most commonly used menu is the standard type.

Standard Menu

The standard menu is printed, recited, or otherwise communicated to the customer. The standard menu is fixed day after day. While an operation may periodically add or delete an item, the standard menu remains virtually constant. There are many advantages to having one. First, the standard menu simplifies ordering products. Since the menu remains constant, it is fairly easy to know which products to secure to produce the menu items. A second advantage is that customer preference data are easily obtained, since the total number of menu items is typically modest, and the preference data can be used to accurately determine production schedules and purchasing requirements. In addition, standard menus become marketing tools for the operation, since customers soon become familiar with and return for their favorite menu items.

The standard menu is most typically found in the restaurant or hotel segment of the hospitality industry. It tends to dominate those segments of the business where the customer selects the location of the dining experience, as opposed to a college dormitory cafeteria, for instance, where students are required to dine frequently. Despite its many advantages, the standard menu does have drawbacks from a control standpoint. First, standard menus are often not developed to utilize carryovers effectively. In fact, in many cases, items that are produced for a standard menu and remain unsold must be discarded because the next day their quality will not be acceptable. An example would be a quick-service restaurant that produces too many hamburgers for lunch and does not sell all of them. Indeed, for many quick-service restaurants, a burger that is made but not sold within ten minutes would be discarded. Contrast that cost control strategy with one that says that burger meat not sold within ten minutes will be chopped and added to the house specialty chili, and it is easy to see how menu design affects food cost control. A second disadvantage of the standard menu is its lack of ability to respond quickly to market changes and product cost changes. A restaurant that does not list green beans on the menu cannot take advantage of the seasonal harvest of green beans, a time when they can be purchased extremely inexpensively. Conversely, if management has decided that its two house vegetables will be broccoli and corn, even considerable price increases in these two items will have to be absorbed by management, since the items are listed on the permanent menu. An extreme example of this kind of problem was found in a quick-service seafood restaurant chain that found itself paying almost three times what it had the previous year for a seafood item that constituted approximately 80% of its menu sales. A foreign government had restricted fishing for this product off its shores, and the price skyrocketed. This chain was nearly devastated by this turn of events. Needless to say, management quickly moved to add chicken and different seafood products to the menu in order to dilute the effect of this incredible price increase. Whenever possible, the effective foodservice manager should monitor food prices with an eye to making seasonal adjustments. The standard menu makes this quite difficult.

In summary, the standard menu presents management with both benefits and liabilities. A careful look at what is being served and how the menu affects costs is in the best interest of every foodservice manager who operates from a standard menu.

Daily Menu

In some restaurants, management elects to operate without a standard or fixed menu and instead changes the menu every day. This concept is especially popular in some upscale restaurants where the chef's daily creations are viewed with great anticipation, and some awe, by the eager customer. The daily menu would seem to offer some advantages over the standard menu, since management can respond very quickly to changes in the price of the raw materials needed to produce the menu items. In fact, that is one of the daily menu's great advantages. In addition, carryovers are less of a problem, because any product unsold yesterday has at least the potential of being incorporated into today's menu. Every silver lining has its cloud, however. For all its flexibility, the daily menu is recommended only for very special situations due to the tremendous control drawbacks associated with its implementation. First, customer percent selecting data is difficult to come by, since the items on any given day's menu may never have been served in that particular combination in that restaurant. Thus, the preparation of specific items in certain quantities is pure guesswork and a dangerous way of determining production schedules. Second, how does one plan to have the necessary ingredients on hand to prepare the daily menu if the menu is not known ahead of time? And how does one decide on Monday whether one should order tuna or sirloin steak for the menu on Thursday? Obviously, this situation requires that even the daily menu be planned far enough in advance to allow the purchasing agent to select and order the items necessary to produce the menu. Third, the daily menu may sometimes serve as a marketing tool, but can just as often serve as a disappointment to the customers who had a wonderful menu item the last time they dined at this establishment, and have now returned to find that the favorite item is not being served. On the other hand, it is very unlikely that any customer will get bored with a routine at a daily menu restaurant, since the routine is, in fact, no routine at all.

Both the standard and the daily menus have advantages and disadvantages. The cycle menu is an effort by management to enjoy the best aspects of both these approaches and minimize their respective disadvantages.

Cycle Menu

A cycle menu is a menu in effect for a specific time period. The length of the cycle refers to the length of time the menu is in effect. We refer to a 7-day cycle menu, 21-day cycle menu, 30-day cycle menu, or one of any other length of time. Typically, the cycle menu is repeated on a regular basis. Thus, a particular cycle menu could consist of four 7-day periods. If the four periods were labeled as A, B, C, and D, the cycle periods would rotate as illustrated in Figure 5.13.

Cycle menus are most often selected by foodservice managers whose guests dine with them on a very regular basis, either through the choice of the individual, such as a college student or summer camper eating in a dining hall, or through the choice of an institution, such as a hospital or prison feeding situation. In cases like this, menu variety is very important. The cycle menu provides a systematic method for incorporating that variety into the menu. At a glance, the foodservice manager can determine how often fried chicken is served per week, month, or year, and also how frequently bread dressing rather than saffron rice is served with baked chicken. In this respect, the cycle menu offers more to the customer than does the standard menu. With cycle menus, production personnel can be trained to produce a wider variety of food than with the standard menu, thus improving their skills but requiring fewer skills than might be needed with a daily menu concept.

Cycle menus have the advantage of being able to systematically incorporate today's carryovers into tomorrow's finished product. This is a key management advantage. Because of the menu's cyclical nature, management should have a good idea of customer preferences and thus be able to schedule and control production to a greater degree than with the daily menu.

Purchasing also is simplified, since the menu is known ahead of time and menu ingredients that will appear on all the cycles can be ordered with plenty of lead time. Inventory levels are easy to maintain because, as is the case with the standard menu, product usage is well known.

To illustrate the differences, and the impact of operating under the three different menu systems, consider the case of Larry, Moe, and Curly Joe, three

Figure 5.13 **Sample Cycle Menu Rotation**

Day	Cycle
1–7	A
8–14	B
15–21	C
22–28	D
29–35	A
36–42	B
43–49	C
50–56	D
57–63	A

foodservice operators who wish to serve roast turkey and dressing for their dinner entrée on a Saturday night in April. Larry operates a restaurant with a fixed menu. If he is to print a fixed menu that allows him to serve turkey in April, he may be required to have it available in January and June also. If he is to utilize the carryover parts of the whole turkey, he must incorporate a second turkey item that also must be made available every day. Larry is not sure all the trouble and cost are worth it!

Moe operates a restaurant with a daily menu. For him, roast turkey and dressing on a Saturday in April is quite easy. His problem, however, is that he has no idea how much to produce, since he has never before served this item at this time of the year in his restaurant. What if no one orders it?

Curly Joe operates on a cycle menu. He can indeed put roast turkey and dressing on the cycle. If it sells well, he will keep it on the cycle. If it does not, he can remove it from the next cycle. Curly Joe makes a note to himself that he should record how well it sells and leave a space in the cycle for the utilization of any carryover product that might exist the next day (although he may prefer to eat all of the carryover himself!)

Menu Specials

Regardless of the menu type used, most foodservice operators can incorporate minor menu changes on a daily basis. These daily or weekly specials are an effort to provide variety, take advantage of low-cost raw ingredients, utilize carryover products, or test market potential for new menu items. The menu special is a powerful cost control tool. Properly utilized, it helps shape the future menu while providing opportunities for the effective foodservice manager to respond to the challenges of utilizing all the food and beverage products available in inventory or on the market.

Related Menu Issues

Some aspects of menu development apply to any of the previously mentioned menu types. Proper employee scheduling, for example, is a key factor in controlling not only labor cost, but food as well. Certainly, the operation's menu must allow for the correct number of employees to be in place and to work at a pace that is productive and not wasteful of time or products. Failure to do so will result in increased costs. If a bar is improperly staffed, for example, so that drink preparation personnel are unduly rushed, product waste is sure to increase. In addition, proper menu planning of all types must include the assessment of equipment utilization. No piece of equipment should be overloaded, even at peak time periods, or product quality as well as customer service may suffer. Another important aspect of menu planning, and the one we shall explore next, is the concept of price and value for each menu item served. Care must be taken to match menu items with a price that customers are willing to pay and for which they feel a fair value is received. Too often, management sees increasing menu price as a way to make up for poor cost control systems. It is never wise, however, to ask customers to subsidize management inefficiency. In the long run, this is simply a bankrupt customer strategy. Pricing is important and must be well understood by management. It is not the total solution to cost control problems but may indeed play a part in assuring that an improper price/value relationship is not the cause of the cost control problem.

Factors Affecting Menu Pricing

A great deal of important information has been written in the area of menu pricing and strategy. For the serious foodservice operator, menu pricing is a topic that deserves its own research and study. Pricing is related to cost control by virtue of the basic formula from Chapter 1:

Income − Expense = Profit

When operators find that profits are too low, they frequently question whether or not price (income) is too low. It is important to remember, however, that income and price are not synonymous terms. Income means amount spent by *all* customers, while price refers to the amount charged to *one* customer. Experienced foodservice managers know that increasing prices without giving value can result in higher prices but, frequently, lower income because of reduced customer counts.

Perhaps no area of hospitality management is less understood than the area of pricing. This is not surprising when we consider the many factors that play a part in the pricing decision. For some foodservice operators, inefficiency in cost control is passed on to the customer in terms of higher prices. In fact, sound pricing decisions should be based on establishing a positive price/value relationship in the mind of the customer. Most foodservice operators face similar product costs when selecting their goods on the open market. Whether the product is oranges or beer, wholesale prices vary little from supplier to supplier. In some cases, this variation is due to volume buying; in others, the relationship established with the vendor. Regardless of the source, the variation is small relative to variations in menu pricing. This is because price is a function of much more than product cost. Menu price is significantly affected by all of the following factors:

1. **Local competition**
2. **Service levels**
3. **Customer type**

4. **Product quality**
5. **Portion size**
6. **Ambience**
7. **Location**
8. **Sales mix**
9. **Discounting**

Local Competition

This factor is often **too** closely monitored by the typical foodservice operator. It may seem to some that the average consumer is vitally concerned with price, and nothing more. In reality, small variations in price make little difference to the average consumer. If a group of young professionals goes out for pizza and beer after work, the major determinant will *not* be that the beer is $2.00 in one establishment and $2.25 in another. The competition is important when establishing price, but it is a well-known fact in foodservice that someone can always sell a lesser-grade product for a lesser price. The price a competitor charges for his or her product can be helpful in setting a price. It should *not*, however, be the only determining factor. Successful foodservice operators spend their time focusing on their own operation, not on the affairs of the competition.

Service Levels

Customers expect to pay more for the same product when service levels are higher. The can of soda sold from a vending machine is less expensive than one served by a human being. This is as it should be. The hospitality industry is, in fact, a service industry. As the personal level of service increases, prices may also increase. This is not to say that the price increase is reserved exclusively to pay for the labor required to increase service levels. Customers are willing to pay more for increased service levels but this higher price should provide for extra profit as well. In our industry, the companies who have been able to survive and thrive over the years have done so because of their uncompromising commitment to high levels of customer service. This trend will continue.

Customer Type

Some consumers are simply less price sensitive than others. All customers, however, want value for their money. The question of what represents value can vary, of course, due to the type of clientele. The effective foodservice operator understands this principle and uses it to his or her advantage. This can clearly be seen in the pricing decisions of convenience stores across the United States. In these facilities, food products such as sandwiches, fruit, drinks, and cookies are sold at relatively high prices. The customers these stores cater to, however, value convenience above all else. For this convenience, and a wider range of products than would be found at a quick-service restaurant, they are willing to pay a premium price. A thorough analysis of who their customers are and what they value most is critical to the success of the foodservice operator.

Product Quality

When the average foodservice customer thinks of hamburger, he or she actually thinks not of one product, but of a range of products. A hamburger may be a rather small one-ounce burger patty on a mini-bun. If so, its price will be low and so perhaps may service levels and quality. If, however, the thought turns to an eight-ounce gourmet burger with avocado slices and alfalfa sprouts, the price will be much higher and so, probably, will service levels and quality. Foodservice operators choose from a variety of quality levels when developing product specifications and consequently planning menus and setting prices. The operator who selects the market's cheapest bourbon as his or her well brand can charge less than a competitor who selects a better brand. Each foodservice operator must, however, select the quality level that best represents his or her customers' anticipated desire and then price the product accordingly.

Portion Size

Portion size plays a large role in determining menu pricing. It is a relatively misunderstood concept, yet it is probably the second most significant factor (next to sales mix) in overall pricing. The great chefs know that people "eat with their eyes first!" This relates to presenting food that is visually appealing. It also relates to portion size. A four-ounce drink in a five-ounce glass looks good. The same four-ounce drink in a six-ounce glass looks as if the operator is attempting to skimp at the customer's expense. A burger and fries may fill an 8-inch plate, but will be lost on an 11-inch plate. Portion size, then, is a function of both food quantity and presentation. It is no secret why some successful cafeteria chains use smaller than average dishes to plate their food. For their customers, the image of price/value comes across loud and clear.

In some dining situations, particularly in an all-you-can-eat operation, the above-mentioned principle again holds true. The proper dish size is just as critical as the proper scoop or ladle size when serving the food.

Of course, in a traditional service operation, management controls (or should control!) portion size. The best way to determine whether portion sizes are too large is simply to watch the dishroom area and see what comes back from the dining room. In this regard, the dishroom operator becomes a key player in the cost control team.

Today's consumers prefer lighter food, more fruits and vegetables, and smaller portions. This is good news for the foodservice operator. Every menu item should be analyzed with an eye toward determining if the quantity being served is the "proper" quantity. We would like to serve this proper amount, but obviously no more than that. Its affect on menu price cannot be overstated, and management must establish and maintain strict control over proper portion size.

Ambience

If people ate only because they were hungry, few restaurants would be open today. People eat out for a variety of reasons, some of which have little to do with food. Fun, companionship, adventure, and variety are just a few reasons diners cite for eating out rather than eating at home. For the foodservice operator who provides an attractive ambience, menu prices can be higher. In fact, the operator in such a situation is selling much more than food and thus justly deserves this higher price. But a caveat is in order, since many foodservice operations that did count on ambience alone to carry their business have not been successful. Excellent product quality with outstanding service go much further over the long run than do clever restaurant designs. Ambience may draw customers to a location. When this is true, prices may be somewhat higher. It is always the price/value relationship, however, that will bring the customer back, again and again.

Location

Location can be a major factor in determining price. One need look no further than America's many themed amusement parks to see evidence of this. Foodservice operators in these places are able to charge premium prices because they have, in effect, a monopoly on food sold to the visitors. The only all-night diner on the interstate highway exit is in much the same situation. Contrast that with an operator of one of ten seafood restaurants on restaurant row. It used to be said of restaurants that success was due to three things: location, location, and location! This may have been true before so many operations opened in the United States. There is, of course, no discounting the value of a prime restaurant location, and location alone can influence price. It does not, however, guarantee success. Each foodservice operator must analyze his or her own operation. Location can be an asset or a liability, and if it is an asset, menu prices may reflect that fact. If location is indeed a liability, menu prices may need to be lower to attract a clientele.

Sales Mix

Of all the factors mentioned thus far, the sales mix will most heavily influence the menu pricing decision, just as customer purchase decisions will influence total product costs. Managers respond to this situation by employing the concept called **price blending**. Price blending refers to the process of pricing products in groups with the intent of achieving a favorable overall cost situation. It is a necessary process, well worth mastering by the effective foodservice manager. Consider, for example, the case of Mark, who operates a quick-service hamburger shop. Let us assume that Mark hopes to achieve an overall food cost of 40%. Figure 5.14 illustrates the three products Mark sells and their corresponding selling price if each is priced to achieve a 40% food cost.

Notice that in Figure 5.14 Mark has assumed that each product should sell at a price that results in a 40% food cost. Certainly under this system, sales mix would not affect overall food cost percentage. The sales mix could, however, have very damaging results on Mark's profitability. The reason is very simple. If Mark uses the price structure indicated, his drink prices are too low. Most customers expect to pay far in excess of 23 cents for a soft drink at a quick-service restaurant. Mark runs the risk in this situation of attracting many customers who are interested in buying only soft drinks at his restaurant. His french fries also are probably priced too low. His burger, however, is priced too high relative to that of his competitors. But if Mark uses the price blending concept, and if he assumes that each customer coming into his restaurant will buy a burger, french fries, and a soft drink, he can still achieve his overall cost objective as seen in Figure 5.15.

Note that Mark has actually achieved food cost slightly lower than 40%. His hamburger price is now less than one dollar and in line with his local competitors. Note also, however, that Mark has assumed that each customer will buy one of each item. In reality, of course, not all customers will select one of each item. Some customers will not elect fries, while others may stop in only for a soft drink. It is for this reason that percent selecting figures, discussed in Chapter 3, are so

Figure 5.14 **Mark's Burgers**

Item	Item Cost	Desired Food Cost %	Proposed Selling Price
Hamburger	$ .75	40%	$1.88
French fries	.16	40	.40
Soft drinks (12 oz)	.09	40	.23
Total	1.00	40	2.51

Figure 5.15 **Mark's Burgers**

Item	Item Cost	Proposed Food Cost %	Proposed Selling Price
Hamburger	$ .75	75.7%	$ .99
French fries	.16	20.2	.79
Soft drinks (12 oz)	.09	11.4	.79
Total	1.00	38.9	2.57

critical. They let Mark know exactly what his customers are buying when they visit his outlet. He can apply percent selecting figures to his menu if he has kept them. In his operation, these figures are not yet available, so he monitors his first 100 customers and finds the results presented in Figure 5.16.

As you see, Mark can use the price blending concept to achieve his overall cost objectives if he has a good understanding of how many people buy each menu item. Mark now has the 40% food cost he sought. It matters little if the burger has a 75.7% food cost *if* the burger is sold in conjunction with the soft drink. Obviously, there is a danger if Mark's customers begin to order nothing but hamburgers when they come to his establishment. Again, careful and continual monitoring of consumer preference will allow Mark to make price adjustments, as needed, to keep his overall costs in line. A word of caution regarding the use of price blending is, however, in order. Since price itself is one of the factors that impact percent selecting figures, a change in menu price may cause a change in item popularity. If, in an effort to reduce overall product cost percentage, Mark were to increase the price of soft drinks, for example, he might find that a higher percentage of customers would elect not to purchase a soft drink. This could have the effect of actually increasing his overall product cost percentage, since fewer customers would choose to buy the one item with an extremely low product cost percentage.

Discounting

Two-for-one specials, discount coupons, and other promotional efforts can have a major impact on menu pricing strategy. When marketing efforts are combined with menu pricing decisions, a great impact on bottom line profits can result. The foodservice manager who desires to fully understand this complex issue is referred to the book *Menu Pricing and Strategy*, by Jack Miller, which contains an excellent, in-depth discussion of this important topic.

The sales mix and the concept of price blending have a major impact on overall menu price structure. Some restaurants offer low-priced specials to attract

Figure 5.16 **Mark's Burgers Sales Mix**

Total Income: $221.43 Customers Served: 100

Total Food Expense: $88.82 Food Cost %: 40.1%

Item	Number Sold	Item Cost	Total Cost	Selling Price	Total Income	Cost %
Hamburger	92	$.75	$69.00	$.99	$ 91.08	75.7%
French fries	71	.16	11.36	.79	56.09	20.2
Soft drink (12 oz)	94	.09	8.46	.79	74.26	11.4
Total			88.82		221.43	40.1

customers who may then also select a higher-priced item. Others adjust prices to meet new competition or changing consumer preferences. In all cases, product pricing is an important, powerful management tool in the hands of an effective foodservice manager. A thorough study of this area is well worth the manager's time investment.

Assigning Menu Price

The methods used to assign menu price are as varied as foodservice managers themselves. In general, however, menu pricing is most often assigned on the basis of one of the following two concepts:

1. **Product cost percentage**
2. **Contribution margin**

Product Cost Percentage

This method of pricing is based on the idea that product cost should be a predetermined percentage of selling price. For example, Tina, a foodservice manager, has a menu item that costs $1.50 to produce, and her desired cost percentage equals 40. She can determine what the item's selling price should be by using the food cost percentage formula as follows:

$$\frac{\textbf{Cost of product}}{\textbf{Selling price}} = \frac{\textbf{\$1.50}}{\textbf{Unknown}} = \textbf{40\%}$$

Or

$$\frac{\textbf{\$1.50}}{\textbf{Unknown}} = \textbf{40\%}$$

To solve for this unknown, one simply divides the cost of food by the desired food cost percentage according to the following formula:

$$\frac{\textbf{Cost of product}}{\textbf{Desired product cost \%}} = \textbf{Selling price}$$

In our example, the result is

$$\frac{\textbf{\$1.50}}{\textbf{.40}} = \textbf{\$3.75}$$

Thus, the recommended selling price, given a $1.50 product cost, is $3.75.

If the item is sold for \$3.75, then a 40% food cost will be achieved for that item. A check on this calculation can be done using the food cost percentage formula:

$$\frac{\$1.50}{\$3.75} = 40\%$$

When management uses a predetermined food cost percentage to price menu items, it is stating its belief that product cost in relationship to selling price is of vital importance. Experienced foodservice managers know that a factor can be assigned to each desired food cost percentage. This factor, when multiplied by the product cost, will result in a selling price that yields the desired food cost percentage. Figure 5.17 details such a factor table.

In each case, the factor is arrived at by the following formula:

$$\frac{100}{\text{Desired product cost \%}} = \text{Pricing factor}$$

Thus, if one were attempting to price a product and achieve a product cost of 40%, the computation would be as follows:

$$\frac{100}{40\%} = 2.5$$

This pricing factor of 2.5, when multiplied by any product cost, will yield a selling price that is based on a 40% product cost. The formula is as follows:

$$\text{Pricing factor} \times \text{Product cost} = \text{Selling price}$$

To return to our example of Tina, she could use the above formula to

Figure 5.17 **Pricing Factor Table**

Desired Product Cost %	Factor
20%	5.000
23	4.348
25	4.000
28	3.571
30	3.333
33⅓	3.000
35	2.857
38	2.632
40	2.500
43	2.326
45	2.222

determine selling price if she hopes to achieve a 40% product cost and her item costs $1.50 to produce.

2.5 × $1.50 = $3.75

As can be seen, these two methods of arriving at a proposed selling price yield the same results. One formula simply relies on division, while the other relies on multiplication. The decision about which formula to use is completely up to the individual foodservice manager. With either approach, the selling price will be determined with a goal of achieving a given product cost percentage for each item. Obviously, due to sales mix and the price blending concept, the appropriate product cost percentage desired for any given item may vary according to management's view of the appropriate selling price for that menu item.

Contribution Margin

A second approach to menu pricing is to focus not on product cost percentage but rather on a menu item's contribution margin. Contribution margin, in this case, is defined as the profit or margin that remains after product cost is subtracted from an item's selling price. Thus, if an item sells for $3.75 and the product cost for this item is $1.50, the contribution margin would be computed as follows:

Selling price − Product cost = Contribution margin

or

$3.75 − $1.50 = $2.25

When this approach is used, the formula for determining selling price is as follows:

Product cost + Contribution margin desired = Selling price

Establishing menu price, in this case, is a simple matter of combining product cost with that predetermined contribution margin. Management's role here is to determine desired contribution margins for each menu item. Generally speaking, when using this approach, management establishes different contribution margins for various menu items or groups. For example, in a cafeteria, entrées may be priced with a contribution margin of $1.50 each, desserts with a contribution margin of $.75, and drinks, perhaps, with a contribution margin of $.50. Again, menu price would be established by combining desired contribution margin with actual product cost.

Product Cost Percentage or Contribution Margin?

Proponents exist for both of these approaches to menu pricing. Indeed, there are additional venues to menu pricing, beyond the scope of an introduction to pricing theory. Some large foodservice organizations have established highly complex computer-driven formulas for determining appropriate menu prices. For the average foodservice operator, however, product cost percentage, contribution margin, or a combination of both will suffice when attempting to arrive at appropriate pricing decisions.

While the debate over the best pricing method is likely to continue for some time, the effective foodservice operator will view pricing not as an attempt to take advantage of the customer, but rather as an important process with an end goal of setting a good price/value relationship in the mind of the consumer.

Each foodservice manager may, of course, have his or her own method of pricing menu items. In all cases, however, pricing is based on the cost of goods sold. This includes all expenses incurred by the operation. It is not appropriate, however, for management to pass on to consumers the cost of production errors or simple managerial inefficiencies. If management is not committed to controlling expenses, and thus providing consumers with high-quality products at fair prices, the operation will suffer. Regardless of whether the pricing method used is based on food cost percentage or contribution margin, the selling price selected must provide for a predetermined operational profit. For this reason, it is important that the menu not be priced so low that no profit is possible or so high that we will never be able to sell the menu items. In the final analysis, it is the market that will eventually determine what our sales will be on any given item. Being sensitive to both required profit and our customers—their needs, wants and desires—is very critical to a pricing philosophy. *Menu Pricing and Strategy*, by Jack Miller, provides an excellent treatment of the menu development, marketing strategies, price support systems, and pricing strategies necessary to effectively design and assign price to a menu. It is highly recommended as a management aid.

Special Pricing Situations

Some pricing decisions faced by foodservice managers call for a unique approach. Note the following:

1. **Salad bars and buffets**
2. **Bottled wine**
3. **Beverages at receptions and parties**

Salad Bars and Buffets

The difficulty in establishing a set price for either a salad bar or buffet is, of course, that total portion cost can vary greatly from one customer to the next. A person weighing 100 pounds will most likely consume less product from a buffet or an all-you-can-eat line than will a 300-pound person. The general rule, however, is that each of these consumers will pay the same price to go through the salad bar or buffet line. Some operators prefer to establish a per-ounce charge, especially for salad bars. In this situation, rather than paying one flat price, patrons actually pay for the amount taken. Short of charging customers for the amount they actually consume, a method of determining selling price must be established. This price must yield an overall acceptable cost for the average diner who selects the all-you-can-eat option.

This price may be different, of course, if the average clients are 300-pound males rather than 100-pound females. The point is that the selling price must be established and monitored so that either customer can be accommodated. This can be accomplished rather easily if record keeping is accurate and timely. The secret to keeping selling price low in a salad bar or buffet situation is to apply the ABC inventory approach. That is, A items, which are expensive, should comprise no more than 20% of the total product available. B items, which are moderate in price, should comprise about 30% of the item offerings. And C items, which are inexpensive, should comprise 50% of the offerings. Using this approach, a menu listing of items can be prepared to ensure that items that stay within these predetermined ranges are selected for sale.

Regardless of the items to be sold, their usage must be accurately recorded. Consider the case of David, who operates Lotus Gardens, an Oriental restaurant where patrons pay one price but may return as often as they like to a buffet table. David closely monitors both product usage and customers served, using a form like the one presented in Figure 5.18. David uses the ABC method to categorize menu items. He also notes the amount of product he puts on the buffet to begin the meal period (beginning amount), any additions during the meal period (additions), and the amount of usable product left at the conclusion of the meal period (ending amount). From this information, David can compute his total product usage, and thus his total product cost.

Based on the data in Figure 5.18, David knows that his total product cost for January 1 was $162.54. He can then use the following formula to determine cost per guest:

$$\frac{\textbf{Total product cost}}{\textbf{Guests served}} = \textbf{Product cost per guest}$$

In this example,

$$\frac{\$162.54}{125} = \$1.30$$

Thus, David has a portion cost per guest of $1.30. He can use this information and establish a menu price that he feels is appropriate. David's product cost per guest will vary somewhat each day. This is not a cause for great concern. Minor variations in product cost per guest should be covered if selling price is properly established. By monitoring buffet costs on a regular basis, management can be assured that it will keep good control over both cost per guest and the appropriate selling price.

Figure 5.18 **Salad Bar or Buffet Product Usage**

Unit Name: Lotus Gardens Date: 1/1/93

Item	Category	Beginning Amount	Additions	Ending Amount	Total Usage	Unit Cost	Total Cost
Sweet & sour pork	A	6 lbs	44 lbs	8.5 lbs	41.5 lbs	$2.20/lb	$ 91.30
Bean sprouts	B	3 lbs	17 lbs	2 lbs	18 lbs	.80/lb	14.40
Egg rolls	B	40	85	17	108	.28 ea	30.24
Fried rice	C	10 lbs	21.5 lbs	8.5 lbs	23 lbs	.30/lb	6.90
Steamed rice	C	10 lbs	30 lbs	6.5 lbs	33.5 lbs	.20/lb	6.70
Wonton soup	C	2 gal	6 gal	1 ½ gal	6.5 gal	2.00/gal	13.00
Total product cost							162.54

Total Product Cost: $162.54

Guests Served: 125 Cost per Guest: $1.30

Bottled Wine

While the National Restaurant Association reports that alcohol consumption in the United States declined from 41.8 gallons per capita in 1980 to 39.5 gallons in 1990, wine sales in restaurants were up during the same period. Part of this increase is accounted for by a realization on the part of the American public that wine is both a beverage of moderation and a wonderful addition to any meal. Just as important, however, may be the fact that restaurant operators are changing the way they price wine by the bottle.

Consider the case of Claudia, who operates a fine Italian restaurant. Claudia attempts to achieve an overall wine cost in her restaurant of 25%. Using the factor method of pricing, Claudia multiplies by four the cost of each bottle of wine she sells to arrive at her desired selling price. Listed below are the four wines she sells, and the costs and selling prices associated with each kind.

Wine	Product Cost	Selling Price	Product Cost %
1	$ 3.00	$12.00	25%
2	6.00	24.00	25
3	15.00	60.00	25
4	20.00	80.00	25

Claudia decides that she would like to explore the contribution margin approach to wine pricing. She therefore computes the contribution margin (selling price − product cost) for each wine she sells, and finds the results below:

Wine	Selling Price	Product Cost	Contribution Margin
1	$12.00	$ 3.00	$ 9.00
2	24.00	6.00	18.00
3	60.00	15.00	45.00
4	80.00	20.00	60.00

Her conclusion is that she may be hurting sales of wines 3 and 4 by pricing these products too high, even though they are priced to achieve a 25% product cost. In the case of bottled wine, the contribution margin approach to price can be used to the operator's advantage. Consumers appear to be quite price conscious when it comes to bottled wine. When operators seek to achieve profits consumers feel are inappropriate, bottled wine sales may decline. Presented below is an alternative pricing structure Claudia has developed for use in her restaurant. She must, however, give this price structure a test run and monitor its affect on overall product sales and profitability if she is to determine whether her pricing strategy will be effective.

Wine	Product Cost	Selling Price	Contribution Margin	Product Cost %
1	$ 3.00	$17.00	$14.00	17.6%
2	6.00	22.00	16.00	27.3
3	15.00	33.00	18.00	45.5
4	20.00	39.00	19.00	51.3

Note that while selling price has been increased in the case of wine #1, it has been reduced for wines #2, #3, and #4. Contribution margin still is higher for wine #4 than for wine #1. The difference, however, is not as dramatic as before. Product cost percentages have, of course, been altered due to the selling price changes Claudia is proposing. Note also that the price spread, defined as the range between the lowest and the highest priced menu item, has been drastically reduced. Where the price spread was previously between $12 and $80, it is now between $17 and $39. This reduction in price spread may assist Claudia in selling more, and higher priced, wine. Again, she must monitor sales and determine if her strategy is successful. As a general rule, pricing bottled wine only by the product percentage method is a strategy that may result in overall decreased bottled wine sales. In this specific case, the effective manager is attuned to both product cost percentage and contribution margin.

Beverages at Receptions and Parties

Pricing beverages for open bar receptions and special events can be very difficult, but the reason for this is very simple. Each consumer group can be expected to behave somewhat differently when attending an open bar or hosted bar function. Clearly, we would not expect the guests at a formal wedding reception to consume as many drinks during a one-hour period as a group of fun-loving individuals who are celebrating a sports victory.

Establishing a price per person in these two cases would result in quite different numbers. One way to solve this problem is to charge each guest for what he or she consumes. In reality, however, many party hosts want their guests to consume beverage products without having to pay for each drink. When this is the case, management is forced to charge the host either for the amount of beverage consumed or on a per person, per hour basis. In this scenario, the foodservice operator estimates how much the average attendee will consume during the party or reception, and a per person charge is established. For example, the food and beverage director of the Carlton Resort is approached by Mr. A. His daughter, Shanna, is marrying Luis. Mr. A. would like all of the wedding guests to drink as much champagne during the reception as they would like. His question is "How much will I be charged if 100 guests attend?" Clearly, an answer of "I don't know" or "It depends on how much they drink" is inappropriate. It is our business to know the answer to such questions. The effective food and beverage director must know from past records what the average consumption *for a group of this type* has been. Records for this purpose must be maintained. Figure 5.19 is an example of one such device, used at the Carlton Resort. Note that average consumption of any product type can be recorded. In this example, the food and beverage director has written down the data from the wedding of Mr. A.'s daughter so that she can be better prepared in the future to answer the question "How much will I be charged if 100 guests attend?"

Note that the form in Figure 5.19 can be used for any type of reception or party where beverages are served. Its correct use requires only a knowledge of total product usage, product cost, and number of guests served. The following formula for determining cost per guest in this case is identical to the one used for determining cost per guest in the salad bar or buffet area:

$$\frac{\textbf{Total product cost}}{\textbf{Guests served}} = \textbf{Product cost per guest}$$

In our example of Shanna A.'s wedding,

$$\frac{\$327}{97} = \$3.37$$

The food and beverage director of the Carlton Resort now has a base on which to build her knowledge of normal or average consumption of champagne at a wedding reception. As stated earlier, every group can be expected to behave somewhat differently, but the experienced food and beverage director or sales

Figure 5.19 **Beverage Consumption Report**

Event: Shanna/Luis Wedding Date: 1/1/93

Unit Name: Carlton Resort

Beverage Type	Beginning Amount	Additions	Total Available	Ending Amount	Total Usage	Unit Cost	Total Cost
Liquor A							
B							
C							
D							
E							
F							
G							
Beer A							
B							
C							
D							
E							
Wine A							
B							
C							
D							
Other: Champagne: A. Sparkling B. Sparkling pink	 8 bottles 8 bottles	 24 24	 32 32	 9 11	 23 21	 $6.00/btl 9.00/btl	 $138.00 189.00
Total product cost							327.00

Total Product Cost: $327.00 Cost per Guest: $3.37

Guests Served: 97

Remarks: Mild group; very orderly; no problems; beautiful bride!

associate takes this variation into account when establishing the selling price for the open bar or open reception situation.

Determining Actual Product Cost

If pricing decisions are to be made on a rational basis, they must be supported by accurate product cost data. For this reason, we now turn our attention to answering an important series of questions:

1. **What are our actual product costs?**
2. **What should our product costs be?**
3. **How close are we to this attainable goal?**

Determining Actual Product Cost

Knowledge of actual product cost begins with a standardized recipe cost for each menu item. Just as each menu item should have a standardized recipe, it should also have a standardized recipe cost sheet on file in the manager's office. This cost sheet provides management with up-to-date information that can help with pricing decisions in addition to assisting in the determination of attainable food cost. Figure 5.20 shows the format Jennifer, who operates a small soup and sandwich carryout kiosk, uses to cost the standardized recipes in her operation. This recipe is for beef stew and, as can be seen, yields a cost per portion of 53.4 cents. A standard recipe cost sheet can be produced today using a personal computer and one of the many software packages on the market. This formerly tedious task has become so simplified there is no reason for management not to have accurate, up-to-date costings on all its recipes. To do any less would mean that we are selling items for a set price when we have no idea what we ourselves are paying for those items!

When costing standardized recipes, most foodservice managers prefer to use whole cent figures rather than fractions of a cent. In addition, many elect to omit individual seasoning costs completely. They prefer to add a predetermined fixed cost to those standardized recipes that contain seasonings. This amount, a percentage of total recipe cost, is determined annually. Thus, if 3% represents the total product category of seasoning cost per year, then 3% would be added to the total ingredient cost of each recipe to account for seasonings. Still others prefer to identify spices as high- or low-cost, and then assign a fixed amount to these categories. In our example, salt is designated as a low-cost spice, and a $.05 cost is assigned to two tablespoons of product. Pepper is identified as a high-cost spice, and $.10 has been added to the total recipe to account for its usage. Note that all ingredients are to be costed in their edible portion or EP state. This is extremely important due to the need for accuracy in costing recipes. If EP costs are to be accurate, the effective foodservice manager must thoroughly under-

Figure 5.20 **Standardized Recipe Cost Sheet**

Menu Item: Beef Stew

Special Notes: All ingredients weighed as EP

Recipe Yield: 40

Portion Size: 8 oz

Portion Cost: $.534

Ingredients		**Ingredient Cost**	
Item	**Amount**	**Unit Cost**	**Total Cost**
Corn, frozen	3 lbs	$ .30/lb	$ .90
Tomatoes	3 lbs	.70/lb	2.10
Potatoes	5 lbs	.20/lb	1.00
Beef cubes	5 lbs	2.79/lb	13.95
Carrots	2 lbs	.18/lb	.36
Water	2 gal	N/A	—
Salt	2 T	.15/lb	.05
Pepper	2 t	6.00/lb	.10
Garlic	1 clove	.40/clove	.40
Tomato juice	1 qt	2.00/gal	.50
Onions	4 lbs	.50/lb	2.00
Total cost			21.36

Total Recipe Cost: $21.36

Portion Cost: $.534

Previous Portion Cost: $.512

Recipe Number: 146

Dated Costed: 1/1/92

Previous Dated Costed: 7/1/91

stand the concept of product yield presented in Chapter 3, and the effect of that yield on costs. It is to this matter that Jennifer must turn her attention if she wants to be sure that her standardized recipe costs data are accurate.

Yield Testing

In order to determine actual recipe costs, it may sometimes be necessary to conduct a yield test to determine actual EP ingredient costs. In our example,

Jennifer costed the beef stew recipe (Figure 5.20) and in the process needed to determine the cost of five pounds of beef cubes to be used in its preparation. Since beef accounts for a major portion of the total recipe cost, Jennifer wants to make sure that she computed the cost of the beef cubes accurately. Jennifer knows that AP meat prices do not account for loss due to trimming, cooking, or carving; thus these activities, if undertaken, will impact the EP cost of the meat products. Of course, the same is true for many vegetables, fruits, seafood, and other products.

To determine actual EP cost of the beef cubes, Jennifer purchases ten pounds of beef short ribs from which she cuts her beef stew meat. She knows that she will have losses because of bone and fat removal, but unlike some other products she sells, such as roast beef, she will have no cooking or slicing loss. Jennifer uses a form such as the one presented in Figure 5.19 to determine all her EP meat yields and thus her cost per portion. In the case of the short ribs for beef stew, Jennifer conducts a yield test and finds the data listed in Figure 5.21.

The net product yield for beef cubes equals 64.4%. This can be determined by the following formula:

$$\frac{\textbf{Product loss}}{\textbf{AP weight}} = \textbf{Net waste \%}$$

In this example total product loss is 3 pounds and 9 ounces. We convert all pounds to ounces for ease of computation; thus our product loss of 3 pounds 9

Figure 5.21 **Butcher's Yield Test Results**

Item: Beef cubes

Unit Name: Jennifer's

Date Tested: 1/1/93

Specification: #842

Item Description: Short ribs

AP Amount Tested: 10 lbs

Price per Pound AP: $1.85

Loss Detail	**Weight**	**% of Original**
AP	10 lbs 0 oz	100%
Fat loss	1 lb 6 oz	13.8
Bone loss	2 lb 3 oz	21.8
Cooking loss	0	0
Carving loss	0	0
Total product loss	3 lb 9 oz	35.6

Net Product Yield: 64.4%

Cost per Servable Pound: $2.87

Yield Test Performed by: T.J.

ounces becomes 48 ounces + 9 ounces, which equals 57 ounces. Our as-purchased or AP weight of ten pounds equals 10 times 16 ounces, or 160 ounces, resulting in the following:

$$\frac{\textbf{57 oz}}{\textbf{160 oz}} = \textbf{35.6\% net waste}$$

To determine product yield %, management simply subtracts net waste % from 1.00. In our example, the net product yield % is therefore determined to be 1.00 − .356 = .644. Another way to determine net product yield % is to compute it directly using the following formula:

$$\frac{\textbf{EP weight}}{\textbf{AP weight}} = \textbf{Product yield \%}$$

In our example, EP weight is equal to AP weight of 10 pounds minus the product loss of 3 pounds 9 ounces. Thus, EP weight equals 6 pounds 7 ounces (103 oz), and product yield % is computed as follows:

$$\frac{\textbf{103 oz}}{\textbf{160 oz}} = \textbf{64.4\%}$$

To compute actual EP cost, Jennifer must now simply divide the AP price per pound by the Product Yield % to determine cost per servable pound. In our example, with AP price per pound of short ribs at $1.85 and a product yield of .644, the cost per servable pound would be $2.87, which is computed using the cost per servable pound formula:

$$\frac{\textbf{AP price per pound}}{\textbf{Product yield \%}} = \textbf{Cost per servable pound}$$

Or

$$\frac{\textbf{\$1.85}}{\textbf{.644}} = \textbf{\$2.87}$$

Jennifer knows now that her actual cost per servable pound when buying short ribs of *this particular specification* is $2.87. Jennifer should conduct additional butcher yield tests if she is considering changing suppliers or her beef short rib specifications. In addition, Jennifer will conduct yield tests on all of her meat items at least twice per year.

Determining Attainable Product Cost

If foodservice managers are to draw reasonable conclusions regarding operational efficiency, they must be able to compare how well they are doing with how well they **should** be doing. This process, which is positively necessary, begins with determining **attainable food cost**. Attainable food cost is defined as the cost of goods consumed figure that should be achievable given the product sales mix of a particular operation. Simply put, when we compare attainable food cost to actual food cost, we get a measure of operational efficiency. The formula for this operational efficiency ratio is as follows:

$$\frac{\textbf{Actual product cost}}{\textbf{Attainable product cost}} = \textbf{Operational efficiency ratio}$$

To illustrate: if Jennifer, operating her kiosk, determines her attainable product cost to be $850 for the week and has an actual product cost of $850 for that same period, her operational efficiency ratio would look as follows:

$$\frac{\textbf{\$850.00 actual product cost}}{\textbf{\$850.00 attainable product cost}} = \textbf{100\%}$$

This would represent perfection in the relationship between attainable and actual operational results. More likely, however, if attainable product cost were $850, actual product cost would be higher, say $900. In this case, the formula would be computed as follows:

$$\frac{\textbf{\$900.00 actual product cost}}{\textbf{\$850.00 attainable product cost}} = \textbf{\$105.9\%}$$

In this case, Jennifer knows that her actual product usage is 5.9% higher than her attainable goal.

Chapter 3 described the method used to determine actual product usage through the cost of goods consumed formula. Attainable food cost is determined through the use of a form as illustrated in Figure 5.22.

As is evident, total product cost for January 1, as determined by the standardized recipes, should have been $187.20. Sales were $727.50. Jennifer would know her attainable food cost through the use of the following formula:

$$\frac{\textbf{Cost as per standardized recipes}}{\textbf{Total sales}} = \textbf{Attainable food cost}$$

In our example then,

$$\frac{\textbf{\$187.20}}{\textbf{\$727.50}} = \textbf{25.7\%}$$

Note that this cost excludes any losses due to overcooking, overportioning, waste, theft, and the like. Therefore, the attainable food cost is rarely achieved. Every foodservice operation employs people, and people make errors at work. Through the use of the operational efficiency ratio, however, management can answer the question made famous by former mayor of New York Ed Koch: "How'm I doing?"

Figure 5.22 **Attainable Food Cost**

Unit Name: Jennifer's

Date Prepared: 1/8/93 Time Period: 1/1/93

Prepared by: J.C.

Item	Number Sold	Portion Cost	Total Cost	Menu Price	Total Sales
Beef stew	50	$.53	$ 26.50	$ .95	$ 47.50
Corn chowder	40	.22	8.80	.95	38.00
Ham & beans	60	.41	24.60	.95	57.00
Turkey	30	.51	15.30	2.95	88.50
Ham	90	.60	54.00	2.60	234.00
Roast beef	25	.87	21.75	2.95	73.75
Coffee	75	.10	7.50	.85	63.75
Soda	125	.23	28.75	1.00	125.00
Total			187.20		727.50

The attainable food cost and thus the operational efficiency ratio are designed to address just that issue. In general, operational efficiency ratings in the 90s are attainable; variances that are too high or too low indicate serious control problems. The operational efficiency rating can, of course, be shared with employees, since they also are interested in the question "How are *we* doing?"

Reducing Overall Product Cost Percentage

Once management has determined what costs actually are and has compared them to what costs should be, we often find that Walt Kelly's Pogo character was correct when he said, "We have met the enemy, and they is us!"

Foodservice managers (and their bosses) seem to be on a never-ending quest to reduce food and beverage production costs. While managers must remember to guard against inappropriate cost cutting, they can find themselves in a position where food and beverage production costs must be reduced. When that is the case, effective managers turn to the solutions inherent in the product cost equation.

The food cost percentage equation is extremely interesting. In its simplest form, it can be represented as follows:

$$\frac{A}{B} = C$$

where

A = Cost of goods consumed
B = Unit sales
C = Cost percentage

This formula can, however, become extremely complex. Its analysis occupies many a food organization staff meeting and can give the foodservice operator many sleepless nights! Essentially, only six reduction strategies are available to impact this rather simple formula. A quick algebra lesson, however, prior to our discussion of these six approaches may be useful. In general, the rules of algebra say the following things about the $A / B = C$ formula:

1. **If A is unchanged and B increases, C decreases.**
2. **If A increases at the same proportional rate B increases, C remains unchanged.**
3. **If A decreases while B stays unchanged, C decreases.**
4. **If A increases and B stays unchanged, C increases.**

Put into simple English, these four statements can be translated as follows:

1. **If total costs can be kept constant but sales increase, cost of goods consumed % goes down.**
2. **If costs go up at the same rate sales go up, costs of goods consumed % is unchanged.**
3. **If costs can be reduced but sales remain constant, cost of goods consumed % goes down.**
4. **If costs go up with no increase in sales, cost of goods consumed % goes up.**

Rarely do foodservice operators feel their product costs are too low. In general, foodservice managers work to control the six variables that impact product cost percentages, and thus hope to reduce the overall value of C in the equation. A list of these six approaches to reducing overall product cost percentage and a summary of each follow.

1. **Decrease portion size relative to price.**
2. **Vary recipe composition.**
3. **Adjust product quality.**

4. **Achieve a more favorable sales mix.**
5. **Ensure that all product purchased is sold.**
6. **Increase prices, relative to portion size.**

To reduce food costs, for example, management selects an appropriate strategy from this relatively small number of alternatives. It is the judicious selection and mixing of these approaches that differentiate the successful operator from the unsuccessful one.

Take, for instance, the problem facing Jim, the operator of a small bar. He computes a liquor cost percentage that is four points higher than he has budgeted for. If he has approximately six cost-reducing options available to him, by the mathematics law of permutations this yields ($6 \times 5 \times 4 \times 3 \times 2$) or 720 possible combinations of these differing cost reduction methods. No wonder, then, there is such a plethora of information written about reducing costs!

It is not the authors' contention that all product cost reduction methods are exhausted by these six points, but rather they are presented here as a means of systematically analyzing the various alternatives available. While for illustration purposes these approaches will be applied to reducing beverage cost percentage, they apply equally to food and the cost of goods consumed formula.

Approaches to Reducing Beverage Cost Percentage

Decrease Portion Size Relative to Price

Too often, bar operators assume that standard drink sizes must conform to some unwritten rule of uniformity. This is simply not the case. Most customers would prefer one ounce of liquor in a three- or four-ounce glass over one and one-half ounces in a seven-ounce glass. The point here is that a smaller, high-quality, well-proportioned drink is preferable to a drink that may include more liquor but is of such a large size that the customer feels his or her drink is "weak." Glass selection becomes very important here, and most glassware salespersons are more than willing to work with an operator in determining optimal glass sizes for a particular operation.

The table in Figure 5.23 represents the effect on liquor cost percentage of varying the standard drink size served in an operation, using $8.00 per bottle as the standard cost of liquor and assuming a 0.8-ounce evaporation per 33.8 oz. liter bottle. Jim's standard $1.75 selling price per drink is used to determine sales value in each Drink Size category.

Certainly the matter of the perfect drink size is subjective. As such, Jim must determine the proper drink size for his establishment, taking into account such variables as location, price structure, competition, bar atmosphere, and clientele, to name just a few. While the decision about the proper alcohol content of a

Figure 5.23 **Impact of Drink Size on Beverage Cost Percentage**

Drink Size	Drinks per Liter	Cost per Liter	Cost per Drink	Income per Liter	Liquor Cost % per Liter
2 oz	16.5	$8.00	48.5¢	$28.88	27.7%
1¾ oz	18.9	8.00	42.3¢	33.08	24.2
1½ oz	22.0	8.00	36.4¢	38.50	20.8
1¼ oz	26.4	8.00	30.3¢	46.20	17.3
1 oz	33.0	8.00	24.2¢	57.75	13.9

drink calls for the balancing of many factors, the effect on liquor cost percentage in varying this content is unmistakable.

Vary Recipe Composition

The proportion of alcohol to mixer has a profound effect on liquor cost percentage. This is especially true for those specialty drinks that many operators find so profitable. One option available is to replace high-cost items (fresh juices, coconut milk, etc.) with less expensive alternatives. Indeed, overall drink sizes can be increased by the additional use of such bar extenders as milk, juices, and soda. This often contributes to a feeling of satisfaction by the consumer, while allowing the operator to increase profitability. This could also mean reducing the quantity of alcohol per drink, that is, moving from a 1¾ ounce drink to one which uses 1½ ounces of liquor.

Adjust Product Quality

This is definitely an area to be approached with caution. It is true, however, that one should strive to use the quality of product appropriate for its intended use. A *specific* coffee liqueur and cream, when called for, must, of course, include **that** name brand liqueur and cream! It may be wise, however, to use an alternative brand for the many specialty drinks (black Russian, brave bull, black magic, etc.) that include coffee liqueur as a major or minor ingredient. In this example, a generic-type coffee liqueur might be used with totally satisfactory results. This is, of course, just one of many possibilities.

With appropriate care, the cost-effective bar operator can determine the quality of ingredients necessary for his or her operation and then purchase that quality. This is a case where the **appropriate** ingredient may be preferable to the **best** possible ingredient.

Achieve a More Favorable Sales Mix

Typically, each drink Jim sells carries a unique liquor cost percentage. This is true because many operators set standard drink prices and ignore minor variances in the cost of differing types of liquor. Most operators, for example, set a particular price for each type of drink they sell. One and one-half ounces of all well liquors plus cola may sell for the same price. The various ingredients that make up these drinks, however, do not all represent the same cost to the operator. There exists small differences in liquor cost percentages for these various drinks. The weighted total of these various percentages, due to the sales mix concept, yields the overall liquor cost percentage.

The selection of drinks that one wishes to market heavily has a distinct effect on total profitability. Figure 5.24 illustrates the effect of a shift in consumer buying habits away from a high-cost item to a more profitable one. That is, it shows how the sales mix concept can be used to vary profitability.

While the difference in overall liquor cost percentage in this illustration is only 2.1% (25.6 − 23.5 = 2.1), it represents an increase in profit per drink of about $.45 minus $.41, or 4 cents. In cost control, it's the little things that add up. If Jim is open 365 days a year and serves 100 drinks per day, and each drink costs 4 cents more than it should, the net result on his costs is an increase of 365 × 100 × .04 = $1,460.00. Effective merchandising of the right product has a positive effect on profitability while at the same time allowing the portion size to remain constant.

Ensure that All Product Purchased is Sold

These seven words have tremendous implications. They include all phases of purchasing, receiving, storage, inventory, issuing, and cash control. Perhaps the hospitality industry's greatest challenge in the area of cost control is ensuring that all products, once purchased, do indeed generate cash that makes it to the bank!

Figure 5.24 **Impact of Sales Mix on Beverage Cost Percentage**

	Income per Drink	Number Sold	Total Income	Cost per Drink	Total Cost	Liquor Cost %
Rum/cola	$1.75	60	$105.00	$.52	$31.20	29.7%
Fruit brandy/cola	1.75	40	70.00	.34	13.60	19.4
Combination #1 total		100	175.00	.45	44.80	25.6
Rum/cola	1.75	40	70.00	.52	20.80	29.7
Fruit brandy/cola	1.75	60	105.00	.34	20.40	19.4
Combination #2 total		100	175.00	.41	41.20	23.5

Increase Prices Relative to Portion Size

This area must be approached with the greatest caution of all. There is no greater temptation in foodservice than to raise prices in an effort to conceal an ineffectiveness at controlling costs. This temptation must be resisted. There are times, of course, when prices on selected items must be increased. This is especially true in inflationary times. Price increases should be considered, however, only when all attempts to control costs have been effectively implemented. Any price increases should reflect only increases in our costs, not our inefficiency.

On the other hand, many operators are afraid to be 25 or 50 cents higher per menu item than their competition. In some instances, keeping prices in line with the competition is a good strategy. Frequently, however, decor, quality of product, and service may indeed allow an effective operator to be slightly higher in price than the competition. Given the proper ambience, most consumers will not react negatively to small variances in prices.

Summary

Managing the food and beverage production process effectively is indeed at the heart of all foodservice operations. The combination of equipment and product, and employee and customer make the foodservice industry one of the most fascinating professions in the world. The foodservice manager who finds joy and a challenge in this process is well on his or her way to a successful foodservice management career. All of the preplanning, ordering, receiving, storing, and issuing systems in the world are for naught if the product cannot be produced well and delivered to the customer with a sense of style and hospitality. Cost control systems can never take the place of the sense of welcome we must impart to our customers. The latter must remain a priority; the former are additions to the personal attention we give our guests—not substitutions for it!

Managing the food and beverage production process is a complex task, but it must, of course, be accomplished with the utmost grace and skill. After the customer has been served, however, management's concern must turn to the analysis of the non-product costs of that service. It is to this task we next turn our attention.

TEST YOUR SKILLS

A. Teri would like to add a new menu item to her standard menu. Upper management has approved such an addition if her total product cost percentage does not exceed 31.5% of her allowable selling price. The selling price allowed is $4.95. Using the standardized recipe cost information below, can Teri add the new menu item?

Standardized Recipe Cost Sheet

Menu Item: Dave's Pork Surprise

Special Notes: Boston butt net product yield = 71.5%

Recipe Yield: 24

Portion Size: 5 oz

Portion Cost:

Ingredients		Ingredient Cost	
Item	**Amount**	**Unit Cost**	**Total Cost**
Boston butt	10 lbs	$2.95/lb	29.50
Jones Spicy Sauce	4 oz	4.00/lb	1.00
Onion	8 oz	.60/lb	.30
Water	1/4 C	N/A	
Salt	2 T	.20/lb	.05
Pepper	1 t	6.00/lb	.10
Garlic	1 clove	.60/clove	.60
Pineapple juice	1/2 C	1.89/gal	.06
Total cost			31.61

Total Recipe Cost: 31.61

Portion Cost: 1.32

Previous Portion Cost:

Recipe Number:

Dated Costed:

Previous Dated Costed:

B. Sabrina operates a take-out cookie store in the mall. Business is good, and customers seem to enjoy the products. Her employees, mostly young teens, are a problem since they seem to like to eat the products also. Sabrina takes a physical inventory on a weekly basis. This week, her total cost of goods consumed figure was $590.95. Sabrina has determined that this week she will also compute her attainable food cost and her operational efficiency ratio.

Help Sabrina by completing the following information using the attainable food cost form.

Actual Product Cost: $580.95

Attainable Product Cost: 623.24 (33.7%)

Operational Efficiency Ratio: 93%

Attainable Food Cost

Unit Name: Sabrina's

Date Prepared: ________ Time Period: 1/1 to 1/7

Prepared by: ________

Item	Number Sold	Portion Cost	Total Cost	Menu Price	Total Sales
Chocolate chip	85 doz	$1.32	112.20	$3.40/doz	289.00
Macadamia	60 doz	1.61	96.60	4.10/doz	246.00
Coconut chip	70 doz	.83	58.10	2.95/doz	206.50
Fudge	141 doz	1.42	200.22	3.80/doz	535.80
M & M	68 doz	1.39	94.52	3.40/doz	231.20
Soft drinks	295	.16	47.20	.85	221.25
Coffee	160	.09	14.40	.75	120.00
Total			623.24		1849.75

C. Mary operates a midsize Bar-B-Q restaurant in a large southwestern town. She specializes in serving mesquite-roasted meats and fresh, tasty salads. Recently, the price of buffalo shank, one of Mary's best-selling items, has doubled.

List the six alternative methods of reducing overall food cost percentage that relate to this problem.

Alternatives

1.
2.
3.
4.
5.
6.

Which alternative or combination of alternatives would you select to solve Mary's problem? Why?

CHAPTER 6

Managing the Cost of Labor

OVERVIEW

This chapter details the techniques used to establish and monitor labor cost standards. Factors affecting labor productivity as well as methods for improving productivity are presented. The chapter will discuss employee scheduling, based on established labor standards, as well as the computation of labor cost percentage and other measures of labor productivity.

HIGHLIGHTS

At the conclusion of this chapter, the manager will be able to

- **A. Develop appropriate labor standards for use in any foodservice operation**
- **B. Schedule employee labor hours required, based on anticipated sales volume**
- **C. Analyze actual labor utilization**

Labor Expense in the Hospitality Industry

Having the correct amount of food and beverage in the operation to serve guests is important. Knowing how those products should be prepared is vital also. Consider, however, the case of Pauline, who operates the cafeteria of a large urban hospital. Generally speaking, the quality of food she provides is quite good. Both hospital staff and patients' visitors, who constitute the majority of her customers, have good things to say about the quality of her food. They complain often, however, about the slowness of her cafeteria line, the dirty tables during the busy lunch hour, and the frequent running out of items on both the beverage and the salad bars. Pauline feels that she needs more people, but remembers a few years ago when she was a line server and realizes that there are actually more people on duty in the cafeteria today than when she was a line worker. Of course, business is now better. Many more customers are served per day than when Pauline was on the line. Her question is "Do I have the right number of workers scheduled at the right times for the number of customers I anticipate today?" Unfortunately, Pauline is so busy helping her employees get through the meal periods that there seems to be little time for thinking and planning about strategies and techniques she will have to apply if she is to solve her labor-related problems. When labor was inexpensive, Pauline might have responded to her employee shortage by simply adding more employees. Today's foodservice manager does not have that luxury. In today's labor market, other methods must be employed to accomplish necessary tasks and stay within the allotted labor budget.

In the past, labor-related expenses were much less important to the foodservice manager than they are today. In some foodservice establishments, the cost of labor actually exceeds the cost of food and beverage products. Today's shrinking work force would indicate that future foodservice managers will find it more and more difficult to recruit, train, and retain an effective cadre of employees. Therefore, the control of labor expenses takes on a greater level of importance than ever before. In some sectors of the foodservice industry, a reputation for long hours, poor pay, and undesirable working conditions has caused quality employees to look elsewhere for a more satisfactory job or career. When labor costs are adequately controlled, however, management has the funds necessary to both create desirable working conditions and pay a wage necessary to attract the best workers the labor pool has to offer.

Labor Expense Defined

Labor expense includes salaries and wages (sometimes called payroll). In addition to salaries and wages, however, the following expenses may be considered as labor-related expenses:

1. **FICA taxes**
2. **Unemployment taxes**
3. **Workmen's compensation**
4. **Group life insurance**
5. **Health insurance**
6. **Pension plan payments**
7. **Employee meals**
8. **Employee training expense**
9. **Employee transportation**
10. **Employee housing**
11. **Vacation/sick leave**

Not all foodservice units will incur all of the above costs. Some will have additional costs, but all operators, regardless of their level of activity, will incur some labor-related expenses. The critical question is "How much should I spend on labor to provide the quality of products and service that I feel is appropriate?" Before turning to that question, it is important to distinguish between the terms **payroll** and **labor expense**.

Payroll

In the general sense, **payroll** refers to the gross pay received by an employee in exchange for his or her work. That is, if an employee earns $5 per hour and works 40 hours for his or her employer, the gross paycheck (the paycheck before any deductions) would be $200 ($5 per hour × 40 hours = $200). This amount is considered a payroll expense.

If the employee is salaried and is paid $800 per week, whether he or she works 40 hours in that week or more than 40 hours, we consider that $800 part of the payroll. Payroll is one part of labor expense.

Labor Expense

Labor expense refers to the **total** of all costs associated with maintaining a foodservice work force and, as such, is always larger than payroll expense. Foodservice managers must keep in mind that total labor expense will always exceed that of payroll. As the cost of providing employee benefits increases or employment taxes go up, labor expense will increase, even if payroll expense remains constant.

Most foodservice operators have total control over their payroll expense. It is therefore often referred to as a **controllable** labor expense. Those labor expenses, on the other hand, over which an operator has little or no control, are called **noncontrollable** labor expenses. These expenses include items such as FICA taxes, insurance premiums, and pension plan payments. In reality, however, the foodservice operator may exert some control even over these noncontrollable labor expenses, as for example, a foodservice manager who works very hard to ensure a well-trained work force in a safe environment and achieves thereby a lower rate on accident and health insurance for his or her employees.

In this chapter, we shall deal primarily with payroll-related expenses. This is in keeping with the concept that they are the most controllable of our labor-related expenses and the ones most managers consider when they are called upon to reduce labor expenses.

Fixed Payroll Versus Variable Payroll

There are generally two types of foodservice payrolls. Some employees are needed simply to open the doors for minimally anticipated business, as for example, a manager whose payroll includes one waiter, one cook, and the manager. In this case, the cost of providing payroll to these three individuals is called a **fixed** or set labor cost. Suppose, however, that the manager anticipates much greater volume on a given day. The increased number of guests expected means that the manager must have two more cooks and two more waitpersons present to handle the additional work load. These additional cooks and waitpersons would be considered **variable** payroll costs. Fixed payroll refers to the minimum number of people or positions necessary to operate the business. Variable payroll is added only when management feels it is necessary to provide extra workers in anticipation of an increase in the number of customers to be served.

Fixed payroll is fixed in the sense that this amount of payroll must be expended to minimally operate the business. Variable payroll is the amount that varies with increased volume and is added by management as needed. As more guests are served, more variable labor is needed. The distinction between fixed and variable labor is an important one, since management has little control over fixed labor expense, but exerts nearly 100% control over variable labor expense.

In order to determine how much labor is needed to operate the business, a foodservice manager must be able to determine how much work each fixed and variable worker can perform. If too few workers are scheduled on any given day, poor service and lack of sales can result as customers go elsewhere. If too many workers are scheduled, payroll and other labor expenses will be too high for the day. The solution is to know how many workers are required, given the estimated number of guests anticipated on any given day. In order to determine this number of workers, management must have a clear idea of the productivity of each employee. **Productivity** is simply the amount of work performed by an employee in a given amount of time.

Assessing Labor Productivity

There are many ways to assess labor productivity. In general, productivity is measured by the following formula:

$$\frac{\textbf{Output}}{\textbf{Input}} = \textbf{Productivity ratio}$$

Take, for example, a restaurant in which 4 waitresses served 60 guests. Using the productivity ratio formula, the **output** is guests served, and the **input** is waitresses employed, as follows:

$$\frac{\textbf{60 guests}}{\textbf{4 waitresses}} = \textbf{15 guests per waitress}$$

This formula demonstrates that for each waitress employed, 15 guests can be served. Our productivity ratio is 1 waitress per 15 guests (1/15), or 15 guests to 1 waitress (15 to 1).

There are many ways of defining foodservice output and input; thus there are several types of productivity ratios. They are helpful in determining the answer to the question "How much should I spend on labor?" The answer, however, is more complicated than it might seem at first glance. Our average waitress can serve 15 guests. How many can a poor waitress serve? How about our best waitress? How much do we pay for our best waitress? Our poorest? Are we better off scheduling our best waitress if we anticipate 20 guests, or should we schedule two of our slower ones? How can the slower waitress be developed into an above average waitress? These are the types of questions that must be answered daily if we are to effectively manage payroll costs. These costs can, however, be managed. Each foodservice operator must develop his or her method for managing payroll because each foodservice unit is different. Consider the differences between managing payroll costs at a small quick-service convenience store and a large banquet kitchen in a convention hotel. While the actual application of the methods may vary, payroll costs in these two units can be controlled by the application of a four-step system designed to aid any foodservice operation.

Managing Payroll Costs

Essentially, the management of payroll costs is a four-step process that includes the following factors:

Step 1. **Determine productivity standards.**
Step 2. **Forecast sales volume.**
Step 3. **Schedule employees using sales forecast and productivity standards.**
Step 4. **Analyze results.**

The first step in controlling payroll costs is to determine productivity standards for the operation. In other words, management must find answers to the questions of how long it should take an employee to do a job and how many employees it takes to do the complete job. It was previously stated that a productivity ratio measured the units of output, such as meals served or guests served, relative to the units of input, such as the number of workers or hours worked. Productivity standards represent what the operation should expect in the way of output per unit of input. Assume, for example, that a cafeteria manager knows that a well-trained, motivated cashier can total seven customer trays per minute during a busy lunch period. Actual payment for these meals will be made at another station at the conclusion of the meal. Seven trays (output) per one minute (input) would be the productivity standard for a cashier totaling trays in this operation. Another standard would be established for the individual responsible for collecting money and making change.

A productivity standard is management's expectation of the productivity ratio of each employee. Establishing productivity standards for every employee is a key management task and the first step in controlling payroll costs. Before we discuss how to establish productivity standards, however, it is important to examine the factors that make workers more productive.

The following are ten key employee-related factors that affect worker productivity:

1. **Training**
2. **Supervision**
3. **Equipment**
4. **Morale**
5. **Scheduling**
6. **Breaks**
7. **Employee selection**
8. **Menu**
9. **Convenience versus scratch preparation**
10. **Service level desired**

Training

Perhaps no area under management control holds greater promise for increased employee productivity than job improvement through training. In fact, the human being is the only asset we can expand without spending large sums of money, but in too many cases, training in the hospitality industry is poor or almost nonexistent. Employees with high productivity ratios are well-trained employees and, frequently, employees with low productivity ratios are poorly trained employees. Every position in a food service operation should have a specific, well-developed, and ongoing training program. Effective training will improve job satisfaction and instill in employees a sense of well-being and accomplishment. It will also reduce confusion, product waste, and loss of customers. In addition, supervisors find that a well-trained work force is easier to manage than one in which the employees are poorly trained. An additional advantage of a well-trained work force is that management will be more effective because of reduced stress, both in terms of work completion and interpersonal relationships.

Effective training begins with a good orientation program. The list below includes some of the questions that most employees raise when they start a new job. The effective manager will identify which items are relevant to the new employee and will take care to provide instruction in each area, in written or verbal form.

1. **Life insurance**
2. **Dental insurance**
3. **Medical insurance**
4. **Payday**
5. **Annual performance review**

6. **Training period**
7. **Dress code**
8. **Telephone call policy**
9. **Smoking policy**
10. **Uniform allowance**
11. **Disciplinary system**
12. **Educational assistance**
13. **Work schedule**
14. **Mandatory meetings**
15. **Tip policy**
16. **Transfers**
17. **Employee meal policy**
18. **Sexual harassment policy**
19. **Lockers/security**
20. **Jury duty**
21. **Leave of absence**
22. **Maternity leave**
23. **Alcohol consumption policy**
24. **Tardy policy**
25. **Attendance**
26. **Sick leave policy**
27. **Vacation policy**
28. **Holidays**
29. **Overtime pay**
30. **Retirement program**
31. **Emergency procedures**
32. **Grievance procedures**

In general, employees want to do a good job for their employer and thus look forward to and enjoy participating in training sessions. Managers who like to train tend to find themselves with motivated workers. Managers who, on the other hand, dislike or can find no time for training usually encounter less-productive, less-motivated individuals.

Training programs need not be elaborate. They must, however, be continual. The development of a training program for any task involves the following:

1. **Determine how the task is to be done.**
2. **Plan the training session.**
3. **Present the training session.**
4. **Evaluate the session's effectiveness.**
5. **Retrain at the proper interval.**

Determine how the task is to be done

Often, jobs can be done in more ways than one. An employee making a salad may elect to clean carrots prior to washing the lettuce, with no effect on the total amount of time it takes to prepare the salad. In other areas, for example, in taking table service orders on a guest check, management may have very specific procedures that must be followed so that both cooks and cashiers can receive the guest's order and process it properly. When management has determined how a task should be completed, that method should be made part of the training program and maintained strictly, unless a better method can be demonstrated. If this is not done, employees will find that "anything goes," and product consistency, along with service levels, will vary tremendously. Employees watch management very carefully. If management is not diligent in the enforcement of standard operating procedures, employees may perform tasks in a manner that is easiest for them. This may, of course, not be the manner that is best for the customer or the operation. This is not to underestimate the value of employee input in job design. Employees should certainly have input into the execution of a task, but once management has made the decision to follow a certain procedure, it must be communicated and enforced. This enforcement is best done through a positive approach. Managers should focus less on people who are "doing it wrong" than on those who are "doing it right." Positive reinforcement and praise, as well as rewarding employees for a job well done, are powerful management tools, since most employees want to be recognized by management for that good job.

Plan the training session

Like any other important management task, the training session must be planned. This includes asking and appropriately answering the following questions:

1. **Who should be trained?**
2. **Who should do the training?**
3. **Where should the training occur?**
4. **When should the session occur?**
5. **What tools, materials, or supplies are needed to conduct the session?**
6. **What should the length of the session be?**
7. **How frequently should the sessions occur?**
8. **How and where will the records regarding each training session be kept?**

Good training sessions are the result of a felt need by management to train personnel, matched with a management philosophy that training is important. Taking time to effectively plan the training session is a good way to let employees know that management takes the training process seriously. Whether the training session is a film, a demonstration, or a lecture/presentation, time spent planning the session is time well spent.

Present the training session

Many managers feel that they have no time for training. This attitude is a bit like the worker who says, "If I don't have time to do it right in the first place, how will I ever find the time to do it over again?" Management is about teaching, encouraging, and coaching. Any manager who is interested in the long-term success of his or her operation and employees will find time each week to conduct a formal training session. Some managers maintain that all of the training in *their* unit must be on-the-job training (OJT). They feel that structured training either takes too long or is inappropriate. In nearly all cases, this is incorrect and is a major cause of the rather low rate of productivity so prevalent in the hospitality industry.

Present the training sessions with enthusiasm and an attitude of encouragement. Make sure that training is presented not because employees "don't know," but rather because management wants them to "know more." Involve employees in the presentation of training exercises. Seek their input in the sessions. Ask questions that encourage discussion, and always conclude the sessions with a positive note.

A brief, but effective, outline for each session could be as follows:

1. **Tell the employees what you hope to teach them and why.**
2. **Present the session**
3. **Reemphasize main points and discuss why they are important**
4. **Ask for questions to ensure understanding.**

Evaluate the session's effectiveness

There is a saying in education that "if the student hasn't learned, then the teacher hasn't taught." This concept, when applied to hospitality training, implies that presenting a training session is not enough. Training should cause behavior to change. Either employees improve and gain a new skill, knowledge, or information, or they have not learned. If we are to know which of these is the case, we must evaluate the training session. This can be as simple as observing employee behavior (to test skill acquisition) or as detailed as preparing written questions (to test knowledge retention). Evaluation should also be directed at how the sessions were conducted. Were they too long? Planned well? Delivered with the appropriate attitude?

The evaluation of training is as important as its delivery. Both the content of the session and the delivery itself should be evaluated. The bottom line, of course, is changed behavior. A work force that is trained well is more productive. In fact, employees who are well trained are both more productive and more highly motivated.

Retrain at the proper interval

Few 35-year-old food managers could walk into a room, sit down, and pass with a good or better grade the algebra final they took in high school some 18 years earlier. Why is that? The answer is not that they did not learn algebra. Clearly, they knew the answers at one time. Humans, however, do not learn and then remain stagnant. We learn, unlearn, and relearn on a regular basis. The telephone number we knew so well ten years ago is now gone from memory. The friend or teacher's name we knew we would never forget is forgotten. In the same way, employees who are well trained in an operation's policies and procedures need to be constantly reminded and updated if their skill level is to remain high. Declines in performance levels can come about through a change in the operational system or equipment. When this is true, management must retrain its employees. Nearly every operating foodservice manager can remember an instance when the conversation went something like this:

Supervisor:	"Joe, I thought I told you to . . ."
Joe:	"I did!"
Supervisor:	"That's not how we do it here!"
Joe:	"Oh yeah, I forgot! I'll get it right next time."
Supervisor:	"Good! Make sure you do!"

The point is that without a regular retraining program, Joe will *not* get it right the next time. It matters little whether Joe never got the correct training, or got it but now has forgotten. Conversations like the one above are a sure sign that effective training sessions are not in place on a regular basis.

Training a work force is one, if not the best, method of improving worker productivity. Effective training costs a small amount in time in the short run but pays off extremely well in dollars in the long run.

The managers who have risen to the top in the hospitality industry have some specific characteristics and traits. Chief among these is their desire to teach and encourage their employees and thus get the best results from each one of them.

Supervision

All workers require proper supervision. This is not to say that all workers desire to have someone tell them what to do. Proper supervision means assisting employees in improving productivity. In this sense, the supervisor is a helper and facilitator and provides assistance. Supervising becomes a matter of assisting employees to do better, not just identifying their shortcomings. It is said that employees think one of two things when they see their boss approaching.

1. **Here comes help!**

   or

2. **Here comes trouble!**

For those supervisors whose workers feel that the boss is an asset to their daily routine, productivity gains are remarkable. Supervisors who associate their position only with wielding power and being a taskmaster can rarely maintain the quality work force necessary to compete in today's competitive market. It is important to remember that it is the employee who services the guest, and not management. When supervision is geared toward helping, the guest benefits and thus the operation benefits. This is why it is so important for managers to be "on the floor," in other words, in the dining area, during meal periods. The foodservice manager is, in the final analysis, the individual in the best position to see what must be done to satisfy the guest. This means being where the action is when meals are served. Greeting guests, solving bottleneck problems, maintaining food quality, and ensuring excellent service are all tasks of the foodservice manager during the service period. When employees see that management is committed to guest service and is there to assist employees in delivering that service, their productivity will improve. Again, most employees want to please both the customer and the boss. When both can be pleased at once, productivity rises. If employees feel that they can satisfy only the guest *or* the operation, difficulties arise.

Consider, for example, the employee who has been instructed to serve one 2-ounce portion of tartar sauce with a particular fried fish dinner. When she does so, she finds that 80% of the customers request a second portion of the tartar sauce. If management does not respond to this consumer demand and adjust the portion size, the employee is faced with a difficult choice: "Do I satisfy management (serve one portion) or the guest (serve two portions)?" Clearly, situations such as this can and do occur, but they must be resolved by management. Good managers do this by involving themselves closely with the work of the employee.

This does not mean that the supervisor *does* the employees' work, but rather that employees know that they can go to management with their problems or, better yet, that they can say "Here comes help" when they see the boss approaching.

Equipment

In most cases, foodservice productivity ratios have not increased in recent years, as have those of other businesses. Much of this is due to the fact that ours is a labor-intensive, not machine-intensive, industry. In some cases, equipment improvements have made kitchen work much easier. Slicers, choppers, and mixers have replaced human labor with mechanical labor. However, robotics and automation are not yet a part of our industry in any major way. Nonetheless, it is critical for the foodservice manager to understand the importance of a properly equipped workplace to improve productivity. This can be as simple as understanding that a sharp knife cuts more quickly and effectively than a dull one, or as complex as deciding to computerize the purchasing function of individual units in a 1,000-store quick-service chain. In either case, management must ask itself the fundamental question "Am I providing my people with the tools necessary to effectively do their job?" The key word in that question is *effectively*. If the proper tools are provided, but they are at the wrong height, in the wrong location, or unavailable at the right time, the tools will not be used effectively. Similarly, if the proper tools are provided, but employees are not adequately trained in their use, productivity will suffer. One need look no further than the 1980s and early 1990s, when large numbers of personal computers were purchased but not effectively used by management, to see evidence of mismanagement, poor training, and its impact on productivity. When tools are provided but instruction in their use is not, productivity gains will not occur.

Equipment should be properly maintained (see Chapter 7) and updated if employees are to be held accountable for productivity standards or gains. It is management's obligation to provide workers with the tools they need to do their jobs quickly and effectively.

Morale

Workers' morale is not often mentioned in a discussion about controlling foodservice costs. Yet, as experienced managers will attest, it is impossible to overestimate the value of a highly motivated worker or crew. While it is a truism that employees motivate themselves, it is also true that effective managers provide an environment that makes it easy for workers to want to be motivated. This environment is created by management. History is filled with examples of groups who have achieved goals that seemed impossible, because they were highly motivated. Serving people is fun. It is exciting. If this fun and excitement can be instilled in each employee, work also becomes fun and exciting.

Volumes have been written about the manner in which managers can create a highly motivated work force. It is the authors' opinion, however, that those work groups with high morale share some common traits. In general, these groups work for a management team that has the following characteristics:

1. **Management has created a vision.**
2. **The vision is constantly communicated to employees.**
3. **The vision is shared by both management and employees.**

Creating a vision is nothing more than finding a purpose for the work force. Any manager who communicates that the purpose for a potwasher is simply to clean pots cannot expect to have a fired-up, turned-on worker. Yet, potwashers can have high morale. They can play a critical role in management's overall purpose for the work crew. If the purpose or vision that management creates is only profit for the organization or owner, the vision will probably not be shared by workers, even if it is strongly communicated. If management's vision, however, includes the vital importance of each employee, each worker can share that vision. This vision might be to be the unit with the highest in sales volume, or the highest percent sales increase, or the lowest cost per unit produced. Whatever management's vision for the unit, it must be communicated to the employees with a sense that they can share and profit from its pursuit. A shared purpose between management and worker is important for the development and maintenance of high morale. It is just not enough for management to feel that workers should be "glad to have a job." This type of attitude by management results in high employee turnover and lost productivity.

Employee turnover **is** high in some sections of the hospitality industry. By some estimates, it exceeds 200% per year. Employee turnover is computed by the following formula:

$$\textbf{Employee turnover rate} = \frac{\textbf{\# of employees separated}}{\textbf{\# of employees in work force}}$$

For example, Julie has a total of 50 workers in her foodservice operation. In the past year, she has hired 35 new employees as replacements. Her turnover rate is computed as follows:

$$\frac{\textbf{35 employees separated}}{\textbf{50 employees in work force}} = \textbf{70\% turnover rate}$$

Separated is the term used to describe workers who have quit, have been terminated, or in some other manner have separated themselves from the operation. The number of employees in the work force is computed by adding the number of employees at the beginning of the accounting period to the number of employees at the end of the accounting period, and dividing the sum by two. The number of employees in the work force, then, refers to the average number of people employed by the operation during a given time period.

Some foodservice operators prefer to use the terms **voluntary termination** and **involuntary termination**. If that is the preference, the formula can be modified to create these two ratios:

$$\textbf{Involuntary employee turnover rate} = \frac{\textbf{\# of employees involuntarily separated}}{\textbf{\# of employees in the work force}}$$

$$\textbf{Voluntary employee turnover rate} = \frac{\textbf{\# of employees voluntarily separated}}{\textbf{\# of employees in the work force}}$$

Involuntary in this case means that the foodservice operator terminated the employee; in other words, the employee left involuntarily. Conversely, voluntary separation means that the employee left of his or her own free will and was not dismissed by management.

Whether termination is involuntary or voluntary, turnover is expensive. Employee turnover causes the operator to incur costs that are both actual and hidden. Actual costs, such as those involved in advertisement of the vacancy, relocation, interviewing and training time, and record keeping are easy to determine. The hidden costs of increased dishroom breakage due to a new warewasher, slower customer service and thus smaller stations in the dining room due to a new waitperson, or increased amounts of improperly prepared food due to a new cook—all are expenses that can cost dearly an operation with high turnover rates. Good foodservice managers calculate and closely monitor their turnover rates. High turnover rates mean trouble. Low rates mean that employees feel good about the operation they work for.

To counteract the turnover syndrome, management can decide to be smart. It can seek to give job satisfaction by providing a healthy environment and wholesome working conditions. It can create and train a strong and loyal work force that will be willing and committed to work under many different conditions, some pleasant, some less so. If the understanding between management and the work force is established over time, on good faith, the relationship will transcend and exceed the monetary value attached to the job and allow for the establishment of a dependable and permanent staff.

A belief that both managers and employees share a common vision, and a noble one at that, creates the kind of environment that yields high worker productivity and reduced turnover rates, and most importantly provides excellent service to the guest.

Scheduling

Poor employee scheduling by management can result in low productivity ratios. Consider the example in Figure 6.1, where management has determined a schedule for potwashers in a unit that is open for three meals a day.

In Schedule A, four employees are scheduled for 32 hours at a rate of $5 per hour. Payroll in this case would be $160 per day (32 hours/day × $5/hour = $160/day). Each shift—breakfast, lunch, and dinner—has two employees scheduled.

In Schedule B, three employees are scheduled for 24 hours. At the same rate of $5 per hour, payroll would be $120 per day (24 hours/day × $5/hour = $120/day). The reduction in wages in this case is $40, not to mention the savings that will be made due to reduced benefits, meals, and other labor-related expenses.

Schedule B covers both the lunch and dinner shifts with two employees but assumes that one potwasher is sufficient in the early morning period. When scheduling is done to meet projected demand, productivity ratios will increase. If production standards are to be established and monitored, management must do its job in ensuring that employees are scheduled only when needed to meet the sales or volume anticipated. Returning to our formula for computing productivity ratio, if 60 guests are served and 5 rather than 4 waitresses are scheduled to work, productivity ratios will go down dramatically as seen below.

Effect of Scheduling on Productivity Ratio

# of Guests Served	# of Waitresses Scheduled	Productivity Ratio
60	4	15 guests/waitress
60	5	12 guests/waitress

Figure 6.1 **Employee Schedules**

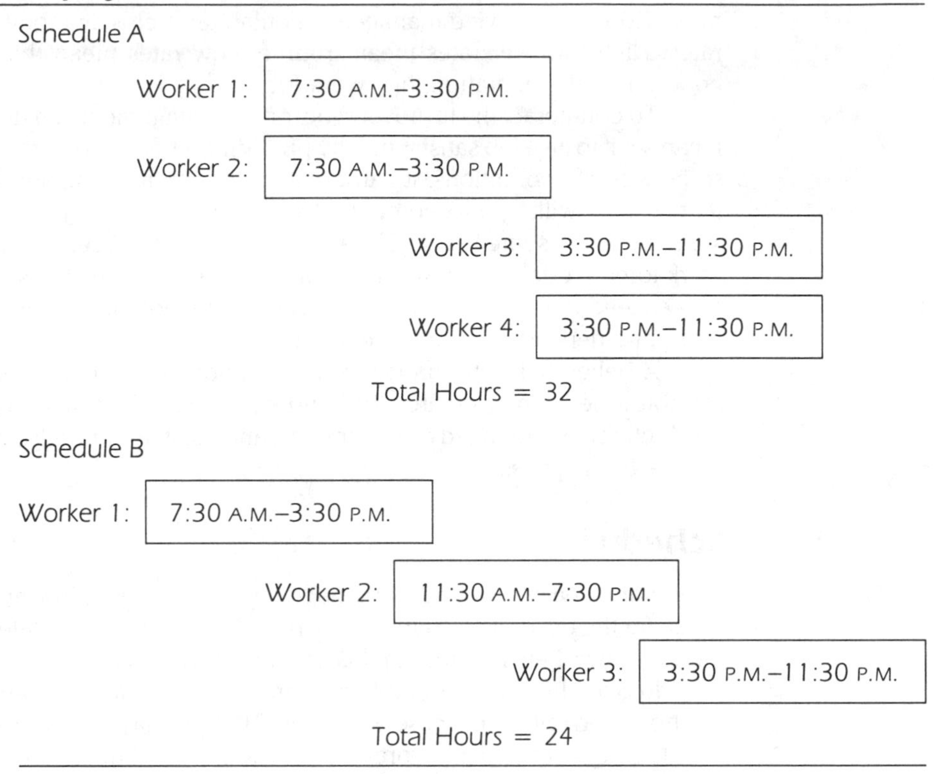

Proper scheduling ensures that the correct number of employees are available to do the necessary amount of work. If too many employees are scheduled, productivity ratios will decline. If too few employees are scheduled, customer service levels may suffer, or necessary tasks may not be completed on time or as well as they should be.

Since work in the foodservice operation tends to come in peaks and valleys, in other words, people in the Unites States tend to eat in three major time periods, the foodservice manager is faced with uneven demands regarding the number of workers needed. In a hotel, the slow period might be weekends, when most business travellers are at home rather than in the hotel. In an upscale restaurant, the slow period may be during the week, with volume picking up on the weekends. In a college foodservice operation, the summers may be slow, but a beach resort may be extremely busy during that time. Demand can also vary from morning to evening. In some restaurants with a busy lunch, 5 cooks and 15 waiters may be necessary. At 3:00 in the afternoon, at the same restaurant, one cook and one waitress may find themselves with few customers to serve. Scheduling efficiency can often be improved through the use of the split shift, a technique used to match individual employee work shifts with peaks and valleys of customer demand. In using a split shift, the manager would require an employee to work a busy period, lunch for example, then be off in the afternoon, only to return for the busy dinner period. Employee scheduling in the hospitality industry is difficult. It is important, however, that it be done well. Productivity standards help the foodservice operator match work load to the number of employees required.

Breaks

Workers cannot work at top speed for eight hours at a time. They have both a physical and mental need for breaks from their work. These breaks give them a chance to pause, collect their thoughts, converse with their fellow workers, and in general, prepare for the next work session. The foodservice supervisor must determine both the frequency and length of designated breaks. Employees need to know that management cares enough about them to establish a break schedule and then maintain it. Of course, workers must be prepared to alter their break schedule when the work load requires it. Short, frequent breaks have been shown to increase worker productivity and morale. Management should not view breaks as lost or wasted time; instead they should be viewed as a necessary part of maintaining a highly productive work force. Workers who are given frequent, short breaks can outproduce those who are not given any.

Employee Selection

Choosing the right employee from the beginning is vitally important in developing a highly productive work force. Good foodservice managers know that proper selection procedures go a long way toward establishing the kind of work force that can be both efficient and effective. This involves matching the right employee with the right job. The process begins with the development of the job description.

Job Description

A job description is a listing of the tasks that must be accomplished by the employee hired to fill a particular position. For example, in the case of a room service delivery person in a large hotel, the tasks might be listed as indicated on the job description card shown in Figure 6.2. A simple job description such as this one should be maintained for every position in the foodservice operation. From the job description, a job specification can be prepared.

Job Specification

A job specification is a listing of the personal attributes needed to perform the tasks contained in a particular job description. Figure 6.3 shows the job specification card that would match the job description in Figure 6.2.

Figure 6.2 **Job Description**

Unit Name: Thunder Motor Lodge   Position Title: Room service delivery person

Primary Tasks:

1. Set up room service trays in steward area
2. Deliver trays to room, as requested
3. Remove tray covers upon delivery
4. Remove soiled trays from floors
5. Maintain guest check control
6. Balance room service cash drawer
7. Answer telephone to receive guest orders
8. Clean room service setup area at conclusion of shift
9. Other duties, as assigned by supervisor
10.
11.
12.

Special Comments:

Salary excludes tips. Uniform allowance is $25.00 per week.

Salary Range: $5.00–$6.25/hour   Signature: Assistant food & beverage director

As can be seen, this position requires a specific set of personal characteristics and skills. When a room service delivery person is hired, the job specification requirements must be foremost in management's mind. If the job specs do not exist or are not followed, it is likely that employees may be hired who are simply not able to be highly productive. Each employee must bring to the operation either the skills necessary to do the job or the ability to acquire those skills. It is management's role to develop both job descriptions and job specifications so that employees know what their job is, and employers know the characteristics that workers must have, or be trained in, to do their jobs well.

Figure 6.3 **Job Specification**

Unit Name: Thunder Motor Lodge   Position Title: Room service delivery person

Personal Characteristics Required:

1. Good telephone skills; clear, easily understood English
2. Ability to operate cash register
3. Bondable
4. Detail-oriented
5. Pleasant personality
6. Discreet

Special Comments: Good grooming habits are especially important in this position as employee will be a primary guest contact person.

Job Spec Prepared by: Chel L.

Menu

A major factor in worker productivity is the foodservice operation's actual menu. The items that management elects to produce have a profound effect on the worker's ability to produce the items quickly and efficiently.

In general, the more items a kitchen is asked to produce, the less efficient that kitchen will be. Of course, if management does not provide the guest with enough choices, loss of sales may result. Clearly, neither too many nor too few menu choices should be offered. The question for management is "How many are too many?" The answer depends on the operation, the skill level of employees, and the level of variety management feels is necessary to properly service the guests.

Menus that continue to grow and grow cost in other ways as well. The quick-service unit that elects to specialize in hamburgers can prepare them quickly and efficiently. The same restaurant that decides to add pizza, tacos, salads, and fried chicken may find that employees are not only less productive, but consumers are confused as to what the operation really is. Again, the dilemma management faces is how to serve the widest variety possible but not so many things as to markedly reduce employee productivity.

While the number of items produced is important, so is the type of item. Obviously, a small diner with one deep-fat fryer will have production problems if the day's specials are fried fish, fried chicken, and a breaded, fried vegetable platter! Menu items must be selected to complement the skill level of the employees and the equipment available to produce the menu item. Most foodservice operations change their menu fairly infrequently. Print costs are often high, and restaurateurs are reluctant to radically change their product offerings. Thus, it is extremely important that the menu items selected by management are items that can be prepared efficiently and well. If this is done, productivity rates will be high, as will customer satisfaction.

Convenience Versus Scratch Preparation

Few if any foodservice operators today make all of their menu items from scratch. Indeed, there is no real agreement among operators as to what "scratch cooking" really is. Canned fruits, frozen seafood, and prebaked pastries are examples of foods that would not be available to many consumers if they were not processed to some degree before they were delivered to the foodservice operator's door. At one time, presliced white bread was considered a convenience item. Today, this is considered a staple. Some foods, like canned cheese sauce, can be modified by the operator to produce a unique item. This can be done by the addition of special ingredients according to the standardized recipe, with the intent of creating a product served only by *that* foodservice operation.

The decision of whether to make or buy involves two major factors. The first is, of course, product quality. In general, if an operation can make a product that is superior to the one it can buy from a supplier, it should produce that item. The second factor, product cost, is also a major issue for management. It is possible that management determines that a given menu item can be made in-house and that it is a superior product. The cost of preparing that product, however, may be so great that it is simply not cost-effective to do so. Consider, for example, the case of Carlos, who operates a quick-service Mexican restaurant. An item used in many of the dishes Carlos' crew prepares is frijoles, or cooked pinto beans, which are seasoned and mashed. Carlos uses 50 pounds of these beans per day. Currently, Carlos buys the beans in a can for 40 cents per pound. His cost per pound with the canned product includes only the cost of the beans; in addition, he incurs the cost of opening the cans and the cost of cooking fuel to heat the beans. If Carlos were to consider making the frijoles from scratch, his food cost would go down to 18 cents per pound (the price of the dried pinto beans), a savings of over 50%. The complete story, however, can only be viewed when we consider the labor required to produce the frijoles. Figure 6.4 details the hypothetical costs involved in the decision that Carlos must make, assuming a usage of 50 pounds of product per day, and a labor cost per hour of $5 for both the cooking and the cleanup of the production process.

As is evident, Carlos experiences a reduction in cost of food, but an increase in the cost of labor, since his own workers must now complete the cooking process. Make-or-buy decisions must be made by management. It is important to note, however, that these decisions affect **both** food and labor costs. One

Figure 6.4 **Frijoles: 50 pounds**

Cost of Product	Convenience Product	Scratch Product
Beans	$20.00	$ 9.00
Seasoning	0	1.00
Labor	2.50	7.50
Fuel	0.20	1.10
Total Cost	22.70	18.60

cannot generally achieve food cost savings without expending labor dollars. Conversely, when a manager elects to buy, rather than make an item from scratch, food costs tend to rise, but labor costs should decline. It is important that management not fall into the trap of electing to buy more convenience-type items but not reducing labor expenditures. When that happens, management loses in terms of both high food costs and higher than required labor costs.

Service Level Desired

The average quick-service employee can serve more customers in an hour than the best waiter can at an exclusive French restaurant. The reason for this is, of course, quite obvious. In the quick-service situation, speed, not total service rendered, is of the utmost importance. In the French restaurant, service is to be more elegant and the total service rendered of a much higher level. When management varies service levels, it varies worker productivity ratios. In the past, foodservice managers focused very heavily on speed of service. While that is still important today, many operators are finding that customers expect and demand higher levels of service than ever before. If this trend continues, one can anticipate that foodservice productivity levels will tend to go down. In order to prevent this from happening, foodservice operators need to become very creative in finding ways to improve worker productivity in other areas, say through training and improving morale, so that these "savings" can be used to provide the higher level of customer service demanded by today's sophisticated foodservice consumer.

Now that we have discussed some of the factors that impact worker productivity, and what management can do to affect them, we return to the question of knowing "how many workers are needed" to effectively operate the foodservice unit. As previously stated, the key to answering that question lies in developing productivity standards for the foodservice unit. There are many measures of worker productivity. We shall discuss the most popular of these and identify their weaknesses and strengths. In the final analysis, the best productivity measure for any unit, of course, is the one that makes the most sense for that unique operation.

Measuring Current Productivity

The Labor Cost Percentage

A very commonly used measure of worker productivity in the foodservice industry is the labor cost percentage. The labor cost percentage is computed as follows:

$$\frac{\textbf{Cost of labor}}{\textbf{Sales}} = \textbf{Labor cost \%}$$

Cost of labor, in this case, may be either payroll, if that is what is of interest to management, or total labor related-expenses. The issue can become cloudy. Where, for instance, should pay for vacations and for sick leave be computed? Are they part of regular payroll, or a benefit, and thus best accounted for in the other expense category? In either case, foodservice operators must know which items they are using to determine cost of labor, and they must know how to accurately compute and interpret labor cost percentage. Controlling the labor cost percentages is extremely important in the foodservice industry, since it is the most widely used measure of productivity and thus is often used to determine the effectiveness of management. If the labor cost percentage increases, management may be held accountable and penalized. Labor cost percentage that increases too much may result in management turnover, even if, as in many cases, the management did not want to turn over!

Labor cost percentages are fairly easy to compute and analyze. Consider the case of Roderick, a foodservice manager in charge of a table-service restaurant in a year-round theme park. The unit is popular and has a $20 per guest check average. Roderick uses only payroll (wages and salaries) when determining labor cost percentage. Other labor-related expenses are considered by Roderick's supervisor to be noncontrollables, beyond Roderick's immediate control. He has computed his labor cost percentage for each of the last four weeks using the labor cost percentage formula. His supervisor has given Roderick a goal of 35% for the four-week period. Roderick feels that he has done well in meeting that goal. Figure 6.5 shows Roderick's four-week performance.

Roderick's supervisor, Madeline, is concerned because she received many comments in week 4 regarding poor service levels in Roderick's unit. As she analyzes the numbers in Figure 6.5, she sees that Roderick exceeded his goal of a 35.0% labor cost in weeks 1 through 3, then reduced his labor cost to 27.9% in week 4. While the monthly overall average of 35.0% is within budget, she knows all is not well in this unit. Roderick elected to reduce his payroll in week 4, and yet it is clear that at 27.9% labor cost, service to guests suffers. That is, too few employees were on staff to provide the necessary guest attention. Unfortunately, one disadvantage of using overall labor cost percentage is that it hides highs and lows. As in Roderick's case, labor costs were too high the first three weeks, too low the last week, but acceptable overall. The total labor cost of 35.0% indicates that for each dollar of sales generated, 35 cents is to be paid to the employees who generated these sales.

Using the labor cost percentage formula and data from Figure 6.5, we find the following:

$$\frac{\textbf{Cost of labor}}{\textbf{Sales}} = \textbf{Labor cost \%}$$

Or

$$\frac{\$29{,}330}{\$83{,}800} = 35\%$$

Thus, management can use the 35% figure to measure worker and management productivity. Notice, however, what would happen to this measure of productivity if all workers were given a 5% raise in pay. If this were the case, Roderick's labor cost percentages for last month would be as follows in Figure 6.6.

Note that labor now accounts for 36.8% of each sales dollar. It is important to realize that Roderick's work force did not become less productive because

Figure 6.5 **Labor Cost Percentage Report**

Unit Name: Roderick's Date: Week 1–4

Week	Cost of Labor	Sales	Labor Cost %
1	$ 7,100.00	$18,400.00	38.6%
2	8,050.00	21,500.00	37.4
3	7,258.00	19,100.00	38.0
4	6,922.00	24,800.00	27.9
Total	29,330.00	83,800.00	35.0

Figure 6.6 **Roderick's Revised Labor Cost Percentage Report**

(Includes 5% Raise)

Week	Original Cost of Labor	5% Raise	Total Cost of Labor	Sales	Labor Cost %
1	$ 7,100.00	$ 355.00	$ 7,455.00	$18,400.00	40.5%
2	8,050.00	402.50	8,452.50	21,500.00	39.3
3	7,258.00	362.90	7,620.90	19,100.00	39.9
4	6,922.00	346.10	7,268.10	24,800.00	29.3
Total	29,330.00	1,466.50	30,796.50	83,800.00	36.8

Figure 6.7 **Roderick's Revised Labor Cost Percentage Report**

(Includes 5% Increase in Selling Price)

Week	Cost of Labor	Original Sales	5% Selling Price Increase	Total Sales	Labor Cost %
1	$ 7,100.00	$18,400.00	$ 920.00	$19,320.00	36.7%
2	8,050.00	21,500.00	1,075.00	22,575.00	35.7
3	7,258.00	19,100.00	955.00	20,055.00	36.2
4	6,922.00	24,800.00	1,240.00	26,040.00	26.6
Total	29,330.00	83,800.00	4,190.00	87,990.00	33.3

they got a 5% increase in pay. Labor cost percentage **varies** with changes in the price paid for labor. When the price paid for labor increases, labor cost percentage increases. When the price paid for labor decreases, labor cost percentage decreases. Because of this, labor cost percentage is not a truly good measure of work force productivity.

Labor cost percentage also varies when selling prices change. Return to the data in Figure 6.5 and assume that Roderick's unit raised prices by 5% prior to the beginning of the month. Figure 6.7 shows how an increase of this size in selling price would affect the labor cost percentage.

As demonstrated, increases in selling prices (assuming no decline in customer count or buying behavior) result in decreases in labor cost percentage. Alternatively, lowering the selling price generally results in increased labor cost percentage. While labor cost percentage is easy to compute and widely used, it is difficult to use as a measure of productivity over time, since it depends on labor dollars spent and sales dollars received for its computation. In addition, those institutional foodservice settings that have no sales figures to report find that it is not possible to measure labor productivity using labor cost percentage, since they generally count customers or meals served rather than sales dollars earned.

Sales Per Labor Hour

It has been said that the most perishable commodity any foodservice operator buys is the labor hour. When not productively used, it disappears forever. It cannot be "carried over" to the next day like an unsold head of lettuce or a slice of ham. Indeed, when one considers the product that a foodservice operator sells as a combination of both food products and labor added to those products, the importance of effectively using each labor hour paid for is very clear. It is for this reason that some foodservice operators prefer to measure labor productivity in terms of the amount of sales generated for each labor hour used. The formula for computing this measure of labor productivity is as follows:

$$\frac{\textbf{Sales}}{\textbf{Labor hours used}} = \textbf{Sales per labor hour}$$

Labor hours used are simply the sum of all labor hours paid for by management in a given sales period. If Roderick had used this measure of productivity for his unit, he would, perhaps, have had data such as that presented in Figure 6.8.

Sales per labor hour ranged from a low of $18.14 in week 1, to a high of $25.08 in week 4. Those operators who compute sales per labor hour tend to do so because they feel it is a better measure of labor productivity than the labor cost percentage. Indeed, while sales per labor hour will vary with changes in menu selling price (as does labor cost percentage), it will not vary based on changes in the price paid for labor. In other words, increases and decreases in the price paid per hour will not affect this productivity measure. On the negative side, however, sales per labor hour neglects to consider the amount paid to workers per hour to generate the sales. Using this measure of productivity, a foodservice unit paying its workers an average of $7.00 per hour could have the same sales per labor hour as a similar unit paying $10.00 for each hour of labor used. Obviously, the manager paying $7.00 per hour has created a lower-cost, yet equally productive work force, if the sales per labor hour used figures are the same in the two units. Sales per labor hour, however, may be useful in some situations and is relatively easy to compute, although it usually is more difficult to determine total labor hours used than total labor dollars spent. This is especially true when large numbers of employees are salaried rather than hourly employees.

Guests Served Per Labor Dollar

Had Roderick preferred, he might have measured his labor productivity in terms of the number of guests served per labor dollar expended. The formula for this measure of productivity is as follows:

Figure 6.8 **Roderick's Sales per Labor Hour**

Week	Sales	Labor Hours Used	Sales Per Labor Hour
1	$18,400.00	1,014.30	$18.14
2	21,500.00	1,150.00	18.70
3	19,100.00	1,036.90	18.42
4	24,800.00	988.80	25.08
Total	83,800.00	4,190.00	20.00

$$\frac{\textbf{Guests served}}{\textbf{Cost of labor}} = \textbf{Guests served per labor dollar}$$

Had Roderick so desired, his productivity data could have been as presented in Figure 6.9.

Dollars Expended Per Guest Served

A variation on the formula for guests served per labor dollar expended is to reverse the formula as follows:

$$\frac{\textbf{Cost of labor}}{\textbf{Guests served}} = \textbf{Dollars expended per guest served}$$

In the example of Roderick's (Figure 6.9) the total dollars expended per guest served for the four-week period would be computed as follows:

$$\frac{\$29{,}330.00}{4{,}190} = \$7.00$$

Roderick prefers to use the method of dividing guests served by cost of labor.

Returning to the guest served per labor dollar method of measuring productivity (Figure 6.9), for the four-week average, Roderick served .143 guests for each labor dollar expended. Guests served per labor dollar can range from only a portion of a guest, such as in this case, to a rather large number of guests, such as in quick-service restaurants. It is important to note, however, that cost of labor in this case represents *all* labor required to serve the guests. This includes cooks, waitstaff, dishwashers, and Roderick himself. It is therefore not surprising that each dollar spent for labor services is often less than one "whole" guest. As a measure of productivity, guests served per labor dollar expended has advantages. It is relatively easy to compute and can be used by foodservice units, such as institutions, that do not routinely record dollar sales figures. When the number of guests to be served stays fairly constant, it can be a good measure of produc-

Figure 6.9 **Roderick's Guests Served per Labor Dollar**

Week	Guests Served	Cost of Labor	Guests Served per Labor Dollar
1	920	$ 7,100.00	.130
2	1,075	8,050.00	.134
3	955	7,258.00	.132
4	1,240	6,922.00	.179
Total	4,190	29,330.00	.143

tivity. If number of guests anticipated varies widely, this measure of productivity will vary widely also, despite management's conscientious efforts at forecasting. Of course, that is true of even the best measures of labor productivity.

Guests Served Per Labor Hour

Guests served per labor hour is the last measure of productivity we shall discuss. Had Roderick elected to use this measure, he would compute it as follows:

$$\frac{\textbf{Guests served}}{\textbf{Labor hours used}} = \textbf{Guests served per labor hour}$$

As is evident, the formula for guests served per labor hour has neither sales figures nor labor expense figures in its computation. It is thus free from both variations due to changes in the price paid for labor and fluctuations due solely to changes in menu selling prices. Guests served per labor hour is a true measure of productivity, not a measure of either cost and productivity or sales and productivity. Guests served per labor hour is powerful in its ability to measure productivity gains across time due to changes that are unrelated to selling price or product cost. It is extremely useful in comparing similar units in areas with widely differing wage rates or selling prices and is thus popular with corporations comparing one operational unit with another. It is also useful in comparing dissimilar facilities with similar wages and selling prices, since it helps identify areas of weakness in management scheduling, worker productivity, facility layout and design, or other factors that can affect productivity.

Had Roderick elected to evaluate his work force productivity through the use of the guest served per labor hour, his data might have looked as follows in Figure 6.10.

As the data demonstrate, Roderick's guests served per labor hour figure ranges from a low of .907 guests per hour (week 1) to a high of 1.254 guests per hour (week 4). The average for the four-week period is 1.00 guest served per labor hour (4,190 guests served / 4,190 hours used = 1.00 guest per labor hour).

Figure 6.10 **Roderick's Guests Served per Labor Hour**

Week	Guests Served	Labor Hours Used	Guests Served per Labor Hour
1	920	1,014.30	.907
2	1,075	1,150.00	.935
3	955	1,036.90	.921
4	1,240	988.80	1.254
Total	4,190	4,190.00	1.000

Those managers who use guests served per labor hour as a measure of productivity generally do so because they like the focus of emphasizing service levels and not just reducing costs.

Since it is widely believed that work really does expand to meet (and exceed) the number of people available to do the job, measures of productivity must be available to guide management in making productivity assessments. The table in Figure 6.11 summarizes the four productivity measures discussed in this text and lists some advantages and disadvantages associated with each.

Each formula for measuring labor productivity has advantages and disadvantages. The effective operator may select one or more of the measures described above or create his or her own measure. The labor cost percentage and at least one other measure of productivity should be monitored regularly by management if it is serious about controlling labor-related expenses.

Figure 6.11 **Productivity Measures Summary**

Measurements	Advantages	Disadvantages
Labor cost % = Cost of labor / Sales	1. Easy to compute 2. Most widely used	1. Hides highs and lows 2. Varies with changes in the price of labor 3. Varies with changes in menu selling price
Sales per labor hour = Sales / Labor hours used	1. Fairly easy to compute 2. Does not vary with changes in the price of labor	1. Ignores price per hour paid for labor 2. Varies with changes in menu selling price
Guests served per labor dollar = Guests served / Cost of labor	1. Fairly easy to compute 2. Does not vary with changes in menu selling price 3. Can be used by non-cash-generating units	1. Ignores average sale per guest and thus total sales 2. Varies with changes in the price of labor
Guests served per labor hour = Guests served / Labor hours used	1. Can be used by non-cash-generating units 2. Does not change due to changes in price of labor or menu selling price 3. Emphasizes serving guests rather than reducing costs	1. Time-consuming to produce 2. Ignores price paid for labor 3. Ignores average sale per guest and thus total sales

Six-Column Daily Productivity Report

Many operators, upon selecting a productivity measure, prefer to compute that measure on a daily rather than weekly or monthly basis. This can easily be done by using a six-column form similar to the one introduced in Chapter 3.

A six-column form for Roderick's restaurant sales and labor cost in week 1 is presented in Figure 6.12. It uses the standard labor cost percentage formula (cost of labor ÷ sales = labor cost percentage). Amounts in the today columns are divided to create labor cost % today, just as amounts in the todate columns are divided to create labor cost % todate.

Roderick's daily labor cost percentage during week 1 ranged from a low of 31.2% (day 7) to a high of 47.8% (day 2). The labor cost percentage for the

Figure 6.12 **Six-Column Labor Cost Percentage**

Unit Name: Rodericks Date: 1/1–1/7

	Cost of Labor		Sales		Labor Cost %	
Weekday	**Today**	**Todate**	**Today**	**Todate**	**Today**	**Todate**
1	$ 800		$2,000		40.0%	
2	880	$1,680	1,840	$ 3,840	47.8	43.8%
3	920	2,600	2,150	5,990	42.8	43.4
4	980	3,580	2,300	8,290	42.6	43.2
5	1,000	4,580	2,100	10,390	47.6	44.0
6	1,300	5,880	4,100	14,490	31.7	40.6
7	1,220	7,100	3,910	18,400	31.2	38.6

week is 38.6%. Again, we see the effect of averaging highs and lows when using measures of labor productivity. Any of the four measures of labor productivity can be calculated on a daily basis using a modification of the six-column form located in the "Management Control Forms" section of this book. Figure 6.13 details the method to be used to establish six-column forms for each of the four productivity measures presented in this chapter.

When using the six-column report, it is important to remember that the todate column value, on any given day, is always the sum of the values of all the preceding today columns, including the current day.

Determining Costs by Labor Category

Many operators find that a single measure of their labor productivity is insufficient for their needs. Consider the case of Otis, the operator of a restaurant called Squirrel Flats, near a logging camp that services both tourists and loggers taking a break from work. Otis's sales last month were $100,000.00. His labor costs were $30,000.00, and thus his labor cost percentage was 30% ($30,000.00 / $100,000.00

Figure 6.13 **Six-Column Labor Productivity Form Format**

Measure of Productivity	**Columns 1 & 2**	**Columns 3 & 4**	**Columns 5 & 6**
Labor cost % =	Cost of labor today	Sales today	Labor cost % today
$\frac{\text{Cost of labor}}{\text{Sales}}$	Cost of labor todate	Sales todate	Labor cost % todate
Sales per labor hour =	Sales today	Labor hours used today	Sales per labor hour today
$\frac{\text{Sales}}{\text{Labor hours used}}$	Sales todate	Labor hours used todate	Sales per labor hour todate
Guests served per labor dollar =	Guests served today	Cost of labor today	Guests served per labor dollar today
$\frac{\text{Guests served}}{\text{Cost of labor}}$	Guests served todate	Cost of labor todate	Guests served per labor dollar todate
Guests served per labor hour =	Guests served today	Labor hours used today	Guests served per labor hour today
$\frac{\text{Guests served}}{\text{Labor hours used}}$	Guest served todate	Labor hours served todate	Guests served per labor hour todate

= .30). Otis, however, knows more about his labor cost percentage than the overall number alone tells him. Figure 6.14 demonstrates the method Otis uses to compute his overall labor cost percentage.

Note that Otis divides his labor expense into four distinct categories. Production includes all those individuals who are involved with the actual preparation of the food products Otis sells. Service includes the waitpersons and cashiers involved in delivering the products to the guests and receiving payment for these products. Sanitation consists of individuals who are responsible for warewashing and after-hours cleanup of the establishment. Management includes the salaries of Otis and his two supervisors.

By establishing four labor categories, Otis has a better idea of where his labor dollars are spent than if only one overall figure had been used. Just as it is helpful to compute more than one food cost percentage, it is often helpful to calculate more than one labor cost percentage. Notice that the sum of Otis's four labor cost percentage categories equals the amount of his total labor cost percentage: 12% + 9% + 3% + 6% = 30%.

An operator may establish any number of categories that make sense for his or her own unique operation. The important points to remember when determining labor productivity measures by category are as follows:

1. **Be sure to include all the relevant data, whether dollars spent, hours used, or guests served.**
2. **Divide each category using the same method to identify numerator and denominator.**
3. **Compute an overall total to ensure that the sum of the categories is consistent with the overall total.**

Keep these points in mind as we examine Figure 6.15, which details Otis's second measure of labor productivity. He has selected guests served per labor dollar as a supplement to his computation of labor cost percentage. Otis feels that this second measure helps him determine his effectiveness with guests without losing sight of the total number of dollars he spends on payroll expense. The formula he uses for his computation is guests served ÷ cost of labor = guests served per labor dollar.

Figure 6.14 **Labor Cost Percentage for Squirrel Flats**

Time Period: 1/1–1/31 Sales: $100,000.00

Labor Category	Cost of Labor	Labor Cost %
Production	$12,000	12%
Service	9,000	9
Sanitation	3,000	3
Management	6,000	6
Total	30,000	30

Figure 6.15 **Guests Served per Labor Dollar for Squirrel Flats**

Time Period: 1/1–1/31 Guests Served: 25,000

Labor Category	Cost of Labor	Guests Served per Labor Dollar
Production	$12,000.00	2.083
Service	9,000.00	2.777
Sanitation	3,000.00	8.333
Management	6,000.00	4.166
Total	30,000.00	.833

Each labor category in Figure 6.15 yields a different guests served per labor dollar figure. As could be expected, when labor dollars expended in a category are small, guests served per labor dollar in that category is relatively high. This is clearly demonstrated in the sanitation category in Figure 6.15. When labor dollars expended are high, as in the total category, guests served per labor dollar is lower. Any measure of labor productivity can be categorized in any logical manner that is of value to management. The purpose of computing numbers such as these is, of course, because of their value in developing staff schedules and estimating future payroll costs.

Steps in Controlling Labor Costs

Step 1. Determine Productivity Standards

Earlier in this chapter, the authors stated that controlling labor-related expense is a four-step process. The first step is the determination of productivity standards. Thus far we have discussed how to measure current productivity ratios based on historical data. This tells us where we **are** in relation to productivity but does not say where we **should be**. To illustrate this concept, consider the case of Lea. She is about to open her own franchise unit in a family-oriented steak house chain. Four units of the same chain exist in her immediate area. Her district supervisor, who measures labor productivity by using labor cost percentage, has shared with her the data shown in Figure 6.16. Units 1–4 figures represent labor cost percentages in those steak house units in Lea's district. The district average is the unweighted mean of those four units. Company average refers to the overall labor cost percentage in the steak house chain that Lea has joined. Industry average refers to the average labor cost percentage of all family steak houses of the type similar to the one Lea will operate.

Using the data presented in Figure 6.16, Lea must now establish her own desired productivity measure. She has no historical data to base her measure on,

Figure 6.16 **Labor Cost Percentage Summary**

Unit Description	Labor Cost %
Unit 1	34.1%
Unit 2	35.5
Unit 3	34.3
Unit 4	35.2
District average	34.9
Company average	34.0
Industry average	35.5

since she has yet to open her restaurant. Using her own judgment and the information she has available, she can choose to use as her goal the lowest labor cost percentage (Unit 1); the highest (Unit 2); the district, company or industry average; or some other number not included in this listing. Any of these numbers could become Lea's ideal labor cost percentage. In the final analysis, management must use whatever data it has available to establish or determine the appropriate productivity standard. A productivity standard is defined as management's view of what constitutes an appropriate productivity ratio in a given foodservice unit or units. Thus, a productivity standard might be, as in Lea's case, a particular labor cost percentage, a specific number of guests served per labor dollar expended, or any other predetermined productivity ratio management wants to utilize. These standards are typically based on the following types of information:

1. **Unit history**
2. **Company averages**
3. **Industry averages**
4. **Management experience**
5. **Combination of the above**

In Lea's case, she chooses a 35% labor cost as her productivity standard. This figure is close to the district average (34.9%), and she feels that this is a realistic goal for her first year. In future years, she hopes to improve profitability by reducing her desired labor cost to 34%. Lea will use the 35% figure as she moves to Step 2 of the labor cost control process, which is forecasting sales volume.

Step 2. Forecast Sales Volume

Sales volume forecasting (discussed in Chapter 2), when combined with established labor standards, allows a foodservice operator to determine the number of employees needed to effectively service those guests who will visit the facility. All foodservice units must forecast volume. This can be done in terms of either sales dollars or number of guests to be served. It is important to note the distinction between forecasting sales volume and forecasting the number of workers needed to service that volume. The distinction is simply that operators see customers coming to an operation in "block" fashion, that is, in groups at a time. Employees, on the other hand, come one individual at a time. A brief example will make this clear. Ted operates a small shop that sells only specialty coffee. His waitstaff productivity standard is 1 waitress to each 30 customers. Thus, his staffing pattern is as shown in Figure 6.17.

When 30 or less customers are expected, Ted needs only one waitperson on duty. In effect, each time a block of 30 customers is added, Ted must add another waitperson. If Ted anticipates 40 customers one day and 50 the next, no change in staff is necessary. That is, an addition of 10 extra customers does not dictate the addition of another waitperson. On the other hand, if Ted anticipates 60 customers one day and 70 the next, an additional staff person is required, since Ted has introduced a new block of customers.

It really does not matter how much of the new block actually arrives, since Ted has staffed for all of it. He hopes, of course, that all or nearly all of the block will arrive, as this will keep his cost per person served lower. If only a small portion of the block comes, Ted's cost per person served will rise unless he takes some action to reduce his labor-related expense.

Step 3. Schedule Employees Using Sales Forecast and Productivity

Forecasting sales volume is important to cost control because it begins to take management out of the past and present and allows it to project into the future and influence what will happen then. To illustrate how established labor standards (Step 1) are combined with sales forecasts (Step 2) to develop employee schedules (Step 3), consider the scenario of Liza, the foodservice director at Langtree, a small women's college in a rural district. Liza operates both a dormitory feeding situation and an open snack bar/cafeteria. The dormitory, Geier Hall, houses 1,000 young women. The snack bar/cafeteria, called Lillie's, is open to the students, staff, and faculty of the school. Liza is committed to controlling her labor-related expense. As such, she has carefully monitored her past labor

Figure 6.17 **Ted's Coffee Shop Staffing Guide**

# of Customers Anticipated	# of Waitpersons Needed
1–30	1
31–60	2
61–90	3
91–120	4

productivity ratios, those of similar schools, and also national averages. In addition, she has considered the facilities she operates, the skill level and morale of her work force, and the impact of her aggressive training program on her future productivity. Taking all of these factors into account, Liza has determined that Lillie's snack bar/cafeteria should be able to operate at a labor cost of 30% of gross sales. In the dormitory, where no dollar sales figures are kept on a daily basis, she has decided that her labor productivity measure should be established in terms of guests served per labor hour used. Her goal is a 30 to 1 ratio, that is, 30 meals served per labor hour used. Liza may now establish her labor cost expense budget both in terms of dollars (Lillie's) and labor hours used (Geier Hall). Let us examine in Figure 6.18 how Liza would establish her labor budget for Lillie's, using her productivity standards and a sales forecast, since sales forecast × labor cost % = labor expense budget.

Figure 6.19 illustrates how Liza would establish a budget for total number of labor hours used to service Geier Hall, since number of meals divided by labor standards equals labor hours budget.

Note that in the case of both Figure 6.18 and 6.19, Liza could have varied her **weekly** productivity standard and still have produced a four-week budget. In other words, on weeks when volume was high, she could have elected to reduce her desired labor cost percentage or increase the meals per hour standard. This can be a logical course of action if the operator feels that increased volume can have the effect of either reducing the cost percentage of fixed labor or increasing the number of meals per hour that can be served by staff persons

Figure 6.18 **Labor Budget for Lillie's**

Time Period	Sales Forecast	Labor Cost Standard	Labor Expense Budget
Week 1	$ 6,550	30%	$1,965
Week 2	6,850	30	2,055
Week 3	6,000	30	1,800
Week 4	8,100	30	2,430
Total	27,500	30	8,250

Figure 6.19 **Labor Budget for Geier Hall**

Time Period	# of Meals Projected	Labor Standard	Labor Hours Budget
Week 1	20,000	30 meals/hr	667
Week 2	18,600	30 meals/hr	620
Week 3	18,100	30 meals/hr	603
Week 4	17,800	30 meals/hr	593
Total	74,500	30 meals/hr	2,483

in fixed positions, such as cashiers and managers. Experience tells Liza, however, that in her case a standard labor productivity ratio that remains unchanged across the four weeks is her best option.

From the labor budgets she has developed, Liza can now schedule her production people, in terms of either dollars to be spent for labor (Lillie's) or labor hours to be used (Geier Hall). *She must be careful to schedule employees only when they are needed.* To do this, she must forecast her volume in time blocks smaller than one-day portions. Perhaps, in her case, volume should be predicted in three groups, such as breakfast, lunch, and dinner, in the dormitory, and in one- or two-hour blocks in her snack bar/cafeteria.

Now let us discuss how Liza might schedule her dormitory staff during week 1 of her four-week projection. Let us assume that Liza's weekly projection of sales volume for Geier Hall is as demonstrated in Figure 6.20.

On any given day, Liza can match volume projections with budgeted hours or dollars. To see exactly how she would use this information to determine her employees' schedules, let us examine day 1 in Figure 6.20, a day when Liza projects 3,000 meals served and 100 labor hours needed. She knows that she should "spend" no more than 100 total hours for labor on that day. She also knows, from recording her productivity ratio in the past (Figure 6.21), where she has spent her labor hours in prior time periods.

Thus, Liza should invest approximately 60 hours (100 hours available × .60 average usage) for production help, 30 hours for service help, and 10 hours of management time for Monday if she is to stay within her budget.

Presented in a different way, Liza knows that each labor category has its own unique guests served per labor hour ratio, as noted in Figure 6.22.

While guests served per labor hour changes by category, the overall total yields 30 guests per labor hour used, which is her productivity standard. Liza's employee schedule for the production area on Monday might look as follows in Figure 6.23.

Figure 6.20 **Weekly Labor Budget for Geier Hall**

Week #: 1

Day	# of Meals Projected	Labor Standard	Labor Hours Budget
1	3,000	30 meals/hr	100
2	2,900	30 meals/hr	97
3	2,900	30 meals/hr	97
4	2,850	30 meals/hr	95
5	3,000	30 meals/hr	100
6	2,700	30 meals/hr	90
7	2,650	30 meals/hr	88
Total	20,000	30 meals/hr	667

Figure 6.21 **Recap of Percentage of Total Usage By Category**

Geier Hall

Labor Category	**% of Total**
Production	60%
Service	30
Management	10
Total	100

Figure 6.22 **Recap of Guests Served per Labor Hour**

Geier Hall

Labor Category	**Guests Served**	**Labor Hours Used**	**Guests Served per Labor Hour Used**
Production	3,000	60	50
Service	3,000	30	100
Management	3,000	10	300
Total	3.000	100	30

Since employee schedules can only be done in terms of either hours scheduled or dollars spent, the form used in Figure 6.23 is effective in any daily analysis of labor productivity. Since most labor is purchased on a daily basis, it should indeed be monitored on a daily basis. It should be modified, as needed, during the day. In other words, if customer demand is lower than expected, employees should be released from the schedule to reduce costs. If volume is higher than expected, additional workers should be available on an as-needed basis.

Some foodservice managers practice an **on-call** system whereby employees who are off duty are assigned to on-call status. This means that these employees can be contacted by management on short notice to service additional volume or to cover for other employees who are absent, for whatever reason. Other managers practice a **call-in** system. In this arrangement, employees who are off duty are required to check in with management on a daily basis to see if the volume is such that they may be needed. This is a particularly good way to make rapid changes in staffing because of unforeseen increases in projected sales volume.

The laws and regulations that govern such arrangements vary by state. Extra compensation for employees who agree to be on call may be required. The effective foodservice manager who wishes to use such an arrangement should check with the agency in his or her state that governs the employer-employee relationship.

Constant adjustment is a key to the quick-service industry's profitability, because schedule modifications by good managers in this segment of the indus-

Figure 6.23 **Employee Schedule**

Unit Name: Geier Hall Date: Monday, 1/1

Labor Category: Production Shift: A.M. & P.M. Labor Budget: 60 hours

Employee Name	Schedule	Hours Scheduled	Rate	Total Cost
Sally S.*	6:00 A.M.–2:30 P.M.	8	N/A	N/A
Tom T.*	6:30 A.M.–3:00 P.M.	8		
Steve J.*	8:00 A.M.–4:30 P.M.	8		
Lucy S.*	10:00 A.M.–6:30 P.M.	8		
Janice J.	7:00 A.M.–11:00 A.M.	4		
Susie T.	6:30 A.M.–10:30 A.M.	4		
Peggy H.	10:30 A.M.–1:30 P.M.	3		
Marian D.	2:00 P.M.–5:00 P.M.	3		
Larry M.*	11:00 A.M.–7:30 P.M.	8		
Curly J.*	1:00 P.M.–7:30 P.M.	6		
Total		60	N/A	N/A

*Includes 30-minute meal break

try are done hourly, not daily! Overtime, which is usually paid at a higher than average rate, should be held to a minimum and should require written management approval before it is authorized. In the case of Geier Hall, the hourly rate and total cost columns are not computed, since in this unit they are not part of our productivity measure. They would, of course, be filled out when establishing the schedule for Lillie's, because in that unit it is labor dollars, not hours used, that is the integral part of our productivity standard. An employee schedule, reviewed on a daily basis, should be established for each unit, labor category, and individual. It is critical to match labor usage with projected volume.

Step 4. Analyze Results

Liza has done a good job of using established labor standards and volume projections in building her employee schedule. To complete the job of managing labor-related expense, she must now analyze her results. Figure 6.24 represents the budgeted and actual results of the operation of Lillie's for the first four weeks of the year.

To determine percent of budget, the following formula, introduced in Chapter 1, is used:

$$\frac{\textbf{Actual amount}}{\textbf{Budgeted amount}} = \textbf{\% of budget}$$

Note that sales were somewhat less than we budgeted (98%), while labor cost dollars were somewhat higher than we budgeted (102%). As a result, labor cost % was somewhat higher than we had anticipated, in other words, a 31% actual result compared to a 30% budget percentage. Notice also that when we project volume perfectly (week 3) but overspend on labor, our actual labor cost will be too high (33%). Conversely, when we spend exactly what we budget for labor (week 4), but sales volume does not reach our estimate, labor cost percentage will similarly be too high (32%).

It may seem that a 1% variation in overall labor cost percentage is insignificant. In fact, in this case it represents only $185 ($8,435 actual − $8,250 budgeted = $185). If a large multiunit foodservice company achieved sales of $30,000,000 per year, however, 1% would represent $300,000 per year in cost overrun! Small percentages can add up! What constitutes a significant budget variation can be determined only by management. Clearly, a company doing $30 million in sales per year should not be concerned about a total labor cost variation of $185. Liza, however, may well want to review standard scheduling techniques with her supervisors, since she exceeded her budgeted amounts in three of the four weeks shown. In Liza's case, $185 is a significant budget variation.

Some foodservice operators prefer to use the term **standard cost** rather than **budgeted cost** when referring to labor. If productivity standards are used

Figure 6.24 **Labor Recap for Lillie's Actual versus Budgeted Labor Cost**

	Sales			Labor Costs			Labor Cost %	
Week	Budgeted	Actual	% of Budget	Budgeted	Actual	% of Budget	Budgeted	Actual
1	$ 6,550	$ 6,400	98%	$1,965	$1,867	95%	30%	29%
2	6,850	7,000	102	2,055	2,158	105	30	31
3	6,000	6,000	100	1,800	1,980	110	30	33
4	8,100	7,600	94	2,430	2,430	100	30	32
Total	27,500	27,000	98	8,250	8,435	102	30	31

to establish budgeted labor costs, then of course, the two terms are synonymous. It is important, however, not to confuse the concept of standard labor cost with that of standard food cost. A simple example will be of help in explaining the difference. Assume a restaurant serves each of four customers a ham steak for dinner. If the restaurant had ten such steaks in the refrigerator, and six remain at the end of the meal period, the food standard of one per customer has been maintained. Assume also, however, that these four customers are the only customers of the night and that labor staffing was established based on five customers. In this case, the labor standard or budget was not met in terms of customers served or perhaps dollar sales, yet management is in control. To further make the point, if one ham steak were missing, our food standard would be off by 10% (1 steak / 10 total). This would represent a serious loss of food product control. In our labor example, our forecast was off by 20% (1 customer short / 5 total projected), yet the variation is not due to lack of management control. In the case of labor, we are still within reasonable budget, though we may vary greatly from standard. For this reason, the authors prefer the term **budgeted labor**, rather than **standard labor**. Labor standards will always vary a bit unless customer counts can be predicted perfectly, which of course is rarely the case. We can, however, compare budgeted with actual results to determine if the reasons for variation from budget are valid and acceptable to management.

Reducing Labor-Related Costs

If management finds through analysis that labor costs are too high, problem areas must be identified and corrective action must be taken. If overall productivity of the work group cannot be improved, other action must be taken by management. The approach taken to reduce labor-related costs, however, is different for fixed payroll costs than for variable costs. Figure 6.25 indicates the steps that can be taken to reduce labor-related expense in each of these two categories.

Notice that the only way to reduce variable expense is to reduce salaries and wages paid or to increase productivity. Fixed expense can be reduced (as

Figure 6.25 **Reducing Labor-Related Expense**

Category	**Steps**
Fixed	1. Reduce wages paid to the fixed-payroll employees. 2. Combine jobs to eliminate fixed positions. 3. Improve productivity. 4. Increase sales volume.
Variable	1. Reduce wages paid to the variable employees. 2. Combine jobs to eliminate variable positions. 3. Improve productivity.

a percentage of income) by increasing sales volume. In all cases, however, the foodservice operation gains when increases in productivity mean that wages can remain high, and in fact increase.

Employee Empowerment

One way of increasing worker productivity, and thus reducing labor-related expense, is through employee empowerment. This is simply a step by management to involve employees in the decision-making process as far as guests and the employees themselves are concerned.

The economic downturn and the concomitant changes in guests' behavior patterns regarding travel and spending money, the changes in tax laws regarding write-offs, the forced closing of many hospitality enterprises and the resulting anxiety caused by this turn of events—all have forced management in the hospitality industry to think creatively. This has resulted in new approaches to evaluate the manner in which the industry has dealt with its operation and employees over time, and the adoption of techniques that lead to improved interpersonal relationships in the workplace.

Contrary to what custom has dictated in the past, the work force today is not as amenable to "forced" labor as in years gone by. In the last decade or so, workers throughout the world have come to the realization that there is more to life than work. Many expect more from life than a 50-hour work week, with little time left for family and kin, and with responsibilities that do not profit the employee. Blind allegiance to an organization, with the likelihood of being dismissed when management is in a squeeze, is no longer acceptable. Workers are seeking job satisfaction in addition to salaries or wages. Absolutely, salaries and wages must be acceptable and fair! It has, however, become critical that management show its human side, its compassionate side, and provide for its employees those amenities that make life gentler, smoother, and more gratifying. Workers have been making demands, and management, unable to offer more money, has found itself in a position where it has had to come up with incentives of a different sort. Many companies are receiving satisfying returns for providing incentives to their employees and creating an open and healthy work environment.

In addition to creating a good working climate, providing decent benefits, and establishing secure and equitable conditions, management has found that one successful way of increasing worker productivity, and thus reducing related expense, is through the use of employee **empowerment**. This term has come into its own in the last decade. It refers simply to the fact that whereas it was customary for management to make all decisions regarding every facet of the operational aspects of its organization, and then present them to its workers as inescapable results to be accomplished, workers are now being given the "power" to get involved. They are being empowered to make decisions with regard to themselves and, most importantly, the guests—the bread and butter of the hospitality industry. Employees generally work closely with guests: they see and observe; they talk to guests; they hear and listen to complaints; they can appease guests, if needed; they can find remedies to rectify problem situations. Most guest-related problems in the hospitality industry could be easily solved if employees were given the power to make it "right" for the guest. Managers have found in many cases that by offering a solid and constant training program, and by giving their employees a share in the decision-making process, they are nurturing a loyal and committed work force, supportive of management and willing to go that extra mile. Employee empowerment, which has been discussed in the hospitality industry primarily in terms of its positive effect on employees and guests, can also be of great assistance in freeing management to concentrate on running the business, while allowing employees to service the guest.

TEST YOUR SKILLS

A. Elizabeth operates a Bar-B-Q restaurant in a quaint southwestern city of the United States. She specializes in beef brisket and blackberry cobbler. Her operation is very popular. The following data are taken from her last month's operation. She would like to establish labor standards for the entire year based on last month's figures because she believes *that* month represents a good level of both customer service and profitability for her operation.

Operating Results for Bessie's

October		
Sales Week	**# of Guests**	**Labor Hours Used**
1	7,000	1,500
2	7,800	1,560
3	7,500	1,555
4	8,000	1,725
Total	30,300	6,340

Elizabeth uses her labor hours in the following ratio:

Meat production	**25%**
Bakery production	**15%**
Salad production	**10%**
Service	**20%**
Sanitation	**20%**
Management	**10%**

Elizabeth has a $5 per guest check average and an overall average payroll cost of $7 per hour.

Given the data above

1. **What is Elizabeth's labor cost percent standard?**
2. **What is her guests served per labor hour standard?**
3. **What is her guests served per labor dollar standard?**
4. **What is her sales per labor hour standard for each of the following categories:**
   a. **Meat production**
   b. **Bakery production**
   c. **Salad production**
   d. **Service**
   e. **Sanitation**
   f. **Management**

B. Jeffrey operates a high-volume, fine-dining restaurant called The Baroness. His labor productivity ratio of choice is guests served per labor hour. His standard for both waitpersons and buspersons is as follows:

1. **Waitperson = 10 guests per labor hour**
2. **Busperson = 25 guests per labor hour**

On a busy Saturday night, Jeffrey projects the following volume in terms of anticipated guests. His projections are made in half-hour blocks. Determine the number of labor hours Jeffrey should schedule for each job classification for each time period.

Volume/Staffing Forecast for Saturday

The Baroness

Time	# of Guests Anticipated	Waitperson Hours Needed	Busperson Hours Needed
5:30– 6:00	170	17/8.5	6.8/3.4
6:00– 6:30	190	19/9.5	7.6/3.8
6:30– 7:00	250	25	10
7:00– 7:30	340	34	13.6
7:30– 8:00	260	26	10.4
8:00– 8:30	285	28.5	11.4
8:30– 9:00	205	20.5	8.2
9:00– 9:30	180	18.0	7.2
9:30–10:00	160	16	6.4
10:00–10:30	90	9	3.6
10:30–11:00	85	8.5	3.4
11:00–11:30	60	6.0	2.4
Total	2,275	227.5	91

How often in the night should Jeffrey check his volume forecast in order to ensure that he achieves his labor productivity standards and thus is within budget at the end of the evening?

C. Steve is in trouble. He has never been a particularly strong labor cost control person. He likes to think of himself more as a "people person." His boss, however, believes that Steve must get more serious about controlling labor costs or he will make Steve an unemployed people person! Steve estimates his weekly sales, then submits that figure to his boss, who then assigns Steve a labor budget for the week. Steve's operating results and budget figures for last month are presented below.

Operating Results

Steve's Airport Deli **For week 1–5**

	Sales			Labor Costs			Labor Cost %	
Week	**Budget**	**Actual**	**% of Budget**	**Budget**	**Actual**	**% of Budget**	**Budget**	**Actual**
1	$2,500	$2,250	90%	$ 875	$ 900	103%	35%	40%
2	1,700	1,610	95%	595	630	106%	35%	39%
3	4,080	3,650	89%	1,224	1,300	106%	30%	35%
4	3,100	2,800	90%	1,085	1,100	101%	35%	39%
5	2,600	2,400	92%	910	980	108%	35%	41%
Total	13,980	12,710	91%	4689	4910 (35%)	105%	34%	39%

Compute Steve's % of budget figures for both sales and labor costs. Also compute Steve's budgeted and actual labor cost percentages per week and for the five-week accounting period. Do you feel that Steve has significant variations from budget? Why do you think Steve's boss assigned Steve a lower labor cost percentage goal during week 3? How do you feel about Steve's overall performance? What would you do if you were Steve's boss? If you were Steve?

CHAPTER 7

Controlling Other Expenses

OVERVIEW

This chapter details the management of foodservice expenses that are not food, beverage, or payroll. These **other expenses** are categorized both in terms of being fixed or variable, and in terms of being controllable or noncontrollable.

Actual other expense computation is demonstrated in terms of both other expense per guest and other expense as a percentage of sales.

HIGHLIGHTS

At the conclusion of this chapter, the manager will be able to

A. Assign other expenses in terms of being either fixed or variable
B. Differentiate controllable from noncontrollable expenses
C. Compute other expense costs in terms of both cost per guest and percentage of sales

Managing Other Expenses

Food, beverage, and payroll expenses represent the greatest cost areas for foodservice operators. **Other expenses,** those cost items that are not food, beverage, or payroll, however, also can account for significant financial expenditures on the part of the foodservice unit. Controlling these costs can be just as important to the success of a foodservice operation as controlling food, beverage, and payroll expenses. An excellent example of this is in the area of energy conservation and waste recycling. In the 1970s, energy shortages caused many foodservice operations to implement a policy of serving water on request rather than with each order. Customers found this change quite acceptable, and the savings in warewashing costs, equipment usage, labor, energy, and cleaning supplies were significant. In a similar vein, many operators today are finding that recycling cans, jars, and paper can be good not only for the environment but also for the bottom line. Source reduction, that is, working with food manufacturers and wholesalers to reduce product packaging waste, is yet another example. When product packaging and wrapping are held to a minimum, delivery and storage costs are reduced, thus reducing the price foodservice operators must pay to wholesalers. In addition, the quantity of trash generated by this packaging is reduced, and this, in turn, reduces garbage pickup fees to the foodservice operator. All of the examples cited point to the importance of controlling other expenses.

Other expenses can constitute almost anything in the foodservice business. If a restaurant is a floating ship, periodically scraping the barnacles off the boat is an other expense. If an operator is serving food to oil field workers in Alaska, heating fuel for the dining rooms and kitchen is an other expense, and probably a fairly large one! If a company has been selected to serve food at the Olympics in a foreign country, airfares for its employees may be a significant other expense. It is important to note that each operation will have its own unique list of required other expenses. It is not possible, therefore, to list all imaginable expenses that could be incurred by the foodservice operator. It is possible, nonetheless, to group them into categories that make them easier to understand and manage. Napkins, straws, paper cups, and plastic lids, for example, might all be listed under the heading **paper supplies,** while stir sticks, coasters, tiny plastic swords, small paper umbrellas, and the like, used in a cocktail lounge, might be grouped under the listing **bar supplies.** Groupings, if used, should make sense to the operator and should be specific enough to let the operator know what is in the category.

The following lists present many common other expense categories grouped under these four headings:

1. **Costs related to food and beverage operations**
2. **Costs related to labor**
3. **Costs related to facility maintenance**
4. **Occupation costs**

Again, it should be pointed out that foodservice managers should analyze their other expense costs in a way that is meaningful to them. Only then can they begin to truly manage and thus control their costs. The following list details many of the other expenses associated with the four groupings listed above.

1. **Costs related to Food and Beverage Operations**
   a. **Direct operating expenses**
      Uniforms
      Laundry and dry cleaning
      Linen rental
      Linen
      China and glassware
      Silverware

Kitchen utensils
Kitchen fuel
Cleaning supplies
Paper supplies
Guest supplies
Bar supplies
Menus and wine lists
Contract cleaning
Exterminating
Flowers and decorations
Auto and truck expense
Parking lot expenses
Licenses and permits
Banquet expenses
Other operating expenses

b. **Music and entertainment**
Orchestra and musicians
Professional entertainers
Mechanical music
Contracted wire services
Piano rental and tuning
Films, records, tapes, and sheet music
Programs
Royalties to ASAP, BMI, and SESAC
Booking agents' fees
Meals served to musicians

c. **Marketing**
Selling and promotion
Sales representative service
Travel expense on solicitation
Direct mail
Telephone and telegraph used for advertising and promotion
Entertainment cost in promotion of business (including gratis meals to customers)
Postage

d. **Advertising**
Newspapers
Magazines and trade journals
Circulars, brochures, postal cards, and other mailing pieces
Outdoor signs
Radio and television
Programs, directories, and guides
Preparation of copy photographs, etc.

e. **Public relations and publicity**
Civic and community projects
Donations

Souvenirs, favors, and treasure chest items

f. **Fees and commissions**
Advertising or promotional agency fees
Franchise fees

g. **Research**
Travel in connection with research
Outside research agency
Product testing

h. **Utilities**
Electric current
Electric bulbs
Water
Removal of waste
Fuel
Engineer's supplies
Ice

i. **Administrative expenses**
Office stationery, printing, and supplies
Data processing costs
Postage
Telegrams and telephone
Management fees
Dues and subscriptions
Executive office expense
Traveling expenses
Insurance—general
Commissions on credit card charges
Provision for doubtful accounts
Cash over or short
Professional fees
Directors' or trustees' fees
Protective and bank pickup services
Bank charges
Miscellaneous

2. **Costs Related to Labor**

a. **Employee benefits**
FICA
Federal unemployment tax
State unemployment tax
Workmen's compensation
Group insurance
State health insurance tax
Welfare plan payments
Pension plan payments
Accident and health insurance premiums
Hospitalization, Blue Cross, and Blue Shield

Employee meals
Employee instruction and education expenses
Employee Christmas and other parties
Employee sports activities
Medical expenses
Credit union
Awards and prizes
Transportation and housing

3. Costs Related to Facility Maintenance

a. Repairs and maintenance

Furniture and fixtures
Kitchen equipment
Office equipment
Refrigeration
Air conditioning
Plumbing and heating
Electrical and mechanical
Floors and carpets
Buildings
Parking lot
Gardening and grounds maintenance
Building alterations
Painting, plastering, and decorating
Maintenance contracts—elevators
Maintenance contracts—signs
Maintenance contracts—office machinery
Autos and trucks
Other equipment and supplies

4. Occupation Costs

a. Rent and other occupation costs, interest, and depreciation

Rent—minimum or fixed
Percentage rent
Ground rental
Equipment rental
Real estate taxes
Personal property taxes
Other municipal taxes
Franchise tax
Capital stock tax
Partnership or corporation license fees
Insurance on building and contents

b. **Interest**
   Notes payable
   Long-term debt
   Other
c. **Depreciation**
   Buildings
   Amortization of leasehold
   Amortization of leasehold improvements
   Furniture, fixtures, and equipment

While there are many ways in which to consider other expenses, the following two views of these costs are particularly useful for the food operator.

1. **Fixed or variable**
2. **Controllable or noncontrollable**

A short discussion of these two concepts will help better understand their relationship to expenses.

Other Expenses as Either Fixed or Variable

A **fixed expense** is one that remains constant despite increases or decreases in sales volume. A **variable expense** is one that generally increases as sales volume increases and decreases as sales volume decreases. Consider, for example, Jo Ann's Hot Dogs Deluxe, a midsize restaurant, located in a shopping center, that serves upscale Chicago-style hot dogs.

Assume that Jo Ann's average sales volume is $28,000 per month. Rent for her facility space is set at $2,000 per month. Each month, Jo Ann computes her rent as a percentage of total sales, using the following standard cost percentage formula:

$$\frac{\textbf{Other expense}}{\textbf{Income}} = \textbf{Other expense percentage}$$

In this case, the other expense category she is interested in looking at is rent; therefore, the formula becomes as follows:

$$\frac{\textbf{Rent expense}}{\textbf{Income}} = \textbf{Rent expense percentage}$$

Jo Ann has computed her rent expense percentage for the last six months. The results are shown in Figure 7.1

Note that Jo Ann's rent expense percentage ranges from a high of 10% (February) to a low of 5.55% (June), yet it is very clear that rent itself was a constant or fixed figure of $2,000.00 per month; thus, rent for her is considered to be a fixed expense. It is important to note that while the rent expense is fixed (as a dollar amount), the rent **percentage** declines as volume increases. Thus the rent payment, as a percentage of sales, is not constant.

It makes little sense for Jo Ann to get concerned about the fact that her rent expense percentage varies by a great amount, based on the time of the year. If Jo Ann is comfortable with the six-month average rent percentage (7.14%), then she is in control of, and managing, her other expense category called rent. If Jo Ann feels that her rent expense percentage is too high, she has only two options. She must increase sales and thereby reduce rent expense percentage, or she must negotiate a lower monthly rental with her landlord. When rent is a fixed expense, as in this case, the expense, as expressed by the percentage of sales, may vary. The expense itself, however, is not affected by sales volume.

Jo Vin operates Quick Wok, an Oriental restaurant in a suburban shopping mall. His rent is based on sales volume. In other words, his lease stipulates that he pay 7.14% of his gross monthly sales as rent. Jo Vin has computed his monthly rental expense for a six-month period. The result is illustrated in Figure 7.2.

Figure 7.1 **Jo Ann's Rent Percentage**

For period 1/1 to 6/30

Month	Rent Expense	Income	Rent %
January	$2,000.00	$23,000.00	8.70%
February	2,000.00	20,000.00	10.00
March	2,000.00	25,000.00	8.00
April	2,000.00	30,000.00	6.66
May	2,000.00	34,000.00	5.88
June	2,000.00	36,000.00	5.55
6-month average	2,000.00	28,000.00	7.14

Figure 7.2 **Quick Wok Rent Expense**

For period 1/1 to 6/30

Month	Rent Expense	Income	Rent %
January	$1,642.20	$23,000.00	7.14%
February	1,428.00	20,000.00	7.14
March	1,785.00	25,000.00	7.14
April	2,142.00	30,000.00	7.14
May	2,427.60	34,000.00	7.14
June	2,570.40	36,000.00	7.14
6-month average	1,999.20	28,000.00	7.14

In Jo Vin's case, the dollar amount paid for rent is variable and increases when sales volume increases. Rent expense goes down when sales volume goes down. Thus, rent expenses range from a low of $1,428.00 (February) to a high of $2,570.40 (June).

In summary, fixed expenses do not vary with volume; variable expenses change as volume changes. A convenient way to remember the distinction is to consider a napkin holder and napkins on a cafeteria line. The napkin holder is a fixed expense. One holder is sufficient whether we serve 10 guests at lunch or 100 guests. The napkins themselves, however, are a variable expense. As we serve more guests (assuming that each one takes one napkin), we will incur a greater paper napkin expense.

It is not possible to categorize fixed or variable costs in terms of being either "good" or "bad." Some expenses, by their very nature, are related to sales volume. Others are not. It is important to remember that the goal of management is not to reduce but to **increase** expenses. Expenses are required if we are to service our guests. In the example of the paper napkins, it is clear that management would prefer to use 100 napkins at lunch rather than 10 if it means serving 100 customers rather than 10. Thus, increasing variable costs is desirable if management increases them in a way that makes sense for both the operation and the satisfaction of the guest.

As we saw in the case of labor expense (Chapter 6), the concept of fixed and variable expense is quite useful. Variations in expense percentage that relate *only* to whether an expense is fixed or variable should not be of undue concern to management. It is only when a fixed expense is too high, or a variable expense is out of control, that management should act. This concept is called **management by exception.** That is, if the expense is within an acceptable range, there is no need for management to intervene. Management must take corrective action only when operational results are outside the range of acceptability. This approach keeps management from overreacting to minor variations in expense, while monitoring all important activities.

Examples of other fixed food service expenses include the areas of advertising (outdoor sign rentals), utilities (restroom light bulbs), employee benefits (employee-of-the-month prizes), repairs and maintenance (parking lot paving), and occupation costs (interest due on long-term debt). Most food operation other expenses, however, are related to sales volume, and thus management control of these items is critical.

Other Expenses as either Controllable or Noncontrollable

While it is useful in some cases to consider other expenses in terms of being fixed or variable, it is also useful to consider some expenses in terms of being controllable or noncontrollable. Consider for a moment the case of Steve, the operator of a neighborhood tavern/sandwich shop. Most of Steve's sales revenue comes from the sale of beer, sandwiches, and his special pizza.

Steve is free to decide on a weekly or monthly basis the amount he will spend on advertising. Advertising expense, then, is under Steve's direct control and is considered a controllable expense. Some of his other expenses, however, are not under his direct control. Taxes are an all too familiar type of noncontrollable expense. The state in which Steve operates charges a liquor tax on all alcoholic beverage sales. As the state in which he operates increases the liquor tax, Steve is forced to pay more. In this situation, the alcoholic beverage tax would be considered a noncontrollable expense. That is, it is an expense beyond Steve's immediate control.

Assume for a moment that you are the manager of a quick-service unit that sells take-out chicken. Your unit is part of a nationwide chain of such stores. Each month, your store is charged a $500 advertising and promotion fee by the regional headquarters' office. The $500 is used to purchase television advertising time for your company. This $500 charge is a noncontrollable expense. A **noncontrollable** expense then is one that the foodservice manager can neither increase nor decrease. A **controllable expense** is one in which decisions made by the foodservice manager can have an effect of either increasing or reducing the expense. Simply stated, management has some control over controllable expenses, but it has little or no control over noncontrollable expenses. Other examples of noncontrollable expenses include some insurance premiums, property taxes, and interest on debt and depreciation. In every one of these cases, the foodservice operator will find that even the best control systems will not impact the specific expense. Operating management should focus its attention on controllable rather than noncontrollable expenses.

It is also important to distinguish between a **necessary** expense and a **noncontrollable** expense. They are not the same. Take, for example, the printing of menus in a restaurant. This is a necessary expense. It is *not*, however, a noncontrollable one. An operator may elect to simply photocopy an 8½-by-11-inch sheet of white paper for the menu, at a cost of 10 cents per copy. On the other hand, he or she may elect to print a full-color, 20-by-24-inch masterpiece, at a cost of $15 per copy. Clearly then, while the expense for a menu is necessary, it is also controllable. Conversely, an expense may be unnecessary, but also noncontrollable. Electing to rent additional parking space from the shopping center next door may not be necessary for the restaurant's survival, although it may help. If the lot is rented, however, the monthly cost becomes a noncontrollable other expense, since the operator has no control over the price paid to rent the space once the owner of the lot has determined the rental fee.

Cost Percentage or Cost per Guest

As we have seen, the computation required to establish the other expense percentage requires the expense category to be divided by sales. In many cases, this approach yields useful management information. In some cases, however, the foodservice manager's sales figure may not provide adequate information.

In a situation such as this, the concept of cost per guest may be of some value. Consider the following example. Scott operates Chez Scot, an exclusive fine-dining establishment in a suburban area of a major city. One of Scott's major expenses is linen. He uses both tablecloths and napkins. Scott's partner, Joshua, believes that linen costs are a noncontrollable expense and should be monitored through the use of a linen cost percentage figure. In fact, says Scott's partner, linen cost percentage has been declining over the past five months; therefore, the control systems must be working. As evident in Figure 7.3, linen cost percentage has indeed been declining over the past five months.

Scott, however, is convinced that there **are** control problems. He has monitored linen cost on a **cost per guest** basis using the following formula:

$$\frac{\textbf{Other expense}}{\textbf{\# of guests served}} = \textbf{Cost per guest}$$

His information is presented in Figure 7.4. It validates Scott's fears. There is indeed a control problem in the linen area.

Figure 7.4 shows that a linen control problem does exist since it is plain that linen cost per guest has gone from $1.06 in January to its May high of $1.22.

Figure 7.3 **Linen Cost Percentage**

Chez Scot

Month	Sales	Linen Cost	Cost %
January	$ 68,000.00	$ 2,720.00	4.00%
February	70,000.00	2,758.00	3.94
March	72,000.00	2,772.00	3.85
April	71,500.00	2,753.00	3.85
May	74,000.00	2,812.00	3.80
Total	355,500.00	13,815.00	3.89

Figure 7.4 **Linen Cost Per Guest**

Chez Scot

Month	Linen Cost	# of Guests Served	Cost per Guest
January	$ 2,720.00	2,566	$1.06
February	2,758.00	2,508	1.10
March	2,772.00	2,410	1.15
April	2,753.00	2,333	1.18
May	2,812.00	2,305	1.22
Total	13,815.00	12,122	1.14

Chez Scot is enjoying increased sales ($68,000 in January versus $74,000 in May), but its customer count is declining (2,566 in January versus 2305 in May). The check average has obviously increased. This is a good sign, as it indicates that each customer is spending more on food. The fact that fewer customers are being served should, however, result in a decrease in demand for linen, and thus a decline in cost. In fact, on a per person basis, linen costs are up. Scott is correct to be concerned about possible problems in the linen control area.

Cost per Guest

Cost per guest may also be useful in a situation where no sales figure is received by the foodservice manager. Consider a college dormitory feeding situation where paper products such as cups, napkins, straws, and lids are placed on the serving line, to be used by the students eating their meals.

In this case, Ann, the cafeteria supervisor, wonders whether students are taking more of these items than is normal. The problem is, of course, that she is not exactly sure what "normal" use is when it comes to supplying paper products to her students. Ann belongs to an association that asks its members to supply annual cost figures to a central location where they are tabulated and sent back to the membership. Figure 7.5 shows the tabulations from five colleges, in addition to those from Ann's unit.

Ann has computed her paper product cost per student for the year and has found it to be higher than at P. University and the University of T., but lower than O. University, C. State University, and Jamestown State. Ann's costs appear to be in line in the paper goods area. If, however, Ann hopes to reduce paper products costs per student even further, she could, perhaps, call or arrange a visit to either P. University or the University of T. to observe their operations or their purchasing techniques.

Figure 7.5 **Average Paper Product Cost**

Campus Association Report for 1992

Institution	Cost of Paper Products	# of Students	Paper Products Cost Per Student
O. University	$140,592.00	8,080	$17.40
C. State University	109,200.00	6,500	16.80
P. University	122,276.00	7,940	15.40
University of T.	184,755.00	11,300	16.35
Jamestown State	61,560.00	3,600	17.10
5-university average	123,676.60	7,484	16.53
Ann's institution	77,220.00	4,680	16.50

The cost per guest formula is of value when management believes it can be helpful in budgeting or when lack of a sales figure makes the computation of other expense percentage impossible.

Figure 7.6 presents a six-column form that is useful in tracking both daily and cumulative cost per guest figures. It is maintained by inserting other expense cost and # of guests served in the first two sets of columns. The third set of columns, cost per guest, is obtained by using the cost per guest formula (page 232).

Figure 7.6 **Cost of Paper Products**

Ann's Institution Date: ______________

	Other Expense Cost		**# of Guests Served**		**Cost Per Guest**	
Weekday	**Today**	**Todate**	**Today**	**Todate**	**Today**	**Todate**

Techniques to Reduce Other Expenses

Since other expenses can be broken down into four distinct areas, it is useful to consider these four areas when developing strategies for reducing overall other expense costs. It is important to remember that each foodservice manager faces his or her own unique set of other expenses. Those operators who are effective are constantly on the lookout for ways to reduce unnecessary additions to other expense categories.

Reducing Costs Related to Food and Beverage Operations

In many respects, some of these other expenses should be treated like food and beverage expenses. For instance, in the case of cleaning supplies, linen, uniforms, and the like, products should be ordered, inventoried, and issued in the same manner used for food and beverage products. In general, fixed costs related to food and beverage operations can only be reduced when measuring them as a percentage of total sales. This is done, of course, by increasing the total sales figure. Reducing total variable cost expenses is generally not desirable, since in fact, each additional sale will bring additional variable expense. In this case, while total variable expense may increase, the positive impact of the additional sales on fixed costs will serve to reduce overall other expense percentage.

To see how this is done, let's examine a shaved ice kiosk called Igloo's, in the middle of a small parking lot. Figure 7.7 demonstrates the impact of volume increases on both total other expense and other expense percentage. We assume, in this example, that some of the other expenses related to food and beverage operations are fixed and others are variable. The variable portion of other expense in this example equals 10% of gross sales. Fixed expense equals $150.

Figure 7.7 **Fixed and Variable Expense**

Igloo's

Income	Fixed Expense	Variable Expense (10%)	Total Other Expense	Other Expense Percent
$ 1,000.00	$150.00	$ 100.00	$ 250.00	25.0%
3,000.00	150.00	300.00	450.00	15.0
9,000.00	150.00	900.00	1,050.00	11.7
10,000.00	150.00	1,000.00	1,150.00	11.5
15,000.00	150.00	1,500.00	1,650.00	11.0

Expense percentage in this case is computed by the following formula:

$$\frac{\textbf{Total other expense}}{\textbf{Income}} = \textbf{Other expense percentage}$$

While variable expense rises from $100 to $1,500, other expense percentage drops from 25% of income to 11% of income. Thus, to reduce costs related to food and beverage operations, increases in income are quite helpful! If **all** other expenses related to food and beverage operations were 100% variable, however, this strategy would not have the effect of reducing other expense percentage, since total other expenses would increase proportionately to volume increases, and other expense percentage would be unchanged.

Reducing Cost Related to Labor

As we saw in Chapter 6, labor-related expenses can also be considered partially fixed and partially variable. To help reduce costs related to labor, it is necessary for the foodservice operator to eliminate wasteful labor expense. This includes the cost of advertising, hiring, and training new employees because of excessive employee turnover. It also means abiding by hiring practices that result in lower health insurance premiums for workers, if this benefit is provided. Proper hiring practices also impact unemployment tax rates paid by the operator. This includes maintaining a safe work environment and providing excellent training to reduce the costs associated with workmen's compensation claims.

Conversely, those operators who attempt to reduce labor-related costs too much, by not providing adequate health care, pension, or sick leave benefits, may find that the best workers prefer to work elsewhere, leaving the operator with a less productive work force than would otherwise be possible. In many ways, employees are the operator's most valuable asset. To reduce employee benefits while attempting to retain a well-qualified work force is simply management at its worst!

Reducing Cost Related to Facility Maintenance

Any worker knows that keeping his or her tools clean and in good working order will make them last longer and perform better. The same is true for foodservice facilities. A properly designed and implemented preventative maintenance program can go a long way toward reducing equipment failure and thus decreasing equipment and facility-related costs. Proper care of mechanical equipment not only prolongs its life, it actually reduces operational costs. As the price of energy needed to operate facilities continues to rise, the effective foodservice manager will strive to operate a repair and maintenance program that seeks to discover and treat minor equipment and facility problems before they become major problems. In the area of maintenance contracts, for either equipment, elevators, or grounds, it is recommended that these contracts go out yearly for bid. This is especially true if the dollar value of the contract is large.

Air-conditioning, plumbing, heating, and refrigerated units should be inspected at least yearly for purposes of preventative maintenance. A form such as the one in Figure 7.8 is useful in this process.

Some operators, like Roscoe (Figure 7.8), are fortunate enough to have their own maintenance people. If this is the case, make sure they have copies of

Figure 7.8 **Equipment Inspection Report**

Unit Name: Roscoe's Time Period: 1/1–1/31

Item Inspected	Inspection Date	Inspected by	Action Recommended
A. Refrigerator #6	1/1	D.H.	Replace gasket
B. Fryer	1/1	D.H.	None
C. Ice machine	1/1	D.H.	Drain, de-lime
D.			
E.			

the operating and maintenance manuals of all equipment. These documents can prove invaluable in the reduction of equipment and facility-related costs.

Reducing Occupation Costs

Occupation costs refer to those expenses incurred by the foodservice unit that are related to the occupation of and payment for the physical facility it occupies.

For the foodservice manager who is not the owner, the majority of occupation costs will be noncontrollable. Rent, taxes, interest, and depreciation are real costs but beyond the immediate control of the foodservice manager. However, for the foodservice operation owner, occupation costs are a primary determiner of both profit on sales and return on dollars invested. When occupation costs are too high because of unfavorable rent or lease arrangements, or excessive debt load, the foodservice operation's owner may face extreme difficulty in generating profit. Food, beverage, and labor costs can only be managed to a point; beyond that, efforts to reduce costs will result in decreased guest satisfaction. If occupation costs are unrealistically high, no amount of effective cost control can help "save" the operation's profitability.

Other expenses can range from 5% to 20% or more of the gross sales. These expenses, while considered as minor expenses, can be extremely important to overall operational profitability. An understanding of their role in the foodservice operation's total expense picture is vital.

TEST YOUR SKILLS

A. Susie operates a restaurant in the ski resort town of Asvail. She has decided to group her other expense categories in terms of being either a fixed expense or a variable expense.

List those expenses that are related to sales volume under the heading variable expense. List those that do not vary with sales under the heading fixed expense. The expenses Susie incurs are as follows:

1. **Linen rental**
2. **Piano rental**
3. **Ice**
4. **Radio advertising fees**
5. **Pension plan payments**
6. **Snow shoveling fees (parking lot)**
7. **FICA**
8. **Kitchen equipment rental (mixer)**
9. **Long-term debt payment**
10. **Real estate tax**

Variable Expense	Fixed Expense
a.	a.
b.	b.
c.	c.
d.	d.
e.	e.
f.	f.
g.	g.
h.	h.
i.	i.
j.	j.

B. John owns and operates the End Zone Steakhouse. He would like to turn the operation over to his son Zeke, a graduate of Cougar High School. Zeke, however, has no foodservice background. Zeke would like to prove that he can effectively operate the restaurant and successfully control costs. John has allowed Zeke to manage End Zone for the past three months. Operating cost categories for the restaurant, in terms of other expenses, are shown below. Place a check in the controllable column for those operating expenses that Zeke could control. If he could not control the cost, check the noncontrollable column.

Other Expenses	Controllable	Noncontrollable
1. Real estate tax		✓
2. Menu printing	✓	
3. Professional musicians	✓	
4. Ice	✓	✓
5. Charitable donations	✓	
6. Cleaning supplies	✓	
7. Flowers and decorations	✓	
8. Water	(✓)	✓
9. Licenses and permits		✓
10. Electric current	(✓)	✓

Some expenses seem to be a mixture of both controllable and noncontrollable expenses. How is that possible?

C. Lea operates a lounge in an extremely popular downtown convention hotel. The hotel regularly operates around the 80% occupancy mark, and its lounge, Luigi's, is very often filled to capacity. On weeks when business at the hotel is slower, Lea attempts to build local sales by scheduling a variety of popular bands to play on the stage. She must select one band to play on Saturday night, six weeks from now, when the hotel is not busy. She has kept records of the costs and sales volume of the last four bands she has booked.

Compute both band expense percentage and cost per guest served. Based on the cost-effectiveness of the bands, which one should Lea select for booking?

Date	Band	Band Expense	Lounge Sales	Expense %	# of Guests Served	Cost per Guest Served
1/1	Tiny and the Boys	$1,400	$11,400		1425	
2/1	Shakin' Bill and the Billfolds	1,900	12,250		1980	
3/1	La Noise	2,000	12,000		2005	
4/1	The Hoppers	2,000	10,250		2100	

Would your answer change if you knew Lea charged a $5 cover charge to enter the lounge on the nights she has a band, and the cover charge is reported separately from the lounge sales? Why?

CHAPTER 8

Analyzing Results Using Basic Accounting

OVERVIEW

This chapter defines the role of the foodservice accountant in producing the balance sheet and the income, or profit and loss (P&L), statement. How to analyze the menu, as well as how to determine the break-even point, is explained. In addition, budgeting and operational budget preparation are discussed, and techniques to analyze operational costs are presented.

HIGHLIGHTS

At the conclusion of this chapter, the manager will be able to

A. Prepare and analyze a weekly or monthly profit and loss statement
B. Prepare and analyze a weekly or monthly budget and performance to budget statement
C. Determine an operational break-even point

Introduction to Financial Analysis

Far too many foodservice managers find that they collect numbers, fill out forms, or generate reams and reams of computer printout paper with little regard for what they should do with all this data. Some have said that managers often make poor decisions because they lack information, but when it comes to the financial analysis of an operation, the opposite is almost always true. Foodservice managers more often than not will find themselves awash in numbers! It is the job of the effective manager to sift through this information and select for analysis those numbers that can shed light on exactly what is *meaningful* and what is happening in the operation. This information, in an appropriate form, is necessary not merely to effectively operate the business, but to serve the many interest groups that are directly or indirectly involved with the financial operation of the facility. Local, state, and federal financial records relating to taxes and employee wages will have to be submitted to the government on a regular basis. In addition, records showing the financial health of an operation may have to be submitted to new suppliers in order to establish credit worthiness. Also, if a foodservice operation has been established with both operating partners and investors, those investors will certainly require accurate and timely updates that focus on the health of the business.

Owners, stockholders, and investment bankers may all have an interest in the day-to-day efficiency and effectiveness of management. For each of these groups and, of course, for the foodservice organization's own upper management, the accurate compilation and analysis of the operation's financial transactions are critical. In the foodservice industry, the average unit manager is concerned with examining the cost of doing business, often called **cost accounting**, and with preparing and maintaining a budget. This budget, or business plan, must detail the operational direction of the unit and the expected financial results. Cost accounting will show management how close actual performance is to this planned budget, while providing the basis for changes if the operation is to achieve the goals of its plan. It is important to note that the business plan is not a static document. It should be modified and fine-tuned as cost accounting presents data about sales and costs that affect the profit, or lack thereof, and the direction of the overall operation.

For example, if Ernie, the manager of a nightclub featuring Latin music, finds that his major competitor in the city has closed its doors, he clearly may decide that he wants to revise his revenue budget upward over the next few months. Not to do so might allow Ernie to meet his original sales goal, but would ignore an event that will definitely impact his business plan.

In a similar vein, if Roberta, the manager of a delicatessen specializing in salads, sliced meats, and related items, finds through her cost records that the price she pays for salami has tripled since last month, she must adjust her budget or find that she has no chance of staying within its guidelines. Again, the point is that the foodservice business plan or budget should be closely monitored through the use of cost accounting that includes the thoughtful analysis of the data this type of accounting provides. Because this is so, it is important for the foodservice manager to be aware of the difference between simply recording and summarizing financial data, and analyzing that data. An excellent example in the foodservice industry can be found in the sale of cash registers that can be programmed to provide data about food and beverage sales per waitperson. In this situation, management can track, per shift, the relative sales effort of each service employee. If this is done with the goal of either increasing the training of the less productive service provider or rewarding the most productive one, the cash register has, in fact, added information that is valuable and assisted in the unit's operation. If, on the other hand, this information is dutifully recorded on a daily basis, sent to the regional office, and then left to collect dust, the cash register has actually harmed the operation by taking management's time away from the more important task of running the business. It has converted the manager's role from that of analyst to that of recordkeeper, and a mindless recordkeeper at that. This type of situation must be avoided at all cost if managers are to be in the production area or dining room during service periods, and not in the office catching up on their paperwork.

One need not be a certified public accountant (C.P.A.) to analyze data related to foodservice income and expense. While this is not meant to discount the value of an accounting professional who assists the foodservice manager, it is important to establish that it is the professional foodservice manager, not an outside expert, who is most qualified to assess the effectiveness of the foodservice team in providing the service levels desired by management, and in controlling production-related costs. Bookkeeping has as its function the recording and summarizing of financial data. The effective foodservice manager must do more. The analyzing of data, the traditional role of the accountant, can also be the role of the manager. The process is not complex and, in fact, is one of the most fun and creative aspects of a foodservice manager's job.

A good foodservice manager is a manager first and not an accountant. It is important, however, for an effective manager to be able to read, analyze, and understand financial information, and be able to converse intelligently and confidently with the many parties outside the operation who will read and use the information generated by accountants. This information will be crucial to the operation's overall health and success, and can provide the needed data that will assist in sharpening the quality of management decisions.

Uniform System of Accounts

Financial statements related to the operation of a foodservice facility are, of course, of interest to management, stockholders, owners, creditors, governmental agencies, and often, the general public. To ensure that this financial information is presented in a way that is both useful and consistent, Uniform Systems of Accounts have been established for many areas of the hospitality industry. The Uniform System of Accounts for Restaurants, for example, has been developed by the National Restaurant Association. Uniform Systems of Accounts also exist for hotels, clubs, nursing homes, schools, and hospitals. Each system seeks to provide a consistent and clear manner in which to record income, expenses, and overall financial condition. Income categories, expense classifications, and methods of computing relevant ratios are included in the uniform systems. These uniform systems are typically available from the national associations involved with each foodservice segment.

It is important to note that the uniform systems attempt to provide operator guidelines, rather than mandated methodology. Small foodservice operations, for example, may use the Uniform System of Accounts for Restaurants in a slightly different way than will large operations. In all cases, however, operators who use the Uniform System of Accounts "speak the same language," and it is truly useful that they do so. If each operator prepared financial statements in any manner he or she elected, it is unlikely that these statements could be properly interpreted by the many external audiences who must use them. Thus, an effective manager will secure a copy of the appropriate Uniform System of Accounts for his or her operation and become familiar with its basic formats and principles.

The foodservice manager who wishes to analyze his or her business must have a thorough understanding of three primary financial summaries as follows:

Summary	Purpose
1. Balance Sheet	1. Tells management *where they are*
2. Income or profit and loss (P&L) statement	2. Tells management *how they performed*
3. Budget or plan	3. Tells management *where they are going*

Analysis of the Balance Sheet

The balance sheet is fundamentally a statement that shows an organization's financial position or strength at a point in time. Its purpose is to communicate the operation's assets, liabilities, and owner's equity, using the following formula:

Assets = Liabilities + Owner's equity

When compiling the balance sheet, the accountant adds up the total value of everything owned by the organization. This includes buildings, land, equipment, inventory, accounts receivable, cash, and anything else that the company owns that has a measurable value. These items, collectively, are called the company's assets.

Next, a determination must be made about what the company owes. This includes accounts payable, accrued taxes and wages, mortgages, dividends due, and any other outstanding long- or short-term debts. These items are called the company's liabilities. The difference between what the company *owns* as assets, and what it *owes* as liabilities is referred to as **owner's equity**, that is, what the owner of the business can call his or her own. An individual buying a car is one simple example of a balance sheet being activated.

Consider the case of Peggi, who has just purchased a new red convertible from the local car dealer. She puts no money down, but agrees to make $500 per month car payments until the car is paid off. This process will take three years, for a total amount to be paid of $18,000 ($500 per month × 12 months × 3 years). Peggi signs an agreement on January 1, 1992, verifying that she will make the payments. Her balance sheet at various points in the life of the loan, assuming no decline in the car's value, would be as shown in Figure 8.1.

Note that each year, Peggi achieves a higher degree of owner's equity. This, of course, indicates that each year Peggi owns more and more of the car, while her lender has less and less of a claim on the vehicle. It is always true, however, that the formula of asset = liability + owner's equity is in balance. That is, the combination of what Peggi **owes** on her car (liability) and the equity she enjoys equals the total value (asset value) of the car in each of the four periods. Of course, the value of any asset can change from month to month or year to year. The market value of real estate, for instance, can go either up or down. Its asset value as reflected on the balance sheet, however, will remain unchanged until some event, such as the asset's sale, causes it to be set at a higher or lower level. If the total assets of an organization increase in value, with no increase in liabilities, the owner's equity portion of the balance sheet improves. If, however, the value of an organization's assets declines, with no corresponding decline in liabilities, owner's equity will be reduced.

Balance sheets for the restaurant industry are similar to those of other businesses; however, some major differences do exist. Since restaurants typically do not extend credit to customers, accounts receivable are generally extremely small. In addition, product inventories are relatively low in relation to sales; thus, total dollars devoted to inventory is somewhat lower than in other businesses. Instead, the typical restaurant balance sheet shows most investment in such assets as land, building, and furniture and equipment.

The balance sheet is a snapshot of an operation's financial position at a specific point in time. The ability to read and understand the balance sheet is a skill that is of great value to the effective foodservice manager.

Figure 8.2 details the balance sheet covering a two-year period for a business owned by Joshua. His complex includes a lounge, two dining areas, banquet space, and a catering business. It is located in a large southwestern city of the United States. Using his balance sheet as his analysis device, Joshua is in the process of examining where he is this year compared to where he was last year. As the sole proprietor of his company, he is not concerned with outstanding stock, as he would be if his company were publicly owned. In this case, all owner's equity belongs to him. Of course, he is personally responsible for all liabilities also. As an independent foodservice owner-operator, Joshua is a mem-

Figure 8.1 **Peggi's Car**

	Asset	Liability	Owners Equity
1/1/92	$18,000	$18,000	$ 0
1/1/93	18,000	12,000	6,000
1/1/94	18,000	6,000	12,000
1/1/95	18,000	0	18,000

Figure 8.2 **Balance Sheet**

Joshua's

	1992	**1991**
Current assets		
Cash	$ 185,250	$ 93,850
Accounts receivable	61,850	57,921
Inventory	37,500	26,380
Total current assets	284,600	178,151
Fixed assets		
Land	300,000	300,000
Building	1,010,000	1,010,000
Furniture & equipment	485,167	468,292
Accumulated depreciation	(328,733)	(241,488)
Total fixed assets	1,466,434	1,536,804
Total assets	1,751,034	1,714,955
Current liabilities		
Accounts payable	80,292	79,582
Wages payable	2,564	3,106
Total current liabilities	82,856	82,688
Mortgage payable	786,541	860,630
Total liabilities	869,397	943,318
Owner's equity	881,637	771,637
Total liabilities & owner's equity	1,751,034	1,714,955

Prepared by: Chaplin, C.P.A.

ber of an elite and exceptionally hardworking sector of the hospitality industry. For most operators, ownership is in one of three major forms:

1. **Proprietorship—an unincorporated business owned by a single individual**
2. **Partnership—an unincorporated business owned by two or more people**
3. **Corporation—a business incorporated under the laws of a state, with ownership held by the stockholders of the corporation**

Joshua is comfortable that his balance sheet accurately reflects his current position, since it was prepared by a C.P.A. As can be seen by Figure 8.2, Joshua's owner's equity portion of the balance sheet is improved over last year (by $110,000).

On the whole, Joshua is quite satisfied. He is, by his accounts, an "almost millionaire" because his owner's equity for 1992 is $881,637. His wife is quick to point out, however, that his mortgage is over $750,000!

Joshua feels that he has done well for his guests, for himself, and for the employees in his organization. He is curious, however, about his total debt. Is it too high? Should he be concerned? What is the "proper" amount of debt for an organization such as his? Answering these questions, of course, requires that Joshua use his managerial analysis skills.

While the balance sheet provides a great deal of information, some key areas that can be analyzed by management are the following:

1. **Current ratio**
2. **Working capital**
3. **Debt to asset ratio**

Current Ratio

One fundamental measure of organizational health that uses information from the balance sheet is the **current ratio**. The current ratio is one of a family of financial ratios called liquidity ratios. Liquidity ratios are those ratios designed to measure the ability of an organization to pay its debts as they become due. The formula for current ratio is as follows:

$$\frac{\textbf{Current assets}}{\textbf{Current liabilities}} = \textbf{Current ratio}$$

In this case, current assets are defined as those assets that are cash or can easily be converted into cash within one year. Current liabilities are those company debts that must be paid within the next year. In Joshua's operation, the current ratio for 1992, based on Figure 8.2, is as follows:

$$\frac{\$284{,}600.00}{\$82{,}856.00} = 3.43 \text{ to } 1$$

To say that Joshua has a 3.43 : 1 current ratio is to state that he has $3.43 of current assets to pay for each $1.00 of current debt. Many operators feel that a current ratio of 2 : 1 is adequate; thus, it appears that Joshua is in a slightly better than average position to pay his bills, in the short term. Obviously, this is a good position to be in! We should not, however, conclude that Joshua's organization is in good financial health simply because he enjoys a strong current ratio position. The balance sheet, remember, indicates where Joshua is now, not where he is going or how he got there. If, for example, he were to lose $100,000.00 per year in his operation, his balance sheet position would be steadily declining, and one could assume that future current ratio computations would not paint such a positive picture.

Some operators prefer to compute the **acid test ratio** rather than the current ratio. Another liquidity ratio, the acid test ratio refers to a measure of assets that can be *quickly* converted to cash. The acid test ratio is similar to the current ratio, except that current assets are modified to include only cash, accounts receivable, and marketable securities. Note that for most restaurants the difference between current ratio and acid test ratio consists of the inclusion or omission of inventory. The choice of which ratio to use is, of course, determined by the needs of management and their view of the liquidity of the inventory.

Working Capital

Another member of the liquidity ratio group is the working capital ratio. **Working capital** is simply the dollar amount of current assets minus the amount of current liabilities. Its formula is as follows:

Current assets − Current liabilities = Working capital

From Figure 8.2, Joshua's working capital for 1992 is as follows:

\$284,600 − \$82,856 = \$201,744

A good question for Joshua, of course, is whether or not this dollar amount is the appropriate amount of working capital. If it is too small, Joshua may not have enough cash to cover unexpected short-term expenses. If it is too large, he may be holding excessive amounts of cash or current assets, which might better be invested elsewhere. To help answer this question, he can compute his working capital ratio, a figure that can be generated by combining information from both the balance sheet and the income statement. This process is described later in this chapter.

Debt to Asset Ratio

In addition to seeking information regarding his ability to meet short-term debt payments, Joshua is also interested in another type of ratio, the **debt to asset ratio**. In the hospitality industry, it is common for foodservice operators to borrow money in order to establish their business. The question always arises, however, about the "proper" amount of debt to incur. If debt load is too high, the operator may have difficulty meeting debt payments. If, on the other hand, debts are too low, the operation may be missing opportunities to borrow money, expand, and thus generate even greater profits, albeit with a higher risk level. Joshua computes his debt to asset ratio using the following formula:

$$\frac{\textbf{Total liabilities}}{\textbf{Total assets}} = \textbf{Debt to asset ratio}$$

For 1992, Joshua's debt to asset ratio is computed as follows:

$$\frac{\$869{,}397.00}{\$1{,}751{,}034.00} = 49.6\%$$

In this case, Joshua knows that 49.6% of his assets are financed by someone other than himself. This is often called the amount of **leverage** a company has. A company that is highly leveraged has a high debt to asset ratio. A company that is not highly leveraged has a low debt to asset ratio. When Joshua computed his 1991 debt to asset ratio, he found it to be 55.0% ($943,318.00 / 1,714,955.00 = 55.0%). Thus, Joshua has reduced his overall debt percentage for the year by 5.4 percentage points (55.0% − 49.6% = 5.4%). He is sure that his spouse will be glad to hear this, and he does feel good about knowing that (1) his assets increased over the year, and (2) his ownership percentage of those assets increased also.

While he is pleased with the picture his balance sheet presents, and thus his overall current financial status, he must still determine how well he is doing in his operation today. He knows that while the balance sheet may tell him where he is now, but his P&L will tell him how he got there, and thus give him an indication of current operational efficiency and financial direction.

Analysis Involving Both the Balance Sheet and the Income Statement

The income statement, often referred to as the profit and loss, or P&L, statement is the key management tool for cost control. Just as many types of analysis can be done on the balance sheet, the P&L statement, in conjunction with the balance sheet, can be a source of great information to the successful operator. Essentially, the P&L statement seeks to show income and expense in a level of detail determined by management after review of the appropriate Uniform System of Accounts.

Figure 8.3 details both the 1992 and 1991 profit and loss statements for Joshua. His fiscal year, that is, his accounting year, begins on October 1 and concludes on September 30 of the next year. This fiscal year coincides with the beginning of his busy season and thus gives him a logical starting point. The word **profit** can mean many things; therefore, the profit and loss statement can be somewhat confusing if one is not familiar with it. Some operators use pretax profit on their P&L statements, while others do not. A tight definition of what is meant by profit must be established for each P&L statement if it is to be helpful. In all cases, however, a purpose of the profit and loss statement is to identify net income, or the profit generated after all appropriate expenses of the business have been paid.

In the case of Joshua's, taxes paid are accounted for on his individual tax return, since sole proprietorship taxes are due at the individual rather than business level. For the year 1992, Joshua achieved a net income (profit) figure of

Figure 8.3 **Income Statement**

Joshua's

	1992	**%**	**1991**	**%**
Revenue				
Food sales	$1,728,020	68.0%	$1,533,564	66.5%
Catering sales	330,356	13.0	357,447	15.5
Total food sales	2,058,376	81.0	1,891,011	82.0
Beverage sales	482,830	19.0	415,099	18.0
Total sales	2,541,206	100.0	2,306,110	100.0
Cost of goods sold				
Meat, seafood	343,063	16.7	297,488	15.7
Fruits, vegetables	127,060	6.2	94,550	5.0
Dairy	40,660	2.0	55,347	2.9
Baked goods	22,870	1.1	16,142	0.9
Other	233,790	11.4	249,060	13.2
Total cost of food sold	767,443	37.3	712,587	37.7
Beverage	96,566	20.0	94,550	22.8
Total cost of goods sold	864,009	34.0	807,137	35.0
Gross profit	1,677,197	66.0	1,498,973	65.0
Controllable expenses				
Salaries & wages	710,585	28.0	641,099	27.8
Payroll taxes & benefits	190,590	7.5	168,346	7.3
Total payroll & related	901,175	35.5	809,445	35.1
Direct operating expenses	180,200	7.1	142,309	6.2
Marketing	99,189	3.9	89,622	3.9
Energy & utility services	119,500	4.7	121,000	5.2
Administrative & general	70,541	2.8	66,000	2.9
Repairs and maintenance	29,520	1.2	17,861	0.8
Total controllable expense	1,400,125	55.1	1,246,237	54.0
Profit before rent, interest and depreciation	277,072	10.9	252,736	11.0
Interest	84,889	3.3	86,750	3.8
Depreciation	82,183	3.2	80,496	3.5
Net income (loss)	110,000	4.3	85,490	3.7

Prepared by: Chaplin, C.P.A.

$110,000 on $2,541,206 of sales. The questions he must ask himself, of course, is "How good is this performance?"

It is important to note that each operation's P&L statement will look slightly different. All of them, however, typically take a similar approach to reporting income and expense. Note that while the detail is much greater, the layout of Joshua's P&L is similar in structure to the abbreviated P&L presented as Figure

1.6 in Chapter 1. Both statements list income first, expense second, and the difference between the income and expense figures third. If this number is positive, it represents a profit. If expenses exceed income, a loss, represented by a negative number or a number in parentheses, is shown. Operating at a loss is, for some unknown reason, often referred to as operating "in the red" or "shedding red ink." Regardless of the color of ink, operating at a loss can cause an operator to shed a few tears! The P&L, used either alone or in conjunction with the balance sheet, allows the foodservice operator to compute many useful ratios, including both return on sales and working capital rates.

Return on Sales

As can be seen in Figure 8.3, Joshua's total sales for fiscal year 1992 were $2,541,206. His operating profit was $110,000. His profit percentage using the profit percentage formula from Chapter 1 (profit ÷ income = profit percentage) is as follows:

$$\frac{\$110{,}000.00}{\$2{,}541{,}206.00} = 4.3\%$$

Thus, 4.3% is both Joshua's operating profit and his ROS, or return on sales. For the foodservice manager, perhaps no figure is more important than the ROS. This percentage is the most telling indicator of a manager's effectiveness and is computed as follows:

$$\frac{\textbf{Profit}}{\textbf{Sales}} = \textbf{Return on sales}$$

While it is not possible to state what a "good" return on sales figure should be for all restaurants, industry averages, depending on the segment, range from 1% to over 20%.

Note that each income and expense category in Figure 8.3 is represented in terms of both its whole dollar amount and its percentage of total sales. Notice also that Joshua's accountant presents this year's (1992) P&L statement along with last year's (1991), as this can help Joshua make comparisons and analyze the trends in his business. With the data from both the balance sheet and the P&L, the effective foodservice manager can also analyze a variety of indicators that relate to the health of his or her business.

Working Capital Ratio

Another area Joshua wishes to analyze is his **working capital ratio**. The working capital ratio relates the number of dollars of sales generated by a business to each dollar of working capital the business has available. It is important to remember that just generating sales is not enough. A profit must be made from those sales. The working capital ratio is important, however, since a business with too large a ratio may not have enough capital to operate fully, while one with too small a ratio may have funds that might be put to better use elsewhere, since they are not being used effectively to generate additional sales.

Joshua knows from his balance sheet that his working capital is $201,744, using the working capital formula. He now computes his working capital ratio, using the following formula:

$$\frac{\textbf{Sales}}{\textbf{Working capital}} = \textbf{Working capital ratio}$$

Or

$$\frac{\$2{,}541{,}206.00}{\$201{,}744.00} = 12.6\%$$

Joshua makes a note to discuss this ratio with his accountant to determine whether, in fact, a 12.6 : 1 working capital ratio is *appropriate for this business.* The decision about whether to change the amount of working capital is, of course, Joshua's. He does, however, look to his accountant for advice on how his operating results compare on a regional and national basis to others.

Other areas involving the balance sheet and P&L statement that foodservice operators may wish to analyze include the following:

1. **Accounts receivable turnover**
2. **Return on assets**
3. **Return on owner's equity**
4. **Return on investment**

Accounts Receivable Turnover

When food and beverage products are sold on credit, the foodservice manager is, in effect, operating a loan program. As with any loan program, some customers will pay their bills quickly, others will take their time. If customers pay quickly, more funds are available for operational needs. If, however, they take their time, dollars that should have been available to operate the business are no longer there. The accounts receivable activity ratio indicates the number of times per year the accounts receivable of an operation are paid back. The formula for this ratio is as follows:

$$\frac{\textbf{Total sales}}{\textbf{Average amount of accounts receivable}} = \textbf{Accounts receivable turnover}$$

In Joshua's case, his total sales figure for 1992 is $2,541,206. He computes his average amount of accounts receivable by using the following formula:

$$\frac{\textbf{1991 accounts receivable + 1992 accounts receivable}}{\textbf{2}} = \textbf{Average amount of accounts receivable}$$

Or

$$\frac{\$57{,}921.00 + \$61{,}850.00}{2} = \$59{,}885.50$$

Thus, Joshua's accounts receivable turnover equals 42.4 (2,541,206.00 / 59,885.50 = 42.4). In reality, it would make sense to compute accounts receivable turnover not on total sales, but rather, on total credit sales. Since most operators do not maintain a separate credit sales figure, using the total sales figure is accepted practice. It should be noted that increases in cash sales, with no change in credit sales, will have the effect of increasing accounts receivable turnover.

Many operators use their receivables turnover to compute the average number of days it takes the customer to pay his or her bill. To compute such a number requires simply that receivables turnover be divided into the number of days per year, as in our example, 365 / 42.4 = 8.6 days. This indicates that the average customer in our example takes 8.6 days to pay his or her bill. Whether this length of time is considered good or bad depends, of course, on the terms of the credit extended. If, for instance, customers are to pay within 30 days, we are doing quite well. If, however, they are supposed to pay within 7 days, we have some very slow-paying customers and may wish to step up our collection efforts.

Return on Assets

This ratio lets Joshua know the total dollar value of profits generated relative to assets owned. The formula for this ratio is as follows:

$$\frac{\textbf{Profit}}{\textbf{Average total assets}} = \textbf{Return on assets}$$

Joshua's return on assets, derived from data contained in Figure 8.2 (balance sheet) and Figure 8.3 (income statement), is as follows:

$$\frac{\$110{,}000}{(\$1{,}751{,}034 + \$1{,}714{,}955)/2}$$

Or

$$\frac{\$110{,}000}{\$1{,}732{,}995} = 6.3\%$$

Many experts suggest that return on assets ratios be calculated without the inclusion of interest expense, since that is a measure of how much debt financing is used by the foodservice organization. Return on assets also is computed prior to the payment of any taxes due on the earned income.

Joshua is able to achieve a 6.3% rate of return for each dollar of assets he controls. The question of whether this rate of return is good or not must focus on how many dollars Joshua has invested in the past to control these assets, and how much it would cost him in today's dollars to control additional assets.

Return on Owner's Equity

The return on owner's equity reflects the dollar amount of profits as it relates to the owner's share of the assets. The formula for return on owner's equity, similar to the one for return on assets, is as follows:

$$\frac{\textbf{Profit}}{\textbf{Average owner's equity}} = \textbf{Return on owner's equity}$$

Based on the data in Figures 8.2 and 8.3, Joshua's return on owner's equity would be computed as follows:

$$\frac{\$110{,}000}{(\$881{,}637 + \$771{,}637)/2}$$

Or

$$\frac{\$110{,}000}{\$826{,}637} = 13.3\%$$

In different words, for every dollar of owner's equity Joshua has in his business, on average, 13.3 cents in profit was generated in the current year.

Return on Investment

Perhaps the most difficult ratio of all to analyze is return on investment, or ROI. The formula for its computation is not particularly difficult, in fact, it is rather easy.

$$\frac{\textbf{Profit}}{\textbf{Total invested}} = \textbf{Return on investment}$$

To understand the complexity of evaluating return on investment, consider the case of Ashley, who has just won a million dollars from the state lottery. All applicable taxes have been deducted, and Ashley finds herself somewhat puzzled as to what to do with her million dollars. She knows that it should be invested, but the question is "*How* should this be done?" Her local banker tells her that if she puts the money in his bank, she can expect a 10% pretax return per year. In other words, Ashley would receive $1,000,000.00 × .10 = $100,000.00 per year from the bank, assuming there is no change in the interest rate. Thus, her ROI would be computed as follows:

$$\frac{\$100{,}000}{\$1{,}000{,}00} = 10\%$$

Ashley's decision to "invest" her money in the bank is one that thousands of Americans make every day. The investment is relatively risk-free, and the money is typically available should the investor wish to withdraw it. In many cases, the security of an investment of this type is locked by a governmental pledge that, should the bank fail, the investor's funds will be replaced by the government up to a predetermined limit.

If Ashley seeks a higher ROI, she will find that, as her willingness to take risks increases, so generally will her ROI. If, for example, she wishes to buy a restaurant with her million dollars, and the restaurant yields $110,000 in profits in the first year. Ashley's ROI would be computed as follows:

$$\frac{\$110{,}000}{\$1{,}000{,}000} = 11\%$$

The question Ashley must ask herself prior to buying the restaurant is simply this: "What rate of return do I want relative to the amount of risk I am willing to take?" If Ashley invests in a restaurant, her million dollars may not easily be converted back into cash. In addition, the government does not stand ready to refund Ashley's money should the restaurant fail. In the hospitality industry, owners would like to maximize ROI while minimizing risk. This is to be expected. Since ROI is dependent in great measure on profits generated, it is easy to see why owners are very interested in the profitable operation of their facilities, and why they require excellent cost control systems to be in place to protect their investments.

ROI Versus ROS

The relationship between ROI and ROS is very important. Obviously, one would prefer to have both strong ROI and ROS positions. It is possible, however, that one of the two will be high, while the other will be low. Consider Ashley's purchase of a restaurant with her million dollars. Figure 8.4 details three scenarios that could occur as a result of her acquisition.

Ashley may, of course, hope for a scenario similar to A. She will, however, not know until she begins her operations exactly how her facility will perform. This is part of the challenge of the job of the foodservice manager. ROI is a measure of an owner's reward for risk, while ROS is a measure of the manager's

Figure 8.4 **Ashley's Million Dollar Scenarios**

	A	B	C
Purchase price (investment)	$1,000,000	$ 1,000,000	$1,000,000
Total sales: Year 1	$1,000,000	$10,000,000	$ 100,000
Total profit: Year 1	$ 100,000	$ 100,000	$ 10,000
ROI	10%	10%	1%
ROS	10%	1%	10%

ability to control costs. Excellent performance in each area makes for profits and gives satisfaction to owners, managers, employees, and most importantly, guests.

Joshua knows from his own records that the total cash investment in his operation was $450,000. His $110,000 net operation profit this year yields a ROI as follows:

$$\frac{\$110{,}000.00}{\$450{,}000.00} = 24.4\%$$

While he realizes that this is an excellent return on investment, he also knows that he is one of the lucky independent owners whose willingness to take risks and work hard has paid off. Many others, who lose their investments, are not quite that lucky!

Analysis of the Profit and Loss Statement

The balance sheet gives the operator valuable information about the current health of the organization. The P&L statement, in conjunction with the balance sheet, can provide useful data regarding rates of financial return based on various sales or profit measurements. The P&L statement alone, however, can yield important information that is critical to the development of future management plans and budgets. The analysis of P&L statements is a fun and very creative process if basic procedures are well understood. In general, the following areas of analysis are undertaken by managers who seek to uncover all that their P&L will tell them:

1. **Sales/volume**
2. **Food expense**
3. **Beverage expense**
4. **Labor expense**
5. **Other expense**
6. **Profits**

Using the data from Figure 8.3, each of these areas will be reviewed in turn.

Analysis of Sales/Volume

As discussed earlier in this text, foodservice operators can measure sales in terms of either dollars or number of customers served. In both cases, an increase in sales volume is usually to be desired. A sales increase must, however, be analyzed carefully if the foodservice operator is to truly understand the direction of his or her business. Consider the sales portion of Joshua's P&L statement as detailed in Figure 8.5.

Based on the data from Figure 8.5, Joshua can compute his overall sales increase or decrease using the following steps:

Step 1. Determine sales for this accounting period.
Step 2. Subtract the prior period's sales from this period's sales.
Step 3. Divide the difference in Step 2 by the prior period's sales to determine percentage variance.

For Joshua, the percentage variance is as indicated in Figure 8.6.

To illustrate the steps outlined, using total sales as an example, we find the following:

Step 1. $2,541,206
Step 2. $2,541,206 – $2,306,110 = $235,096
Step 3. $235,096 / $2,306,110 = 10.2%

As can be seen, it appears that Joshua has achieved an overall increase in sales of 10.2%. Note, however, that his catering sales have actually declined in 1992.

Figure 8.5 **Joshua's P&L**

		Sales		
Income	**1992**	**%**	**1991**	**%**
Food sales	$1,728,020.00	68.0%	$1,533,564.00	66.5%
Catering sales	330,356.00	13.0	357,447.00	15.5
Beverage sales	482,830.00	19.0	415,099.00	18.0
Total sales	2,541,206.00	100.0	2,306,110.00	100.0

Figure 8.6 **Joshua's P&L Sales Comparison**

Income	**% Variance from Last Year**
Food sales	+ 12.7%
Catering sales	– 7.6
Beverage sales	+ 16.3
Total sales	+ 10.2

There are two ways Joshua could have experienced total sales volume increases in the current year. If Joshua served more customers at the same check average, or the same number of customers at a higher check average, he would, of course, have achieved overall sales increases. It is also true, however, that Joshua could have experienced sales volume increases if he had served the same amount of food and beverage products as during the prior year but sold these at a higher price than he did last year. To determine which of these two alternatives is indeed the case, Joshua uses a sales adjustment technique.

Assume for a moment that Joshua raised prices by 5% at the beginning of fiscal 1992. If this were the case, and he wishes to determine fairly his sales increase, he must adjust for that 5% menu price increase. The procedure he would use to adjust sales variance for known menu price increases is as follows:

Step 1. Increase prior period sales by amount of the price increase.
Step 2. Subtract the result in Step 1 from this period's income.
Step 3. Divide the difference in Step 2 by the value of Step 1.

Thus, in our example, Joshua would follow the steps outlined above to determine his real sales increase. In the case of total sales, the procedure would be as follows:

Step 1. $2,306,110 × 1.05 = $2,421,416
Step 2. $2,541,206 − $2,421,416 = $119,790
Step 3. $119,790 / $2,421,416 = 4.95%

Figure 8.7 details the results that are achieved if this 5% adjustment process is completed for all sales areas.

Joshua's total sales figure would be up by 4.95% if he adjusted it for a 5% menu price increase. The P&L statement tells Joshua more about his sales, however, than simply their movement up or down. It also tells him where his sales originate. Figure 8.5 shows that Joshua's beverage sales are a higher percentage of total sales in 1992 (19%) than they were in 1991 (18%). From this trend, he can expect that his beverage purchases will likely represent a larger dollar amount in 1992, and that purchases in some other product area should decline proportionately. In this example, it was purchases in the catering area that should

Figure 8.7 **Joshua's P&L Sales Comparison with 5% Menu Price Increase**

Income	**Adjusted % Variance from Last Year**
Food sales	+ 7.3%
Catering sales	− 12.0
Beverage sales	+ 10.8
Total sales	+ 4.95

decline, since sales in that area dropped from 15.5% of total sales in 1991, to 13.0% in 1992.

There is still more, however, that the P&L can tell Joshua about his sales. If he has kept accurate customer count records, he can compute his sales per guest figure (see Chapter 2). With this information, he can determine whether his sales are up because he is serving more customers, or because he is serving the same number of guests, but each one is spending more per visit. In fact, if each customer is spending quite a bit more per visit, Joshua may even have experienced a decline in **total** customer count yet an increase in total sales. If this were the case, he would want to know about it, since it is unrealistic to assume that revenue will continue to increase over the long run if the number of customers visiting his establishment is declining.

Other Factors Influencing Sales Analysis

In some foodservice establishments, other factors must be taken into consideration before sales revenue can be accurately analyzed. Consider the case of the Copper Caboose. It is a restaurant across the street from a professional basketball stadium. If the owner is to compare revenue from this May with revenue from last May, the number of home games in May for this professional team would have to be determined before reasonable assumptions about customer count increases or decreases could be made. Also, if a foodservice facility is open only Monday through Friday, the number of operating days in two given accounting periods may be different for the facility. When this is the case, percentage increases or decreases in sales volume must be based on average daily sales, rather than the total sales figure. To illustrate this, look at a hot dog stand that operates in the city center, Monday through Friday only. In October of this year, the stand was open for 21 operating days. Last year, however, because of the number of weekend days in October, the stand operated for 22 days. Figure 8.8 details the comparison of sales for the stand, assuming no increase in menu selling price this year compared with last year.

While at first glance it appears that October sales this year are 1.2% lower than last year, in reality, average daily sales are up 3.6%! Are sales for October up or down? Clearly, the answer must be qualified in terms of monthly or daily sales. For this reason, effective foodservice managers are careful to consider all of the relevant facts before making determinations about unit sales direction.

Every critical factor must be considered when evaluating sales revenue, including the number of operating units or days; changes in menu prices, cus-

Figure 8.8 **Hot Dog! Sales Data**

	This Year	Last Year	Variance
Total sales (October)	$17,506.00	$17,710.00	− 1.2%
# of operating days	21 days	22 days	1 day
Average daily sales	833.62	805.00	+ 3.6%

tomer counts, and check average; and special events. Only after carefully reviewing all details can management feel confident about generalizing statements concerning increases or decreases in revenue.

Analysis of Food and Beverage Expense

In addition to income analysis, the P&L statement , whether weekly, monthly, or annual, can provide information about other areas of operational interest. For the effective foodservice manager, the analysis of food and beverage expense is a matter of major concern. Figure 8.9 details the food and beverage expense portion of Joshua's P&L.

At first glance it appears that Joshua's cost of goods sold expense has declined 1%, from 35% overall in 1991 to 34% in 1992. Closer inspection reveals, however, that while the dairy, other, and beverages categories showed declines, meats and seafood, fruits and vegetables, and baked goods showed increases. Figure 8.10 shows the actual differences in food cost percentage for each of Joshua's food and beverage categories.

Figure 8.9 **Joshua's P&L**

Food and Beverage Expense

Cost of Goods Sold	**1992**	**%**	**1991**	**%**
Meats and seafood	$343,063.00	13.5%	$297,488.00	12.9%
Fruits and vegetables	127,060.00	5.0	94,550.00	4.1
Dairy	40,660.00	1.6	55,347.00	2.4
Baked goods	22,870.00	.9	16,142.00	.7
Other	233,790.00	9.2	249,060.00	10.8
Beverages	96,566.00	3.8	94,550.00	4.1
Total cost of goods sold	864,009.00	34.0	807,137.00	35.0

Figure 8.10 **Variation in Food and Beverage Expense**

Category	**1992 %**	**1991 %**	**Variance***
Meats and seafood	13.5%	12.9%	+ .6%
Fruits and vegetables	5.0	4.1	+ .9
Dairy	1.6	2.4	− .8
Baked goods	.9	.7	+ .2
Other	9.2	10.8	− 1.6
Beverages	3.8	4.1	− .3
Total	34.0	35.0	− 1.0

*A plus sign indicates an unfavorable change in costs; a minus sign represents a favorable change.

While it is true that Joshua's overall food cost percentage is down by one percentage point, the variation among categories is quite marked. It is clear that it is to his benefit to categorize food and beverage products so that he can watch for fluctuations within and among groups, rather than merely monitor his overall increase or decrease in food and beverage costs. Without such a breakdown of categories, he will not know exactly where to look if costs get too high.

It would also be helpful for Joshua to determine how appropriate the inventory levels are for each of his product subgroups so that he can adjust the inventory sizes accordingly. To do this, Joshua must be able to compute his inventory turnover.

Inventory Turnover

The formula used to compute inventory turnover is as follows:

$$\frac{\textbf{Cost of goods sold}}{\textbf{Average inventory value}} = \textbf{Inventory turnover}$$

Inventory turnover is a measure of how many times the inventory value is purchased and sold to the customer. Each time the cycle is completed once, we are said to have "turned" the inventory. In the foodservice industry we are, of course, interested in high inventory turnover. It simply makes sense that if 5% profit is made on the sale of an inventory item, we would like to sell that item as many times (turns) per year as possible. If the item were sold from inventory only once a year, one 5% profit would result. If the item turned ten times, a 5% profit on each of the ten sales would result.

Figure 8.11 details the average inventory value and turnover notes for each of Joshua's food and beverage categories. Average inventory value is computed, in Joshua's case, by adding his beginning inventory for 1992 to the ending in-

Figure 8.11 **Inventory Turnover**

Unit Name: Joshua's Date: 10/31/92

Inventory Category	Cost of Goods Sold	Average Inventory	Inventory Turnover
Meats and seafood	$343,063.00	$15,547.00	22.0
Fruits and vegetables	127,060.00	1,080.00	117.6
Dairy	40,660.00	452.00	89.9
Baked goods	22,870.00	116.00	197.1
Other	233,790.00	8,651.00	27.0
Beverages	96,566.00	6,094.00	15.8
Total	864,009.00	31,940.00	27.0

ventory, and dividing by two. Thus, his average inventory (from Figure 8.2) is as follows:

$$\frac{\$37{,}500 + \$26{,}380}{2} = \$31{,}940$$

If Joshua has inventory figures for each month of his current year, he could compute average inventory value as the sum value of each inventory taken, divided by the number of times the inventory was counted and valued. This method has the advantage of increased accuracy and takes seasonal variation of inventory size into account. The balance sheet and P&L statement provide the data to compute inventory turnover. If the operator has kept accurate records of the value of inventory subgroups, however, inventory turnover can be computed for each subgroup.

As can be seen, Joshua's overall inventory turnover occurs 27 times per year. In categories such as dairy, baked goods, and fruits and vegetables, the turnover is understandably higher. Joshua may want to examine his wine and spirits inventory, since their turnover is rather low. Perhaps he will find that he is stocking too many products that are slow-moving. Alternatively, if Joshua stocks many expensive but slow-selling wines, he may find this turnover rate quite acceptable.

Analysis of Beverage Expense

Figure 8.9 lists beverage expense for the year as $96,566. From Figure 8.3, we see that beverage sales were $482,830. Using the formula for beverage cost percentage, Joshua determines this cost as follows:

$$\frac{\$96{,}566}{\$482{,}830} = 20\%$$

The previous year's beverage cost percentage was $94,550 / $415,099 or 22.8%. A first glance would indicate that beverage costs have been reduced, not in total dollars spent, since sales were up, but in percentage terms. In other words, a cost of 22.8% last year versus 20% this year indicates a 2.8% overall reduction.

Assume for a moment, however, that Joshua raised drink prices by 10% this year over last year. Assume also that Joshua pays, on average, 5% more for beverages this year compared with last year. Is his beverage operation more efficient than last year, less efficient, or the same? To determine the answer to this question, Joshua must make adjustments both in last year's sales figures, as previously discussed, and also in his beverage expense category. Similar to the method for adjusting sales, the method for adjusting expense categories for known cost increases is as follows:

Step 1. Increase prior period expense by amount of cost increase.
Step 2. Determine appropriate sales data, remembering to adjust prior period sales, if applicable.
Step 3. Divide costs determined in Step 1 by sales determined in Step 2.

Thus, in our example, Joshua's beverage expense last year, adjusted for this year's costs, would be \$94,550 × 1.05 = \$99,278. His beverage sales from last year, adjusted for this year's menu prices, would be \$415,099 × 1.10 = \$456,609. His 1991 beverage cost percentage, using *1992 costs and selling prices*, would be computed as follows:

$$\frac{\$99{,}278}{\$456{,}609} = 21.7\%$$

In this case, Joshua's real cost of beverage consumed has, in fact, declined, although not by as much as he had originally thought. That is, a 21.7% adjusted cost for 1991 versus 20% for 1992 equals a reduction of 1.7%, not 2.8% as originally determined.

All food and beverage expense categories must be adjusted both in terms of costs and selling price if effective comparisons are to be made **over** time. It would not be possible to compare efficiency in food and beverage usage unless we were making that comparison in equal terms. As product costs increase or decrease, and as menu prices change, so too will food and beverage expense percentages.

Analysis of Labor Expense

It is interesting to note that while the total dollars Joshua spent on labor increased greatly from 1991 to 1992, his labor cost percentage increased only slightly. This was true in both the salaries and the wages categories. Whenever labor costs are not 100% variable costs, increasing volume will help decrease labor cost percentage, even though total dollars spent for labor will increase. The reason for this is simple. When total dollar sales volume increases, fixed labor cost percentages will decline. In other words, the dollars paid for fixed labor will consume a smaller *percentage* of total income. Thus, as long as any portion of total labor cost is fixed, increasing volume will have the effect of reducing labor cost percentage. Variable labor costs, of course, will increase along with sales volume increases, but the percentage of income they consume should stay constant. When we add a declining percentage (fixed labor) to a constant one (variable labor), we achieve a reduced overall percentage, even though total labor dollars expended can be higher. This is an excellent example of the reason operators seek to increase labor expense, rather than reduce it. If expenses are controlled properly, we will find that an increase in the number of guests and sales will result in increased costs to service those guests. We must be careful, however, to always ensure that increased costs are *appropriate* to increases in sales volume. An effective foodservice manager hopes to see declines in operational expense because of operational efficiencies, not reduced sales. Figure 8.12 details the salaries and wages portion of Joshua's P&L.

Just as adjustments must be made for changes in food and beverage expenses, so too must adjustments be made for changes, if any, in the price an operator pays for labor. In Joshua's case, assume that all employees were given

Figure 8.12 **Joshua's P&L**

Salaries and Wages Expense

	1992	%	1991	%
Salaries and wages	$710,585.00	28%	$641,099.00	27.8%
Taxes/benefits	190,590.00	7.5	168,346.00	7.3
Total labor cost	901,175.00	35.5	809,445.00	35.1

a 4% salary increase at the beginning of fiscal year 1992. This, coupled with an assumed 10% menu price increase, would have the effect of changing overall labor cost percentage. Joshua can see that his actual labor cost percentage increased from 35.1% in 1991 to 35.5% in 1992, an increase of .4%. To adjust for the changes in the cost of labor and selling prices, if these indeed occurred, Joshua uses the techniques previously detailed in this chapter. Thus, based on his earlier assumption of a 4% increase in the cost of labor and a 10% increase in selling price, he adjusts both sales and cost of labor using the same steps as those employed for adjusting food or beverage cost percentage and computes a new labor cost for 1991 as follows:

Step 1. Determine sales adjustment: **$2,306,110 × 1.10 = $2,536,721**

Step 2. Determine cost of labor adjustment: **$ 809,449 × 1.04 = $ 841,827**

Step 3. Compute adjusted labor cost percentage: $$\frac{\$841{,}827}{\$2{,}536{,}721} = 33.2\%$$

As can be seen, Joshua would have experienced a slight increase (35.5% − 33.2% = 2.3%) in his labor cost percentage if these increased menu prices and increased costs of labor had been taken into account.

This is certainly an area that Joshua would want to investigate. The reason is simple. If he were exactly as efficient this year as he was last year, and if he assumes 10% menu price increases and 4% wage and salary increases, Joshua's cost of labor for this year should have been computed as follows:

This year's sales × Last year's adjusted labor cost percentage = Projected labor cost this year

The computation in our example would be as follows:

$2,541,206 × .332 = $843,680

Put in another way, Joshua would have expected to spend 33.2% of sales for labor this year, given his 4% payroll increase and 10% menu price increase. In actuality, Joshua's labor cost was $57,495 higher ($901,175 actual − $843,680 projected = $57,495). A variation this large could obviously be of concern to

Joshua. Increases in payroll taxes, benefit programs, and employee turnover all can impact labor cost percentage. In using his P&L statement and in analyzing changes in his overall cost of labor, he must be careful to consider these items in addition to changing menu prices and wages paid. Indeed, employee-related costs are expected to rise faster than any other type of cost the operator will encounter over the next decade.

Analysis of Other Expense

The analysis of other expense, like that of cost of goods sold and labor, should be performed each time the P&L is produced. Figure 8.13 details the other expense portion of Joshua's P&L statement.

As discussed in Chapter 7, Joshua's other expense category consists of both controllable and noncontrollable items, and he must review them carefully. His repairs category is higher this year than it was last year. This is one area in which he both expects and approves a cost increase. It is logical to assume that kitchen repairs will increase as a kitchen ages. In that sense, a kitchen is much like a car. Even with a good preventative maintenance program, Joshua does not expect an annual decline in kitchen repair expense. In fact, he would be somewhat surprised and concerned should this category be smaller one year than in the previous year. In the same way, his contributions to his state and national association political action funds, charged to administrative and general expense, were up significantly. This is due to Joshua's belief that he, as part of the hospitality industry, needs to make his voice heard to his local and national political leaders. Joshua is a strong believer in taking a leadership role in his association on the local, state, and national levels. Indeed, one of his goals is to someday serve on the board of his national association! He knows that membership in that organization gives him a voice straight to the nation's law- and policy-makers.

An analysis of other expense always proves difficult for Joshua since he is not sure how he compares with others in his area or with operations of a similar nature. For comparison purposes, he is, however, able to use industry trade

Figure 8.13 **Joshua's P&L**

Other Expenses

	1992	**%**	**1991**	**%**
Direct operating expense	$180,200.00	7.1%	$142,309.00	6.2%
Marketing	99,189.00	3.9	89,622.00	3.9
Energy and utility services	119,500.00	4.7	121,000.00	5.2
Administrative and general	70,541.00	2.8	66,000.00	2.9
Repairs and maintenance	29,520.00	1.2	17,861.00	.8
Interest	84,889.00	3.3	86,750.00	3.8
Depreciation	82,183.00	3.2	80,496.00	3.5

publications to get national averages on other expense categories. On the other hand, Joanna, who operates a quick-service hamburger restaurant, knows exactly how she stands in the area of other expense. Her corporation keeps meticulous records on each of its thousands of operations. By doing so, Joanna's district and regional managers can chart her performance against those of other operators in the city, region, state, and nation. From this aspect, an operator like Joanna has a better gauge of operating expenses than does an independent operator such as Joshua.

Interest and Depreciation

These noncontrollable expenses figure prominently in Joshua's overall profit picture. Interest, both paid (income statement) and accrued (balance sheet) represents the price paid for the use of borrowed funds. As such, this is a real expense of the business. Depreciation is also a real expense of the business and must be accounted for. In its simplest sense, depreciation is a systematic method of allocating the costs associated with the acquisition of an asset over the life of that asset.

If, for example, Joshua were to buy a piece of equipment for his kitchen, and the equipment had a life of seven years, Joshua would want to "charge" the cost of the equipment over its seven-year life. He does this by expensing one-seventh of the value of the equipment each year. This value is charged to the depreciation section of the P&L, and its cumulative total is kept in the accumulated depreciation section of Joshua's balance sheet. Depreciation, as an expense, is unique in that it serves to generate cash flow for the foodservice operation. For a thorough discussion of this topic, the reader is referred to one of the many fine texts on the market that deal with hospitality accounting. For the purposes of cost control, it is enough to note that depreciation seeks to accurately reflect all costs associated with the generation of sales, including the cost of equipment wearing out or reaching the end of its useful life cycle.

Analysis of Profits

Joshua's net operating profit for the year was $110,000, or 4.3% of total sales. This is an improvement over last year's figure of $85,490, or 3.7% of total sales. He realizes, however, that increased sales rather than great improvements in operational efficiency could have caused this progress, because his sales volume in 1992 was greater than in 1991. In order to analyze his profitability appropriately, he must determine how much of this increase was due to increased menu prices as opposed to increased customer count or check average. Joshua's improvement in profits for the year can be measured by the following formula:

$$\frac{\textbf{Profit this period} - \textbf{Profit last period}}{\textbf{Profit last period}} = \textbf{Profit variance}$$

For Joshua, the computation is as follows:

$$\frac{\$110{,}000 - \$85{,}490}{\$85{,}490} = +28.7\%$$

How much of this improvement is due to improved operational methods versus increased sales will depend, of course, on how much Joshua actually did increase his selling prices relative to increases in his costs. Monitoring selling price, customer count, sales per guest, operating days, special events, and actual operating costs is necessary for accurate profit comparisons. Without knowledge of each of these areas, the effective analysis of profits becomes a risky proposition.

Menu Analysis / Break-Even Analysis

In addition to analyzing the balance sheet and P&L statement, the effective foodservice manager should undertake a thorough study of two other areas prior to the preparation of the operating budget or plan. These two forms of analysis, to which we now turn our attention, are menu analysis and break-even analysis. Whereas **menu analysis** concerns itself with the profitability of each item the foodservice manager elects to sell, **break-even analysis** deals with the minimum sales volume required by a foodservice unit in order to avoid an operating loss. In other words, the break-even analysis seeks to determine the precise sales point at which an operation becomes profitable, given the fixed and variable costs that operation must incur.

Menu Analysis

As with menu pricing, a large number of methods for menu analysis exist in the foodservice industry. All of them, however, should seek to answer the question "How does the sale of this menu item contribute to the overall success of the operation?" It is unfortunate, in many ways, that the discussion of menu analysis typically leads one to elaborate mathematical formulas and computations. This is, of course, just one component of the analysis of a menu. It is not, however, nor should it ever be, the only component. Consider the case of Danny, who operates a successful family restaurant called Twins in a rural location. The restaurant has been in his family for three generations. One item on the menu is mustard greens with scrambled eggs. It does not sell often, but both mustard greens and eggs are ingredients in other, more popular items. Why does Danny keep the item in a prominent spot on the menu? It was Danny's grandfather's favorite. As a thank you to his grandfather, who started the business and inspired Danny to become service and guest oriented, the menu item survives every menu reprint. Menu analysis, then, is about more than just numbers. It involves marketing, sociology, psychology, and emotions. Guests respond, not to weighty financial analyses, but rather to menu copy, the description of the menu item, the placement of items on the menu, their price, and their current popularity. For the serious foodservice manager, the analysis of a menu deserves special study, like that required for a thorough knowledge of menu pricing. Indeed, menu layout, design, copy, and pricing play a key role in the overall success of a foodservice operation. The foodservice manager who does not seek to understand how a menu works is akin to the manager who does not seek to understand the key components of making a good cup of coffee!

While the financial analysis of a menu is indeed done "by the numbers," the effective foodservice manager realizes that it is just one part, albeit an important part, of the total menu analysis picture.

As in the case of menu pricing, most foodservice operators who do a financial analysis of their menu do so on the basis of one or a combination of the variables listed below:

1. **Food cost percentage**
2. **Popularity**
3. **Contribution margin**
4. **Selling price**
5. **Variable expenses**
6. **Fixed expenses**

Three of the most popular systems of menu analysis, shown in Figure 8.14, will be discussed. Each one has its proponents and detractors, but an understanding of each will help the foodservice operator as he or she attempts to develop his or her own philosophy of menu analysis.

Figure 8.14 **Three Methods of Menu Analysis**

Title	Variables Considered	Analysis Method	Goal
1. Food cost %	a. Food cost % b. Popularity	Matrix	Minimize overall food cost %
2. Contribution margin	a. Contribution margin b. Popularity	Matrix	Maximize contribution margin
3. Goal value	a. Contribution margin % b. Popularity c. Selling price d. Variable cost % e. Food cost %	Algebraic equation	Achieve predetermined profit % goals

Food Cost Percentage

When analyzing a menu using the food cost percentage method, the foodservice operator is seeking menu items that have the effect of minimizing overall food cost percentage. The rationale is that a lowered food cost percentage leaves more of the sales dollar to be spent for other operational expense. A criticism of the food cost percentage approach is that items that have a higher food cost percentage may be sacrificed in favor of items that have a lower food cost percentage, but also contribute fewer dollars to overall profit. To illustrate the use of this method, consider the case of Erin, who operates a steak and seafood restaurant near the beach in a busy resort town. Erin sells seven items in the entrée section of her menu. The items, and information related to their costs, selling price, and popularity, are presented in Figure 8.15.

To determine her average selling price, Erin divides total sales by the total number of items sold. In this case, the computation is $8,083.00 / 700 = $11.55. To determine her total food cost percentage, she divides total cost by total sales ($2,828.47 / $8,083.00 = 35%). To determine average contribution margin, she divides total contribution margin by total number of customers ($5,254.53 / 700 = $7.51). This computation is discussed more fully later in this chapter.

To analyze her menu, using the food cost percentage method, Erin must segregate her items based on the following two variables:

1. **Food cost percentage**
2. **Popularity**

Since her overall food cost is 35%, she determines that any item with a food cost percentage above 35% will be considered *high* in food cost percentage, while any menu item with a food cost below 35% will be considered *low*. In a similar vein, with a total of 700 customers served in this accounting period and seven possible menu choices, each menu item would sell 700 / 7, or 100 times, if all were equally popular. Given that fact, Erin determines that any item sold more than 100 times during this accounting period would be considered high in popularity, while any item selling less than 100 times would be considered low in popularity. Having made these determinations, Erin can produce a matrix labeled as follows:

	Low popularity (Below 100 sales)	High popularity (Above 100 sales)
High food cost % (Above 35%)	1	2
Low food cost % (Below 35%)	3	4

Figure 8.15 **Menu Analysis—Food Cost %**

Unit Name: Erin's Date: 1/1/92–1/7/92

Menu Item	# Sold	Item Cost	Total Cost	Selling Price	Total Sales	Item's Contrib. Margin	Total Contrib. Margin	Food Cost %
Steak	73	$5.83	$ 425.59	$12.95	$ 945.35	$7.12	$ 519.76	45%
Shrimp	121	3.59	434.39	11.95	1,445.95	8.36	1,011.56	30
Swordfish	105	5.18	543.90	12.95	1,359.75	7.77	815.85	40
Chicken	140	1.97	275.80	8.95	1,253.00	6.98	977.20	22
Lobster	51	8.64	440.64	16.95	864.45	8.31	423.81	51
Scallops/pasta	85	2.39	203.15	9.95	845.75	7.56	642.60	24
Beef medallions	125	4.04	505.00	10.95	1,368.75	6.91	863.75	37
Total/average	700		2,828.47	11.55	8,083.00	7.51	5,254.53	35

The squares can be further defined as follows:

Square	Characteristics
1	High food cost %, low popularity
2	High food cost %, high popularity
3	Low food cost %, low popularity
4	Low food cost %, high popularity

Based on the number sold and food cost percentage data in Figure 8.15, Erin can classify her menu items in the following manner:

Square	Characteristics	Menu Item
1	High food cost %, low popularity	Steak, lobster
2	High food cost %, high popularity	Swordfish, beef medallion
3	Low food cost %, low popularity	Scallops, pasta
4	Low food cost %, high popularity	Shrimp, chicken

Note that each menu item finds itself in one, and only one, square. Using the food cost percentage method of menu analysis, Erin would like as many menu items as possible to fall within square 4. These items have the characteristics of being low in food cost percentage, but high in customer acceptance. Thus, both shrimp and chicken have below average food cost percentages and above average popularity. When developing a menu that seeks to minimize food cost percentage, items in the fourth square are highly desirable. These, of course, are kept on the menu. They should be well promoted and have high menu visibility. Promote them to your best customers and take care not to develop and attempt to sell a menu item that is similar enough in nature that it could detract from the sales of these items!

Each of the menu items that fall in the other squares requires a special marketing strategy, depending on its square location. These strategies can be summarized as shown in Figure 8.16.

It is quite effective to use the food cost percentage method of menu evaluation. Again, however, the operator should be cautioned against promoting low cost items with low selling prices at the expense of higher food cost percentage items that contribute greater gross profits.

Contribution Margin

When analyzing a menu using the contribution margin approach, the operator seeks to produce a menu that maximizes the overall contribution margin. The two variables to be analyzed, using this system, are **contribution margin** and **item popularity**. A criticism of the contribution margin approach to menu analysis is that it tends to favor high-priced menu items over low-priced ones, since higher priced menu items tend to have higher contribution margins. Over the

Figure 8.16 **Analysis of Food Cost Matrix Results**

Square	Characteristics	Problem	Marketing Strategy
1	High food cost %, low popularity	Marginal due to both high product cost and lack of sales	A. Remove from the menu. B. Consider current food trends to determine if the item itself is unpopular, or if its method of preparation is. C. Survey customers to determine current wants. D. If this is a high contribution margin item, consider reducing price and portion size.
2	High food cost %, high popularity	Marginal due to high product cost	A. Increase price. B. Reduce its prominence on the menu. C. Consider reducing portion size. D. "Package" the sale of this item with one that has a lower cost, and thus provide better overall profit.
3	Low food cost %, low popularity	Marginal due to lack of sales	A. Relocate on the menu for greater visibility. B. Take off the regular menu and run as specials. C. Reduce menu price. D. Eliminate other unpopular menu items in order to increase demand for this one.
4	Low food cost %, high popularity	None	A. Promote well. B. Give good visibility on menu.

long term, this can result in sales techniques and menu placement decisions that tend to put in the customer's mind a higher check average than the operation may warrant or desire. To illustrate the use of the contribution margin approach to menu pricing, the data in Figure 8.15 are again used.

In this case, Erin must again separate her items based on high or low popularity. This, of course, results in the same figures as those obtained when using the food cost percentage method; thus, any item that sells 700 / 7, or 100 times or more, is considered to be a high popularity item, while any menu choice selling less than 100 times would be considered low in popularity. To employ the contribution margin approach to menu pricing, Erin must first determine her average item contribution margin.

In Chapter 5, the following formula was presented:

$$\textbf{Product cost} + \textbf{Contribution margin desired} = \textbf{Selling price}$$

This same formula, stated in another way, indicates the following:

$$\textbf{Selling price} - \textbf{Product cost} = \textbf{Contribution margin desired}$$

When applying this formula to the data in Figure 8.15, we determine the following information for the total menu:

$$\textbf{Total sales} - \textbf{Total product costs} = \textbf{Total contribution margin}$$

Or

$$\$8{,}083.00 - \$2{,}828.47 = \$5{,}254.53$$

With a total of 700 menu items sold, we can determine the average contribution margin per item, using the following formula:

$$\frac{\textbf{Total contribution margin}}{\textbf{\# of items sold}} = \textbf{Contribution margin per item}$$

And in our own example,

$$\frac{\$5{,}254.53}{700} = \$7.51$$

To develop the contribution margin matrix, we proceed along much the same lines as we did with the food cost percentage matrix. In this case, average item popularity is 100 and average item contribution margin is $7.51. The matrix is developed as follows:

	Low popularity (Below 100 sales)	High popularity (Above 100 sales)
High contribution margin (Above $7.51)	1	2
Low contribution margin (Below $7.51)	3	4

The squares can further be defined as follows:

Square	Characteristics
1	High contribution margin, low popularity
2	High contribution margin, high popularity
3	Low contribution margin, low popularity
4	Low contribution margin, high popularity

Erin now classifies her menu items according to the contribution margin matrix in the following manner:

Square	Characteristics	Menu Items
1	High contribution margin, low popularity	Lobster, scallops, pasta
2	High contribution margin, high popularity	Shrimp, swordfish
3	Low contribution margin, low popularity	Steak
4	Low contribution margin, high popularity	Chicken, beef medallion

Again, each menu item finds itself in one and only one matrix square. Using the contribution margin method of menu analysis, Erin would like as many of her menu items as possible to fall into square 2, that is, high contribution margin and high popularity. From this analysis, Erin knows that both shrimp and swordfish yield a higher than average contribution margin. In addition, these items sell very well. Just as Erin would seek to give high menu visibility to items with low food cost percentage and high popularity, using the food cost percentage method of menu analysis; she would seek to give that same visibility to items with high contribution margin and high popularity when using the contribution margin approach.

Each of the menu items that fall in the other squares require a special marketing strategy, depending on their square location. These strategies can be summarized as shown in Figure 8.17.

The selection of either food cost percentage or contribution margin as a menu analysis technique is really an attempt by the foodservice operator to answer the following questions:

1. **Are my menu items priced correctly?**
2. **How much sales volume is needed on an item to justify keeping that item on the menu?**
3. **Is the overall profit margin on my menu items satisfactory?**

In reality, however, with the matrix method, neither approach is tremen-

Figure 8.17 **Analysis of Contribution Margin Matrix Results**

Square	Characteristics	Problem	Marketing Strategy
1	High contribution margin, low popularity	Marginal due to lack of sales	A. Relocate on menu for greater visibility. B. Consider reducing selling price.
2	High contribution margin, high popularity	None	A. Promote well. B. Give good visibility on menu.
3	Low contribution margin, low popularity	Marginal due to both low contribution margin and lack of sales	A. Remove from menu. B. Consider offering as a special occasionally, but at a higher menu price.
4	Low contribution margin, high popularity	Marginal due to low contribution margin	A. Increase price. B. Reduce menu visibility. C. Consider reducing portion size.

dously effective in analyzing menus. Because the axes on the matrix are determined by an *average* of food cost percentage, contribution margin, or sales level, some items will *always* fall into the less desirable categories. This is so because high food cost percentage, for instance, really means food cost percentage above the mean or average. Obviously then, some items will fall below the mean. Eliminating the poorest items only shifts *other* items into undesirable categories. To illustrate the problem, consider the following example. Homer, one of Erin's competitors, sells only four items, as listed below:

Homer's #1 Menu

Item	Number Sold
Beef	70
Chicken	60
Pork	15
Seafood	55
Total	200
Average sold	50 (200 / 4)

Homer may elect to remove the pork item, since its sales range is below the average of 50 items sold. If Homer adds turkey to the menu and removes the pork, he could get the following results:

Homer's #2 Menu

Item	Number Sold
Beef	65
Chicken	55
Turkey	50
Seafood	30
Total	200
Average sold	50 (200 / 4)

As can be seen, the turkey item draws sales away from the beef, chicken, and seafood dishes. In this case, it is now the seafood item that falls below the menu average. Should it be removed because its sales are below average? Clearly, this would not be wise. Removing the seafood item might serve to draw sales *from* the remaining items *to* the seafood replacement item. Obviously, the same type of results can occur when the operator uses a matrix to analyze food cost percentage or contribution margin. As someone once stated, half of us are always below average in anything. Even so, the matrix approach forces some items to be below average. How then can an operator answer questions related to price, sales volume, and overall profit margin? One answer is to employ a method of menu analysis called goal value analysis.

Goal Value Analysis

Returning to the data in Figure 8.15, we see that Erin has an overall food cost of 35%. In addition, she served 700 customers at a check average of $11.55. If we know Erin's overall fixed and variable costs, we could, in effect, create a P&L statement for each of Erin's menu items. One difficulty in creating such P&L's resides in the assignment of fixed and variable costs to individual menu items. The issue is complex, since deep-fried chicken, for example, might require more electricity in its preparation than an egg salad sandwich. For most operators, however, it is convenient to assign variable costs on the basis of menu price, while fixed costs must be assigned equally to each menu item or category. Not to do so would penalize those menu items that are forced to carry a larger than appropriate share of fixed costs. For the purpose of her goal value analysis, Erin determines her total variable costs. These are all the costs that vary with her sales volume, excluding the cost of the food itself. She computes those variable costs from her P&L statement and finds that they account for 30% of her total sales. Fixed costs for this accounting period were determined to be $1,400. Using this information, Erin assigns a fixed cost of $200 to each menu item ($1,400 total fixed costs / 7 menu items = $200).

Data from Figure 8.15 are now used to prepare the seven individual P&L statements associated with Erin's menu items. Figure 8.18 details the results of this process, rounded to the nearest whole dollar.

Figure 8.18 **Erins' Seven Individual P&L Statements**

	Steak		Shrimp		Swordfish		Chicken		Lobster		Scallops/ Pasta		Beef Medallions	
Sales	$945	1.00%	$1,446	1.00%	$1,360	1.00%	$1,253	1.00%	$864	1.00%	$846	1.00%	$1,369	1.00%
Food cost	426	.45	434	.30	544	.40	276	.22	441	.51	203	.23	507	.37
Variable cost	284	.30	434	.30	408	.30	376	.30	259	.30	254	.30	411	.30
Fixed cost	200	.21	200	.14	200	.15	200	.16	200	.23	200	.24	200	.15
Total cost	910	.96	1,068	.74	1,152	.85	852	.68	900	1.04	657	.78	1,118	.82
Net profit (loss)	35	.04	378	.26	208	.15	401	.32	(36)	(04)	189	.22	251	.18

Listed in order of their profitability, Erin's menu items rank as shown in Figure 8.19. Erin's ROS in this case is computed as $1,426.00 profit / $8,083.00 sales, or 17.6%.

The question for Erin, of course, is whether she should she revise her menu. Note that she has a 17.6% profit margin, an $11.55 check average, and a 35% food cost. The steak and lobster are rather unprofitable items. Should they be replaced? The answer, most likely, is no, *if* Erin is satisfied with her current food cost percentage, profit margin, check average, and customer count. Every menu will have items that are more or less profitable than others. In fact, some operators develop items called **loss leaders**. A loss leader is a menu item that is priced very low, sometimes even below cost, for the purpose of drawing large numbers of customers to the operation. If, for example, Erin has the only operation in town that serves outstanding lobster, that item may, in fact, contribute to the overall success of the operation by drawing people who will buy lobster, while their fellow diners may order other items that are more profitable.

Erin can use a shorthand method to **predict** an item's profitability. This method creates a goal value for the average menu item. Menu items that achieve goal values higher than this average will contribute greater than average profit percentages. As the goal value for an item increases, so does its profitability percentage. The goal value formula is as follows:

$$A \times B \times C \times D = \text{Goal value}$$

where

A = 1.00 − Food cost %
B = Item popularity
C = Selling price
D = 1.00 − (Variable cost % + Food cost %)

The computed goal value carries no unit designation; that is, it is neither a percent nor a dollar figure, because it is really a numerical target or score. If we

Figure 8.19 **Profit Contribution of Seven Menu Items**

Rank	Item	Profit
1	Chicken	+ $ 401.00
2	Shrimp	+ 378.00
3	Beef medallions	+ 251.00
4	Swordfish	+ 208.00
5	Scallops/pasta	+ 189.00
6	Steak	+ 35.00
7	Lobster	− 36.00
Total		+ 1,426.00

assume that Erin is pleased with the current performance of her operation, the goal value for her *average* menu item, using the formula above, would be as follows.

$$\overset{A}{(1.00 - .35)} \times \overset{B}{100} \times \overset{C}{11.55} \times \overset{D}{1.00 - (.30 + .35)} = \textbf{Goal value}$$

or

$$.65 \times 100 \times 11.55 \times .35 = \textbf{Goal value}$$

thus

$$263 = \textbf{Goal value}$$

According to this formula, any menu item whose goal value equals or exceeds 263 will achieve at least a 17.6% profit margin. Figure 8.20 details the goal value computation for each of Erin's seven menu items.

The usefulness and accuracy of goal value analysis are well documented. Simply put, it is a convenient way for management to make shorthand decisions regarding required profitability, sales volume, and pricing. Because all of the values needed for the goal value formula are readily available, management need not concern itself with puzzling through endless decisions about item replacement. Items that do not achieve goal value tend to be deficient in one or more of the key areas of food cost percentage (*A*), popularity (*B*), selling price (*C*), or the percentage amount available to fund fixed costs and profit (*D*). In theory, *all* menu items have the potential of reaching goal value, although management may determine that some menu items can indeed best serve the operation as loss leaders. Goal value analysis is also useful because it is not dependent on past performance, but can be established by management. Assume for a moment that Erin wished to achieve a greater profit margin and a $12 check average for next year. She plans to achieve this through a reduction in her food

Figure 8.20 **Goal Value Analysis**

Unit Name: Erin's Date: 1/8/92

Rank	Item	*A*	*B*	*C*	*D*	Goal Value
1	Chicken	.78	140	8.95	.48	469
2	Shrimp	.70	121	11.95	.40	405
3	Scallops/pasta	.76	85	9.95	.46	296
4	Beef medallions	.63	125	10.95	.33	285
5	Swordfish	.60	105	12.95	.30	245
6	Steak	.55	73	12.95	.25	130
7	Lobster	.49	51	16.95	.19	80

Target Goal Value: 263 Completed by: E.H.

cost to 33%, and her other variable costs to 29%. Her goal value formula for *next* year, assuming no reduction or increase in customer count, would be as follows:

$$\overset{A}{(1.00 - .33)} \times \overset{B}{100} \times \overset{C}{12.00} \times \overset{D}{1.00 - (.33 + .29)} = \textbf{Goal value}$$

or

$$.67 \times 100 \times 12.00 \times .38 = \textbf{Goal value}$$

thus

$$305 = \textbf{Goal value}$$

It is important to remember, however, that Erin's actual profit percentage will be heavily influenced by sales mix. Thus, each pricing, portion size, or menu placement decision becomes critical. Note that Erin can now go to each menu item in Figure 8.20 and determine whether she wishes to change any of the items to meet her goals. It is at this point that she must remember that she is a foodservice operator and not merely an accountant. A purely quantitative approach to menu analysis is neither practical nor desirable. Menu analysis is always somewhat a matter of educated guessing because operators cannot know in advance how changing any one menu item may affect the sales mix of the remaining items. Goal value analysis can be modified a bit if management prefers to do so. In the area of variable costs, a menu item might be assigned a low, medium, or high variable cost. If overall variable costs equal 30%, for example, management may choose sometimes to assign a variable cost of 25%, and at other times, 30% or 35%. This adjustment affects only the *D* variable of the goal value formula and can be accommodated quite easily. Goal value analysis will, however, allow an operator to make better decisions more quickly. This is especially true if the operator knows a bit of algebra and realizes that anytime he or she determines the desired goal value and any three of the four variables contained in the formula are known, he or she can solve for the fourth unknown variable. In other words, the operator can use the chart in Figure 8.21 to solve for any unknown variable.

Figure 8.21 **Solving for Goal Value (GV) Unknowns**

	Known Variables	**Unknown Variable**	**Method to Find Unknown**
1	*A, B, C, D*	*GV*	$A \times B \times C \times D$
2	*A, B, C, GV*	*D*	$\frac{GV}{A \times B \times C}$
3	*A, B, D, GV*	*C*	$\frac{GV}{A \times B \times D}$
4	*A, C, D, GV*	*B*	$\frac{GV}{A \times C \times D}$
5	*B, C, D, GV*	*A*	$\frac{GV}{B \times C \times D}$

To illustrate this, assume that Erin wishes to know how many servings of steak would have to be sold to bring its goal value to the 263 current target. Since popularity is value *B* and is unknown, we apply the following algebraic equation:

$$B = \frac{GV}{A \times C \times D}$$

In the case of the steak item from Figure 8.20, we determined the following:

$$A = .55$$
$$C = 12.95$$
$$D = .25$$
$$GV = 263$$

thus

$$B = \frac{263}{.55 \times 12.95 \times .25}$$

or

$$B = \frac{263}{1.78}$$

or

$$B = 148$$

According to these formulas, 148 servings of steak would have to be sold to achieve goal value. Again, goal value analysis is a very useful estimation tool for management.

Break-Even Analysis

Each foodservice operator knows that some accounting periods are more profitable than others. Often, this is due to the fact that sales volume is higher or costs are lower during certain periods. The ski resort that experiences tremendous sales during the ski season, but has a greatly reduced volume or may even close during the summer season, is a good example. Profitability, then, can be viewed as existing on a scale similar to the one below:

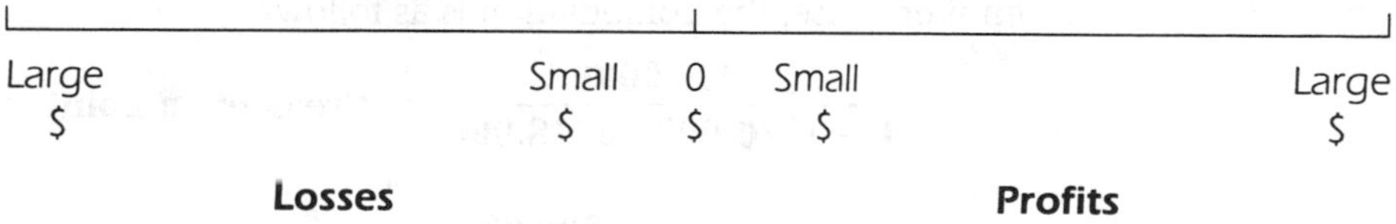

Large $	Small $	0 $	Small $	Large $
Losses			**Profits**	

The midpoint on the scale, indicated by the zero, is called the break-even point. At the break-even point, operational expenses are **exactly** equal to sales income. Stated in another way, when sales volume in an operation equals the sum of the operation's variable and fixed costs, the break-even point has been reached. Most operators would like to know their break-even point on a daily, weekly, or monthly basis. In effect, by determining the break-even point, the operator is answering the question "How much sales volume must I generate before I begin to make a profit?"

The answer to this question may be found either by constructing a break-even graph or by arithmetical calculation. While there are advantages to both methods, the arithmetical calculation is typically the most accurate. Break-even calculations can be done either on the dollar sales volume required to break even or on the basis of the number of customers required.

Consider the case of Jennifer, who operates an oriental restaurant in a suburban northwestern city. Based on her P&L statement and sales records of last month, Jennifer has the following information:

	Jennifer's		1/1/31
Total sales	$118,000	Sales per guest	$8.00
Variable costs	70,000	Guests served	14,750
Fixed costs	20,000		
Net profit (before tax)	28,000		

As discussed in Chapter 7, foodservice expenses can generally be classified as either fixed or variable. Of course, some expenses have both a fixed and a variable component and thus are, in reality, semivariable. For the purpose of engaging in a break-even analysis, however, it is necessary for the operator to assign costs to either a fixed or a variable category, as Jennifer has done. Once this has been accomplished, she can proceed to determine her operational break-even point. She wants to do this based both on dollar sales required to break even and on the number of customers required to do so.

To determine the sales volume required to break even, Jennifer uses the following formula:

$$\frac{\textbf{Fixed costs}}{\textbf{1 − (Variable cost / Total sales)}} = \textbf{Break-even point in sales}$$

In Jennifer's case, the computation is as follows:

$$\frac{\$20{,}000}{1 - (\$70{,}000 / \$118{,}000)} = \text{Break-even point in sales}$$

or

$$\frac{\$20{,}000}{1 - (.593)} = \text{Break-even point in sales}$$

or

$$\frac{\$20{,}000}{.407} = \$49{,}140.05$$

Thus, Jennifer must generate \$49,140.05 in sales per month *before* she begins to make a profit. At a sales volume of less than \$49,140.05, she would be operating at a loss. In terms of the number of customers that must be served in order to break even, Jennifer uses the following formula:

$$\frac{\textbf{Fixed costs}}{\textbf{Sales per guest} - (\textbf{Variable cost \%} \times \textbf{Sales per guest})} = \textbf{Break-even point in guests served}$$

Using the data from the previous computation, we know that fixed costs equal \$20,000.00 and that variable cost percentage equals .593 (\$70,000 / \$118,000 = .593). With an \$8.00 average sale per guest, Jennifer completes the computation as follows:

$$\frac{\$20{,}000.00}{\$8.00 - (.593 \times \$8.00)} = \textbf{Break-even point in guests served}$$

or

$$\frac{\$20{,}000.00}{\$8.00 - (4.744)}$$

or

$$\frac{\$20{,}000.00}{\$3.256} = 6{,}142.5 \textbf{ guests}$$

Minimum Sales Point

Every foodservice operator should know his or her break-even point. The concept of **minimum sales point** or **MSP** is related to this area. MSP is the dollar sales volume required to justify staying open for a given period of time. The information necessary to compute MSP is as follows:

1. **Food cost %**
2. **Minimum payroll cost for the time period**
3. **Variable cost %**

Fixed costs are eliminated from the calculation because even if volume of sales equals zero, fixed costs still exist and must be paid. Consider the situation of James, who is trying to determine whether he should close his steak house at 10:00 P.M. or 11:00 P.M. James wishes to compute the sales volume necessary to justify staying open the additional hour. He can make this calculation because he knows that his food cost equals 40%, his minimum labor cost to stay open for the extra hour equals \$150, and his variable costs (taken from his P&L statement) equal 30%. James applies the MSP formula as shown below:

$$\frac{\textbf{Minimum labor cost}}{1 - \textbf{Minimum operating cost \%}} = \textbf{MSP}$$

In James' case, the computation would be as follows:

$$\frac{\$150.00}{1 - (.40 + .30)} = \text{MSP}$$

or

$$\frac{\$150.00}{1 - .70} = \text{MSP}$$

or

$$\frac{\$150.00}{.30} = \text{MSP}$$

thus

$$\$500.00 = \text{MSP}$$

If James can achieve a sales volume of $500 in the 10:00 P.M. to 11:00 P.M. time period, he should stay open. If this level of sales is not feasible, he should consider closing the operation at 10:00 P.M. By doing an analysis of this type, James may be able to determine when he should offer promotions and specials during his off-periods. He can also use MSP to determine the hours his operation is most profitable. Of course, some operators may not have the authority to close the operation, even when remaining open is not particularly profitable. Corporate policy, contractual hours, promotion of a new unit, competition, and other factors must all be taken into account before the decision is made to modify operational hours.

The Budget

Just as the balance sheet tells management where they are, and the P&L analysis describes how they got there, the budget tells management where they are going. For practical purposes, the budget is the same as the profit plan. In effect, the budget tells management what must be done if predetermined profit and cost objectives are to be met. In this respect, management hopes to modify the profit formula, as presented in Chapter 1. With a well-thought out and attainable budget, management's profit formula would read as follows:

Budgeted income − Budgeted expense = Budgeted profit

To prepare this budget and stay within it assures predetermined profit levels. Without such a plan, management is left to guess about items such as expenditures and acceptable sales levels. The effective foodservice operator builds his or her budget, monitors it closely, modifies it when necessary, and achieves the desired results. Yet, many operators do not develop a budget. Some say that the process is too time-consuming. Others feel that a budget, especially one shared with the entire organization, is too revealing. Budgeting can also cause conflicts. This is true, for example, when the budget for new equipment must be used for either a new kitchen stove or a new beer-tapping system. Obviously, the kitchen manager and the beverage manager may hold different points of view on where these funds can best be spent!

Despite the fact that some operators avoid budgets, they are extremely important. The rationale for having and using a budget can be summarized as follows:

1. **It is the best means of analyzing alternative courses of action and allows management to examine these alternatives prior to adopting a particular one.**
2. **It forces management to examine the facts regarding what is necessary to achieve desired profit levels.**
3. **It provides a standard for comparison essential for good controls.**
4. **It allows management to anticipate and prepare for future business conditions.**
5. **It helps management to periodically carry out a self-evaluation of the organization and its progress toward its financial objectives.**
6. **It provides a communication channel whereby the organization's objectives are passed down to its various departments.**
7. **It encourages department managers who have participated in the preparation of the budget to establish their own operating objectives and evaluation techniques and tools.**
8. **It provides management with reasonable estimates of future expense levels and serves as an instrument for setting proper prices.**

Budgeting is best done by the entire management team, for it is only through participation in the process that the whole organization will feel compelled to support the budget's implementation. Budgets can be considered as one of three main types:

1. **Long-range budget**
2. **Annual budget**
3. **Achievement budget**

Long-range Budget

The long-range budget is often called the strategic plan. It is typically done for a period of three to five years. While its detail is not great, it does provide a long-term view about where the operation should be going. It is also particularly useful in those cases where additional operational units may increase sales volume, or planned construction projects may restrict volume.

Annual Budget

The annual, or yearly, budget is the type most operators think of when the word budget is uttered. As it states, the annual budget is for a one-year period or, in some cases, one season. This would be true, for example, in the case of a church summer camp that is open and serving meals only while school is out of session and campers are attending.

Achievement Budget

This budget is of a shorter range, perhaps a month or a week. It provides current operating information and thus assists in making current operational decisions. A weekly achievement budget might, for example, attempt to predict the number of gallons of milk needed for this time period or the number of waitpersons to be scheduled on Tuesday.

Developing the Budget

To establish any type of budget, management must have the following information available:

1. **Prior period operating results**
2. **Assumptions of next period operations**
3. **Goals**
4. **Monitoring policies**

Prior Period Operating Results

Consider the case of Levi, who is preparing the annual foodservice budget for his 100-bed extended care facility. Levi's facility operates at an average occupancy of 80% and serves 300 additional meals per day to staff and visitors. He is given a flat dollar amount by the administration for each meal he serves. His operating results for last year are detailed in Figure 8.22.

Patient and additional meals served were determined by actual count. Revenue and expense figures were taken from Levi's P&L statements from the prior year. It is important to note that Levi must have this information if he is to do any meaningful profit planning. Foodservice unit managers who do not have access to their operating results are at a tremendous managerial disadvantage. Levi has his operational summaries and the data that produced them. He is now ready to proceed to the assumptions section of the planning process.

Figure 8.22 **Levi's**

1/1/90–1/1/92

Patient Meals Served: 29,200 Revenue per Meal: $3.46

Additional Meals Served: 109,500

Total Meals Served: 138,700

	Amount	Percentage
Total department revenue	$480,000	100%
Cost of food	192,000	40
Cost of labor	153,600	32
Other expense	86,400	18
Total expense	432,000	90
Net	48,000	10

Assumptions of Next Period Operations

If Levi is to prepare a budget with enough strength to serve as a guide and enough flexibility to adapt to a changing environment, he must factor in the assumptions he and others feel will impact the operation. While each operation will arrive at its own conclusions, Levi makes the following assumptions regarding next year:

1. **Food costs will increase by 3%.**
2. **Labor costs will increase by 5%.**
3. **Other expenses will rise by 10% due to a significant increase in utility cost.**
4. **Revenue received for all meals will be increased by no more than 1%.**
5. **Patient occupancy of 80% will remain unchanged.**

Levi would be able to establish these assumptions through discussions with his suppliers and union leaders, his own records, and most importantly, his sense of the operation itself. In the commercial sector, when arriving at assumptions, operators must also consider new or diminished competition, changes in traffic patterns, and national food trends. At the highest level of foodservice management, assumptions regarding the acquisition of new units or the introduction of new products will certainly affect the budget process. As an operator, Levi predicts items 1, 2, and 3 by himself, while his supervisor has given him input about items 4 and 5. Given these assumptions, Levi must consider what his operational goals are.

Establishing Goals

Given the assumptions he makes, Levi can now determine actual goals for the coming year. He will establish them for each of the following areas:

1. **Meals served**
2. **Revenue**
3. **Food**
4. **Labor**
5. **Other expense**
6. **Profit**

Meals Served

Given the assumption of no increase in patient occupancy, Levi budgets for 29,200 patient meals. He feels, however, that he can increase his visitor and staff meals a little by being more customer-driven and offering a wider selection of items on the cycle menu. He decides, therefore, to raise his goal for additional meals to 115,000 for the coming year. Thus, his total meals to be served will equal 29,200 + 115,000, or 144,200 meals.

Revenue

Levi knows that his total revenue is to increase by only 1%. His revenue per meal will be \$3.46 × 1.01 = \$3.49. With 144,200 meals to be served, Levi will receive 144,200 × \$3.49, or \$503,258.00, if he meets his meals served budget.

Food

Since Levi is planning on serving more meals, he expects to spend more on food. In addition, he assumes that this food will cost, on average, 3% more than last year. To determine a food budget, Levi computes the sales value of 144,200 meals using *this* year's revenue per meal as follows:

144,200 meals projected for next year × \$3.46 = \$498,932.00 revenue

At a 40% food cost, Levi would have spent \$498,932.00 × .40 = \$199,573.00 to serve 144,200 meals at current prices. Next year's prices, however, are to be 3% higher, and given that 144,200 meals are to be served, Levi budgets \$199,573.00 × 1.03 = \$205,560.00 for next year's food expense.

Labor

In order to determine how much labor is required to serve one meal, Levi employs the following formula:

$$\frac{\textbf{Cost of labor}}{\textbf{Meals served}} = \textbf{Labor cost per meal}$$

His data for the previous year are as follows:

$$\frac{\$153{,}600}{138{,}700} = \$1.11 \text{ per meal}$$

Since Levi assumes that next year his labor cost will increase by 5%, he determines that his labor cost per meal will be $1.11 × 1.05 = $1.17 per meal. Given an estimate of 144,200 meals to be served, Levi's budgeted labor cost for the coming year would be 144,200 × $1.17 = $168,714.00.

Other Expense

Since Levi assumes a 10% increase in other expense, it is budgeted as $86,400 × 1.10 = $95,040. Based on his previous assumptions, Figure 8.23 details Levi's budget summary for the next year.

Figure 8.23 **Budget For Next Year**

Levi's

Patient Meals Budgeted: 29,200 Budgeted Revenue per Meal: $3.49

Additional Meals

Budgeted: 115,000

Total Meals Budgeted: 144,200

	Amount	Percentage
Total budgeted revenue	$503,258.00	100.0%
Budgeted expenses		
Food	205,560.00	40.8
Labor	168,714.00	33.5
Other	95,040.00	18.9
Total	469,314.00	93.3
Income over expense	33,944.00	6.7

Note that the increased costs Levi will be forced to bear, when coupled with his minimal revenue increase, caused his income over expense to fall from $48,000 for last year to a projected $33,944 for the coming year. If this is not acceptable, Levi must either increase his revenue beyond his assumption or look to his operation to reduce costs. In any event, he has developed concrete guidelines for his operation. Since his supervisor has approved his budget as submitted, Levi is now ready to enter into the budget's monitoring stage.

Budget Monitoring Policies

An operational plan has little value if it is not used by management. In general, the budget should be monitored in each of the following three areas:

1. **Income**
2. **Expense**
3. **Profit**

Income Analysis

If income should fall below projected levels, management selects from a handful of alternative strategies. As discussed in Chapter 2, income variance should be monitored on a very regular basis. If income consistently exceeds projections, the overall budget must be modified or the expenses associated with these increased sales will soon exceed budgeted amounts. It is clear that increases in operational income should dictate proportional increases in variable expense budgets, although fixed expenses, of course, need not be adjusted for these increases. For those foodservice operations with more than one meal period, monitoring budgeted volume may mean monitoring each meal period. Consider the case of Ruthann, the night (P.M.) manager of a college cafeteria. She feels that she is busier than ever, but her boss, Lois, maintains that there can be no increase in Ruthann's labor budget, since the overall cafeteria sales volume is exactly in line with projections. Figure 8.24 shows the reality of the sales volume

Figure 8.24 **College Cafeteria Income/Budget Summary**

1/1/92–6/30/92

Meal Period	Budget	Actual	% of Budget
A.M.	$480,500	$166,698	35%
P.M.	350,250	248,677	71
Total	830,750	415,375	50

situation at the college cafeteria after six months of the fiscal year. Note that the year is half (or 50%) over at the time of this analysis.

Based on the sales volume she generates, Ruthann *should* have an increase in her labor budget. This, however, does not mean that the labor budget for the entire cafeteria should be increased. In fact, the labor budget for the A.M. shift should be reduced, as those dollars are more appropriately needed in the evening meal period. Some foodservice operators relate income to the number of seats they have available in their operation. Since the size of a foodservice facility affects both total investment and operating costs, this can be a useful number. The formula for the computation of sales per seat is as follows:

$$\frac{\textbf{Total sales}}{\textbf{Number of seats}} = \textbf{Sales per seat}$$

To illustrate this, let's assume that if Ruthann's cafeteria had 120 seats, her P.M. sales per seat thus far this year would be as follows:

$$\frac{\$248{,}677}{120} = \$2{,}072.31$$

The A.M. sales per seat, given the same number of seats, would be computed as follows:

$$\frac{\$166{,}698}{120} = \$1{,}389.15$$

As can be seen, Ruthann's sales per seat is much higher than that of her A.M. counterpart.

When sales volume is lower than originally projected, management must seek ways to increase income. As stated earlier, one of management's main tasks is to generate customers, while the employee's main task is to service these customers to the best of his or her ability. The typical methods for increasing volume include the use of coupons, increased advertising, price discounting, and specials. For the serious foodservice manager, a thorough study of the modern techniques of foodservice marketing is mandatory.

Expense Analysis

Effective foodservice managers are careful to monitor operational expense because costs that are too high *or* too low may be cause for concern. Just as it is not possible to estimate future sales volume perfectly, it is also not possible to estimate future expense perfectly, since some expenses will vary as sales volume increases or decreases. To know that an operation spent $500 for produce in a given week becomes meaningful only if we know what the sales volume for that week was. In the same vein, knowing that $200 was spent for labor during a given lunch period can be analyzed only in terms of the amount of sales achieved in that same period. Some operators, therefore, elect to utilize the yardstick method of determining expense standards. To illustrate this, consider the case of Marion, who operates a college cafeteria during nine months of the year in a small southeastern city. Marion has developed both income and expense budgets. His problem, however, is that variations in income cause variations in expense. This is true in terms of both food products and labor. He wishes to know whether changes in his expenses are due to inefficiencies in his operation or normal sales variation. To begin his analysis, Marion establishes a purchase standard for food products using a seven-step model.

Developing Yardstick Standards for Food

Step 1. Divide total inventory into management-designated subgroups, for example, meats, produce, dairy, and groceries.
Step 2. Establish dollar value of subgroup purchases for prior accounting period.
Step 3. Establish sales volume for prior accounting period.
Step 4. Determine percentage of purchasing dollar spent for each food category.
Step 5. Determine percentage of income dollar spent for each food category.
Step 6. Develop weekly sales volume and associated expense projection. Compute % cost to sales for each food grouping and sales estimate.
Step 7. Compare weekly income and expense to projection. Correct if necessary.

To develop his yardstick standards for food, Marion collects the following data from last year.

Marion's College Cafeteria

Last School Year/9 Months

Total Sales: $450,000.00 — Average Monthly Sales: $50,000

Purchases	
Meats	$ 66,600
Fish/Poultry	36,500
Produce	26,500
Dairy	20,000
Groceries	18,300
Total	167,900

Assuming that Marion has created an income estimate of $52,000 per month for this year, and that he was satisfied with both last year's food cost percentage and profits, he can now follow the steps outlined above to establish his yardstick standards for food. Marion estimates weekly sales volume of $52,000 / 4, or $13,000, for this year.

Marion's Yardstick Standards for Food

Step 1. Meat
Fish/poultry
Produce
Dairy
Groceries

Step 2.

Step 2.	**Meat**	**$ 66,600**
	Fish/poultry	**36,500**
	Produce	**26,500**
	Dairy	**20,000**
	Groceries	**18,300**
	Total	**167,900**

Step 3. **$450,000 / 9 months**

Step 4.	**Meat**	**$ 66,600 / 167,900 =**	**39.7%**
	Fish/poultry	**36,500 / 167,900 =**	**21.7**
	Produce	**26,500 / 167,900 =**	**15.8**
	Dairy	**20,000 / 167,900 =**	**11.9**
	Grocery	**18,300 / 167,900 =**	**10.9**
	Total	**167,900**	**100.0**

Step 5.	**Meat**	**$ 66,600 / 450,000 =**	**14.8%**
	Fish/poultry	**36,500 / 450,000 =**	**8.1**
	Produce	**26,500 / 450,000 =**	**5.9**
	Dairy	**20,000 / 450,000 =**	**4.4**
	Grocery	**18,300 / 450,000 =**	**4.1**
	Total	**167,900**	**37.3**

Step 6.

			Weekly Sales Estimate				
Category	**% Cost to Total Cost**	**% Cost to Total Sales**	**$11,000**	**$12,000**	**$13,000**	**$14,000**	**$15,000**
Meat	39.7%	14.8%	$1,628	$1,776	$1,924	$2,072	$2,220
Fish/poultry	21.7	8.1	891	972	1,053	1,134	1,215
Produce	15.8	5.9	649	708	767	826	885
Dairy	11.9	4.4	484	528	572	616	660
Groceries	10.9	4.1	451	492	533	574	615
Total	100	37.3	4,103	4,476	4,849	5,222	5,595

Note that to compute the data for Step 6, one must multiply % cost to total sales by sales estimate. To use the sales estimate of $13,000.00, for example, the meat budget would be computed as follows:

.148 × $13,000.00 = $1,924.00

Fish/poultry would be computed as follows:

.081 × $13,000.00 = $1,053.00

Step 7. Analysis
Marion can now compare his budgeted expense performance with actual performance over several volume levels. In a week in which sales volume equals $14,000.00, for example, Marion would expect that total meat invoices for that period, according to his yardstick measure, would equal approximately $14,000.00 × 14.8%, or $2,072.00. Of course, this assumes that Marion has not changed the level of his meat inventory. If his invoices, or in the case of an issues and requisition system, his issues, exceed $2,072.00, he would know exactly where to direct his attention. Using the yardstick system, Marion can easily monitor any expense over any number of differing volume levels. The yardstick method of purchase estimation is especially helpful for those operations that experience great variation in sales volume. A hotel that has a slow and busy season, for instance, will find that the use of this method is quite helpful in predicting working capital needed for inventory acquisition.

Developing Yardstick Standards for Labor

Just as Marion used the yardstick method to estimate food expense, he can also use it to estimate labor cost expenditures. To develop such a yardstick, he follows these steps:

Step 1. Divide total labor cost into management-designated subgroups, for example, cooks, warewashers, and bartenders.
Step 2. Establish dollar value spent for each subgroup for prior accounting period.
Step 3. Establish sales volume for prior accounting period.
Step 4. Determine percentage of labor dollar spent for each subgroup.
Step 5. Determine percentage of income dollar spent for each labor category.
Step 6. Develop weekly sales volume and associated expense projection. Compute % cost to sales for each labor category and sales estimate.
Step 7. Compare weekly income and expense to projection. Correct if necessary.

Marion collected the following labor-related data from last year's operation.

Marion's College Cafeteria

Last School Year/9 Months

Total Sales: $450,000.00 | Average Monthly Sales: $50,000

Labor Costs	
Management	$ 40,000
Food production	65,000
Service	12,000
Sanitation	18,000
Total	135,000

It is important to note that Marion can develop a labor yardstick based on customers served, labor hours worked, or, as is his preference, labor cost percentage. To develop the labor standard, Marion follows the seven-step process as outlined.

Marion's Yardstick Standards for Labor

Step 1. **Management**
Food production
Service
Sanitation

Step 2.		
	Management	**$ 40,000**
	Food production	**65,000**
	Service	**12,000**
	Sanitation	**18,000**
	Total	**$135,000**

Step 3. **$450,000**

Step 4.			
	Management	**$ 40,000 / 135,000 =**	**29.6%**
	Food production	**65,000 / 135,000 =**	**48.2**
	Service	**12,000 / 135,000 =**	**8.9**
	Sanitation	**18,000 / 135,000 =**	**13.3**
	Total	**135,000**	**100.0**

Step 5.			
	Management	**$ 40,000 / 450,000 =**	**8.9%**
	Food production	**65,000 / 450,000 =**	**14.4**
	Service	**12,000 / 450,000 =**	**2.7**
	Sanitation	**18,000 / 450,000 =**	**4.0**
	Total	**135,000**	**30.0**

Step 6.

Category	% Cost to Total Cost	% Cost to Total Sales	Sales Estimate				
			$11,000	**$12,000**	**$13,000**	**$14,000**	**$15,000**
Management	29.6%	8.9%	$ 979	$1,068	$1,157	$1,246	$1,335
Food production	48.2	14.4	1,584	1,728	1,872	2,016	2,160
Service	8.9	2.7	297	324	351	378	405
Sanitation	13.3	4.0	440	480	520	560	600
Total	100	30.0	3,300	3,600	3,900	4,200	4,500

Note that to compute the data for Step 6, one must multiply % cost to Total Sales by sales estimate. To use the sales estimate of $13,000.00, for example, the management budget would be computed as follows:

.089 × $13,000.00 = $1,157.00

Food production cost expense would be estimated as follows:

.144 × $13,000.00 = $1,872.00

Step 7. Analysis
It is now easy for Marion to identify exactly where his labor variations, if any, are to be found.

The yardstick method may, of course, be used for any operational expense, be it food, labor, or one of the many other expenses incurred by the operator. In all cases, however, the effective foodservice manager must monitor actual expenditures as they relate to budgeted expenditures, while keeping changes in sales volume in mind.

Profit Analysis

Chapter 1 of this text presented the following formula:

Income − Expense = Profit

In analyzing profit, a more accurate formula would be as follows:

Budgeted income − Budgeted expense = Budgeted profit

If budgeted profit is not realized, it must be due to unanticipated sales levels, unanticipated expenditure, or a combination of these. It is important to note that the budget is not a static device. As business conditions change, changes in the budget are to be expected. This is because budgets are based on a given set of assumptions, and as these assumptions change, so too does the budget that follows from the assumptions.

Budgeted profit must be realized if the operation is to provide adequate returns for owner and investor risk. Consider the case of James, the operator of a foodservice establishment with excellent sales but below-budgeted profits. James budgeted a 5% profit on $2,000,000 of sales; thus, $100,000 profit ($2,000,000 × .05 = $100,000) was anticipated. In reality, at year's end, James achieved only $50,000 profit, or 2.5% of sales ($50,000 / $2,000,000 = 2.5%). If the operation's owners feel that $50,000 is an adequate return for their risk, James' services may be retained. If they do not, he may lose his position *even though* the operation is profitable. A primary goal of management is to generate the profits necessary for the successful continuation of the business. Budgeting for these profits is a fundamental step in the process. Analyzing the success of achieving budget forecasts is of tremendous managerial concern.

If profit goals are to be met, safeguarding operational income is critical. It is to that task we now turn our attention. The proper collection and accounting for guest payment of services is the last step in a successful food and beverage cost control system.

TEST YOUR SKILLS

A. Given the information below, complete the P&L statement for Bobbie's restaurant. Compute the real increase in sales this year over last, assuming a 5% increase in selling prices at the beginning of the fiscal year. Also, what should have been the labor cost percentage for Bobbie's, if you assume no change in operational efficiency but a 5% increase in selling prices at the beginning of the fiscal year and a 10% increase in labor costs for the same period?

Bobbie's P&L

	This Year	%	Last Year	%
Sales	$2,315,000	100%	$1,865,000	100%
Cost of food	?	.31	?	.33
Cost of labor	671,350	?	540,850	?
Other expense	?	.21	?	.23
Profit	?	?	?	?

B. Elizabeth operates a pizza parlor in a college town. Her volume varies tremendously, based on whether school is in or out of session. Due to this fact, budgeting her income and costs is of extreme importance to her. She budgets both income and expense on a quarterly basis. Given the information below, develop a budget for each of the four quarters of her fiscal year. Use the income and expense data from last year, as well as the following assumptions she and her supervisor have developed:

1. **A 5% increase in guests served for each of the four quarters**
2. **A 3% increase in the cost of food for each of the four quarters**
3. **A 10% increase in the cost of labor for the fourth quarter only**
4. **A 5% increase in average sales per guest for the fourth quarter only**

Last Year's Results

Elizabeth's Pizza Parlor

	Quarters			
	1	2	3	4
Sales	$192,045.00	$189,720.00	$117,250.00	$209,250.00
Food expense	65,295.00	30,505.00	41,038.00	73,238.00
Labor expense	57,614.00	56,916.00	35,175.00	62,775.00
Other expense	38,409.00	37,944.00	23,450.00	41,850.00
Total expense				
Profit				
Guests served	29,500.00	30,600.00	17,500.00	31,000.00
Average sale per guest	6.51	6.20	6.70	6.75

C. Tony operates a seafood house in Miami, Florida. He is a very successful operator. Tony would like to compute his operational break-even point in terms of both dollar sales required and guests required to be served. Based on last year's information, and assuming no changes in either menu prices or costs, compute these two numbers for him.

Total sales:	$3,465,000	(100%)	Sales per guest:	$16.50
Variable costs:	______	(68%)	Guests served:	______
Fixed costs:	______	(20%)		
Net profit:	$ 415,800	(12%)		

Break-even point in sales: ______

Break-even point in guests served: ______

CHAPTER 9

Maintaining and Improving the Income Control System

OVERVIEW

In this chapter, the basic principles of income control will be presented. In addition, the use of computers in the cost control process and the elements necessary to effectively select computer assistance for the cost control system are detailed and discussed. This chapter, the last one in this textbook, concludes with a summary of the cost control function.

HIGHLIGHTS

At the conclusion of this chapter, the manager will be able to

A. **Develop an income control system for a foodservice operation**
B. **Wisely shop for the basics of a computer-assisted control system**
C. **Outline a complete food and beverage cost control system for a new foodservice operation**

Income Security

All the cost control systems an operator can develop will be of no use if the foodservice operator is unable to collect the income generated by product sales, and then deposit that income into the proper bank account. Errors in income collection can come from simple employee mistakes or, in some cases, outright theft by either customers or employees. The effective foodservice manager must devise security systems to protect income, whether income is in the form of cash, checks, credit card receipts, coupons, meal cards, or any other method of guest payment.

In its simplest form, income security is a matter of matching product sold with funds received. An income security system does nothing more than ensure that the following formula reflects what really happens in the foodservice establishment.

Product sales	=	**Guest check totals**	=	**Sales receipts**	=	**Sales deposits**

The potential for employee theft exists in any of the above areas, and it behooves management to remain vigilant. To illustrate this, consider the case of Lonnie's Pie Parlor. Lonnie sells pies of many varieties, all for the same price of $2 per slice or $15 for a whole pie, consisting of eight slices. In addition, coffee is sold for $1 per cup. Figure 9.1 details the sales record for Monday's pie and coffee sales.

If Lonnie has a system of controlling his income, he should have total receipts of $1,200 for January 1, 1992. If, in fact, at the conclusion of the day, Lonnie has only $1,100 in income, a security problem exists, not perhaps in the control of products, but rather in the control of receipts. There are several reasons why Lonnie may be short in income. A discussion of the potential problems he may be facing will be helpful as we proceed to develop income security systems designed to address these issues. Income security problems can exist in any or all of the following three areas:

1. **Customer theft**
2. **Service personnel theft**
3. **Cashier theft**

Figure 9.1 **Sales Record**

Unit Name: Lonnie's Pie Parlor Date: 1/1/92

Item	# Sold	Selling Price	Total Sales
Apple pie			
Slices	60	$ 2	$ 120
Whole	11	15	165
Pumpkin pie			
Slices	40	2	80
Whole	14	15	210
Cherry pie			
Slices	75	2	150
Whole	5	15	75
Peach pie			
Slices	25	2	50
Whole	10	15	150
Coffee	200	1	200
Total			1,200

Customer Theft

Lonnie could, of course, have lost sales income because some customers simply try to defraud foodservice operators. This activity can take a variety of forms, and a very common one is for a customer to "walk" the bill or guest check. A customer is said to have walked a check when he or she has consumed a product but has left the foodservice operation without paying the bill. This type of theft is obviously not present in a quick-service operation, where payment is received at the time the food is given to the customer. In cases where a guest is in a busy dining room, however, it is quite possible for one or more members of a dining party to slip outside while the waiter or waitress is busy with other guests. This type of theft can be prevented only by instructing waitstaff to keep a close watch on all of their tables. It is also possible that a customer truly forgets to pay his or her bill and leaves the establishment without paying. In cases such as this, it is up to management to remind the customer that the bill is due and payable, if the customer can be located prior to leaving the premises. If many of his customers walked their bills on Lonnie's day of $1,200 sales, he would find that while the products had indeed been consumed, the income in his cash register would not equal the sales value of the pie and coffee served.

A second form of consumer theft that management must guard against is that of passing bad checks or using invalid credit cards. In our society, fewer and fewer consumers carry large amounts of cash. Thus, more and more foodservice operators accept credit cards, and many accept a variety of different cards. Since they are billed by a third party, the foodservice operator must pay a percentage of each credit card sale back to the credit card company. If, for example, the credit card sale is $10.00 and an operator is charged 4% for accepting the card, the credit card company would receive $10.00 × .04, or $.40, from the restaurant for the use of the card. The number of stolen and fraudulent credit cards in use today is very high. It is therefore important for the foodservice operator to check the validity of the credit card before accepting it for payment. This may be done manually through the use of a published listing of stolen or missing credit cards or, as is more common today, through the use of a computer coding system. A small magnetic tape on the back of the credit card can be read by machine to ensure that the card is indeed valid. Rapid advances in computer technology virtually guarantee that this system will soon become part of even the most basic cash register systems.

Credit card companies do charge the foodservice operation that agrees to accept the cards. The operator, of course, hopes that by accepting credit cards, overall sales volume will increase. Some operators, however, have found that the cost of accepting credit cards exceeds the amount of additional revenue they generate. Each operation must carefully weigh the decision of which, if any, credit cards to accept.

In the past, those foodservice operations that accepted personal checks ran the risk of being handed checks with insufficient funds in the bank to cover the expense. While many operations no longer accept checks, those that do find that they too must use a verification service prior to accepting these instruments for payment. These services do not actually certify that there are sufficient funds in the bank to complete the transaction, but rather they notify the foodservice operator if that particular checking account or individual has had difficulty in the past in covering checks written on that account.

The cost of verifying credit, cash, and personal checks prior to acceptance is an expense that foodservice managers simply must bear. Of course, these costs, as all others, will be reflected in higher menu prices. It is imperative, however, that customer theft of this type be kept to an absolute minimum. The last method of customer theft Lonnie must be aware of is that employed by the quick-change artist. A customer, who has practiced the routine many times, attempts to confuse the cashier, and in his or her confusion, the cashier gives the customer too much change. For example, a customer who should have received $5 in change may use a confusing routine to secure $25. To prevent this from happening, management must train its cashiers well and instruct them to notify management immediately if there is any suspicion of attempted fraud to the operation through quick-change routines by a customer.

Service Personnel Theft

While most foodservice employees are honest, some are not. Since cash is the most readily usable asset in a foodservice operation, it is a major target for dishonest employees. In general, theft from service personnel is not a matter of removing large sums of cash at one time, since this is too easy for management to detect. Rather, service personnel can use a variety of techniques to cheat an operation a small amount at a time. One of the most common methods involves the omission of writing the customer's order on the guest check. If, for example, a customer ordered both pie and coffee, but the pie sale is not recorded on the guest check, Lonnie may find that a piece of pie was missing, but no record of sale was ever made. In this situation, the cashier might have chosen to charge the customer and keep the income from the piece of pie, or might have attempted to build favor with the customer by not charging for the product at all. This type of theft is especially prevalent in bars. As an old foodservice story goes: "A customer walks into a bar that sells drinks for $3, has five drinks, and places $15 on the counter as he leaves. The bartender then turns to the manager and says, 'Hey, that guy didn't pay for his drinks, but he left a great tip!' " The manager was not amused. The point, however, is that all sales must be recorded if management is to develop a system that matches products sold to income received. In reality, income control is a matter of developing checks and counterchecks to ensure that the value of products sold and the amount of income received do indeed equal each other.

A second method of server theft is to use the same guest check for more than one customer. If, for example, one of Lonnie's customers orders peach pie and coffee and the service person collects the income for these products, the same guest check could be used one hour later for another customer who orders peach pie and coffee. The waitperson could then keep the money from the second sale, and at the end of the day, the operation would find itself short on income relative to product used. It is important to note that most customers do not know or care if the guest check presented to them is actually theirs or belongs to someone else. In fact, if the guest check is accurate in terms of total charges and items ordered, customers would have no way of knowing if they are paying their own bill or someone else's. To prevent fraud of this type, the effective foodservice manager must have a system of guest check controls in place so that each check can be used one time only and is subsequently put under the safe-keeping of management. It should not be possible, for example, for a waitperson to submit a guest check that had previously been used, while keeping a blank one. Guest checks should be recorded by number and then safely stored or destroyed, as management policy dictates.

Another method of service personnel fraud also involves the use of guest checks. In this case, the waiter or waitress gives the guest check to the customer, collects payment, and *destroys* the guest check but keeps the money. Management may find that receipts in the cash register equal the sum of the guest checks. The cash drawer and guest checks will balance, but the amount of food products sold does not equal this total. In Lonnie's case, he would find that more pie and coffee had been served to customers than payment had been received. To prevent this type of service personnel fraud, management must make sure that all guest checks are accounted for.

In a similar vein, cashiers can bring in their own guest checks, record sales, collect funds, and then destroy the check. This can occur when management uses a guest check that can be purchased outside of the operation by service personnel. To keep this from happening, management must have guest checks that are both numbered and not easily secured by employees. In addition, managers should be constantly aware of the type of check used by each server. They should not allow employees to bring in checks purchased or stolen from other operations. Prevention of this is possible only through constant management vigilance. Recording guest orders on anything other than a management-issued guest check must be strictly prohibited.

In a foodservice operation, guests frequently place an order and then change their mind and order something else. When this happens, so too does the opportunity for fraud. Service personnel may charge the customer for a higher priced item while serving a lower priced one, and then keep the difference in selling price. Similarly, the operation can be defrauded if a higher priced item is sold, but the customer is charged for a lower priced menu selection. To prevent this kind of abuse, guest checks should be filled out in pen, never pencil, and any changes should be made by drawing a line through the original item and writing the new item below it. In no case should service personnel be provided with guest checks that can be erased. Many types of guest checks manufactured today are done so on nonerasable paper. This is an excellent control device.

Not all service personnel are dishonest, of course, and sometimes honest mistakes can be made. This usually occurs when service personnel are required to total their guest checks by hand. Simple errors in addition and subtraction can cost an operation dearly in lost revenue. For this reason, it is critical that service personnel do not total guest checks without the use of a cash register, adding machine, or calculator. Customers also prefer to see that the guest check is totalled by machine. It strengthens their belief that the total they have been charged does indeed match the items they have consumed, and that no errors in arithmetic have been made.

Cashier Theft

If a cashier is responsible for the collection of money, several areas of potential fraud can exist. The cashier may collect payment from a guest but proceed to destroy the guest check that recorded the sale. Another method of cashier theft involves failing to ring up the sale indicated by the guest check, while pocketing the money. Management must have systems in place to identify missing checks that cannot be accounted for and to match guest check totals with those of cash register sales.

Cashiers may also shortchange customers. This involves, for example, giving a customer change from a $10 bill when in fact the customer paid with a $20 bill. This can occur when an operation is very busy, or when a customer is distracted by surrounding incidents or perhaps has overindulged in alcohol. Cashiers rarely steal directly from the cash drawer, but management must make it a policy that any cash shortages over a predetermined amount will be investigated. If the cash register has a void key, a dishonest cashier could enter a sales amount, collect for it, and then void the sale after the customer has departed. In this way, total sales would equal the amount of the cash drawer. If the cashier then destroys the guest check involved with this sale, the remaining guest checks, cash register sales figure, and cash drawer would all balance. To prevent this, management should insist that all cash register voids be performed by a supervisor or at least be authorized by management on an individual basis.

A final method of cashier theft to be discussed here involves the manipulation of complimentary meals or meal coupons. Assume, for example, that at his establishment, Lonnie has produced a large number of guest coupons good for a free piece of pie. If the cashier has access to these coupons, it is possible to collect the income from a guest *without* a coupon and then add the coupon to the cash drawer while simultaneously removing sales income equal to the value of the coupon. A variation on this theme is for the cashier to declare a check to be complimentary after the guest has paid the bill. In cases like this, the cashier would again remove sales income from the cash register in an amount equal to the "comped" check. This kind of fraud can be prevented by denying cashiers access to unredeemed cash value coupons and by requiring special authorization from management to "comp" guest checks.

While the scenarios above do not list all possible methods of income loss, it is clear that Lonnie must have a complete income security system if he is to ensure that all product sold generates sales income that finds its way into his deposit report. It is to this matter, the development of an income control system, that we now turn our attention. It is important to remember that even good income control systems present the opportunity for theft if management is not vigilant or if two or more employees conspire to defraud the operation. It may not be possible to prevent all types of theft, but a good income control system should help management determine if, in fact, a theft has occurred. It is then up to management to take appropriate action.

Bonding

While it may not be possible to collect funds that are stolen by customers, employees of a foodservice establishment may be bonded, as a method of insuring against theft. Bonding is simply a matter of purchasing an insurance policy against the possibility that an employee will steal. If an employee has been bonded, and an operation can determine that he or she was indeed involved in a theft of a specific amount of money, the operation will be reimbursed for the loss by the bonding company. It is relatively inexpensive and well worth the cost to require that all employees who handle cash or other forms of operational income be bonded. It is also an excellent preemployment check to verify an employee's track record in prior jobs.

Developing the Income Security System

As presented earlier in this chapter, an effective income security system involves the following four key points:

1. **Verify product sales**
2. **Verify guest check totals**
3. **Verify sales receipts**
4. **Verify sales deposits**

The effective foodservice manager must consider each of these four areas when developing a total income security system. Obviously, each foodservice operation will have a different manner of both selling products and accounting for income. It is useful, however, to see the income control system for any unit in terms of these four key points and how they relate to each other. In an ideal world, a product would be sold, its sale recorded, its selling price collected, and the funds deposited in the foodservice operation's bank account, all in a single step. While this is not the case as of yet, rapid advances in the area of computers and debit cards will surely make this a reality someday. Consider, for example, the grocery store customer who uses his or her bank-issued automatic teller machine (ATM) debit card when buying a frozen TV dinner. The cashier, in this instance, uses a scanner to read the bar code printed on the TV dinner. This action has the following effect:

1. **To reduce store inventory by one TV dinner**
2. **To print sales slip (guest check) for customer, including name of item**
3. **To record selling price on cash register**
4. **To accept debit card in payment, which results in transfer of funds from customer's bank account to grocery store's account**

If the foodservice industry is to keep up with today's technology, systems such as the one described in our grocery store example must and will be developed in our industry. In the meantime, foodservice operators must adapt the technology they currently have available to the development of good income control systems. This can be done without the use of computers, although computers can assist in the task. It is important to note, however, that the foodservice manager designs the control system *first* and then decides whether to use a computer in its implementation. Computers do not **bring** controls to an operation; they can, however, assist the foodservice manager in making his or her control system work faster and with less human effort. In all cases, the foodservice manager should have a thorough understanding of how the income security system works, and thus what is required to maintain it.

To illustrate the four-step process of income security, consider the situation of Henry, who operates an Austrian restaurant in New York City. Henry considers his restaurant to be a family-oriented establishment. It has a small cocktail area and 100 guest seats in the dining room. Total revenue at Henry's exceeds $1 million per year. In the past, he did not have anything approaching an income control system. Due to the discovery of some recent thefts of sales income, he has moved to develop an income security system, concentrating on the following formula:

Product sale = Guest check totals = Sales receipts = Sales deposits

He knows that sophisticated computer systems are on the market, because he regularly attends restaurant trade shows. However, he does not wish to overspend on an income security system in terms of either equipment or time. He wants to make sure that he does not find himself spending hours of labor or thousands of dollars trying to account for 2 cents' worth of product or a 5-cent cash shortage. Obviously, these are cases where the demand for 100% accuracy and total control exceeds the actual value of that control. As the first step in his system, Henry considers the issue of verifying product sales.

Step 1. Verify Product Sales

The key to this step in the income security system is to follow one basic rule: *No product should be issued from the kitchen or bar unless a written record of issue is made.* In its simplest terms this means that the kitchen should not fill any order for food unless that order is accompanied by a written record (guest check). This could be the duplicate portion (top copy) of the guest check, or the order information could be sent to the kitchen by way of computer or other device. In every case, however, there should be a written order that authorizes the kitchen to prepare food or the bar to prepare a drink. In a quick-service restaurant, no food should be given to the customer unless that sale has been recorded. If a foodservice operation elects to supply its employees with meals during work shifts, they should also be issued along with a guest check. In the bar, this principle is even more important. Bartenders should be instructed *never* to issue a drink unless that drink has been recorded on a guest check first. This should be the procedure, even if the bartender is working alone. This rule regarding product issuing is important for two reasons. In the first place, requiring a written food order helps ensure that there is a record of each product sale. Secondly, this written record of product sales can be used to verify both proper inventory usage and guest check totals. Henry implements this basic rule by requiring that nothing leave either the kitchen or the bar without a written record of the sale. For Henry, this means the use of a precheck-postcheck system.

The precheck-postcheck system is used to match product issues with sales receipts. When a service person places an order for either a food product or drink, he or she writes the request on a guest check. This is the precheck portion of the system. Each cook and bartender at Henry's must be instructed not to issue products unless a prechecked guest check accompanies the order. As guests complete their meal, these precheck sales totals will be compared to postcheck sales to see that the totals match. Postcheck sales refers to the actual amount billed to and collected from the customer. In the case of employee or comp meals, the precheck-postcheck system will identify these as authorized, but nonbilled, sales. If the precheck-postcheck system is working correctly, Henry will find that the following formula should hold true:

Precheck product issues = Postcheck sales

The precheck-postcheck system may be done manually or by machine. In either case, good income control demands that no product be issued without a *written* guest check or its equivalent.

Step 2. Verify Guest Check Totals

The key to this step of income control is simply to require that the following principle be put into place and enforced: *All guest checks will be numbered and tightly controlled.* If Henry is to ensure that product issues equal guest check totals, all guest checks used should be numbered. In a situation where there is no physical guest check, each transaction should be assigned a transaction number, either manually or by machine. Figure 9.2 details the guest check in use at Henry's. Note that each check is numbered on both the top and the bottom, or customer receipt portion.

Figure 9.2 **Guest Check**

Henry's, NY

New York **Phone: xxx-xxxx**

Date	Table	Server	Guests	Check Number 123456
Date	Table	Server	Guests	Check Number 123456

Many foodservice managers use numbered guest checks. It is important to note, however, that the numbers themselves are of no operational value if the checks are not tightly controlled. Each guest check must be accounted for, and employees must know that they will be held responsible for each check they are issued. To keep track of the checks he issues to service personnel, Henry uses a form similar to the one in Figure 9.3. Note that this form recognizes that some guest checks can be lost or destroyed. Management must, however, be aware of these incidents when they occur and must investigate when it is determined that a check is missing. Each lost or destroyed check should be "approved" by management. That is, management should know why and how each missing check got to be missing!

Figure 9.3 **Guest Check Control**

Henry's

Date: 1/1/92 Shift: Lunch

Check Numbers Issued			Check Numbers Returned				
From	**To**	**Issued To**	**From**	**To**	**Checks Used**	**Checks Accounted For**	**Number Missing**
00001	00100	Beth	00055	00100	45	44	1
00101	00200	Sally	00130	00200	70	70	0
00201	00300	Jerry	00264	00300	36	36	0

Unaccounted Checks:

Check Number	Issued To	Explanation	Manager's Initials
00035	Beth	Torn by accident	D.K.H.

It is not necessary to actually count each individual server's checks if the total number of guest checks used equals the number accounted for. In a good guest check control system, this will usually be the case. It is only when a guest check is missing and unaccounted for that management must audit the guest checks to determine which server's check is missing.

Henry now has two major income control components in place. The first one is that no product can be served unless the order is written on a guest check; the second one is that all guest checks are numbered and closely monitored. With these two systems in place, he can deal with many problems. If, for example, a guest has walked his or her check, the kitchen would have a duplicate of the order. This allows management to know which products were sold to this guest, which server sold them, and perhaps additional information, such as the time of the sale, the number of guests in the party, and, of course, the sales value of the products. The precheck system Henry has in place is also useful in ensuring that service personnel do not attempt to write one item on the guest check but charge the customer a higher or lower price. A periodic audit of checks by management would help detect such fraud. Henry's strict policy regarding a written, prechecked record of employee meals has the added advantage of giving him a monthly total for employee meals. He needs this to compute his cost of food consumed percentage (see Chapter 3). Henry is now ready for the next major component in an income security system, and that is the actual collection of guest payment.

Step 3. Verify Sales Receipts

Sales receipts, as defined in this step, refer to actual income received by the cashier or other designated personnel, in payment for product served. In Henry's case, this means all sales revenue from his restaurant and lounge. In terms of the precheck-postcheck system, sales receipts refer to the postcheck sales totals.

Henry knows that in a perfect system the precheck sales total, verified by written guest checks, should equal postcheck sales. In fact, if the income security system is functioning properly, the following formula would be in place:

Precheck sales = Postcheck sales = Actual sales receipts

Verifying sales receipts is more than a simple matter of counting cash at the end of a shift. In fact, cash handling, while it is an important part of the total sales receipt reconciliation, is only one part of the total sales receipt verification system. To illustrate this, consider Figure 9.4, the form Henry uses to verify his total sales receipts. He wishes to ensure that the amount of cash and credit card charges in his cash register matches the dollar amount of his guest checks. If this is so, he has accounted for all of his sales receipts, given that he has controlled for both product issues and guest checks. As can be seen, the form in Figure 9.4 registers both guest check totals and sales receipts. Depending on the type of operation, guest check totals may be done by machine only. This is the case in

Figure 9.4 **Sales Receipt Report**

Henry's

		Performed by:	
Date: 1/1/92		Cashier: Tammi F.	
Shift: Dinner		Supervisor: Henry S.	
Revenue Per Guest Checks			
Guest check totals		$7,500.00	
Service charges		450.00	
Tax		410.00	
Total guest check revenue			$8,360.00
Receipts			
Charge Cards			
Visa		A. $ 685.00	
M/C		B. 495.00	
Discover		C. 1,200.00	
Amex		D. 975.00	
Total charge cards receipts		3,355.00	
Cash			
Twenties & larger		$4,840.00	
Tens		1,480.00	
Fives		240.00	
Ones		196.00	
Change		68.20	
Total cash		6,824.20	
Less: Bank	$ 500.00		
Tip-outs	1,320.00		
Net cash receipts		$5,004.20	
Net total receipts			$8,359.20
Variance check revenue to net receipts			$(0.80)

a cafeteria, where food purchases may be totalled and paid for at the same time. In such instances, the cash register itself provides the guest check total. In Henry's case, guest checks are used, along with this key principle: *Verification of sales receipts must be made by both the cashier and a supervisor.* Figure 9.4 indicates that the sales receipt verification is made by both the cashier and the supervisor. While this will not prevent possible collusion by this pair, it is extremely important that verification be a two-person process.

Note that Figure 9.4 requires Henry's staff to reconcile guest check totals with actual income (net receipts). Overage or shortages are entered, and if they exceed predetermined allowable limits, are investigated by management. Service charges, the second entry on the form, are special charges assessed to guests. Henry assesses a service charge of 15% on all parties larger than eight persons. Observe also that guest check revenue consists of all sales, service charges, and taxes. This is the total amount of income the operation *should* have received on this date. Receipts refer to all forms of income, such as cash, checks (which Henry does not accept), or credit cards. In addition, note that he must subtract the value of his starting cash bank and any tip-outs or gratuities due to service personnel. These gratuities are typically added to charge card vouchers by the customer, but paid out to the service personnel by management, since the latter would not have collected the credit card income. In the example of January 1, 1992, Henry finds that he is 80 cents short. This could have been due to a cashier error or miscalculation. It is up to Henry to determine the level of variance he is comfortable with as far as this reconciliation is concerned. Some foodservice operators allow no variance whatsoever.

The level of variance that is tolerated is greatly affected by the method of guest payment collection that is in place. In general, there are three basic payment arrangements in use in the normal foodservice operation. They are as follows:

1. **Customer pays cashier.**
2. **Customer pays service personnel, who pay cashier.**
3. **Customer pays service personnel, who have already paid cashier.**

Customer Pays Cashier

In this situation, a common one in the hospitality industry, losses can occur primarily due to guest walks. Obviously, this collection system works best in quick-service and cafeteria settings, where a customer does not actually receive his or her food or beverage until the bill has been paid. It works less well in a busy table-service restaurant, where a cashier may simply be too preoccupied to notice whether each individual who has consumed a product has indeed paid their bill before leaving. Only a few customers are dishonest, but these few will account for some walked checks in this collection system. In addition, under this system, cashiers could collect funds, destroy a ticket, and claim a customer has walked his or her bill.

Since the cashier has no way of knowing whether each item served to the guest was entered on the guest check, the potential for fraud exists here also. Of course, if the precheck-postcheck system is in use, and if no food is issued without a written order, the chance for theft or error of this type is greatly reduced.

Customer Pays Service Personnel, Who Pay Cashier

In this situation, the server simply transports the bill to the guest and then accepts payment, which is taken to the cashier for processing. Under this system, the customer's change is returned by the service personnel along with the receipt, if appropriate. An advantage of this system is that it is more difficult for customers to walk their checks, since it is easier for a waiter or waitress to watch their own tables than it is for a cashier to observe an entire dining room. A second advantage is that the guest is not required to stand in line to pay his or her bill during a busy period. A disadvantage of the system is that customers may have to wait longer than they like to settle their bill if service personnel do not notice when they are finished with their meal. This can be the case especially when the operation is very busy.

From a control point of view, it is good practice to separate into at least two parts the processes of requesting food, delivering it, totalling the check, and collecting payment. While this does not prevent collusion on the part of the service personnel and cashier, it does make it more difficult to defraud the operation.

Customer Pays Service Personnel, Who Have Already Paid Cashier

This method of payment, also known as working with individual cash drawers or banks, is popular in some restaurants and many beverage operations. In this scenario, each server begins his or her shift with a predetermined cash bank. As customer orders are filled by the kitchen or bar, the service personnel purchase these products and use their own bank to collect later from the customer. In this manner, each server is responsible for the total of his or her bank only, since all food and beverages were purchased at the time they were issued. In some beverage operations, a record is made of each drink issued to an individual server. Funds equal to the sales value of those drinks are then collected from the server at the conclusion of the shift rather than having the bartender and waitperson settle their cash accounts after each drink. In a very busy operation, this would require much time and effort. Money could be cleared and exchanged between server and bartender on the hour or at the conclusion of the shift.

Using this system where the customer pays the service personnel, who have already paid the cashier, management has less concern regarding the cash overage or shortages of each server's bank, since all products are paid for at the time they are issued. It is important to note, however, that this collection system is not under direct management control. Customers can be defrauded by service personnel, and guest checks can be walked without management's knowledge.

Some employees resent this system as it makes them personally responsible for customer walks, instead of the operation itself sharing some of the risk.

Special Income Collection Situations

In some cases, variations on the three systems can be in place, for example, the drink coupon, often sold in hotel reception areas for use in a given reception. These coupons should be treated as if they were cash, for in fact, they are its equivalent. Thus, those individuals who are selling the coupons should not be the same ones as those dispensing the beverages. In addition, the collected drink coupons should equal the drinks served. While the form required to verify this will vary, based on each operation's drink price policy, such an instrument should be in use.

In Henry's situation, no such special coupons or discount tickets are used. Henry prefers to use the second method: customer pays service personnel, who pay cashier. He feels that this extra bit of service adds to the charm of his operation. It also prevents his customers from ever standing in line.

With his check revenue reconciled to net receipts, Henry now has only to complete Step 4 of the income security process.

Step 4. Verify Sales Deposits

It is recommended that only management make the actual bank deposit of daily sales. The deposit slip may be completed by a cashier or other clerical assistant, but management alone should bear the responsibility for the actual deposit of sales. This concept can be summarized as follows: *Management must personally verify all bank deposits.* This involves the actual verification of the contents of the deposit *and* the process of matching bank deposit with actual sales. These two numbers obviously should match.

Henry has now completed his income security system. Its four key principles are as follows:

1. **No product shall be issued from the kitchen or bar unless a written record is made of its issue.**
2. **All guest checks shall be numbered and tightly controlled.**
3. **Verification of sale receipts must be made by both the cashier and supervisor.**
4. **Management must personally verify all bank deposits.**

The most significant aspect of Henry's system is that he owns *no cash register* of any kind! His system is 100-percent manual. The only mechanical assistance he employs is a 50-year-old adding machine he was given by his grandfather. Is Henry's income security system good? Yes, it is. Can it be made better by the addition of high-tech machinery or computers? Perhaps. Perhaps not. The point is that a good control system *can* be executed manually. It can, however, be done **faster** and in most cases with greater **accuracy** if today's technology is applied, but this in itself is *not* control. It is also dangerous for a foodservice operator to expect that a computer will "bring" control to an operation. That happens rarely! A computer may, however, take good control systems already in place and add even more in terms of speed, accuracy, or additional information. If a foodservice manager hopes to improve his or her income security, or any other cost control system in the operation, a computerized system may be of value. If, however, an operation has no controls, and management is not committed to the control process, the computer will simply become a high-tech adding machine, used primarily to sum up guest checks and nothing more. Properly selected and understood, the computer can be a powerful ally in the cost control/income security system. To understand how it can play this role, a brief overview of computers and their operation is in order.

Computer Systems: A Brief Overview

Computer systems consist of two parts. The first part is called **hardware**. Computer hardware consists of the machines and equipment that we normally associate with the term **computer**. More accurately, however, hardware should be viewed as the equipment necessary to operate or run the second major part of a computer system, namely the **software**. Software can be defined as the set of instructions that control the workings of the hardware and direct the processing of data. Over the past two decades, the cost of computer hardware has tended to decline, while the cost of software, which has become ever more sophisticated and easier to operate, has tended to increase. For the foodservice operator, the selection of the right hardware coupled with the right software is of the utmost importance.

System Hardware

Figure 9.5 shows the basic hardware components of a simplified computer system.

Figure 9.5 **Computer System**

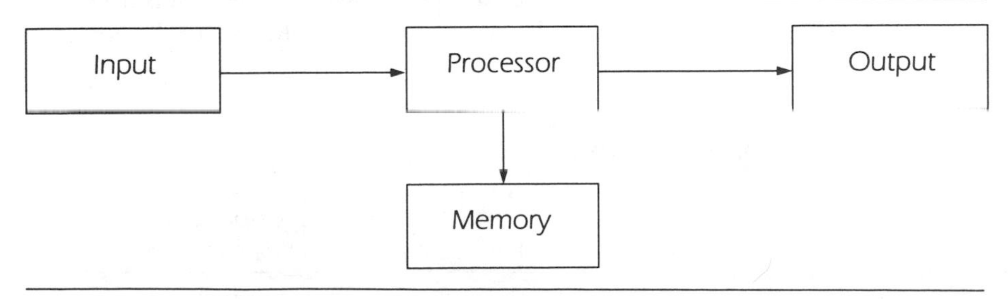

Input devices, often called terminals, are used to enter data and information into the processing unit. These input devices can consist of a typewriter keyboard or a cash register that enters an item's sale, a magnetic strip reader that enters information from a credit card, a bar code reader that assists in taking inventory, or a hand-held unit that records item sales in a dining room and automatically prints them in the kitchen! In all cases, it is the objective of the input device to send to the processor the information that is of importance to the computer system operator.

The processor is the part of the hardware system that most people think of when they hear the term **computer**. The processor takes the information from the input unit and using the instructions given to it by the software system, manipulates the data it has received in the appropriate manner. Sometimes this data must be stored for extended periods of time. The processor will then rely on extra storage space, called **memory**, to save the information. Depending on the quantity of information to be stored, it may be held in the memory on a magnetic tape, on a magnetic disk, or within the processor itself. In any case, the memory capability of the computer must be equal to the task the computer system has been asked to perform.

Output devices, which actually provide the information requested by the system user, usually take the form of either a printer or video screen. With the video screen, information can be quickly and easily viewed by the computer system operator. If, however, the operator wishes to have a paper copy of the information displayed on the screen, a printer must be used. A printed copy of the information a computer operator wishes to receive is called **hard copy**.

Because one central processor works fast, it is possible for several input devices to feed information into the computer system at the same time. In that case, many users can operate within the same computer system by using their own computer input terminals.

System Software

Just as computer systems consists of two main parts, **software** can be divided into two main parts as demonstrated in Figure 9.6.

Systems software consists of the set of instructions that coordinate the activities of all input, processing, memory, and output devices. When one processor serves many users, it is the systems software that acts as a "traffic cop" to allow information to flow in a timely manner to each relevant part of the computer

Figure 9.6 **Computer Software**

Systems software	Applications software

system. Applications software, often referred to as **programs**, tells the computer to perform specific tasks of interest to the user.

Applications software may be purchased by the foodservice operator for a variety of uses. If a foodservice manager finds, for example, that the time involved in the many hand calculations of payroll has become excessive, he or she may elect to purchase an application program to do the payroll. This program could be of a general nature, that is, one that is marketed by its manufacturer as appropriate for a wide variety of business operations. If, however, special characteristics of the foodservice payroll prevented the use of the general program, a special application's program could be written for use by this particular foodservice operator. In this case, the price of the software would obviously be higher, but its usefulness might indeed justify the higher price.

System Integration

Some units combine all aspects of a computer system into one electromechanical unit. To illustrate this, consider the case of a simple cash register in today's foodservice operation. The register itself serves as an input device when sales, in terms of either dollar amounts or items being sold, are entered by the cashier (operator). The sale of several items is totaled by the unit (processor), and this information is held in the machine's interior sales total (memory). A guest check may then be imprinted with the information on the sale (output) so that it can be physically presented to the guest (hard copy). From the simplest single-unit computer system to the most complex system possible, the future of computer applications in the foodservice industry is great.

Applications Programs for Food Cost Control

For purposes of cost management, the computer can be helpful in a large number of areas. The following represent some of the applications foodservice operators have found useful:

1. **Menu construction**
2. **Sales forecast**
3. **Recipe expansion**
4. **Recipe costing**
5. **Menu analysis**
6. **Purchase order preparation**
7. **Storeroom issues**
8. **Inventory extension**
9. **Labor forecasting**
10. **Payroll**
11. **Income security**

Menu Construction

Because of its great memory ability, a computer system can be of tremendous assistance in developing cycle menus based on past percent selecting data. The relative popularity of many menu items can be simultaneously weighed to produce a menu that maximizes both variety and item popularity. If the foodservice operator so chooses, predetermined instructions can be programmed into the system. For example, if a college dormitory foodservice manager wishes to produce a 21-day cycle menu but wants to include pizza no more than three times, regardless of its popularity, this can be done. The computer can also be very helpful in making sure that menu offerings provide the guest with nutritional adequacy, as for instance in a nursing home whose foodservice director wants to ensure in the menu adequate quantities of calcium or other nutrients.

Sales Forecast

If the foodservice manager assumes that the best prediction of what customers will do in the future is what they have done in the past, the computer can be an excellent sales forecaster. Consider, for example, a Tuesday in a given fried chicken restaurant in a busy shopping mall. Management may have data on sales from last Tuesday, but the computer can take sales data from the last 20 Tuesdays, calculate the sales for Tuesday a year ago, consider the upward or downward movement of overall unit sales in the last six months, and *then* predict sales for the Tuesday in question. Obviously, information such as this, generated in seconds, is of great assistance to a foodservice manager who is trying to efficiently schedule both incoming product and product preparation. There is computer software on the market to help forecast sales for tomorrow, next week, next month, or next year! As indicated in Chapter 2, estimating sales volume is a major step in the development of effective income and expense management systems. Using the computer to help predict sales volume puts the foodservice manager in an advantageous position.

Recipe Expansion

There is a problem if sales forecast for a given day indicates that 32 servings of a given product will be sold, but the standardized recipe is developed on the basis of 25 and 50 servings. Management can elect to produce 25 servings, but will probably run out of the item too early during the meal period. If, however, 50 servings are produced and in fact only 32 servings are sold, 18 servings must be carried over to the next meal period. This can cause product and quality loss, especially if the menu item cannot be sold in its original form the next day. If the foodservice operator has a recipe expansion system on the computer, however, it can be instructed to expand the recipe to *exactly* 32 servings. This process, which is complicated and time-consuming to do manually, can be accomplished in seconds with the computer. With a recipe expansion program in place, management can produce the number of menu items it believes are appropriate, without being tied to standardized recipes whose quantities are not exact. This will produce savings both in terms of product cost, since less overproduction will occur, and in terms of labor, since extra time will not be devoted to producing unwanted menu items or figuring out a recipe conversion.

Recipe Costing

One of the major difficulties facing many cost-conscious foodservice managers today is that the price he or she pays for basic food and beverage products changes slightly each day. If an operation is large, or part of a major chain, prices may be negotiated on a long-term basis. A major steak house chain, for example, may negotiate a price for salad dressing that stays constant for six months or a year. If so, the foodservice operator knows his or her cost on that item exactly. For other operators, however, the price of salad dressing can fluctuate on a regular basis from a few pennies to dollars per case. This means that the operator may find his or her costs varying on a daily or weekly basis. In some cases, menu selling prices can be adjusted to accommodate these changes. In others, the operator must wait for a new menu to be printed or contract to be signed before prices can be adjusted. In order to know precisely what each menu item costs to produce on a daily basis, many foodservice operators select applications software designed to do recipe costing. This time-consuming and tedious task can be completed by computer in seconds for each menu item to be produced on any given day. In addition, management can establish predetermined upper and lower cost limits for menu items, which prevent items from being put on the menu when costs get too high, or identify items as good ones to put on the menu when costs are low. Even if an operator does not have the flexibility to change the menu, a knowledge of how much each recipe costs to produce is of great value. With this knowledge, an attainable food cost can be generated, and from that, an operational efficiency ratio can be established (see Chapter 5). Recipe costing is indeed one of the best examples of how computer systems can assist the effective foodservice manager. Everyone would agree that recipe costing is an important aspect of a cost control system. Everyone would also agree that the process is extremely time consuming, especially when one realizes that a recipe that has been costed on Monday may well be inaccurate by a few pennies on Tuesday. With the computer, however, one need only enter the current prices paid for goods, the recipes themselves, and the frequency with which management desires output. In the case of recipe costing, a computer system is truly well worth the funds invested.

Menu Analysis

In Chapter 8 we detailed the advantages of using any one of a number of possible menu analysis systems. One reason many operators decline to do extensive menu analysis calculations is because they are complex and time-consuming. Once again, this is the type of situation best suited for computer application. Anytime an operator's need for information is met with the objection "It takes too long to get it," or "It is too complicated to compute on a regular basis," the astute operator should consider the possibility of applications software suited to handle the problem. This clearly could be the case with menu analysis.

Purchase Order Preparation

Once the foodservice manager has forecasted sales volume and expanded recipes to meet that volume, the computer can be used to actually generate the purchase order itself. If vendors have been established for each inventory item, and if product specifications make those items clearly definable, the computer can analyze competitive prices and produce a purchase order for each vendor a foodservice operator does business with. The advantages with such a system are very evident. A manual control device, the purchase order, can be put on computer so that management can be free to service guests, build employee morale, and plan for the future of the business. It should be pointed out that in a case like this the computer is not actually *doing* the purchasing. Management is doing the purchasing, but is simply using the computer as a tool to do the job faster and, perhaps, with a greater degree of accuracy. Note that computers do not manage food and beverage facilities; managers can, however, use computers to help **themselves** manage food and beverage facilities. Computers are not a replacement for skilled management, but are rather a part of a skilled manager's managerial techniques.

Storeroom Issues

For those foodservice operations that include an ingredient room or are set up to control food costs through the use of an issues or a requisition system, the computer can be of great assistance. If management has forecast sales and recipes have been expanded to meet those sales, a storeroom requisition can be prepared by computer to give the foodservice production workers the ingredients necessary to produce these products. If the required level of product is currently not held in inventory, management can be informed of the situation so that appropriate action can be taken. If desired, the actual cost or sales value of the storeroom issues can be printed along with the list of items being used by the production personnel. This can be a powerful reminder that all food products have a cost, even in their as yet unprocessed state. With a storeroom issues system in place, costs can be better controlled in terms of both products and labor. In a large operation, storeroom personnel can be scheduled based on the quantity of product to be issued on any given day.

Inventory Extension

Every foodservice operator knows that frequent physical inventories are necessary if one is to compute accurately the cost of goods consumed, and to verify, if used, perpetual inventory systems. An extremely time-consuming task, however, is the physical extension of that inventory. With applications software designed for inventory purposes, the foodservice manager need merely enter the amount of each product currently on hand, and the computer will tabulate the actual product value. The total inventory value can then be broken into as many subunits as the operator sees fit, and this data can be used to compute subunit cost of goods consumed percentages, inventory turnover values, or inventory yardsticks, as described in Chapter 8. Applications software of this type can be modified to calculate the value of incoming products using either the LIFO or FIFO method, and the total product usage by subunit. If an efficient usage recording system is in place, this software can be helpful in comparing projected or attainable food cost values with actual usage.

Frequent physical inventories of all food products are an extremely useful management tool. The computer can make this task more accurate and save a great deal of management time in the process.

Labor Forecasting

If management is to forecast sales volume, it can also forecast the labor necessary to service that volume. Assume, for example, that an operator has acquired a computer software package that will forecast sales volume for next week, on an *hourly* basis. Using the information from this sales forecast, management can develop a staffing schedule that will match the labor needs of the forecast. This schedule can be preprogrammed for any parameters management feels are appropriate, such as seniority scheduling and minimum shift length. In addition, these labor schedules can be broken down into any worker category subunit that management desires. Thus, if the operation is a quick-service hamburger unit, forecasted sales volume levels may determine the number of hours that cooks, counter personnel, and dining room attendants are to be scheduled.

Payroll

The advent of the computer has changed immeasurably the process of doing payroll. Where in the past, cumbersome and tedious hand calculations were required in order to correctly issue payroll checks, today's computers can be programmed to compute state, local, and federal taxes; FICA; other deductions; and overtime and tip payments. This same data can then be used at year's end to produce the employees' W-2 statements. The W-2 statement, required by federal law, is a summary of wages and taxes paid for the year. Computers can be programmed to generate payroll reports, which can be combined with sales reports to generate labor cost percentages and other employee productivity ratios.

When combined with labor forecasting and sales forecasting programs, the payroll report can identify variation in budgeted labor costs as well as the direction and magnitude of the variation. From this, management can determine how well it is doing in matching actual payroll with payroll forecasts, as determined by volume estimates. If variation exceeds predetermined limits, management can investigate to see if the problem lies in the sales forecast, labor forecast, or actual paid wages that have been authorized.

Income Security

While it is possible to have a completely manual system of income security, the arrival of the computer has allowed even the smallest foodservice operators to take advantage of this powerful tool. In the example of Henry's restaurant, a clear difference was established between a good control system and one that is simply computerized. Computers can, however, be of great value in developing an income security system. From the moment the order for the food or beverage item is entered in the point of sale terminal to be fed into the processor, the computer or cash register system can maintain all of the following types of information related to sales and income security:

1. **Daily sales with tax**
2. **Daily sales without tax**
3. **Tips**
4. **Guest check number**
5. **Server number**
6. **Number of customers served**
7. **Average sale per customer**
8. **Guest checks used**
9. **Open checks**
10. **Sales in a given time frame**
11. **Customers in a given time frame**
12. **Menu items served**
13. **Sales by form of payment**
14. **Cumulative sale totals**
15. **Complimentary/coupon sales**

Additional programs exist and they can be selected for inclusion.

While most of these items could be monitored using a paper and pencil system, the effective foodservice manager would prefer to use his or her time for better purposes. All of the above information is of importance, however, and can be extremely useful in management's decision-making process.

System Selection

There is no question that the future of foodservice income and expense management is dependent on the ever-expanding capabilities of computer systems. Inexpensive ones are now within the budget of even the smallest-volume foodservice operator. While it is not expected, or even desirable, that foodservice managers become experts in computer programming, these computer systems will play an ever larger role in the operation of the foodservice unit. While the rapid advances in technology have made computer systems ever more versatile and flexible, there are disadvantages as well as advantages in using them. They can become so complicated that they generate great quantities of financial data, much of which is ignored by management. For our discussion on selecting a computerized system, a system will encompass everything from a simple electronic cash register to the most sophisticated multiterminal system.

Prior to shopping for a computer system, the foodservice manager should analyze his or her operation with an eye toward answering the following questions related to software selection:

1. **What information am I currently collecting?**
2. **What information would be valuable to collect, if time permitted?**
3. **What specific management actions could be undertaken if the information in question 2 were known?**
4. **What routine managerial tasks can best be accomplished by computer?**

All managers collect information, either formally or informally. The problem is knowing what information is worth collecting and, most importantly, what to do with that information. That is, how will management use the information collected to make better decisions? If this question cannot be answered specifically, the information will be of little use. Once the operator knows what information is desirable, software packages can be purchased or developed to provide it. In addition, routine tasks like payroll can be computerized to free either labor dollars or management time.

Hardware Selection

Once a foodservice director has determined the type of information he or she desires in a computer system, the following questions for selecting appropriate hardware must be addressed:

1. **How many input devices are needed? Where should they be located?**
2. **How much data must be stored?**
3. **How much, if any, hard copy will be required? What quality level of hard copy is desirable?**

For the foodservice operator, the number and type of input devices required for the operation is a key question. In addition, the location of these devices is of importance to operational productivity. If too few input devices are made available, service may be slowed down as waiters and waitresses line up to enter their orders or process guest payment. If too many units are provided, equipment may stand idle and costs will be higher than necessary to service the operation.

The quantity of memory required in a system must also be considered when selecting computer hardware. In effect, the computer's memory is much like a file cabinet. Each file cabinet has a finite quantity of storage space. In a similar way, each computer system will have a finite quantity of storage available. This memory capacity, measured in bytes, should be equal to the tasks management has designed for the system.

If hard copy is to be produced by the computer system, the speed with which this hard copy will be produced and the quality of print required will greatly impact the type of printer appropriate to the task. If, for example, a word processing program is to be purchased so that promotional fliers can be mailed to select customers, the quality of print and printer needed may be quite high. If, on the other hand, the only hard copy required of the system is the printing of guest checks, speed, not print quality, may be of utmost concern. As in the case of input devices, the location of output devices, be they screens or printers, is of great importance to operational efficiency.

System Implementation

It is not easy to convert from a manual control system to a computerized one. In fact, if this is to be done, it is of great value to run the manual and automated systems in parallel until the automated system runs well enough so that the manual system can be discontinued. It is also important to remember that computers, like any other piece of foodservice equipment, can break down. When this happens, it is imperative that both management and employees understand the basic income and expense control systems well enough to revert to a manual system until the mechanical problem is resolved.

It is important to remember that computers can only be programmed to imitate processes that are already understood. This is not to imply that computers should be used only for those tasks that management currently performs. Indeed, a creative foodservice manager should be able to use the computer to do things that were never attempted because they were too complex or time-consuming. It is true, however, that a computer will not do the thinking required to initiate the new process. That task is up to management! Once again, computers will not bring controls to an operation, but an effective computer system can free management from routine data collection and analysis tasks so that it can get on with the business of serving guests.

A generation of foodservice managers were trained in the 1940s, 50s, and 60s, when computers were not readily available. Many of these individuals use computers today; a great number still don't. Today's young foodservice manager, however, understands computers and their capabilities. Where foodservice operators in the past would go to a print shop each time they wanted to create a new menu or change prices, today's foodservice managers can design and print in a matter of hours their own menus on their own computers. These and other changes seem radical to the foodservice manager who is not computer literate, but are as normal as using a telephone to today's computer-literate managers. The application of the computer's abilities to the needs of the foodservice industry has only just started. The decade of the 1990s will see tremendous growth in the creative use of the foodservice computer. The future clearly holds the prospects of input devices, in even the smallest production areas, as well as voice-activated ordering systems. The computer will have no less impact on foodservice than did the advent of canned or frozen foods. Computers have changed the way foodservice managers manage, and this change is still in its infancy.

TEST YOUR SKILLS

A. Carl and Sue operate a restaurant in the theater district of a large western city. Lately they have found that their food cost percentage is higher than it should be. Their operational cost controls are excellent, and thus they feel that their problem lies in income security. Assuming that they operate a table-service restaurant, outline four basic steps to help them ensure that they in fact collect all of the income they generate.

B. JoAnn is the district manager of a regional fried chicken chain. She supervises 15 units in the Indiana-Ohio-Kentucky area. She wants to computerize both product usage and sales income for each of these 15 units. What should JoAnn ask herself prior to beginning her selection of a computer system? What specific questions should she ask regarding the appropriate hardware for her operation? The software?

C. You, who operate or hope to operate a foodservice facility, must develop your own income and expense control system. Using the information from this textbook and the operation's activities listed below, name the systems you will put into place in order to manage in your enterprise most effectively and efficiently.

1. **Forecast sales volume**
2. **Manage food cost**
3. **Manage beverage cost (if applicable)**
4. **Manage the production process**
5. **Manage labor cost**
6. **Control other expense**
7. **Control income**
8. **Summarize and analyze results**

Whatever your answer, keep guest service foremost in your mind, be creative, and most of all, have fun!

TEST YOUR SKILLS

APPENDIX A

Frequently Used Formulas for Managing Costs

CHAPTER 1

Managing Income and Expense

1. $$\text{Income} - \text{Expenses} = \text{Profit}$$

2. $$\text{Income} - \text{Desired profit} = \text{Ideal expense}$$

3. $$\frac{\text{Part}}{\text{Whole}} = \text{Percent}$$

4. $$\frac{\text{Expense}}{\text{Income}} = \text{Expense \%}$$

5. $$\frac{\text{Profit}}{\text{Income}} = \text{Profit \%}$$

6. $$\frac{\text{Actual}}{\text{Budget}} = \text{\% of Budget}$$

CHAPTER 2

Determining Sales Volume

1. $$\text{Average sales per guest} = \frac{\text{Total sales}}{\text{\# of guests served}}$$

CHAPTER 3

Managing the Cost of Food

1. $$\text{Percent selecting} = \frac{\text{Total \# of specific menu items sold}}{\text{Total \# of all menu items sold}}$$

2. # guests expected × % selecting = Predicted # sold

3. $$\frac{\text{Yield desired}}{\text{Current yield}} = \text{Conversion factor}$$

4. $$\text{Waste \%} = \frac{\text{Product loss}}{\text{AP weight}}$$

5. Yield % = 1.00 − Waste %

6. $$\frac{\text{EP required}}{\text{Yield \%}} = \text{AP required}$$

7. EP required = AP required × Yield %

8. Item amount × Item value = Inventory value

9. Cost of food consumed = Beginning inventory
   + Purchases
   Goods available for sale
   − Ending inventory
   − Employee meals
   Cost of food consumed

10. $$\frac{\text{Cost of food consumed}}{\text{Sales}} = \text{Food cost \%}$$

CHAPTER 4

Managing the Cost of Beverages

1. $$\frac{\text{Cost of beverages consumed}}{\text{Beverage sales}} = \text{Beverage cost \%}$$

2. $$\frac{\text{Item dollar sales}}{\text{Total sales}} = \text{Item's \% of total sales}$$

CHAPTER 5

Managing the Food and Beverage Production Process

1. $$\frac{\text{Issues today}}{\text{Sales today}} = \text{Beverage cost estimate today}$$

2. $$\frac{\text{Issues todate}}{\text{Sales todate}} = \text{Beverage cost estimate todate}$$

3. $$\frac{\text{Cost in product category}}{\text{Total cost in all categories}} = \text{Proportion of total product cost}$$

4. $$\frac{\text{Cost of product}}{\text{Desired product cost \%}} = \text{Selling price}$$

5. $$\frac{100}{\text{Desired product cost \%}} = \text{Pricing factor}$$

6. $$\text{Pricing factor} \times \text{Product cost} = \text{Selling price}$$

7. $$\text{Product cost} + \text{Contribution margin desired} = \text{Selling price}$$

8. $$\frac{\text{EP weight}}{\text{AP weight}} = \text{Product yield \%}$$

9. $$\frac{\text{AP price per pound}}{\text{Product yield \%}} = \text{Cost per servable pound}$$

10. $$\frac{\text{Actual product cost}}{\text{Attainable product cost}} = \text{Operational efficiency ratio}$$

11. $$\frac{\text{Cost as per standardized recipes}}{\text{Total sales}} = \text{Attainable food cost}$$

CHAPTER 6

Managing the Cost of Labor

1. $$\frac{\text{Cost of labor}}{\text{Sales}} = \text{Labor cost \%}$$

2. $$\frac{\text{Sales}}{\text{Labor hours used}} = \text{Sales per labor hour}$$

3. $$\frac{\text{Guests served}}{\text{Cost of labor}} = \text{Guests served per labor dollar}$$

4. $$\frac{\text{Cost of labor}}{\text{Guests served}} = \text{Dollars expended per guest served}$$

5. $$\frac{\text{Guests served}}{\text{Labor hours used}} = \text{Guests served per labor hour}$$

CHAPTER 7

Controlling Other Expenses

1. $$\frac{\text{Other expense}}{\text{Income}} = \text{Other expense percentage}$$

2. $$\frac{\text{Other expense}}{\text{\# of guests served}} = \text{Cost per guest}$$

CHAPTER 8

Analyzing Results Using Basic Accounting

1. Assets = Liabilities + Owner's equity

2. $$\frac{\text{Current assets}}{\text{Current liabilities}} = \text{Current ratio}$$

3. Current assets − Current liabilities = Working capital

4. $$\frac{\text{Total liabilities}}{\text{Total assets}} = \text{Debt to assets ratio}$$

5. $$\frac{\text{Profit}}{\text{Sales}} = \text{Return on sales (ROS)}$$

6. $$\frac{\text{Sales}}{\text{Working capital}} = \text{Working capital ratio}$$

7. $$\frac{\text{Total sales}}{\text{Average amount of accounts receivable}} = \text{Accounts receivable turnover}$$

8. $$\frac{\text{Profit}}{\text{Average total assets}} = \text{Return on assets}$$

9. $$\frac{\text{Profit}}{\text{Average owner's equity}} = \text{Return on owner's equity}$$

10. $$\frac{\text{Profit}}{\text{Total invested}} = \text{Return on investment (ROI)}$$

11. $$\frac{\text{Cost of goods sold}}{\text{Average inventory value}} = \text{Inventory turnover}$$

12. $$\frac{\text{Profit this year} - \text{Profit last period}}{\text{Profit last period}} = \text{Profit variance}$$

13. Selling price − Product cost = Contribution margin desired

14. $$\frac{\text{Fixed costs}}{1 - (\text{Variable costs} / \text{Total sales})} = \text{Break-even point in sales}$$

15. $$\frac{\text{Fixed costs}}{\text{Sales per guest} - (\text{Variable cost \%} \times \text{Sales per guest})} = \text{Break-even point in guests served}$$

16. $$\frac{\text{Minimum labor cost}}{1 - \text{Minimum operating cost}} = \text{Minimum sales point}$$

17. $$\frac{\text{Cost of labor}}{\text{Meals served}} = \text{Labor cost per meal}$$

18. $$\frac{\text{Total sales}}{\text{Number of seats}} = \text{Sales per seat}$$

19. Budgeted income − Budgeted expense = Budgeted profit

APPENDIX B

Management Control Forms

Attainable Food Cost

Unit Name: ______________________________

Date Prepared: ____________________ Time Period: ____________________

Prepared by: ____________________

Item	Number Sold	Portion Cost	Total Cost	Menu Price	Total Sales	Attainable Food Cost
Total						

Beverage Consumption Report

Unit Name: ______________________________

Event: ______________________ Date: ______________________

Beverage Type	Beginning Amount	Additions	Total Available	Ending Amount	Total Usage	Unit Cost	Total Cost
Liquor							
1.							
2.							
3.							
4.							
5.							
Etc.							
Beer							
1.							
2.							
3.							
Wine							
1.							
2.							
3.							
Other							
1.							
2.							
3.							
						Total Product Cost	

Total Product Cost: ______________ Cost per Guest: ______________

Guests Served: ______________

Remarks: ____

Bid Sheet

Unit Name: ______________________

Vendors:

A. ______________________

B. ______________________

C. ______________________

D. ______________________

Category: ______________________

Date Bid: ______________________

Item	Quantity	Vendor A		Vendor B		Vendor C		Vendor D	
		Unit	Total	Unit	Total	Unit	Total	Unit	Total
Total									

Bid Method: Telephone ______________ Written ______________________

Bid Reviewed by: ______________

Bin Card

Product Name: ________________ Bottle Size: ________________

Balance Brought Forward: ________ Date: ________________

Date	In	Out	Total on Hand

Butcher's Yield Test Results

Unit Name: ______________________________

Item: ______________________ Date Tested: ______________________

Specification: ______________________ Item Description: ______________________

AP Amount Tested: ______________

Price per Pound AP: ______________

Loss Detail	Weight Loss (Pounds)	% of Original
AP		
Fat loss		
Bone loss		
Cooking loss		
Carving loss		
Total product loss		

Net Product Yield: ______________ Cost per Servable Pound: ______________

Yield Test Performed by: ______________

Cost of Beverage Consumed

Unit Name: ______________________________

Accounting Period: ________ to ________

Beginning inventory	$ ________	
plus		
Purchases	$ ________	
Goods available		$ ________
less		
Ending inventory		$ ________
less		$ ________
Transfers from bar		$ ________
plus		$ ________
Transfers to bar		$ ________
Cost of beverage consumed		$ ________

Cost of Food Consumed

Unit Name: ______________________________

Accounting Period: ________ to ________

Beginning inventory	$ ________	
plus		
Purchases	$ ________	
Goods available		$ ________
less		
Ending inventory		$ ________
less		$ ________
Employee meals		$ ________
Cost of food consumed		$ ________

Credit Memo

Unit Name: ____________________

Credit Memo #: ____________ Date: ____________

Vendor: ____________

Vendor Invoice Number: ____________

Item	Quantity	Correction		Price	Credit Amount
		Short	Refused		
Total					

Explanation: ____________________

____

Vendor Representative: ____________

Operation Representative: ____________

Employee Schedule

Unit Name: ______________________________

Shift: ______________________ Date: ______________________

Labor Category: ______________ Labor Budget: ______________

Employee Name	Schedule	Hours Scheduled	Rate	Total Cost
Total				

Equipment Inspection Report

Unit Name: ______________________________

Time Period: __________ to __________

Item Inspected	Inspection Date	Inspected by	Action Recommended
A.			
B.			
C.			
D.			
E.			

Goal Value Analysis

Unit Name: ____________________

Date: ____________________

Rank	Item	A	B	C	D	Goal Value
1						
2						
3						
4						
5						
6						
7						

Target Goal Value: ____________________ Completed by: ____________________

Guest Check

Unit Name: ______________________________

Phone: xxx-xxxx

Date	Table	Server	Guests	Check Number
Date	Table	Server	Guests	Check Number

Guest Check Control

Unit Name: ______________________________

Date: ______________________ Shift: ______________________

Check Numbers Issued		Issued To	Check Numbers Returned		Checks Used	Number Accounted For	Number Missing
From	To		From	To			

Unaccounted Checks:

Check Number	Issued To	Explanation	Manager's Initials

Inventory Valuation Sheet

Unit Name: ______________________________

Inventory Date: ________________

Item	Item Amount	Item Value	Inventory Value
		Page Total	

Extended by: __________________ Page ________ of ________

Counted by: __________________

Job Description

Unit Name: ______________________

Position Title: ______________________

Primary Tasks

1. ______________________

2. ______________________

3. ______________________

4. ______________________

5. ______________________

6. ______________________

7. ______________________

8. ______________________

9. ______________________

10. ______________________

11. ______________________

12. ______________________

Special Comments: ______________________

Salary Range: ______________________

Report to: ______________________

Job Specification

Unit Name: ______________________________

Position Title: ____________________

Personal Characteristics Required

1. ______________________________
2. ______________________________
3. ______________________________
4. ______________________________
5. ______________________________
6. ______________________________

Special Comments: ______________________________

____

____

Job Spec Prepared by: ____________________

Date Prepared: ____________________

Labor Budget

Unit Name: ______________________________

Time Period	Sales Forecast	Labor Cost Standard	Labor Expense Budget
Week 1			
Week 2			
Week 3			
Week 4			
Total			

Labor Recap
Actual Versus Budgeted Labor Cost

Unit Name: ______________________________

	Sales			Labor Costs			Labor Cost %	
Week	Budgeted	Actual	% of Budget	Budgeted	Actual	% of Budget	Budgeted	Actual
1								
2								
3								
4								
Total								

Liquor Requisition

Unit Name: ____________________

Shift: ____________________ Date: ____________________

Service Area: ____________________

Product	# Empties	Bottle Size	Verified by Management	
			Bar	Management

Performance to Budget Summary

Unit Name: ______________________________

Item	Budget	Actual	% of Budget
Meals served			
Income			
Food expense			
Labor expense			
Other expense			
Total expense			
Profit			

Product Request Log

Unit Name: ______________________________

Date	Item Requested	Entry by

Product Specification

Unit Name: ______________________________

Product Name: ____________________ Spec #: ______________________

Pricing Unit: ____________________

Standard/Grade: ____

____

____

____

Weight Range: ____

____

____

Packaging: ____

____

____

Container Size: ____

____

Other Information: ____

____

____

____

____

Production Schedule

Unit Name: ______________________________

Date: ______________________

	Menu Item	Sales Forecast	Prior Day Carryover	New Production	Total Available	# Sold	Carryover

Special Instructions: ____

____

____

Prepared by: ____________________

Purchase Order

Unit Name: ______________________

Vendor: ______________________ Delivery Date: ______________________

Vendor's Telephone #: ______________

Item Purchased	Spec #	Qty Ordered	Quoted Price	Ext Price
1.				
2.				
3.				
4.				
5.				
6.				
7.				
8.				
9.				
10.				
11.				
12.				
13.				
14.				
15.				
16.				

Order Date: ______________________

Ordered by: ______________________

Received by: ______________________

Delivery Instructions: ______________

____

Comments: ______________________

____

____

____

____

Quarterly Sales Forecast

Unit Name: ______________________________

Month/Year	Customer Counts			Check Average			Projected Sales
	Last Year	Projected % Increase	Total Expected	Last Year	Projected Increase	Check Average Forecast	
Quarter total							

Quarterly Sales History

Unit Name: ______________________________

Month	Sales This Year	Sales Last Year	Variance	Percentage Variance
January				
February				
March				
Total				

Month	Sales This Year	Sales Last Year	Variance	Percentage Variance
April				
May				
June				
Total				

Month	Sales This Year	Sales Last Year	Variance	Percentage Variance
July				
August				
September				
Total				

Month	Sales This Year	Sales Last Year	Variance	Percentage Variance
October				
November				
December				
Total				

Quarterly Sales Projection

Unit Name: ______________________________

Month	Sales Last Year	Predicted Change	Projected Sales Increase
January			
February			
March			
Total			

Month	Sales Last Year	Predicted Change	Projected Sales Increase
April			
May			
June			
Total			

Month	Sales Last Year	Predicted Change	Projected Sales Increase
July			
August			
September			
Total			

Month	Sales Last Year	Predicted Change	Projected Sales Increase
October			
November			
December			
Total			

Receiving Report

Unit Name: ______________________

Date: ______________________

Supplier	Invoice #	Item	Unit Price	# of Units	Total Cost	Distribution				
						A	B	C	D	E
Total Units										
Total										

Distribution Key:

A. ______________________ D. ______________________

B. ______________________ E. ______________________

C. ______________________ ______________________

Comments:

____

____

____

Salad Bar or Buffet Product Usage

Unit Name: ____________________

Date: ____________________

Item	Category	Beginning Amount	Additions	Ending Amount	Total Usage	Unit Cost	Total Cost
Total product cost							

Total Product Cost: ____________________

Guests Served: ____________________ Cost per Guest: ____________________

Sales History
Average Sales per Guest

Unit Name: ______________________

Sales Period	Date	Sales	Guests Served	Sales per Guest
Monday				
Tuesday				
Wednesday				
Thursday				
Friday				
Saturday				
Sunday				
Week's total				

Sales Period	Date	Sales	Guests Served	Sales per Guest
Monday				
Tuesday				
Wednesday				
Thursday				
Friday				
Saturday				
Sunday				
Week's total				

Sales History
Daily Guests

Unit Name: ______________________________

Number Sold

Serving Period	Mon	Tues	Wed	Thurs	Fri	Sat	Sun	Total

Serving Period	Mon	Tues	Wed	Thurs	Fri	Sat	Sun	Total

Sales History
Menu Items

Unit Name: ______________________________

Date: ______________________

Menu Item	Mon	Tues	Wed	Thurs	Fri	Sat	Sun	Total	Wk Avg
Total									

Sales History
Weekly Sales

Unit Name: ______________________________

Sales Period	Date	Sales	Sales to Date
Monday			
Tuesday			
Wednesday			
Thursday			
Friday			
Saturday			
Sunday			
Week's total			

Sales Period	Date	Sales	Sales to Date
Monday			
Tuesday			
Wednesday			
Thursday			
Friday			
Saturday			
Sunday			
Week's total			

Six-Column Form

Unit Name: ______________________________

Date: __________ to __________

Date	Today	Todate	Today	Todate	Today	Todate

Six-Column Beverage Cost Estimate

Unit Name: ______________________________

Date: __________ to __________

Date	Issues		Sales		Beverage Cost Estimate	
	Today	Todate	Today	Todate	Today	Todate
Subtotal						
+/–						
Total						

Standardized Recipe

Unit Name: ______________________

Menu Item: ______________________

Special Instructions: ______________________

____

____

____

Recipe Yield: ______________________

Portion Size: ______________________

Portion Cost: ______________________

Ingredients		Method
Item	Amount	

Standardized Recipe Cost Sheet

Unit Name: ______________________________

Menu Item: ____________________

Special Instructions: ______________
____
____
____

Recipe Yield: ____________________
Portion Size: ____________________
Portion Cost: ____________________

Ingredients		Ingredient Cost	
Item	**Amount**	**Unit Cost**	**Total Cost**

Total Recipe Cost: ______________
Portion Cost: __________________
Previous Portion Cost: ____________

Total Portions: __________________
Dated Costed: __________________
Previous Dated Costed: ____________

Storeroom Requisition

Unit Name: ______________________

Requisition #: ______________ Date: ______________

Item	Storage Unit	Requested Amount	Unit Cost	Total Cost
Total				

To: Kitchen ______________ Requisition Approved by: ______________

Bar ______________ Requisition Filled by: ______________

Wine Cellar Issue

Unit Name: ______________________

Date: ______________

	Product	Vintage	# of Bottles	Guest Check #	Removed by
1.					
2.					
3.					
4.					
5.					
6.					
7.					
8.					
9.					
10.					
11.					
12.					
13.					
14.					
15.					

Remarks: ____

Glossary

Acceptance hours. The hours of the day in which an operation is willing to accept food and beverage deliveries.

Accounting period. A period of time, that is, hour, day, week, or month, in which an operator wishes to analyze income and expenses.

AP (as purchased). This term refers to the weight or count of a product as delivered to the foodservice operator.

AP required. As purchased amount necessary to yield the desired EP weight. AP required is computed as EP required divided by yield percentage.

As needed. A system of determining purchase point by using sales forecasts and standardized recipes to decide how much of an item to place in inventory.

Attainable food cost. That cost of goods consumed figure that should be achievable given the product sales mix of a particular operation.

Average. The value arrived at by adding the quantities in a series, and dividing the sum of the quantities by the number of items in the series.

Average sales per guest. The mean amount of money spent per customer during a given financial accounting period.

Balance sheet. A statement showing an organization's assets, liabilities, and owner's equity.

Beginning inventory. The dollar value of all products on hand at the beginning of the accounting period. This amount is determined by completing a physical inventory.

Bid sheet. A form used to compare prices among many vendors in order to select the best prices.

Bin card. An index card with both additions to and deletions from inventory of a given beverage product. To facilitate its use, the card is usually affixed to the shelf that holds the given item. Used in a perpetual inventory system.

Blind receiving. Signing to accept delivered products without checking the product for performance to specifications or verifying quantity ordered.

Bonding. Purchasing an insurance policy to protect the operation in case of employee theft.

Broken case. A case of beverage products in which several different brands or products make up the contents of the case.

Budget. A projection or estimate of future income, expense, and profit over a given accounting period.

Call liquors. Those spirits that are requested (called for) by a particular brand name.

Carryover. A menu item prepared for sale during a meal period but carried over for use in a different meal period.

Check average. Commonly known as average sale per guest. In some cases, a check may refer to more than one guest.

Cherry picking. The act of buying only those items from a supplier that are the lowest in price among the supplier's competition.

Comp. Short for the word **complimentary**, which refers to the practice of management giving a product to a guest without a charge. This can be done for a special customer, or as a way of making amends for an operational error.

Contract price. A price mutually agreed upon by supplier and operator. This price is the amount to be paid for a product or products over a prescribed period of time.

Contribution margin. The profit or margin that remains after product cost is subtracted from an item's selling price.

Controllable expense. An expense in which the decisions made by the foodservice manager can have the effect of either increasing or reducing the expense.

Cost per guest. A method of analyzing other expense categories that uses the total expense and total number of guests served to establish an actual cost of servicing each guest.

Credit memo. An addendum to the vendor's delivery slip (invoice) that reconciles differences between the delivery slip and purchase order.

Current ratio. A liquidity ratio computed as the ratio between current assets and current liabilities.

Cycle menu. A menu that is in effect for a predetermined length of time such as 7 days or 14 days.

Desired profit. The profit level that management desires to achieve on a given quantity of sales.

Draft. Term used to identify beer products sold in a keg.

Ending inventory. The dollar value of all products on hand at the end of the accounting period. This amount is determined by completing a physical inventory.

EP (edible portion). This term refers to the weight or count of a product after it has been trimmed, cooked, and portioned.

Extended price. The extended price is the price per unit multiplied by the number of units. This refers to a total unit price on a delivery slip or invoice.

FIFO. With the first-in, first-out method of storage, the operator intends to sell his or her oldest product before selling the most recently delivered product.

Fiscal year. Start and stop dates for a 365-day accounting period. This period need not begin in January and end in December.

Fixed average. The average amount of sales or volume over a specific series or time period, for example, first month of the year or second week of the second month.

Fixed expense. An expense that remains constant despite increases or decreases in sales volume.

Fixed payroll. Those dollars spent on employees such as managers, receiving clerks, and dietitians whose presence is not generally directly dependent on the number of guests served. Also the minimum amount of money required for labor to operate the foodservice unit.

Forecasting. The process of estimating future income or expenses of a hospitality operation.

Half bottle. A bottle of wine that is approximately one-half the size of the standard 750-milliliter wine bottle. Typically sold for either room service or dining room consumption.

Hard copy. A printed copy of data or information produced by a computer system's output device.

Hardware. The machines and equipment used to operate computer software.

Head size. The amount of space on the top of a glass of beer that is made up of foam. Thus, a glass of beer with one inch of foam on its top is said to have a one-inch head.

Ideal expense. Management's view of the correct or appropriate amount of expense necessary to generate a given quantity of sales.

Income statement. A detailed listing of income and expenses for a given accounting period. Also called a profit and loss (P&L) statement.

Ingredient room. A storeroom or section of a storeroom where ingredients are weighed and measured according to standardized recipes, and then delivered to the appropriate kitchen production area.

Issues. When food or beverage products are supplied from storage by management for use in an operation, these products are called management issues.

Jigger. A bar device used to measure predetermined quantities of alcoholic beverages. Jiggers usually are marked in ounces and portions of an ounce, for example, 1 ounce, 1¼ ounces, or 1½ ounces.

Job description. A listing of the tasks to be performed in a particular position.

Job specification. A listing of the personal skills and characteristics needed to perform those tasks pertaining to a particular job description.

Labor expense. All expenses, including payroll, required to maintain a work force in a foodservice operation.

LIFO. With the last-in, first-out method of storage, the operator intends to sell his or her most recently delivered product before selling the older product.

Liquidity ratio. A family of ratios designed to measure the ability of an organization to pay its short-term debts as they become due.

Loss leader. A menu item that is priced very low for the purpose of drawing large numbers of customers to the operation.

Menu copy. The description of menu items delivered to the customer in either written or verbal form.

Menu forecasting. The process of determining the expected demand for each menu item sold, based on a knowledge of the total number of customers expected.

Minimum sales point. The minimum sales point or MSP refers to the dollar sales volume required in order to justify staying open.

Net profit. The profit realized after all expenses and appropriate taxes for a business have been paid.

Noncontrollable expense. An expense that the foodservice manager can neither increase nor decrease.

Occupation costs. Expenses related to occupying and paying for the physical facility that houses the foodservice unit.

OJT (on-the-job training). A method of training in which workers are training while they actually are performing their required tasks.

Open bar. A bar in which no charge for an individual drink is made to the customer, thus establishing an all-you-can-drink environment. Sometimes referred to as a hotel bar.

Par level. A system of determining purchase point by using management-established minimum and maximum allowable inventory levels for a given inventory item.

Payroll. Total wages and salaries paid by a foodservice operation to its employees.

Percent. The number "out of each hundred." Thus, 10 percent means 10 out of each 100. This is computed by dividing the part by the whole.

Percent selecting. A formula for determining the proportion of people who will buy a given menu item from a list of menu choices.

Perpetual inventory. An inventory control system in which additions to and deletions from total inventory are noted as they occur.

Physical inventory. An inventory control system in which an actual or physical count and valuation of all inventory on hand is taken at the beginning and close of each accounting period.

POS (point of sale). A system of controlling hospitality operations' cash and product usage by using a computer processor and, depending on operational size, additional computer terminals.

Predicted number to be sold. A method of determining the number of a given menu item that is likely to be sold if the total number of customers to be served is known.

Price blending. The process of assigning prices based on product groups for the purpose of achieving predetermined cost objectives.

Price spread. The difference in price on a menu between the lowest and highest priced item of a similar nature.

Productivity. The amount of work performed by a worker in a set amount of time.

Productivity ratio. This formula refers to the total unit output divided by the total unit input.

Productivity standard. Management's expectation of the productivity ratio of each employee. Also management's view of what constitutes the appropriate productivity ratio in a given foodservice unit or units.

Product mix. *See* Sales mix.

Product specification. A detailed description of an ingredient or menu item.

Profit and loss statement. A detailed listing of income and expenses for a given accounting period. Also referred to as an income statement.

Projected sales. Sales that may be determined by either cash sales or customer count. Projected sales are established by using sales histories and other knowledge the operator may have that could impact total volume. They are predictions of future sales volume.

Pull date. Expiration date on beverage products, usually beers, after which they should not be sold, but rather pulled and sent back to the distributor.

Purchasing agent. The individual charged with the responsibility of developing and completing a purchase order.

Purchase order. A listing of products requested by the purchasing agent. The purchase order or PO lists various product information, including quantity ordered and price quoted by the vendor.

Purchase point. The point in time when an item held in inventory reaches a level that indicates it should be reordered.

Refusal hours. Those hours of the day in which an operation refuses to accept food and beverage deliveries.

Reporting period. The process of reporting a time period for which records are being maintained. This may be of the same duration as an accounting period.

Requisitions. When food or beverage products are requested from storage by employees for use in an operation, these products are called employee requisitions.

ROI. Return on investment. As is the case with ROS, ROI can be expressed either in whole dollar terms or as a percentage.

Rolling average. The average amount of sales or volume over a changing time period, for example, the last ten days or the last three weeks.

ROS. Return on sales, often referred to as operating profit percentage. ROS can be stated in whole dollar terms.

Safety stock. These are additions to working stock, held as a hedge against the possibility of extra demand for a given product. This helps reduce the risk of being out of stock on a given item.

Sales history. A record of sales achieved by an operator in a given sales outlet during a specifically identified time period.

Sales mix. The series of consumer purchasing decisions that result in a specific food and beverage cost percentage. Sales mix affects overall product cost percentage anytime menu items have varying food and beverage cost percentages.

Sales to date. The cumulative sales figures reported during a given financial accounting period.

Shelf life. The period of time an ingredient or menu item maintains its freshness, flavor, and quality.

Short. A vendor is said to "short" an operator on a delivery item when the vendor is unable to deliver the quantity of item ordered for the appointed delivery date.

Software. The set of instructions that control the workings of computer hardware and direct the processing of data.

Spec. *See* Product specification.

Split. *See* Half bottle.

Split shift. A scheduling technique used to match individual employee work shifts with the peaks and valleys of customer demand.

Spotter. An individual employed by management for the purpose of inconspicuously observing bartenders and waitstaff in order to detect any fraudulent or policy violating behavior.

Standard menu. A printed and otherwise fixed menu that stays the same day after day.

Variable expense. An expense that generally increases as sales volume increases and decreases as sales volume decreases.

Variable payroll. Those dollars expended on employees whose presence is directly dependent on the number of guests served. These employees include waitpersons, bartenders, and dishwashers, for example. As the number of guests served increases, the number of these individuals required to do the job also increases. As the number of guests served decreases, variable payroll should decrease.

Walk. A term used to describe a customer who has consumed a product, but leaves the foodservice operation without paying the bill.

Waste percentage. This formula is defined as product loss divided by AP weight and refers to product lost in the preparation process.

Well liquors. Those spirits that are served by an operation when the customer does not specify a particular brand name.

Working capital. A dollar figure computed by subtracting current liabilities from current assets.

Working capital ratio. A ratio that relates the number of dollars of sales generated to each dollar of working capital available.

Working stock. The quantity of goods from inventory reasonably expected to be used between deliveries.

Yield percentage. This formula is defined as 1.0 minus waste percentage, and refers to the amount of product available for use by the operator after all preparation-related losses.

Bibliography

American Hotel and Motel Association. *Uniform System of Accounts and Expense Dictionary for Small Hotels and Motels* 4th ed. East Lansing, MI: Educational Institute of the American Hotel and Motel Association, 1987.

Bell, Donald A. *Food and Beverage Cost Control.* Berkeley: McCutcheon Publishing Corporation, 1984.

Chaban, Joel. *Practical Foodservice Spreadsheets with Excel.* New York: Van Nostrand Reinhold, 1989.

Coltman, Michael M. *Cost Control for the Hospitality Industry.* New York: Van Nostrand Reinhold, 1989.

Coltman, Michael M. *Financial Control for Your Foodservice Operation.* New York: Van Nostrand Reinhold, 1989.

Dittmer, Paul R., and Gerald G. Griffin. *Principles of Food, Beverage and Labor Cost Controls for Hotels and Restaurants.* New York: Van Nostrand Reinhold, 1989.

Fay, Clifford T., Jr. *Basic Financial Accounting for the Hospitality Industry.* East Lansing, MI: Educational Institute of the American Hotel and Motel Association, 1982.

Gisslen, Wayne *Professional Cooking.* 2d ed. New York: John Wiley & Sons, 1989.

Haines, Robert G. *Math Principles for Food Service Occupations.* 2d ed. Albany, NY: Delmar Publishers, Inc., 1988.

Hayes, David K. *Bar and Beverage Management and Operations.* New York: Chain Store Publishing Corp., 1987.

Katsigris, Costas, and Mary Porter. *The Bar and Beverage Book.* 2d ed. New York: John Wiley & Sons, 1991.

Keiser, James, and Elmer Kallio. *Controlling and Analyzing Costs in Food Service Operations.* New York: Macmillan, 1989.

Keister, Douglas C. *Food and Beverage Control.* 2d ed. Englewood Cliffs, NJ: Prentice Hall, 1990.

Knight, John B., and Lendal H. Kotschevar. *Quantity Food Production, Planning, and Management.* 2d ed. New York: Van Nostrand Reinhold, 1989.

Kotschevar, Lendal H. *Management by Menu.* 2d ed. Chicago: The Educational Foundation of the National Restaurant Association, 1987.

Laventhol & Horwath. *Uniform System of Accounts for Restaurants: Adopted and Recommended by the National Restaurant Association.* 5th ed. Washington, DC: National Restaurant Association, 1989.

Levinson, Charles. *Food and Beverage Operation: Cost Control and Systems Management.* 2d ed. Englewood Cliffs, NJ: Prentice Hall, 1989.

Messersmith, Ann M., and Judy Miller. *Forecasting in Foodservice*. New York: John Wiley & Sons, 1992.

Miller, Jack E. *Menu Pricing and Strategy*. 3d ed. New York: Van Nostrand Reinhold, 1990.

Ninemeier, Jack D. *Planning and Control for Food and Beverage Operations*. East Lansing, MI: The Educational Institute of the American Hotel & Motel Association, 1982.

Paige, Grace. *Catering Costs and Control*. London, UK, Cassell, 1977.

Zaccarelli, Brother Herman E., C.S.C. *Food Service Management by Checklist: A Handbook of Control Techniques*. New York: John Wiley & Sons, Inc., 1991.

Index